Francisca Wood and Nineteenth-Century Periodical Culture

Pressing for Change

CLÁUDIA PAZOS ALONSO

LEGENDA

Studies in Hispanic and Lusophone Cultures 35
Modern Humanities Research Association
2020

Published by Legenda
an imprint of the Modern Humanities Research Association
Salisbury House, Station Road, Cambridge CB1 2LA

ISBN 978-1-78188-799-8

First published 2020

Copy-Editor: Richard Correll

CONTENTS

Acknowledgements   x

Introduction: Pressing Matters   I

    Women's Exclusions: The Perpetuation of Unconscious Bias
    The Regeneration
    Francisca Wood and Nineteenth-Century Print Culture: Achieving
      Recognition
    Content Overview

1   Piecing Together the Life-histories of Francisca de Assis Martins Wood
   and William Thorold Wood   25

    Francisca de Assis Martins Wood
    Picturing a Victorian Gentleman
    The Woods' Twilight Years

2   In the Public Eye: Women in Print Culture (1848–1867)   55

    Asymmetrical Positions
    Two Mid-Century Pioneers
    Riding the Wave
    Conclusion

3   The Editor and her Team   83

    A Distinctive Editorial Vision
    The Female Cast at the Heart of *A Voz Feminina*
    Male Champions
    Conclusion

4   Questioning Subordi/Nation   III

    Cultivating the Thinking Woman
    Critiquing Religious Subordination: Anticlericalism in Action
    Exposing the Naturalization of Male Privilege
    The Structural Inequality of Access to Education
    Biology is not Destiny
    Political and Economic Emancipation: 'a mulher livre'
    Rethinking Hegemonic Masculinity: 'o homem livre'
    Conclusion

5   Activism through Open Letters   139

    Petitions for the Protection of Animals
    Address to the Pope
    Letter to Emilio Castelar
    Backlash in *Bem Público*
    Letter to Subscribers about the Closure of *O Progresso*
    Conclusion

6   Spreading the Word   159
        Border Crossings
        Female Suffrage through Portuguese Eyes
        Hot Off the Press: Ammunition from Abroad
        After the Demise of O *Progresso*
        Conclusion

    Conclusion   185

    Bibliography   195

    Appendix 1. Tipografia Luso-Britânica   217

    Appendix 2. List of Editorials by Francisca Wood   225

    Appendix 3. List of Editorials (Alphabetically by Author) 227

    Index   231

To Maria Lúcia Dal Farra and Hilary Owen
for their inspirational example
and enduring friendship

ACKNOWLEDGEMENTS

This book owes a great deal to many colleagues, friends and family. It was meant to be written, even if it took me a long time to realize it. Maria Lúcia kindly encouraged me at the outset of my career with a generosity I will never forget, and her scholarship opened my eyes to the transformative value of blending together archival work, biography and textual criticism. The many productive conversations I have had with Hilary Owen, some dating all the way back to 1997, when we set ourselves the challenge to act on the political imperative of recovering Portuguese women writers of the last 150 years, have been instrumental in shaping my work and thought.

In Oxford, I will always be grateful to Tom Earle and Stephen Parkinson who believed in this book even before it got underway. My close colleagues in the Portuguese Sub-faculty, Claire Williams, Phillip Rothwell, Simon Park, Gui Perdigão and Maria Luisa Coelho, have been wonderfully supportive throughout the extended process of researching and writing up this monograph in more ways than I can ever hope to list here. I trust they all know how much their intellectual companionship means to me. In the English Faculty, I am grateful to Pelagia Goulimari, with whom it was a privilege to co-direct the MSt in Women's Studies for three years. Wadham College provided an exceptionally congenial environment in which to conduct research. I am particularly indebted to Jane Garnett, who offered crucial early guidance and personal encouragement, and all my Modern Languages colleagues, especially Olivia Vázquez-Medina, for their conviviality.

Further afield, two other trusted colleagues were invaluable in helping me to bring this book to completion. Pat Odber de Baubeta, who kindly agreed to undertake all the translations into English, kept me going with a steady supply of bibliographical suggestions and her wicked sense of humour. Bruno Silva Rodrigues transcribed more than 50,000 words, mainly from editorials, sent me numerous photocopies from the Biblioteca Nacional de Portugal, often at short notice, and formatted the final manuscript. Since Pat and Bruno's attention to detail is second to none, it goes without saying that any remaining faults are entirely my own.

Research for this monograph could not have been completed without three terms' sabbatical leave in Michaelmas 2014, Michaelmas 2016, and Hilary 2017, the latter funded by the European Humanities Research Centre. I was also fortunate to receive generous financial assistance from Wadham College, the Faculty of Modern Languages and the Humanities Division. Aside from covering multiple research costs, including the index, ably carried out by Kirsty Adegboro, such funding enabled me to present work-in-progress in the UK, Portugal, France, Italy, and Brazil, where I benefitted considerably from informal interactions with scholars in related fields. Although their names are too numerous to list here, I should like to single out Paulo de Medeiros, Anna Klobucka, Chatarina Edfeldt, Ana Luísa Amaral, Maria Irene Ramalho, Irene Vaquinhas, Teresa Pinto Coelho, and Fabio Mario da Silva for the interest they took in my work in progress.

I wish to record my sincere thanks to many others who helped me in practical ways too, especially Ana Teresa Marques dos Santos who sent me material from Coimbra and with whom it has been a pleasure to work on the Portuguese and Brazilian translations of *Jane Eyre*. Alison Howe first prompted me to search records available online and taught me how to navigate them. Andrew Swinnerton, Honorary Administrator of the British Cemetery in Lisbon, identified Francisca Wood's tombstone and verified Church records for me. Filipe Botelho Correa and Vanessa Domingos shared information about the location of rare material. In Portugal, the staff at Biblioteca Nacional de Portugal and the Biblioteca Municipal do Porto deserve my special gratitude. Closer to home, in the Taylorian Library, Joanne Ferrari regularly went out of her way to help; and Jon Edwards and his team in the Faculty of Modern Languages dealt with computer-related matters with impeccable goodwill.

This project started in earnest in 2014, the year my mother died. My father was exemplary in the way he read and commented on every single draft chapter, always asking pertinent and searching questions. My sons Alex and Miguel cheered from the sidelines, although they couldn't refrain from commenting on my 'online stalking', after I joined Ancestry.com and just occasionally (!) found it hard to tear myself away from the computer. Miguel navigated several technological 'emergencies' with characteristic cool and Alex was kind enough to read several chapters, thereby acting as an excellent 'educated general reader'. Last but not least, I was most fortunate to be able to count once more on the unsurpassed wisdom of Legenda's Managing Editor, Graham Nelson, and the impressive attention to detail of Richard Correll as copy-editor.

Earlier versions of some chapters were first published as articles and I thank the relevant publishers for permission to use them. Chapter 3 started out as 'Modernity in the Making: The Women at the Heart of *A Voz Feminina* and *O Progresso*', in *O Feminino e o Moderno*, ed by Ana Luísa Vilela, Fabio Mario da Silva and Maria Lúcia Dal Farra (Lisbon: CEPUL, 2017). Chapter 5 was published as 'A public intellectual in nineteenth-century Portugal: Francisca Wood's editorials', *Journal of Romance Studies*, 19.3 (2019), while Chapter 6 is a reworked version of 'Spreading the Word: The "Woman Question" in the periodicals *A Voz Feminina* and *O Progresso* (1868–9)', *Angelaki. Journal of the Theoretical Humanities*, 22 (2017). The portrait of William Thorold Wood is reproduced in Chapter 1 with permission from Bridgeman.

C.P.A., Oxford, November 2019

INTRODUCTION:
PRESSING MATTERS

The conceptualization of pre-1900 women writers as agents of modernity in their own right still presents a challenge in a Portuguese context. The prevailing consensus is that the publication of Ana de Castro Osório's *Às Mulheres Portuguesas* in 1905 marks the symbolic start of an organized first-wave feminist movement, and articulates a modern sense of female agency.[1] This monograph, however, seeks to nuance such received wisdom by uncovering how, nearly half a century earlier, when women first began to press for political change in countries like Britain and the US, Francisca de Assis Martins Wood (1802–1900) became one of the most vocal advocates of progressive causes in Portugal, through her trail-blazing journalism and serialized fiction.

Wood's ground-breaking cultural — and, to all intents and purposes, political — intervention in mid-nineteenth-century Portugal will be examined through the prism of the weekly periodical that she headed for two years (1868–69), initially titled *A Voz Feminina*, and subsequently renamed *O Progresso*. Crucially, in nineteenth-century Portugal, as elsewhere, the press fostered the circulation of ideas and the forging of transnational connections. Wood functions as a cultural mediator who sought to provide a modernizing perspective on sociopolitical issues that were relevant to the situation of Portugal during the second half on the nineteenth century, a period known as the Regeneração [Regeneration].[2] Her journalism regularly exposed the detrimental effect of the monopoly of the Catholic Church and, conversely, unapologetically promoted Enlightenment rationality and freedom of thought. This dovetailed with an early brand of 'equal rights' feminism, informed by her first-hand experience of living in Victorian England for several decades and, after her return to Portugal, by keeping abreast of contemporary debates in the Victorian press.

Traditional Portuguese nineteenth-century literary history enshrines and praises the combative reformist cultural and political thrust of male public intellectuals with cosmopolitan credentials, such as the Anglophile Almeida Garrett (1799–1854) in the first half of the century and Eça de Queirós (1945–1900) in the second half.[3] Given that, chronologically, Francisca Wood sits between these two giants, this monograph interrogates why her progressive ideas were vilified at the time, not least through a sustained public hate campaign in one Portuguese periodical, the today little-known *Bem Público*. In fact, a detailed analysis of Wood's modernizing agenda in the late 1860s highlights the extent to which it anticipated and in some cases overlapped with the anticlericalism of the *Geração de 70* [Generation of 1870].[4] As such, today, her contribution to the history of ideas deserves to be properly recovered and understood.

Owing to her explosive combination of forward-thinking writings with gender, Wood became so marginalized that, one hundred and fifty years on, the present monograph constitutes the first book-length study in any language to provide an in-depth survey of her outspoken and wide-ranging intervention. Although the return to democracy in 1974 ensured the gradual recovery of her protagonism in Portuguese scholarship, the lack of availability of any study in English up to now has had adverse ramifications insofar as she has remained overlooked in textbooks dealing with nineteenth-century European feminisms, whether published in English or in French, such as the classics *Histoire des femmes en occident* and *Women's Emancipation Movements in the Nineteenth Century: A European Perspective*.[5] One commendable recent exception is her presence — albeit fleeting — in João Esteves's overview chapter in *A New History of Iberian Feminisms*, among a handful of Portuguese women who gained prominence through the press, such as Antónia Gertrudes Pusich (1805–1883), Guiomar Torresão (1844–1898), Angelina Vidal (1853–1917) and Alice Pestana (1860–1929), the latter explicitly 'associated with the establishment of feminist and pacifist movements in Portugal'.[6]

Women's Exclusions: The Perpetuation of Unconscious Bias

The processes by which Portuguese women were excluded from the construction of an imagined national community deserve close scrutiny. With regard to the nineteenth century, one example should suffice to illustrate the current state of affairs. The landmark Lisbon statue of Eça de Queirós, produced by Teixeira Lopes and placed in 1903 in the Largo Barão de Quintela, portrays him holding in his arms a life-size woman, whose transparent cloak has come undone, revealing her naked body (Fig. I.1).[7]

In symbolic terms, the sculpture vividly captures and embodies the asymmetry of gender roles pre-1900: on the one hand, the male creator and public intellectual, on the other the excessively corporeal female muse. Over one century later, in 2012, this time in Porto, little seems to have changed in public perceptions and discourses, judging by the inauguration of a statue celebrating yet another canonical male, Camilo Castelo Branco (1825–1890) (Fig. I.2).

If anything, the same clichés are now heightened by the disturbing fact that the female body on display is no longer an allegorical figuration, but Castelo Branco's long-standing companion, the writer Ana Augusta Plácido (1831–1895). Castelo Branco, fully dressed, protectively attempts to cover the visibly naked body of Plácido. Furthermore, this twenty-first-century statue, through its allusions to the earlier one, effectively reinforces intertextual dialogue between two male artists predicated upon their unspoken assumptions of a genealogy of male genius. In a nutshell, these visual illustrations help us to grasp the damaging yet deeply seated gender asymmetries that continue to circulate in the public space and collective imaginary.

FIG. I.1. 1903 sculpture of statue of Eça de Queirós
by Teixeira Lopes, Museu da Cidade, Lisbon.

FIG. I.2. 2012 sculpture of Ana Augusta Plácido and Camilo Castelo Branco
by Francisco Simões, Campo dos Mártires da Pátria, Porto.

Unexamined discursive practices remain profoundly disempowering for women. Even in the new millennium, visitors to the former Porto prison Cadeia da Relação are likely to accept at face value the informative plaque that states that Ana Plácido was a 'escritora sem talento' [a writer devoid of talent].[8] For how many people know that *Luz coada por ferros* (1863), a compilation of short stories and meditations partly composed in prison while awaiting trial for adultery, was favourably reviewed by her contemporaries? In fact, as far afield as Brazil, a young Machado de Assis concluded that 'Uma mulher de espírito é brilhante preto; não é coisa para deixar-se cair no fundo da gaveta' [a spirited woman is a rough diamond; she is not an object that can be dropped in the bottom of the drawer].[9] This suggests not only that Plácido enjoyed transatlantic circulation, but that she was welcomed by some of her peers in the republic of letters. What is more, she was not the only one, as Chapter 2 will reveal.

It is worth stating at the outset of this book, echoing the words of Filipa Lowndes Vicente, that 'não está aqui em causa a competência *daqueles* que estão [no cânone], mas sim a ausência *daquelas* que não estão' [What is at stake here is not the competence of those *men* who are in [the canon] but rather the absence of those *women* who aren't].[10] At stake is the fact that Portuguese literary historiography has seldom sought to identify, let alone promote, any nineteenth-century female gems. The Marchioness of Alorna, Maria Browne, Ana Plácido, Guiomar Torresão and Maria Amália Vaz de Carvalho are among the handful of names that traditional literary scholars are most likely be able to identify.[11] Even this sketchy list might be presuming too much, if we pause to consider the results of a survey undertaken by Fabio Mario da Silva in 2014: the only nineteenth-century women mentioned by his admittedly small sample of interviewees were the Marchioness of Alorna and Ana Plácido.[12] The former certainly seems to have entered the literary canon, in no small part due to the efforts of Vanda Anastácio, who has already spent more than a decade engaged in her recovery, with modern re-editions of her work.[13] As for Plácido, despite the publication of her biography in the new millennium, by and large she remains a historical curiosity as one of Camilo's muses, generally presented as an isolated female voice, decontextualized from broader trends in women's literary history.[14] This distorted image is in dire need of re-examination, and for this reason Chapter 2 will place Plácido, alongside others, in the context of a thriving periodical culture where female production was ongoing.

Part of the issue lies in a narrow understanding of what constitutes 'literature' and indeed the unspoken exclusionary assumptions underpinning definitions of 'good literature' (the label used in Silva's questionnaire). It is worth quoting here Joanna Russ, writing in 1983 about the Black novelist Zora Neale Hurston: Russ exemplifies anecdotally how unconscious bias can insidiously permeate critical assessments, even those of an unbiased critic such as she assumed herself to be *a priori*. When she first read Hurston's 1937 classic, *Their Eyes Were Watching God*, she thought 'it was clearly inferior to the great central tradition of Western Literature'. After researching the context of production, however, and rereading the very same novel, she wryly noted 'it was astonishing how much the novel had improved in the interval'.[15]

We might add that, specifically in terms of the academic practice of literary studies in Portugal and the training of the next generation of scholars, the underlying issue was succinctly identified and summarized more than a decade ago by Chatarina Edfeldt, as follows: 'Dá maior prestígio académico ser a décima sétima pessoa a estudar um autor canonizado, sob qualquer perspectiva exótica, do que dar visibilidade à vasta obra duma autora nunca antes estudada'[16] [There is greater academic prestige to be had from being the seventeenth person to study a canonical author from no matter how exotic a perspective, than from bestowing visibility on the vast oeuvre of a female author who has never been studied]. As such, it is encouraging to come across theses on the subject of nineteenth-century women writers completed in the last few years.[17] In Portugal, a broader historical cultural studies approach was recently offered by the Brazilian researcher Elen Biguelini's doctoral thesis, 'Tenho escrevinhado muito: mulheres que escreveram em Portugal (1800–1850)'.[18] Her archival research uncovers and maps female authorship in unexpectedly large numbers, listing over one hundred women who published, either in periodicals or in book-form, during the first half of the nineteenth century. In so doing, she considerably nuances the prevailing image in literary history of the Marchioness of Alorna as the exception to the rule during this fifty-year period.

The Regeneration

In order to bring out the profound originality and coherence of Francisca Wood's project it is crucial to immerse ourselves fully in the setting of her time, anchoring our study in the cultural transformations that occurred in Portugal in the second half of the nineteenth century, and specifically in the omnipresence of periodical culture, thereby adopting a broad perspective that straddles literary and cultural studies. Dillane argues that 'periodical research expresses a reasonable and proper leaning towards material approaches that have been democratizing and have positively disrupted canon hierarchies'.[19] But this alone can only be the first step. In addition, it will be necessary to think through the asymmetrical circumstances affecting nineteenth-century culture makers. As Filipa Lowndes Vicente contends, in a context of institutionalized gender discrimination sedimented over time, awareness of the positionality of a given artist (or writer) is crucial: 'Ignorar a identidade sexual, em defesa dos supostos critérios de qualidade artística e da análise formal de uma obra, significa desprezar um dado significativo na construção e percepção contemporâneas da obra, tal como no percurso da artista' [Ignoring sexual identity, in defence of the putative criteria of artistic quality and the formal analysis of a work, means disregarding a significant fact in the contemporary construction and perception of the work, as well as in the artist's trajectory].[20]

The period that specifically interests us, roughly the third quarter of the nineteenth century, is well-known to Portuguese cultural historians. From 1851 onwards, after decades of political instability, the period conventionally known as the Regeneração [Regeneration] ushered in modernization. Politically speaking, in the course of the 1860s, progress resulted in important symbolic legal changes, notably the extinction of *morgadios* (compulsory first-born inheritance) in 1863;[21]

the abolition of the death penalty for civil crimes in 1867;[22] and the abolition of slavery in Portuguese colonies in 1869. The first two topics featured in Wood's novel, *Maria Severn*, while the third was reported in the periodical, suggesting that all three were matters dear to her heart.[23]

The Regeneração also promoted technological advances, notably the use of the telegraph (1857) and the construction of a railway network. The telegraph accelerated the dissemination of up-to-date news across countries, while the railways facilitated the speedy importation of culture from elsewhere in Europe after the network reached the Spanish border, in 1863, as Eça de Queirós famously reminisced:

> Coimbra vivia então numa grande atividade, ou antes num grande tumulto mental. Pelos caminhos de ferro, que tinham aberto a Península, rompiam cada dia, descendo da França e da Alemanha (através da França) torrentes de coisas novas, ideias, sistemas, estéticas, formas, sentimentos, interesses humanitários.[24]

> [Coimbra then experienced great activity, or rather great mental turmoil. Through the railways that had opened up the Peninsula, new things, ideas, systems, aesthetics, forms, feelings, humanitarian interests came flooding in every day from France and from Germany (through France).]

The two main cities, Lisbon and Porto, became connected by railway line up to Vila Nova de Gaia in 1864.[25] Lisbon underwent a makeover, and the description that Wood offers of the capital in one of her 1868 editorials vividly highlighted this:

> Vejo as lojas da Baixa, ostentando luxo asiático no seu interior assim como no seu exterior; vejo belíssimas casas aformoseando as ruas da capital, e outras em construção; vejo os jardins públicos da cidade primorosamente conservados; o delicioso aterro tão favorável aos viandantes; uma polícia civil que faria honra às primeiras capitais do mundo; vejo grande abundância de ónibus lindos, asseados e baratos; vejo as pobres e sujas casas de pasto substituídas por belíssimos hotéis. (*A Voz Feminina*, 11: 1)[26]

> [I see the shops in the Baixa district, flaunting Oriental luxury both inside and outside; I see the most beautiful houses embellishing the streets of the capital, while others are being built; I see the public gardens of the city exquisitely maintained; the delightful embankment so favourable to the passer-by; a civil police force that would do honour to the first capitals of the world; I see a great abundance of pretty omnibuses, clean and cheap; I see the poor, dirty eating houses replaced by splendid hotels.]

Nonetheless, while Wood commented approvingly on urban modernization, she was simultaneously keenly aware that the money showered on these expensive improvements had done little to change the material conditions of the lower classes. Cosmetic changes concealed the fact that, both in economic and educational terms, the broader picture in the country at large remained dismal.

The truth of the matter is that the majority of the population was illiterate: in 1878 female illiteracy stood at around 89.3%; male illiteracy was 10% lower. According to Rui Ramos, however, basic female literacy in the urban centre of Lisbon was unexpectedly high at 49%, although falling to 12% for the surrounding area.[27] Perhaps it was in the light of this anomalous pocket of educated women that the Civil Code of 1867 had enforced the model of the patriarchal family, through a series of articles which effectively enshrined women's legal subordination to the control of their husbands. As Vaquinhas reminds us, a woman required her husband's permission in order to publish (article 1187), or to exercise a profession, or run a business, or make financial transactions (articles 1192–94, and 1196).[28] Yet if the need to regulate women's writing was felt, it was surely because periodical culture had increasingly been opening up new opportunities for women determined to play a role with greater public visibility.

The omnipresence of the periodical press in mid-nineteenth-century Portugal

It is impossible to understand nineteenth-century culture without reference to its thriving periodical culture. Indeed, as Kathryn Bishop-Sánchez observes:

> The emergence of a relatively broader reading public [...] the development of means of communication, the greater circulation of culture and knowledge and the growing influence of the press are some of the many aspects that radically changed nineteenth-century life.[29]

In the same article where Wood approvingly described the outward signs of modernization in central Lisbon, she went on to comment on the presence of newspapers in daily life as another tangible sign of progress:

> Vejo sete diários de província aqui sobre a minha mesa, seis dos quais saíram à luz ainda não há um ano. O sétimo — folha grande, escrita por penas áticas, e dirigido por cabeças iluminadas pelos fachos intelectuais do século XIX — *A Voz da Liberdade* de Ponta Delgada, esse, já passou os umbrais do seu segundo ano. Pode haver outros jornais de províncias, que datem da mesma época, mas os sete presentes bastam para provar os gigantescos passos do progresso nacional. ([n.a.], *VF*, 11: 1)

> [I see seven provincial newspapers here on my desk, six of which have not been in existence for a full year yet. The seventh — a broadsheet, written by wise authors, and directed by heads illuminated by the intellectual beacons of the nineteenth century — *A Voz da Liberdade* of Ponta Delgada, that one has already crossed the threshold of its second year. There may be other provincial papers dating from the same time, but the seven I have before me are sufficient to confirm the gigantic steps of national progress]

Silva Pereira lists eighty-seven new periodicals launched in 1868 alone, although most of them were to be short-lived.[30] The significance of the regional press is especially noteworthy. As is common knowledge, only the previous year Eça de Queirós had made his debut as Editor of the *Distrito de Évora*, which he wrote almost single-handedly from January to August 1867.[31] In addition, it is worth mentioning that if Wood had more than half a dozen provincial papers sitting on her desk, it was no doubt because she was following the common practice of exchanging her own with others, a practice which boosted the circulation of ideas.

The press, then, became a vehicle for the dissemination of ideas, endowed with intellectual weight and capacity to produce an impact. Furthermore, Wood did not see readers as passive consumers, but rather stressed the participative nature of reading in the formation of critical thought:

> Em toda a parte do reino se faz sentir a férvida ação da inteligência; ação necessariamente muito generalizada pois sem leitores não haveria tantos indivíduos que se dedicassem à transmissão de ideias.
>
> O escritor pensa e escreve — o leitor lê e pensa; ambos são pensadores em maior ou menor grau. ([n.a.], *VF*, II: I)

> [Throughout the kingdom the heated workings of the mind are felt; workings that are necessarily very widespread because without readers there would not be so many individuals who devoted themselves to transmitting ideas.
>
> The author thinks and writes — the reader reads and thinks; both are thinkers to a greater or lesser extent.]

Wood then turned her attention to the two main cities placing them on an equal footing:

> Nas duas cidades principais do reino, que chusma de jornais! E todos acham leitores e todos acham compradores.
>
> Lembro-me mui distintamente de ler o *Jornal do Comércio* quando este era pouco maior do que o meu lenço de assoar, e agora?! Agora vai tomando as dimensões de uma tolha de mesa, da qual uma quarta parte é ocupado por anúncios — provas incontestáveis de florescente comércio. Dizem-me também que lhe estão construindo um magnífico palácio: é natural. 'Picollo passaro piccolo nido', mas se o pássaro passa de pintassilgo a águia, necessita de grande ninho.
>
> O *Diário de Notícias* suscita também meia dúzia de pontos de admiração. Há dias, achei cobrindo a capa de um livro o *Diário de Notícias* na sua infância. O livro é quarto, e a folha apenas o cobria. E agora que corpulento está o tal senhor! Que bela máquina de vapor me dizem possui; que belos escritórios mobilados de mogno e mantidos na melhor ordem e asseio!
>
> Estes diários, estas máquinas, estes palácios são outras tantas bocas que proclamam prosperidade, progresso, riqueza, inteligência. ([n.a.], *VF*, II: I)

> [In the two main cities of the kingdom, what a lot of newspapers! And they all find readers and they all find people to buy them.
>
> I remember very clearly reading the *Jornal do Comércio* when it was not much bigger than my pocket handkerchief, and now?! Now it has grown to the size of a tablecloth, of which one quarter is taken up by advertisements — irrefutable proof of flourishing commerce. I am told that they are building a magnificent palace for it. Quite right too. 'Picollo passaro piccolo nido' — tiny bird, tiny nest, but if the bird goes from goldfinch to golden eagle, it needs a very big nest indeed.
>
> The *Diário de Notícias* also gives rise to half a dozen exclamation marks. Some days ago, I found the *Diário de Notícias* in its infancy, covering a book jacket. The book is quarto size and the page barely covered it. Now how corpulent the gentleman has grown! What a beautiful steam powered engine I'm told he possesses; what beautiful offices furnished in mahogany and kept as clean and tidy as can be!
>
> These dailies, these machines, these palaces are so many more mouths that proclaim prosperity, progress, wealth, intelligence.]

Moreover, Wood underlines not just technical progress (i.e. the steam engine) but also a new conception of commercial journalism which hinged on advertising: as she makes clear, a quarter of *Jornal do Comércio* was now taken up with advertisements. The launch of the *Diário de Notícias* in late 1864 represented a landmark. New press laws in 1866, abolishing restrictions, fuelled its extraordinary expansion in the space of a few years.[32] A table supplied by Sousa et al. documents the exponential increase in circulation enjoyed by this daily over a twenty-year period. In the first five years alone, sale figures rose from 5,000 a day to 17,000.[33]

While the format of dailies produced for mass consumption heralded a new era for commercial journalism,[34] the new model continued to coexist for some time with periodicals of various kinds, including literary magazines. Many of the latter were headed by writers, whether aspiring or established ones: for instance, in 1868 in the capital of the North, Camilo launched the monthly *Gazeta literária do Porto*. For men, the press was often a stepping stone, leading to publication in book-format and a career as a man of letters, or even political office. The two were not mutually exclusive, as Maria de Lourdes Lima dos Santos demonstrates in *Intelectuais portugueses na primeira metade de oitocentos*.[35] The generic designation of man of letters neatly avoids creating an artificial divide between journalism and literature, an opposition that makes little sense in the context of the period. But on closer scrutiny, this category was heavily gendered: access to knowledge in the form of broad reading and study was often difficult for women in the first place; and secondly, women did not have the opportunities to belong to an intellectual peer group in the way most men did. It comes as no surprise therefore that the sample of fifty Portuguese intellectuals on whom Santos based her study were all men.[36]

Female intellectuals

Since women were debarred from a career in the public eye, writing in the press often became their most obvious, and often their only, public avenue for engaging in intellectual pursuits and/or activism, insofar as the press provided a virtual meeting point for an imagined community of like-minded individuals. It also gave them a modicum of access to partake in ideological debates. Yet, although women participated in periodical culture, the label of 'mulher de letras' [woman of letters] remained for the most part inexistent or still had little currency in mid-nineteenth-century Portugal. Moreover, alternative terms such as 'literata' [lettered woman] or 'mulher letrada' [learned woman] were as likely to be deployed as an accusation as an accolade. It is perhaps unsurprising that, in a climate where prejudice was rife and female intellectuals had to contend with structural inequalities and double standards, conservative positions were often also perpetuated by women themselves. This self-sabotaging tendency was dealt with head-on by Francisca Wood in one of her early editorials, where she addressed opposition from other women in order to lay to rest the ever-present ghost of the *sabichona* [know-it-all]. Her point-by-point response to commonly held views succinctly encapsulates the deep-seated opposition with which learned women routinely had to contend:

> 'Não gosto de senhoras sabichonas'. Primeira objeção da generalidade. Nem nós tão-pouco, minhas senhoras. A sabichona é a pedante — a *femme savante* de quem Monseigneur l'Evêque d'Orléans diz: 'É necessário não confundir, não

envolver no mesmo anátema as mulheres estudiosas com as mulheres *savantes*; as mulheres instruídas com as mulheres ridículas; as mulheres sensatas, pensadoras, aplicadas, sérias, com as pedantes.

'É literata? Basta para mim. Estão as informações tiradas'. Segunda objeção da generalidade, a qual pode significar, de duas insensatezes uma: ou que despreza a mulher literata; ou que a crê alheia às virtudes do seu sexo.

'As mulheres letradas são insofríveis'. Terceira objeção da generalidade. Agora pergunto eu, e as iletradas são invariavelmente sofríveis? A meu ver nada há mais insofrível que a estolidez trajando sedas com guarnição de *pretensões*. [...]

Mas passemos a outra objeção. Elas são tantas como as uvas a que a raposa, não podendo chegar, dizia que as não queria porque estavam verdes. 'As mulheres literatas carecem de graças feminis; querem-se fazer homens'.

Oh! Minhas senhoras das objeções, estudem: não percam tanto tempo com as horrorosas cuias [...] se é perder as graças feminis, e querer fazer-se homem, não passar as horas preciosas que nunca mais voltam, diante do toucador, despenteando-se, pondo aqui um lacinho e ali um *suivez-moi*, prendendo a cauda e desprendendo a cauda, estudando os figurinos, falando, com a maninha ou com a amiguinha, do vestido que trajava D. Fulana ou D. Sicrana, e espiando os viandantes, então nenhuma mulher, não digo sábia, mas sensata, pode ter graças feminis. (*VF*, 17: 1–2)

['I don't like ladies who are know-it-alls'. First general objection. Nor do we, my ladies. The know-it-all is a pedant — the *femme savante* of whom Monseigneur the Bishop of Orleans says: 'It is necessary to not confuse, to not involve in the same anathema studious women with *femmes savantes*; educated women with ridiculous women; sensible, diligent, serious thinking women with pedants'.

'She is lettered? That's enough for me. That's all we need to know'. Second general objection, which can mean one of two idiocies: either the speaker despises the lettered woman, or believes she lacks the virtues of her sex.

'Learned women are insufferable'. Third general objection. Now I ask, are illiterate women invariably tolerable? In my opinion there is nothing more insufferable than obtuseness dressed up in silks trimmed with *pretensions*. [...]

But let us consider another objection. They are as numerous as the grapes that the fox, unable to reach them, said he did not want because they were not ripe. 'Lettered women lack feminine graces; they want to become men'.

Oh! My ladies full of objections, do study: don't waste so much time with those horrendous hairpieces [...] if losing feminine graces, and wanting to become a man, means not spending precious hours that will never return in front of the dressing table, disarranging your hair, placing a bow here and a floating ribbon there, catching up your train and undoing your train, studying dress patterns, talking with your darling sister or dearest friend about the dress that Madame So-and-so or Madame What's-her-name was wearing, and spying on passers-by, then no woman, I won't say learned, but sensible, can have feminine graces.]

As Wood rightly points out, if the only measure of femininity is being a slave to the latest fashion, then by definition this exclude all sensible women.

Notwithstanding deeply ingrained prejudices against learned women, by the time that the nineteenth century drew to a close those female intellectuals who had succeeded in maintaining a high-profile presence in the press, sometimes over several decades, did often become *de facto* public intellectuals, the best-known cases being those of Guiomar Torresão and Maria Amália Vaz de Carvalho. The former was one of the founding members of the Association of Portuguese Journalists and Writers, formed in 1880,[37] while the consecration of the latter by her peers was ultimately sealed under the new Republican regime, when she became the first woman to join the Academia das Ciências de Lisboa in 1912.[38] In order to survive as women of letters in a male-dominated environment, however, both had to navigate codes of femininity with the utmost care. What is of particular interest to us is how, as emerging young writers, both positioned themselves in relation to Wood's periodical: Torresão embraced it, but subsequently seems to have strategically distanced herself from her youthful enthusiasm in order to build a name for herself, as Chapter 3 discusses at greater length. Vaz de Carvalho, conversely, rejected any involvement in Wood's project.

Francisca Wood and Nineteenth-Century Print Culture: Achieving Recognition

It is precisely because *A Voz Feminina* fulfilled such a ground-breaking function in the 1860s that Francisca Wood's inspirational cultural intervention caught the eye of several Portuguese researchers in the aftermath of the 1974 Revolution, when gender equality was finally enshrined in the 1976 Constitution. After all, the motto of the paper 'A mulher livre ao lado do homem livre' [the free woman beside the free man] resonated with the zeitgeist. As such, a pioneering 1981 overview by Leal enthusiastically considered *A Voz Feminina* 'o primeiro jornal feminista da Europa' [the first feminist newspaper in Europe].[39] It duly paved the way for Brito et al.'s succinct but excellent article titled 'Um Jornal feminista' (1986).[40]

By the close of the twentieth century, Ernesto Rodrigues devotes ten pages to 'jornalismo feminino' [female journalism] in his 1998 *Mágico Folhetim*.[41] Yet, retrospectively at least, this might seem rather perfunctory, considering that Leal's engagement with women's periodical culture, undertaken in her 1981 survey, and expanded and reprinted in 1992, had unearthed well over one hundred periodicals edited by women. Rodrigues tentatively suggests 'talvez, aí [in Wood's pioneering paper], o dealbar, mais consciente, de um longo processo, a cada passo torpeado' [there, perhaps, the dawning, more conscious, of a long process, torpedoed at every stage],[42] but does not explore the issues of its awakening or of systemic resistance to woman's voices any further. By contrast, Ildefonso's unpublished Open University master's thesis under the aegis of a women's studies programme had provided the first full-scale treatment of the periodical.[43] And by the new millennium, Outeirinho devoted a full chapter of *O Folhetim em Portugal no Século XIX: uma nova janela no mundo das letras* (2003) to the non-negligible contingent of women who were active in the press, under different guises, especially in the 1860s and the 1870s: as translators, as poets and as producers of *crónicas* and serialized fiction.[44] Simultaneously, the genealogy of female-led periodicals and their analysis in their own right came to the fore in Lopes's 2003 doctoral thesis, published in book-form in 2005 as *Imagens da Mulher na Imprensa Feminina de Oitocentos*. The result of a considerable amount of archival work, it was subtitled precisely and not by chance, 'percursos de modernidade' [pathways to modernity].[45]

Leal's overviews had granted pride of place to Antónia Gertrudes Pusich's (1805–1883) and Francisca Wood's projects, in the late 1840–50s and late 1860s respectively. Lopes follows in her footsteps, noting that women journalists in the middle of the century (1850–70) seemed to be more outspoken than later ones (1870–90). Such an assessment was made largely, one might add, on the basis of Pusich's three periodicals and, crucially, Wood's *A Voz Feminina* and *O Progresso*. To the latter, Lopes devoted over one third of her monograph, amounting to around one hundred and fifty pages across four chapters. As such, it is disappointing to see that, even in the aftermath of Lopes's ground-breaking work, the detrimental effects of 're-mediation' conspire to maintain women's invisibility in general surveys to this day.[46] A striking example is the case of Tengarrinha: his seminal *História da Imprensa Periódica Portuguesa* published in 1965 during the New State, did not refer to women's periodicals at all. Nearly half a century later, his 2013 *Nova História da Imprensa Portuguesa: das Origens a 1865*, which stands at over one thousand pages, only devotes two meagre pages to women's periodicals and does not include Pusich in this context. He had however mentioned two of her periodicals, *A Cruzada* (1858) and *A Beneficência* (1852–55) earlier, when evoking journals that promoted conservative religious views, though without citing her name as Editor.[47] Equally unfortunate is the fact that the first history of Lusophone journalism to be published in English, edited by Sousa et al., doesn't recall either Pusich's or Wood's ground-breaking periodicals, selecting instead *O Correio das Damas* as the sole representative of 'feminine [*sic*] periodicals'.[48]

There remains an urgent need for recognition [valorizar], as Teresa Salvador rightly intimated a decade ago:

> As revistas femininas não são o género menor de uma espécie. Para o reconhecer, basta atender à crítica situacional e às propostas reformistas de certos artigos [...]. As revistas femininas são, como quaisquer revistas, plataformas de fixação de ideias e, por conseguinte, suportes incontornáveis para a história das mentalidades e dinâmicas sociais.[49]

> [Women's magazines are not the minor genre of a species. In order to recognize it, it is sufficient to note the contextual criticism and reformist proposals of certain articles [...]. Women's magazines are, like any other magazines, platforms for establishing certain ideas and, consequently, indispensable sources for the history of mentalities and social dynamics.]

While some recent overviews fail to do justice to the wealth and diversity of female periodical culture, and pressing for change therefore continues to be imperative, not all is gloom and doom. Since the start of the new millennium, the woeful neglect of Portuguese women as culture makers in the second half of the nineteenth century is being redressed through focus on a few key names. Two politically active public intellectuals who made their names through periodical culture have been profiled in book-length studies: the afore-mentioned Antónia Gertrudes Pusich and the republican Angelina Vidal (1853–1917).[50] If Wood, located chronologically in between these two pioneers, still awaits a book of her own, one explanation may be that the multifaceted interventions of Pusich and Vidal extended over several decades, whereas Wood's presence through print culture seemed more circumscribed in time. The recent surge of interest in Vidal also derives from her role as precursor of the First Republic, which she lived to witness. Fina d'Armada goes as far as suggesting that her wearing a red and green outfit may have provided a source of inspiration for the Republican flag.[51] While Vidal does not seem to acknowledge the pioneering efforts of Wood — either because she was unaware of her predecessor or because, strategically, it may have seemed easier to start with a clean slate — recovering Wood as an even earlier precursor of first-wave feminism is one of the over-riding aims of the present monograph.

Women and the transnational circulation of ideas

As Lopes readily surmised, Francisca's two journals would justify a whole PhD dissertation in their own right 'tão rico e multifacetado é o material nelas contido'[52] [so rich and multi-faceted is the material contained within them]. Of the several angles that necessarily fell outside the scope of Lopes's recuperation of the contribution of Portuguese women to nineteenth-century print culture, in-depth consideration of transnational aspects is particular relevant to the present monograph. In so doing, we build on Brito et al.'s 1986 article, in order to interrogate the interrelated strands of feminism, transnationalism and the dialogic nature of the periodical culture.

The focus on comparative European women's history, exemplified since the 1990s by edited collections such as *Histoire des femmes en occident*; *Writing Women's History in Southern Europe 19th–20th Centuries;* and *Women's Emancipation Movements in the Nineteenth Century: A European Perspective*, has been generating important historical insights that inform the thinking of this volume.[53] More particularly, the emergence of transnational networks is highly relevant to our discussion, especially since, in the case of Portugal, such networks typically only start to be considered in a later time-span than the one that will presently occupy us here.[54] Simultaneously, the transnational lens is currently producing thought-provoking approaches to the study of nineteenth-century women's cultural production. Examples include the completed Hera-funded project *Travelling Texts, 1790–1914*, and the ongoing ERC-funded Belgium-based 'Agents of Change: Women Editors and Socio-Cultural Transformation in Europe, 1710–1920'.[55] Although Portugal remained marginal in the first project, Christina Bezari's ongoing doctoral research as part of the latter network has recently led to a fascinating article about *Sociedade Futura*, a periodical initially jointly directed by Ana de Castro Osório and Maria Olga Morais Sarmento da Silveira in 1902.[56]

The focus on networks is also generating interest from a transatlantic perspective. In particular, the ongoing *Almanaque das Lembranças* project brings together researchers from both sides of the Atlantic, spanning the period 1851–1932.[57] There are plans to follow up with the publication of biographies of individual women contributors, and one of the first volumes, on Maria José da Silva Canuto, a contemporary of Wood, came out in 2018.[58] As such, the *Almanaque* project promises to add significantly to the recovery of neglected Portuguese women writers in the second half of the nineteenth century. Nonetheless, it will not incorporate Francisca Wood for the simple reason that, as far as we know, she was not a contributor to any of the *Almanaques*. Annuals strove to have wide appeal, and no doubt she was perceived as far too radical to be in demand at home.

The fact remains that it was precisely because of her radical ideas that Wood registered abroad with emergent feminist networks, as we shall see in Chapter 6, and thus she deserves to be understood and celebrated as an early example of European first-wave feminism. This monograph will explore the extent to which, in the absence of any formal organizations for women's emancipation in Portugal in the 1860s, Wood's journalism reflects, or at least shares, some of the priorities in evidence elsewhere. According to Paletschek and Bianka Pietrow-Ennker's summary, emerging nineteenth-century women's organizations were committed to:

1. debate on the rights and duties of women and on gender relations;
2. improvement of women's education;
3. better employment opportunities for women;
4. civil and political rights for women;
5. the social-purity movement, i.e., the fight against the double standard in sexual morality and the regulation of prostitution; and
6. social and charitable work.[59]

Wood's editorials repeatedly touch on such topics. When discussing them in greater depth, we will be guided by Lorna Finlayson's contention that

Theory and practice are not two cleanly separate types of feminism, or alternative forms that feminism can take: the protest and the treatise. To expound a theory is also an action, and sometimes an important political intervention — as we'll see, the insight that *to say something is to do something* has been an extremely important one for some feminists.[60]

This insight that 'to say something is to do something' is particularly relevant in 1860s Portugal, because raising awareness of women's systemic subaltern status was a necessary first step before any collective movement had a realistic chance of gathering momentum.

Broader aspects of Francisca Wood as cultural agent

Finally, it is essential to remember that the reach of Wood as a cultural agent extends beyond her periodicals. Three other aspects of her activities fall outside the scope of this study, although they will be touched upon in the course of it: firstly, her novel, *Maria Severn*, initially serialized in the pages of *A Voz Feminina* and *O Progresso*, deserves a separate study of its own, as well as a new edition. As Cristo notes, during the nineteenth century 'muitas das obras literárias dos mais consagrados escritores europeus e nacionais foram previamente publicadas, em variados jornais, no folhetim, espaço que ocupava o rodapé da primeira página' [many of the literary works written by the most consecrated European and Portuguese authors were first published in various newspapers, in the *folhetim*, the space at the foot of the first page].[61] Of the seven papers mentioned by Wood in the citation transcribed earlier, it is worth noting that the *Jornal do Comércio* had printed in instalments Camilo Castelo Branco's *A Queda de um Anjo* in 1865. Five years later, in 1870, the *Diário de Notícias* serialized the joint Eça de Queirós/Ramalho Ortigão venture, *O Mistério da Estrada de Sintra*. *Maria Severn* is no exception and Wood duly took advantage of her periodical as a platform that provided the impetus both to entertain her readers and to raise their expectations through fiction.

Although the serialized version remained incomplete, it was followed by publication in book-form by Tipografia da Voz Feminina, in two volumes. Yet, remarkably, the online catalogue Porbase does not register the existence of any copies of the novel in Portugal, while the online catalogue WorldCat only shows the existence of one copy, held by the British Library. Other copies can been located in Portugal through *in situ* consultation: both volumes are in the Biblioteca Municipal do Porto, and vol. II is in the Fundação Gulbenkian Library, in Lisbon (it bears a stamp of Instituto Britânico em Portugal; as well as an earlier stamp which reads 'António Joaquim da Silva vendilhão ambulante de livros com depósito em Braga, Campo de Sant'Ana 56 A'). In addition, according to its online catalogue, the Real Gabinete de Leitura, in Rio de Janeiro, holds both volumes.

The difficulty of locating copies in Portugal may explain why until recently, to the best of our knowledge, only one unpublished doctoral thesis, Gabriela Gândara Terenas's 'Diagnoses Especulares: Imagens da Grã-Bretanha na Imprensa Periódica Portuguesa, 1865–1890' and one published article dealt with *Maria Severn*. Moreover, both relied on the incomplete serialized version as their source. Attached to the Universidade Nova, both scholars adopted the perspective of Anglo-Portuguese studies. A more recent article, the first to work from the complete book-version, tackles *Maria Severn* afresh.[62] It argues that Wood presented her readers with a heroine who proved herself to be unusually spirited, in a work where what is fundamentally at stake is a progressive versus a conservative outlook. Thus, through the accessible format of the serial, by contrasting the ideological positions of Maria and her fiancé Henrique, Wood raised a number of pertinent questions about topics close to her heart, including politics, education, class and gender.

Secondly, in broader terms, the Tipografia Luso-Britânica warrants a study of its own from the perspective of the history of the book. Readers will find in Appendix I a list of more than ninety items published under its imprint, uncovered during the research for this monograph. The press was created at the end of 1868, initially with the aim of ensuring the orderly weekly printing of *A Voz Feminina*, as was subsequently detailed in a letter from William Wood to the American Theodore Stanton: 'at the end of last year, we set on foot a printing office, not finding any such establishment equal to our requirements, in point of neatness, correctness, punctuality and economy' (in English in the original, *VF*, 73: 4). Initially known as Tipografia da Voz Feminina, from no. 44 (i.e. November 1868 onwards), each issue of *A Voz Feminina* featured at the bottom of the last page the indication that the paper was printed by Tipografia da Voz Feminina, 29 Rua de S Domingos.

The services of the press were advertised in nos. 45 and 46 and prominently in no. 56. The name was subsequently changed to Tipografia Luso-Britânica from no. 64 (April 1869 onwards), perhaps to emphasize its transcultural nature. It is interesting to note, however, that even after the new designation became operational two early works were published in book-form with the indication of Tipografia da Voz Feminina: Francisca's own novel, *Maria Severn*, and a scientific translation, *História natural ou descrição de todas as classes de animais*, carried out by a woman, Maria Isabel Fernandes.

Jointly owned by the Woods (if we take at face value the plural pronoun 'we set on foot a printing office'), Tipografia Luso-Britânica seemed to gain a life of its own, especially after the demise of the periodical and remained active between 1868 and 1877, as far as we have been able to ascertain. The list in Appendix 1, which is not exhaustive, nevertheless suggests that Tipografia Luso-Britânica was instrumental in the spread of evangelical ideas.[63] All Protestant Churches in Portugal in the nineteenth century, irrespective of denomination, were closely linked with efforts to disseminate and encourage reading of the Bible and the Tipografia Luso-Britânica was no exception, with two editions of the New Testament in Portuguese translation (1870 and 1873), one of them a reprint of António Pereira de Figueiredo's *O Novo Testamento de Jesus Cristo*. The press also produced the monthly *O Amigo da Infância*, a religious magazine that survived into the twentieth century, and more than a dozen short evangelical pamphlets, suggesting there was steady demand for such materials. Among these, a few were translated from English and three others were transcribed from the periodical press in Brazil. The link with Brazil was probably Robert Kalley, a Presbyterian priest who had to leave Madeira in the 1840s, due to persecution, and eventually settled in Brazil.[64] Aside from the dissemination of an alternative understanding of Christianity, Tipografia Luso-Britânica engaged in range of other publications, in particular some literary translations from English that included an early version of Dickens's 'A Christmas Carol' (*Cânticos de Natal*, 1873, translated by Eugénio de Castilho) and Wilkie Collins's 1866 novel *Armadale* (*Armadeile*, 1873).

A third aspect of Francisca's activities that falls outside the purview of this monograph is the translation studies perspective introduced by Cortez's examination of her versions of Grimm's tales published in *A Voz Feminina*, which documents her tendency towards feminist rewriting.[65] Translation was a well-trodden path for learned women, but the most unexpected finding uncovered in the course of the research undertaken for this book is that Francisca Wood may have been the anonymous translator of Charlotte Brontë's famous novel *Jane Eyre*, published under the title *Joana Eyre* in the pages of *O Zoofilo* (1877–1882). *O Zoofilo*, a fortnightly magazine launched in January 1877, was sponsored by the newly created Portuguese Society for the Protection of Animals, but printed by the Tipografia Luso-Britânica during the first year of its life, according to the information given at the bottom of the last page of each issue. The Woods were listed within the pages of *O Zoofilo* as paid-up members of the Society. Moreover, as will be discussed in Chapter 5, even before the Portuguese Society for the Protection of Animals came into existence,

Francisca had not been slow to use her own periodicals to put pressure on the local authorities in Lisbon to clamp down on widespread animal cruelty.

Future detailed stylistic analysis may help to determine conclusively whether Francisca Wood was indeed responsible for *Joana Eyre*, but suffice to note here that the novel provided an empowering model of womanhood for Portuguese readers. The small, plain governess was a woman determined to earn her keep, and intent on self-determination, uttering unforgettable lines such as 'I am no bird; and no net ensnares me; I am a free human being with an independent will'. This attitude of self-respect chimed with Wood's feminist convictions and may support the speculation that she chose to translate this particular novel.[66]

Content Overview

Since this is the first monograph to examine the contribution of Francisca Wood to the history of ideas in nineteenth-century Portugal, the opening two chapters begin by focusing on contextual matters, in order to gain a better understanding of the Woods and the intellectual background that gave rise to the spirited intervention of a periodical guided by the supremely revolutionary concept of 'A mulher livre ao lado do homem livre'. Thereafter, the next four chapters are devoted to *A Voz Feminina* and *O Progresso*, moving from scrutiny of the overall design and cast, through to an analysis of the radical ideas propounded by Wood. Drawing primarily but not exclusively on her editorials as the intellectual *pièce de résistance*, we interrogate the markedly dialogical nature of her discourse, in a process that will involve careful consideration of both her allies and her opponents.

Chapter 1 pieces together new biographical information about Francisca and her husband William, in a bid to bring to light and interpret their life-long engagement with progressive ideas and principles. Drawing on a range of digitized archival material not previously considered, as well as information gleaned from *A Voz Feminina*, *O Progresso* and *Maria Severn*, it speculates that Francisca Wood left her homeland around 1817 only to return four decades later, probably sometime in 1858, imbued with liberal attitudes and values that were whole-heartedly shared by her upper-class husband. First-hand exposure to Victorian print culture over a long period of time decisively shaped the subsequent intervention undertaken by the Woods, through print media, on settling in Portugal.

Chapter 2 introduces readers to the shifting intellectual landscape in Portugal, providing an overview of women's involvement in the 1860s press industry as a continuum. Given the impossibility of examining in detail the presence of all women in print culture, the analysis will primarily focus on the intersection of journalism and literature, through four representative female prose-writers as case studies. The first two, Antónia Gertrudes Pusich and Maria Peregrina de Sousa, active from the 1840s onwards, had built a significant public profile by the early 1860s. Their visibility no doubt encouraged other women to make their mark in print. Of those others, we discuss Ana Augusta Plácido and the today unknown Josephina Neuville and consider how their swift rise to fame in the early 1860s was partly fuelled by controversy. Together, they offer an illustration of how the press helped to amplify shifting roles and identities for Portuguese women of letters.

Chapter 3 focuses on the symbolic significance of having a female public intellectual at the helm of a periodical endowed with a distinctive progressive ethos. It examines the emergence of the sense of a nationwide female community generated from the pages of the newspaper, while bringing out the role of Francisca Wood as a mentor to a younger generation with literary aspirations. We focus on half a dozen female contributors, including three major participants — Emília da Maia, Mariana Angélica de Andrade and most importantly Guiomar Torresão — and briefly touch upon male contributors too. This and subsequent chapters further contextualize the radical novelty and disquiet generated by Wood's project by bringing to light and examining the ongoing hate campaign waged by the conservative periodical, *Bem Público*.

Chapter 4 discusses how Wood's editorials cogently critiqued the dominant assumptions underpinning gender in nineteenth-century Portugal. As well as identifying some of the pressing 'equal rights' issues that would subsequently become associated with Portuguese first-wave feminism some thirty years later (women's education; intellectual aspirations; employment opportunities), her lead articles provided a discursive platform that allowed Wood to critique gendered norms. She tackled head-on the widespread culture of low expectations for women, predicated upon biological assumptions. Even more ambitiously, her modernizing agenda explicitly signposted the need to deconstruct what R. W. Connell calls 'hegemonic masculinity', in ways that productively interrogate and denaturalize the unconscious gendering of the Portuguese nation.

In her self-appointed mission to promote debate, Wood deployed a variety of tactics. Chapter 5 examines one recurrent discursive strategy, namely the publication of open letters, some in the form of petitions, addressed to men in positions of authority. When she began to petition men in power she started on a relatively modest scale with a seemingly self-contained and practical issue, entreating the local authorities in Lisbon to deal with widespread cruelty to animals. Within a matter of weeks, however, two other pieces broaden her scope to more inflammatory issues: the right of women to education, and the thorny question of the vote. In so doing, her public interventions addressed to figureheads endowed with transnational significance — Pope Pius IX (1792–1878), and at the opposite end of the spectrum, the Spanish Republican leader Emilio Castelar (1832–1899) — must necessarily be understood as political statements at a time when women's voices were not easily heard in the public sphere.

Finally, Chapter 6 situates the Portuguese periodical within the emergence of a transnational network of progressive women. It examines how, on the cusp of modernity, Wood used the space of the periodical strategically, as she embraced the transnational cause of women's rights. In Britain, the so-called Woman Question had become a burning issue in 1866, after Barbara Leigh Smith Bodichon collected 1499 signatures in favour of female suffrage within a fortnight, in advance of the Second Reform Bill. The petition was presented to Parliament by John Stuart Mill.

Taking its cue from the unexpected fact that one of the most influential periodicals of the Victorian period, *The Athenaeum*, registered the launch of *A Voz Feminina*, this chapter considers Wood in her role as cultural mediator, through her interactions with Lydia Becker (England), André Léo (France), and Marie Goegg (Switzerland), noting that her deployment of ammunition from abroad simultaneously included references to mid-Victorian male advocates of the female cause such as John Stuart Mill and F. W. Newman.

As A. S. Byatt reminds us in *Possession*, a novel whose main protagonist undertakes conventional archival research in the context of the nineteenth century, with transformative effects that eventually spills into every aspect of his life: 'All scholars are a bit mad. All obsessions are dangerous. This one's got a bit out of hand'.[67] Indeed, the appeal of thinking outside the box when researching the nineteenth century, at the intersection of periodical studies, gender studies, transnational studies, and the history of ideas, soon became dangerously addictive, thanks to the unprecedented opportunities offered in the twenty-first century by '[digital] archives [that] house corpora brimming with potential life, spirits clamorous to return'.[68] By engaging with periodical culture and other digital archives the following chapters will take us, over six instalments, on a journey brimming with discovery. The first instalment begins by fleshing out the background of Francisca de Assis Martins Wood. She is assuredly a spirited writer clamouring to return, yet one about whom so little was known that even her dates of birth and death had remained a mystery prior to the start of this project.

Notes to the Introduction

1. The centenary of the Republic in 2010 has finally ensured the wider availability of this work. See Ana de Castro Osório, *As Mulheres Portuguesas*, ed. by Andreia Neves and Filipa Catarino (Lisbon: Bibliotrónica Portuguesa, 2015). Another edition is available online at <https://bibliotronicaportuguesa.pt/wp-content/uploads/2015/03/ana_de_castro_osorio_as_mulheres_portuguesas_3.pdf>. For a discussion of Osório, see Deborah Madden, 'Historical Context in Portugal', in *A New History of Iberian Feminisms*, ed. by Silvia Bermúdez and Roberta Johnson (Toronto: Toronto University Press, 2018), pp. 199–203 and 'Feminist Thought in Portugal, 1900–1926', pp. 204–12.

2. See Maria Manuela Tavares Ribeiro, 'A Regeneração e o seu significado', in *História de Portugal*, ed. by José Mattoso, 8 vols (Lisbon: Estampa, 1993–1994), V: *O Liberalismo*, ed. by Luís Reis Torgal and João Lourenço Roque (1993), pp. 121–29.

3. For a general overview of their trajectory, see the relevant chapters in *A Companion to Portuguese Literature*, ed. by Stephen Parkinson, Cláudia Pazos Alonso and T. F. Earle (Woodbridge: Tamesis, 2009). For more in-depth studies of their interaction with Britain, see José B. Sousa, *Almeida Garrett (1799–1854), Founder of Portuguese Romanticism: A Study in Anglo-Portuguese Cultural Interaction* (Lewiston, NY: Edwin Mellen Press, 2011) and Maria Teresa Pinto Coelho, *Eça de Queirós and the Victorian Press* (London: Tamesis, 2014).

4. For further details about the *Geração de 70*, see the entry under that name in *Dicionário de Eça de Queiroz*, ed. by A. Campos Matos (Lisbon: Caminho, 1993), pp. 471–76.

5. *Histoire des femmes en occident*, ed. by Georges Duby and Michelle Perrot, 5 vols (Paris: Plon, 1991), vol. IV: *Le XIXe Siècle*, ed. by Geneviève Fraisse and Michelle Perrot; and *Women's Emancipation Movements in the Nineteenth Century: A European Perspective*, ed. by Sylvia Paletschek and Bianka Pietrow-Ennker (Stanford, CA: Stanford University Press, 2004). Wood is also present in Spanish scholarship where her progressive anticlerical thinking is briefly situated

within the broader landscape of 'librepensadoras' [freethinking women] in an article by Rosa María Ballesteros García, 'El despertar de un movimiento social: el feminismo en Portugal', in *Discursos, realidades, utopías: la construcción del sujeto femenino en los siglos XIX–XX*, ed. by María Dolores Ramos Palomo and María Teresa Vera Balanza (Barcelona: Anthropos Editorial, 2002), pp. 165–212 (pp. 173–74).

6. João Esteves, 'Historical Context of Feminism and Women's Rights in Nineteenth-Century Portugal', trans. by Deborah Madden, in *A New History of Iberian Feminisms*, ed. by Silvia Bermúdez and Roberta Johnson (Toronto: Toronto University Press, 2018), pp. 101–10 (pp. 102–05).

7. The inscription at the base features Eça de Queirós's epigraph to *A Relíquia*, 'Sob a nudez forte da verdade — o manto diáfano da fantasia' [Over the stark nakedness of truth — the diaphanous cloak of fantasy (my translation)], thereby allowing viewers to interpret the *female figure* allegorically, as an embodiment of Truth.

8. Deolinda Adão, 'Ecos na escuridão: escritoras portuguesas, vozes controladas, silenciadas, ou de outra forma ignoradas', in *Judith Teixeira: ensaios críticos*, ed. by Fábio Mário da Silva and others ([n.p.]: Edições esgotadas, 2017), pp. 169–82 (p. 180).

9. Machado de Assis, 'Crônica', *O Futuro*, 15 March 1863, pp. 434–36 (p. 436). Machado de Assis, an aspiring young writer at the time, would go on to become Brazil's most famous novelist.

10. Filipa Lowndes Vicente, *A Arte sem História: mulheres e cultura artística (séculos XVI–XX)* (Lisbon: Athena, 2012), p. 239.

11. The last four have individual entries in *Dicionário do Romantismo Literário Português*, ed. by Helena Carvalhão Buescu (Lisbon: Caminho, 1997). Alorna features indirectly as the compiler of her father's biography.

12. Fábio Mário da Silva, *A Autoria feminina na Literatura Portuguesa: reflexões sobre as teorias do cânone* (Lisbon: Edições Colibri, 2014).

13. Marquesa de Alorna, *Obras Poéticas: antologia*, ed. by Vanda Anastácio (Lisbon: Imprensa Nacional–Casa da Moeda, 2015). More broadly speaking, Vanda Anastácio's recovery of pre-1800 women is visible in *Uma Antologia Improvável: a escrita das mulheres (sécs. XVI a XVIII)* (Lisbon: Relógio d'Água, 2013).

14. Maria Amélia Campos, *Ana, a lúcida: biografia de Ana Plácido, a mulher fatal de Camilo* (Lisbon: Parceria A. M. Pereira, 2008).

15. Joanna Russ, *How to Suppress Women's Writing* (London: The Women's Press, 1984), p. 136.

16. Chatarina Edfeldt, *Uma História na História: representações da autoria feminina na História da Literatura Portuguesa do século XX* (Montijo: Câmara Municipal do Montijo, 2006), p. 144.

17. See for instance Juliana de Souza Mariano's master's thesis, 'A Personagem Feminina nos Romances de Maria Peregrina de Sousa: ambiguidades e dualidades' (unpublished master's thesis, Universidade do Rio de Janeiro, 2015).

18. Elen Biguelini, 'Tenho escrevinhado muito: mulheres que escreveram em Portugal (1800–1850)' (unpublished doctoral thesis, Universidade de Coimbra, 2017) <https://estudogeral.sib.uc.pt/bitstream/10316/79402/1/Tenho%20escrevinhado%20muito.pdf>. Biguelini lists ninety-two authors who opted for their full names or initials, and a further twenty-three women who used a generic label such as 'uma menina' to ensure anonymity. Information about these writers and their works are listed in an appendix (pp. 275–391).

19. Fionnuala Dillane, 'Researching a Periodical Genre: Classifications, Codes and Relational Terms', in *Researching the Nineteenth-Century Periodical Press: Case Studies*, ed. by Alexis Easley, Andrew King and John Morton (London: Routledge, 2018), pp. 74–90 (p. 78).

20. Vicente, p. 32.

21. See Maria de Fátima Coelho, 'O Instituto vincular, sua decadência e morte: questões várias', *Análise Social*, 61–62 (1980), 111–31 <https://www.fd.unl.pt/Anexos/Investigacao/7696.pdf>.

22. The news led Victor Hugo to write to *Diário de Notícias* on 10 July 1867, congratulating Portugal on being at the forefront of legislative change. See Leonídio Paulo Ferreira, 'Quando Victor Hugo elogiou Portugal por abolir a pena de morte', *Diário de Notícias*, 1 January 2017 <https://www.dn.pt/portugal/interior/quando-victor-hugo-elogiou-portugal-por-abolir-a-pena-de-morte-5580047.html>.

23. See 'Variedades', *VF*, 61: 4. Henceforth all references to articles from *A Voz Feminina* and *O Progresso* will be given in the main body of the text. *A Voz Feminina* will be abbreviated to *VF* and *O Progresso* to *P*. The later has continuous pagination.

24. Eça de Queirós, 'Um Génio que era um Santo', in *Almanaques e outros dispersos*, ed. by Irene Fialho (Lisbon: Imprensa Nacional–Casa da Moeda, 2009), p. 289.

25. The Linha do Norte only reached Porto itself in 1877, because it took over a decade to build a bridge to cross the river Douro.

26. For reasons of readability, the Portuguese spelling has been modernized throughout. In doing so, I am merely taking my cue from Francisca Wood herself, since she argued for the need of a spelling reform in an early editorial ([n.a.], *VF*, 12: 1–2).

27. Rui Ramos, 'Culturas de alfabetização e culturas de analfabetismo em Portugal: uma introdução à História da Alfabetização em Portugal', *Análise Social*, 24 (1988), 1067–1145. See tables on p. 1116 and 1136.

28. Irene Vaquinhas, 'A Família, essa "pátria em miniatura" ', in *História da vida privada em Portugal*, ed. by José Mattoso, 4 vols (Lisbon: Temas e Debates, 2010–11), III: *A Época contemporânea*, ed. by Irene Maria Vaquinhas (2011), pp. 118–51 (p. 125). For a more in-depth discussion of the 1867 Civil Code, see *Mulheres Portuguesas*, ed. by Irene Flunser Pimentel and Helena Pereira de Melo (Lisbon: Clube do Autor, 2015).

29. Kathryn Bishop-Sanchez, 'Why "The Other Nineteenth Century"?', *Portuguese Literary & Cultural Studies*, 12 (2007), pp. xiii–xxv (pp. xiii–xiv) <http://www.portstudies.umassd.edu/plcs/docs/plcs12/plcs12_introduction.pdf>.

30. Augusto Xavier da Silva Pereira, *O Jornalismo português* (Lisbon: Tip. Soares, 1895), pp. 109–12.

31. See Ana Teresa Fernandes Peixinho de Cristo, *A Epistolaridade nos textos de imprensa de Eça de Queirós* (Lisbon: Fundação Calouste Gulbenkian, 2010).

32. José Tengarrinha, *História da imprensa periódica portuguesa*, 2nd edn (Lisbon: Caminho, 1989), p. 184.

33. Jorge Pedro Sousa, Elsa Simões and Sandra Tuna, 'The Portuguese Press during the Monarchy: From its Origins to 1910', in *A History of the Press in the Portuguese-speaking Countries*, ed. by Jorge Pedro Sousa and others (Porto: Media XXI, 2014), pp. 11–178 (p. 116).

34. Ibid., p. 105.

35. Maria de Lourdes Lima dos Santos, *Intelectuais portugueses na primeira metade de oitocentos* (Lisbon: Editorial Presença, 1988).

36. The table at the back of Santos's book, *Intelectuais portugueses*, usefully provides a summary of their main activities in different fields (ibid., pp. 341–48).

37. Esteves, p. 104. The very existence of an association that brought together journalists and writers demonstrates the intertwining between the press and literature.

38. See entry in *Dicionário do romantismo literário português*, ed. by Helena Carvalhão Buescu, p. 80.

39. Maria Ivone Leal, 'A Voz Feminina: jornal semanal scientífico, litterário e noticioso', *Comissão da Condição Feminina*, 3 (1981), 18–26 (p. 25). <http://cid.cig.gov.pt/Nyron/Library/Catalog/flexpaper.aspx?skey=CDB781C63EB344EAAAEA6D9208D065C7&doc=9636&img=139967&save=true>. This article was expanded and published as Maria Ivone Leal, *Um Século de periódicos femininos: arrolamento de periódicos entre 1807 e 1926* (Lisbon: Comissão para a Igualdade e para os Direitos da Mulher, 1992), pp. 65–71. The Comissão da Condição Feminina, subsequently renamed Comissão para a Igualdade e para os Direitos da Mulher, and today known as the Comissão para a Cidadania e a Igualdade de Género, was instrumental in promoting women's studies in Portugal.

40. Manuela Araújo Brito, Fernanda Robalo and Carlota Guimarães, 'Um Jornal feminista no Portugal de 1868', *História*, 92 (1986), 48–59.

41. Ernesto Rodrigues, *Mágico folhetim: literatura e jornalismo em Portugal* (Lisbon: Notícias, 1998), pp. 160–69.

42. Ibid., p. 169.

43. Maria Isabel Moutinho Duarte Ildefonso, 'As Mulheres na imprensa periódica do séc. XIX' (unpublished master's thesis, Universidade Aberta, 1998). See also her article 'As Mulheres na imprensa periódica do século XIX: o jornal *A Voz feminina* (1868–1869)', in *Novos olhares: passado*

e presente nos estudos sobre as mulheres em Portugal, ed. by Teresa Joaquim and Anabela Galhardo (Oeiras: Celta, 2003), pp. 15–21. Ildefonso restricts herself to *A Voz Feminina*, leaving aside *O Progresso*.

44. Maria de Fátima Outeirinho, 'O Folhetim em Portugal no Século XIX: uma nova janela no mundo das letras' (unpublished doctoral thesis, Universidade do Porto, 2003).

45. Ana Maria Costa Lopes, *Imagens da mulher na imprensa feminina de oitocentos: percursos de modernidade* (Lisbon: Quimera, 2005).

46. For a discussion of the practice of re-mediation see Lilie Chouliaraki, 'Re-Mediation, Inter-Mediation, Trans-Mediation: The Cosmopolitan Trajectories of Convergent Journalism', *Journalism Studies*, 2 (2013), 267–83 <https://doi.org/10.1080/1461670X.2012.718559>.

47. José Tengarrinha, *Nova história da imprensa portuguesa: das origens a 1865* (Lisbon: Temas e Debates, 2013), pp. 825–27, p. 758 and p. 761 respectively.

48. *A History of the Press in the Portuguese-speaking Countries*, ed. by Jorge Pedro Sousa and others, p. 54. *O Correio das Damas* (1838) was headed by a man, J. S. Mengo, according to Lopes, *Imagens da mulher*, p. 691.

49. Teresa Salvador, 'Em torno dos periódicos femininos', *Cultura: revista de história e teoria das ideias*, 26 (2009), 95–117 (p. 95) <http://cultura.revues.org/425>.

50. Nikica Talan, *Antónia Pusich: vida e obra* (Zagreb: Hrvatska Akademija znanosti i umjetnosti; Dubrovnik: Zavod za povijesne znanosti u Dubrovniku, 2006) and Mário de Campos Vidal, *Angelina Vidal: escritora, jornalista, republicana, revolucionária e socialista* (Lisbon: Tribuna da História, 2010) respectively.

51. Fina d'Armada, *As Mulheres na implantaçñao da República* (Lisbon: ésquilo, 2010), p. 93.

52. Lopes, *Imagens da mulher*, p. 361.

53. *Histoire des femmes en occident*, vol. IV: *Le XIXe Siècle*, ed. by Geneviève Fraisse and Michelle Perrot; *Writing Women's History in Southern Europe, 19th–20th Centuries*, ed. by Gisela Bock and Anne Cova (Oeiras: Celta Editora, 2003); and *Women's Emancipation Movements in the Nineteenth Century: A European Perspective*, ed. by Sylvia Paletschek and Bianka Pietrow-Ennker.

54. See Anne Cova, 'The National Councils of Women in France, Italy and Portugal: Comparisons and Entanglements, 1888–1939', in *Gender History in a Transnational Perspective: Networks, Biographies, Gender Orders*, ed. by Oliver Janz and Daniel Schönpflug (New York: Berghahn, 2014), pp. 46–76.

55. <http://travellingtexts.huygens.knaw.nl> and <http://www.wechanged.ugent.be> respectively. See also Henriette Partzch, 'Danger, You Are Entering the Garbage Vortex! Salvaging the History of Women's Participation in European Literary Culture', *Nora: Nordic Journal of Feminist and Gender Research*, 4 (2017), 334–39.3

56. Bezari, Christina, 'Transnational Perspectives in Early Twentieth-Century Portugal: The Emergence of the Periodical *Sociedade Futura* (Lisbon, 1902–04)', *Portuguese Studies*, 35.1 (2019), 39–54.

57. Publications so far include *As Senhoras do almanaque: catálogo da produção de autoria feminina*, ed. by Isabel Lousada, Vânia Pinheiro Chaves and Carlos Abreu (Lisbon: Biblioteca Nacional de Portugal, 2014). For a wider timespan see *As Mulheres e a imprensa periódica*, ed. by Laura Areias and others, 2 vols (Lisbon: CLEPUL, 2014), II (2014), ed. by Isabel Lousada and Vânia Pinheiro Chaves.

58. Eduardo da Cruz, *Maria José Canuto, 1812–1890* (Lisbon: Biblioteca Nacional de Portugal, 2018). According to 'Ana Cristina Comandulli da Cunha' <https://www.escavador.com/sobre/6101641/ana-cristina-comandulli-da-cunha> ('Projectos de pesquisa': para. 1) other Portuguese women featured will include Maria Peregrina de Sousa, Guiomar Torresão, Alice Moderno, Elisa Curado and Matilde Isabel de Santana e Vasconcelos.

59. Sylvia Paletschek and Bianka Pietrow-Ennker, 'Women's Emancipation Movements in the Long Nineteenth Century: Conclusions', in *Women's Emancipation Movements in the Nineteenth Century: A European Perspective*, ed. by Sylvia Paletschek and Bianka Pietrow-Ennker (Stanford, CA: Stanford University Press, 2004), pp. 301–33 (p. 318).

60. Lorna Finlayson, *An Introduction to Feminism* (Cambridge: Cambridge University Press, 2016), p. 5. Italics in the original.

61. Cristo, p. 195. The word *rodapé* is a translation of the French *bas de page* [bottom of the page].

For further information on 'folhetim', see the entry by M. de L. Lima dos Santos in *Dicionário do romantismo literário português*, pp. 190–93. Santos usefully clarifies that there are two different types of *folhetim*: the *folhetim-crónica* and the *folhetim-série*. In the course of this monograph, to distinguish them, the former will be translated generically as 'commentary column' or simply 'commentary' or 'column', and the second as 'serialized fiction' or simply 'serial'.

62. Cláudia Pazos Alonso, 'A Newly Discovered Novel and its Transnational Author: *Maria Severn* by Francisca Wood', *Portuguese Studies*, 32 (2016), 48–61.

63. The proximity of the Convento dos Marianos, located at number 2, Rua das Janelas Verdes, and acquired in 1872 by the Presbyterian Church, may explain the number of evangelical publications by the imprint from 1872 onwards.

64. See Joyce E. Winifred Every-Clayton, 'The Legacy of Robert Reid Kalley', *International Bulletin of Missionary Research*, 26 (2002) 123–27. Tipografia Luso-Britânica published *Exposição de factos: relativos à agressão contra os protestantes na Ilha da Madeira* (1875), a Portuguese translation of Robert Reid Kalley, *An Account of the Recent Persecutions in Madeira* (London, 1844).

65. Maria Teresa Cortez, *Os Contos de Grimm em Portugal: a recepção dos Kinder- und Hausmärchen entre 1837 e 1910* (Coimbra: Minerva Coimbra, 2001), pp. 89–117.

66. The serialization was left incomplete. The first complete translation of *Jane Eyre* seems to have been published in 1916, in Brazil, nearly forty years after the serialized version in *O Zoófilo*, while the first translation published in Portugal did not come out until 1941. See <https://prismaticjaneeyre.org>.

67. A. S. Byatt, *Possession* (London: Vintage, 1990), p. 332.

68. Alexis Easley, Andrew King and John Morton, 'Introduction', in *Researching the Nineteenth-Century Periodical Press: Case Studies*, ed. by Alexis Easley, Andrew King, and John Morton (London: Routledge, 2018), pp. 1–13 (p. 10).

CHAPTER 1

Piecing Together the Life-histories of Francisca de Assis Martins Wood and William Thorold Wood

Information on Francisca Wood is remarkably scant. In fact, up to now scholars have primarily relied on two main biographical recollections, both gleaned from the pages of *A Voz Feminina*. The first is her statement that she was born and raised for the first fourteen years of her life in the parish of Santos-o-Velho ('Declaração', *VF*, 35: 1); the second is her husband's indication that she had spent thirty-five years in England (*VF*, 73: 4). Beyond that, a 2012 article by Lopes acknowledged that 'nada pudemos apurar acerca da sua [Francisca's] permanência naquele país [Britain]'[1] [we have not been able to clarify anything about her stay in that country].

Fortunately, research through a variety of sources, including periodicals, census and parish records, electoral rolls and probate documents, allows us to piece together previously unknown information about Francisca de Assis Martins Wood and her British husband, William Thorold Wood. The fact that William was British, male, and born into an upper-class family inevitably means that it is easier to find out about his background than about Francisca's. An enquiry into his family soon began to unearth a fascinating story, whereas insights into her experience of England, by virtue of necessity, come primarily from both her periodicals and her novel. These were, however, supplemented by the discovery of three official documents: a census record, a marriage certificate and a probate document.

The Great Reform Bill of 1832, and, more broadly speaking, the early Victorian period provided a fertile breeding ground for the radical ideas that would eventually flourish in *A Voz Feminina* and *O Progresso*, almost one decade after the couple's move to Portugal. This chapter will shade in the cultural and political landscape of the first half of the nineteenth century through the couple's dual subjective perspective. It first spotlights Francisca de Assis Martins, before reconstructing William Thorold Wood's biography in more detail, mindful that an understanding of his circumstances also helps us to shed further light on her unconventional trajectory and beliefs.

Francisca de Assis Martins Wood

The 1851 census shows that 'William T Wood' resided in London, at 7 Albion Road, Clapham, where Francisca Martins was named as a visitor. At present, this is the earliest record of her name found in an English official document. She was listed as a Teacher of Languages, while William's occupation was given as Professor of Music. The fact that in 1851 William and Francisca appeared to be living under the same roof is fairly sensational by the standards of the day. Even more tantalizing, however, is the fact that the records revealed that were two other people in that household: a nineteen-year-old servant (Harriet Skinner) and a four-year-old visitor, Charles T. A. Bollard [*sic*]. While a servant simply provides material evidence of William's comfortable status, the unexpected presence of a child, and moreover one with an unrelated surname, naturally begs the question of his exact relationship to the three adults.

In the event, an archival search clarified that the little boy was the eldest son of William Bollaert and Susannah McMorran, a married couple. According to his baptism certificate, his full name was Charles Thorold Alexander Bollaert, which means that he shared William's middle name. The most likely scenario is that William Wood would have been godfather, since the baby was christened eleven months after his parent's marriage (in October 1846, from a marriage which had taken place in November 1845). The Bollaerts' second child, born in 1848, was christened Francisca Maria Augusta Bollaert. Her name suggests that Francisca Martins may have been godmother, all the more so because Francisca (as opposed to Francesca) was a very unusual name for a baby born in mid-nineteenth-century England. William Bollaert (1807–1876) had spent time in Portugal in 1832–33, where his talents in artillery assisted Queen Maria II in retaining her throne.[2] This background provides an explanation of why his path may have crossed with Francisca's. If these speculations are correct, then at the very least William Thorold Wood and Francisca de Assis Martins would surely have heard about each other by 1848, if not before. And, by 1851 Francisca was unconventional enough to go on official record as spending time under the same roof as an unmarried man — implying that they were lovers, and possibly that they used the four-year-old boy as cover.

The known facts surrounding their relationship thus communicate liberal views. In the early 1850s, another couple, George Eliot (the pen name of Mary-Ann Evans) and George Lewes, had famously also embarked on a romantic liaison which led to a lifelong partnership. Their circumstances were even more unfavourable, for Lewes had a wife, a fact which precluded the couple from marrying. The scandal alienated Eliot from her brother as well as polite society.[3] By contrast, official records show that Francisca and William were married on 17 July 1852 at the church of St Dunstan-in-the-West, in London. This Fleet Street church had been refurbished twenty years earlier, in 1831 and the central location suggests that the wedding was not celebrated in secret. That said, it looks as though neither of the witnesses, William Harris and Olivia-Lucy Darell, were relatives. The marriage certificate includes the name of fathers on both sides: hers was Narciso Martins, his

Charles Thorold Wood, both deceased. Curiously, the wedding took place scarcely four months after the death of William's father, Charles Thorold Wood (15 June 1777–13 March 1852). Should something be read into this? Wood senior may have been reluctant to condone such a marriage, or it is conceivable that his legacy gave greater financial security to his offspring.

The 1851 census registered approximate ages for William and Francisca, which place their birthdates around 1816 and 1811 respectively. The former date is confirmed by records showing that William Wood was baptized on 25 March 1816 in Cumberland. Armed with the name of Francisca's father and her place of birth (Narciso Martins and the parish of Santos-o-Velho), I naively imagined it would be fairly straightforward to confirm the exact date of her birth in the Torre do Tombo archives, but I was wrong: there was no record within five years on either side of 1811. I was about to concede defeat when I realized that, in all likelihood, Francisca and William would have been buried in the British cemetery in Lisbon (where Fielding is also buried). Indeed, they were there, in a joint grave, united in death as they had been in life. The inscription concerning her simply read 'nasceu em 1802, faleceu em 1900' (Fig. 1.1), but Church records were more precise and recorded Francisca's death as taking place on 27 November 1900; and William's on 22 April 1888.

This timeline was an unexpected twist, for the age gap between wife and husband appeared to be much greater than the 1851 census had intimated. 1802 seemed implausibly early for Francisca's birthdate, so, for the sake of completeness, it was checked in the Torre do Tombo archives against baptism records for the parish of Santos-o-Velho. There were several Franciscas born in 1802, but only one had a father whose name matched that of Narciso Martins. The relevant entry confirmed that Francisca was born in October 1802 (day of the month illegible). In a nutshell, she was a contemporary of Garrett (1799–1854), albeit one who outlived him by more than forty years. This timeline meant, furthermore, that Wood lived to a ripe old age. In point of fact, she died in the same year as Eça de Queirós (1845–1900), another long-term resident in England. Why then was so little known about her existence after 1869, and no trace of her at all after 1882, given that she lived on for a good deal longer? Had she really retreated into silence, had she become too frail and elderly, or was this another symptomatic example of cultural memory loss in Portuguese literary historiography? The scenario called to mind the marginalization of the provocative Judith Teixeira (1880–1959), whose last three decades remain more or less unaccounted for to this day.[4]

And what about her early life? Bearing in mind, then, that her early formative years coincided with a time of unprecedented political upheaval for Portugal during and after the Peninsular wars, what were the reasons behind her family's move to England? If she was only fourteen, as stated in A Voz Feminina, this would have happened around 1817. The link that immediately sprang to mind was the trial and execution of Gomes Freire de Andrade, in October 1817. A Freemason accused of conspiracy, he died along with another eleven men — his silencing powerfully captured in the 1961 play by Sttau Monteiro, ironically titled Felizmente há Luar! These summary executions led to the emigration of several Freemasons to England.

FIG. 1.1. Tombstone of Francisca Wood and William Thorold Wood,
British Cemetery in Lisbon

Could the relocation of Francisca's father have been part of that movement or was its timing fortuitous? Either way, it seemed reasonable to speculate that Narciso Martins must have been an enlightened man, given the extent of his daughter's learning, and such a profile would go hand-in-hand with liberal convictions. The circulation of freethinking ideas in the aftermath of the French Revolution had led a number of individuals to champion women's education, and even rights. A striking example is that of the Brazilian-born Domingos Borges de Barros, the first politician to call for women to be given the vote in Portugal, on 22 April 1822: 'Domingos Borges de Barros, deputado baiano nas Cortes Gerais, ousa propor que "uma mãe de seis filhos legítimos" possa exercer o direito do voto' [Domingos Borges de Barros, the Bahian born senator in the General Cortes, dares propose that a 'mother of six legitimate children' may exercise the right to vote].[5]

As José B. Sousa points out in his monograph on Almeida Garrett, aptly subtitled *A Study in Anglo-Portuguese Cultural Interaction*, the waves of political refugees that arrived in England at various points during the first three decades of the nineteenth century are 'best explained by political reasons'. Sousa goes as far as labelling the phenomenon 'an exodus of political refugees'.[6] While in exile in England, many of them actively fought to spread liberal ideas, and the press became their greatest weapon. Garrett himself would become the editor of two periodicals printed in England, during his second stay in England (1828–1831): *O Chaveco Liberal* (1829) and *O Precursor* (1831). In doing so, he was following in the tradition of the unusually high number of papers published in London in the previous decade and a half.[7] One of the most long-lasting of such papers, although not one included by Sousa in his list, was *O Português* (1814–19 and then 1823–26). Its editor was the Freemason João Bernardo da Rocha Loureiro. According to Maria Helena C. dos Santos, the paper's readership included 'o grupo de assinantes que o mantêm: comerciantes portugueses radicados em Inglaterra'[8] [the group of subscribers who maintain it: Portuguese merchants settled in England]. If Narciso Martins was one such merchant, Francisca would have had access to the Portuguese liberal press that circulated in England during her adolescence.

We do not know anything about Francisca's mother, but we know Francisca had at least one sibling, since she dedicated her novel *Maria Severn* to her nephew Clarimundo Martins, who wrote to thank her from the Cape Verde Islands (*VF*, 38: 4). Further excavation led to a surprising find: an entry in the *History of the Essex Lodge of Free Masons*, by William Leavitt, registers that Clarimundo was in born in Buena Vista (i.e. Boavista), Cape Verde Islands, on 5 April 1834.[9] His parents were António Joaquim Martins (Francisca's brother) and Apolónia Ferreira Martins. The migration of Francisca's brother to Cape Verde is unexpected but it reinforces the theory of a merchant background. Clarimundo Martins's Masonic credentials indicate that he later went to Salem (Massachusetts, United States), in 1855, and was admitted to the Lodge on 7 August 1860. His links with Freemasonry bolster the hypothesis of similar sympathies in the older Martins generation too.

Although the exact circumstances surrounding the Martins' family move to England remain a matter of speculation, information gleaned from the pages of *A Voz Feminina* confirms that Francisca had opportunities to engage in elite cultural activities such as theatre-going. For instance, she alludes to the various performances and actors she saw on stage:

> Tenho visto algumas das melhores produções dramáticas dos grandes génios: Ricardo III, Henrique VI [*sic*], Othello, Romeo e Julieta, Hamlet, Marino Faliero, Phèdre, e muitas outras antigas e modernas, e também tenho visto os melhores atores estrangeiros, Ristori, Rachel, Helen [*sic*] Faucit, Macready, John Kemble. ('O Teatro D. Maria II', *VF*, 68: 3)

> [I have seen some of the best dramatic productions of the great geniuses: *Richard III, Henry IV, Othello, Romeo and Juliet, Hamlet, Marino Faliero, Phèdre*, and many others ancient and modern, and I have also seen the best foreign actors, Ristori, Rachel, Helena Faucit, Macready, John Kemble.]

Two of the items in this list enable us to date the beginning of her stay in England with some degree of certainty. Her reference to Faliero must be to *Marino Faliero, Doge of Venice*, a tragedy in five acts penned by Byron, first performed in 1821. Even more useful for our purposes, however, is her allusion to John Kemble, for it is known that he took his final leave of the stage in the role of *Coriolanus* on 23 June 1817.[10] This supports the hypothesis that she arrived on British shores no later than the first half of 1817. That being so, the family's relocation was probably unrelated to the assassination of Gomes Freire, since the latter only occurred four months later.

The other names cited also give us an indication about her familiarity with the British stage over several decades: Helena Faucit and Macready, who joined the Covent Garden company in 1836, performed in several Shakespeare plays until 1843, when Macready left for the United States. Rachel [Felix aka Mademoiselle Rachel], best known for her role in *Phèdre*, only became famous after performing in London in 1841. As for the Italian Adelaide Ristori, she only made her debut in England and France in 1856. In short, the dates involved in these passing recollections demonstrate that Francisca was in England for approximately four decades. If we bear in mind that, in the same article, Francisca recounted that she attended a performance in Lisbon in the D. Maria II Theatre on 13 July 1858, this surprisingly precise date suggests that she would have moved back to Portugal by then.

One cannot help noticing that none of these references seem to relate to the late 1820s and early 1830s. Naturally, the possibility that she may have spent a spell outside England should not be discounted. Even if she was in England it is possible that she resided for some years in the countryside. Francisca does not seem to have been married prior to her wedding to William, given that her marriage certificate listed her as a 'spinster' rather than a widow, though earlier romantic interests and even a previous marriage cannot be ruled out. If she did not have a husband to provide for her as was customary, she may have had to work for a living. One possible scenario is that she would have secured employment as a governess, since this was one of the few available respectable means of livelihood for an educated young woman. There were thousands of governesses in England, and Francisca may have been one of them.

In particular, it is conceivable that she took up a position in Hampshire, bearing in mind that *Maria Severn* is set between Newbury and Andover and she appears to have a detailed knowledge of the area. Of course, Hampshire calls to mind Jane Austen's work and therefore, by setting her own novel there, Francisca may simply be following in the footsteps of her literary predecessor. Her first-hand familiarity with the county in question, however, transpires from the following footnote about a local girl:

> O leitor sem dúvida pensará e com razão que a linguagem de Nell não é adaptada a campesina inculta. Nell expressava-se no dialeto do condado em que nascera, tão diferente da língua inglesa que *só depois de se residir muito tempo nas aldeias de Hampshire* é que se pode entender [my italics][11]

> [The reader will no doubt, and correctly, think that Nell's language is not that of an uneducated peasant. Nell expressed herself in the dialect of the county in which she was born, so distinct from the English language that it can only be understood *after residing for a long time in the villages of Hampshire*]

The pages of *A Voz Feminina* also give us an inkling of one of the interests that may have brought William and Francisca together: music. In particular, Francisca's editorial entitled 'A cadeira de Mendelssohn' recounts:

> Eu tive a dita de ver este glorioso artista tocar um trio com Thalberg e Moscheles na sala de Hanover Square em Londres, a um auditório seleto. O trio era um concerto por Sebastian Bach para três pianos; composição que requer de cada executante um *solo* improvisado, o qual necessariamente aquilata o gosto e perícia do improvisador. [...] [Q]uando chegou a vez de Mendelssohn, já não era assombro meramente, era êxtase o que se sentia: o seu *solo* terminou numa trovoada de oitavas com ambas as mãos, de força e presteza quase sobrenaturais. (*VF*, 75: 2)

> [I had the good fortune to see this glorious artist play a trio with Thalberg and Moscheles in the Hanover Square rooms in London, to a select audience. The trio was a concerto by Sebastian Bach for three pianos, a composition that requires each performer to improvise a cadenza, which necessarily measures the taste and skill of the improviser. [...] When it came to Mendelssohn, it was no longer mere astonishment, but ecstasy that was felt: his cadenza ended in a storm of octaves with both hands, of an almost supernatural strength and speed]

It is possible to identify this particular concert as having taken place in the Hanover Square rooms in 1844, since one of Mendelssohn's former pupils, Charles Edward Horsley, described it in a recollection published in 1891:

> Great as Mendelssohn's pianoforte triumphs were, there was one occasion in which he excelled them all. The concert had been arranged at the Hanover Square Rooms, at which Thalberg, Moscheles and Mendelssohn were announced to play Sebastian Bach's Triple Concerto for three pianofortes, in D minor. [...] I wish I had the pen of the Dickens, or Scott (had either of them had any knowledge of music) to describe in fitting terms this performance. It began very quietly, and the themes of the concerto, most scientifically varied, gradually crept up in their new garments. A crescendo then began, the themes ever newly presented, rose higher and higher, and at last a storm, nay a perfect

hurricane of octaves, which must have lasted for five minutes, brought to a conclusion an exhibition of mechanical skill, and the most perfect inspiration, which neither before nor since that memorable Thursday afternoon has ever been approached. The effect on the audience was electrical.[12]

The significance of this particular recollection is twofold. Firstly, it confirms that Francisca, as part of a 'select audience', had access to exclusive spaces like the Hanover Square rooms, several years prior to her marriage to William. What is not yet known is in exactly what circumstances. Secondly, it suggests that William and Francisca shared a love of music. In fact, in the same editorial, Francisca also alludes to a subsequent memorial concert, Mendelssohn's oratorio *Elijah*, performed on 15 December 1848 in Exeter Hall. Elsewhere she mentions in passing a performance by the famed opera singer Madame Viardot Garcia (*VF*, 76: 1).

As well as the theatre and music, her cultural interests extended to the visual arts, and she cites the painters Henrietta Browne and Rose Bonheur. This is also documented in *Maria Severn* where one of the secondary characters, Lionel, is a society painter. His genuine interest, however, lay in the depiction of animals, for which we are told he achieved some recognition, successfully exhibiting at the Royal Academy. As Gabriela Gândara Terenas perceptively demonstrates, the style of this imaginary character brings to mind that of Edwin Landseer, providing a further window into Francisca's artistic tastes as well as her love of animals.[13]

The intellectually curious Francisca was not just attentive to a variety of cultural fields, but was equally at home with developments in psychology and 'popular science'. For instance, in the pages of *A Voz Feminina*, in a lengthy article against animal cruelty, she is complimentary about the American John Solomon Rarey, an early animal psychologist known for his ability to tame violent horses. She also cited William Banting (1796/7–1878), 'author of a pamphlet entitled *A Letter on Corpulence, Addressed to the Public* (1863), in which he singled out sugar and fats as the chief causes of obesity. Written in plain, sensible language, this tract became an overnight success'.[14] The latter is interesting, since it appeared that the Woods were by then based in Portugal. Therefore, it can be inferred that she would have familiarized herself with Banting's ideas through the press.

Politics

During her lengthy residence in England Francisca would have witnessed first-hand major political shifts and read about them regularly, given the explosion of the periodical press as a mass phenomenon. Landmark moments were the debates surrounding the Reform Act of 1832; the Slavery Abolition Act of 1833; the accession to the throne of Queen Victoria in 1837; the physical transformation of London and the Great Exhibition of 1851. Several moments in her novel, as well as a range of articles, confirm Wood's familiarity with British politics and, moreover, her lifelong sympathy for reformers intent on promoting social justice and human dignity.

Maria Severn was set after the Great Reform Bill of 1832, a momentous event described early on in the novel, in Chapter 6, in the following words: 'a promulgação da Reforma Parlamentar, operando como uma portentosa alavanca, deu impulso irresistível ao espírito de reforma geral' (I: 54) [the promulgation of the Parliamentary Reform, operating as a powerful lever, gave an irresistible impulse to the spirit of general reform].[15] The choice to go back in time to an earlier period enables Francisca's identification with progressive politics to come to the fore. In fact, there are allusions to early radical thinkers such as William Wilberforce (1759–1833), one of the leading abolitionist campaigners, invoked as an example of principled action: 'O que fez Wilberforce quando os gemidos da escravidão chegaram a seus ouvidos?' (I: 286) [What did Wilberforce do when the cries of slavery reached his ears?].

A Voz Feminina too offers several tantalizing snippets about Francisca's direct engagement with the British political landscape. The practical involvement of women in the fight for the abolition of slavery is underlined by Wood as an example of early female activism:

> Posso porém assegurar-lhes que em Londres quando se tratava de resgatar os escravos da Jamaica, medida que, como todo o arrojo de benevolência civilizadora, teve que arcar com poderosa e enérgica oposição, a arraia-miúda *recusava* comprar açúcar fabricado por escravos. A mulher que entrava numa tenda a comprar o seu vintém de açúcar tinha sempre o cuidado de recomendar que lhe não dessem *trabalho de escravos*. Ela pouco entendia da questão, mas o marido que lia os jornais ou os ouvia ler e frequentava os *meetings* públicos ensinava-lhe o recado. O senhor abastado ainda quando não apostolizasse aberta ou directamente a emancipação dos escravos, não era *indiferente*, e dava ordens em sua casa para que não comprassem o trabalho de mãos agrilhoadas.
>
> Este expediente não deu, por certo, a liberdade aos escravos, mas sendo forçoso interpretá-lo como expressão de uma grande maioria, deu grande preponderância à opinião reformadora. (*VF*, 67: 1–2)
>
> [I can, however, assure you that in London when there was a move to free the slaves of Jamaica, a measure that, like any courageous act of civilizing benevolence, meant taking on powerful and energetic opposition, the lower orders *refused* to buy sugar manufactured by slaves. The woman who went into a shop to buy her two ha'p'orth of sugar always made a point of urging them not give her the *fruit of slave labour*. She understood little of the matter, but her husband who read the newspapers or heard them read out and who attended public meetings taught her the message. The well-to-do gentleman, even when he did not preach the emancipation of slaves directly or indirectly, was not *indifferent*, and gave orders in his home so that they should not buy the work of shackled hand.
>
> This expedient certainly did not give freedom to the slaves, but as it had necessarily to be interpreted as the expression of a great majority, lent great weight to reformist opinion.]

Francisca Wood's alignment with activism linked to the protection of the most lowly and vulnerable members of society can also be surmised from an unsigned article published in the periodical *O Amigo da Infância* in 1873, titled 'Isabel Fry'.[16] The article offers a biography of the English Quaker, Elizabeth Fry (1780–1845), 'one of the most celebrated women of the nineteenth century'.[17] The author of the

1827 handbook *Observations on the Visiting, Superintendence, and Government, of Female Prisoners*, Fry was:

> a pioneer in her attempts to improve significantly the situation of female prisoners' through her work in Newgate prison from December 1816, whose work gained a more permanent basis in April 1817 with the creation of the Ladies' Association for the Reformation of the Female Prisoners in Newgate, extended in 1821 into the British Ladies' Society for Promoting the Reformation of Female Prisoners, with correspondents in Russia, Italy, Switzerland, and the Netherlands. The British Ladies' Society appears to have been the first nationwide women's organization in Britain.[18]

The article published in *O Amigo da Infância* highlights the sobriety of Fry's Quaker appearance and the righteousness of her behaviour, as well as official government endorsement of her intervention to ensure a more humane and compassionate treatment of female prisoners. But what is of crucial import for our purposes is that Fry's biographical sketch is followed by a first-person account of a visit to Newgate in the company of Fry. The vignette begins as follows:

> Foi alguns anos depois do seu começo que na companhia daquela ilustre filantropa visitei Newgate, uma das principais prisões da Inglaterra e a de mais infausto prestígio. (p. 22)

> [It was a few years after the beginning [of her prison visits] that, in the company of that illustrious philanthropist, I visited Newgate, one of the main prisons in England, of the greatest ill-repute.]

It is almost certain that the author of this article was Francisca Wood herself. Quite aside from the fact that *O Amigo da Infância*, a monthly religious magazine for children, was published by Tip. Luso-Britânica, the above quotation includes a footnote about the word Newgate, which instructs the reader: 'Pronuncie — Niu-guei-te' [to be pronounced — Niu-guei-te]. Footnotes about pronunciation are one of Francisca's signature peculiarities, both throughout her novel *Maria Severn* and her periodicals. Ascribing authorship of this piece to Wood enables us to speculate that her active commitment to humanitarian causes originated in the 1820s — that is, a few years after Fry's work on prison reform at Newgate had began, well before Francisca met her future husband.

Another biographical sketch, this time in *A Voz Feminina*, titled 'Lord Brougham', reads as an obituary of sorts, prompted by the death of the famous antislavery campaigner, Henry Brougham (1778–1868), (n.a., 'Lord Brougham', VF, 23: 2). Additionally, the article emphasizes that he was behind the establishment of the Society for the Diffusion of Useful Knowledge (SDUK), a society founded in 1826, though closed in 1848. The Society was well known for the excellent quality of its European maps, and Francisca writes she was able to acquire maps of Lisbon and Porto whilst in Britain. Another of Brougham's endeavours was the *Penny Magazine*, from which she recalls 'se obtinham excelentes biografias e instrução literária e científica de toda a espécie' [excellent biographies and literary and scientific instruction of all kinds could be obtained] at a very modest price ([n.a.], 'Lord Brougham', VF, 23: 2). At its peak, it enjoyed a circulation of around 200,000 copies a week, and was therefore an instrument for widening its readers' general education. In fact, the *Penny Magazine* was known in Portugal, since *O Panorama: Jornal Literário e Instrutivo da Sociedade Propagadora dos Conhecimentos Uteis* (Lisbon, 1837–68), as its very title implies, drew its inspiration from it.[19] Her article also alludes to Lord Brougham's numerous writings, including a book about the French Revolution of 1848. This obituary helps us to visualize how print culture had a radical effect on the democratization of access to knowledge.

Another telling reference in the context of *A Voz Feminina* was to the radical politician Edward Miall (1809–1881), founder of the Liberation Society, which campaigned for the disestablishment of the Church ([n.a.], *VF*, 78: 117).[20] This would become one of the Republican causes in Portugal, demonstrating what an avant-garde thinker Francisca was for her time.

Print culture is certainly fundamental to an understanding of the Victorian era on multiple levels. Francisca Wood was a consumer of the press, and this was vital to her self-appointed role as cultural mediator, especially in the context of *A Voz Feminina*, as we shall discuss in subsequent chapters. The fundamental importance of the press in the propagation of democratic ideas at the time of the upheaval of the Great Bill of 1832 is highlighted early on in *Maria Severn* too:

> *Squire Severn lia os jornais a sua mulher e a sua filha, e explicava-lhes o que elas não tinham podido entender; inundava o vale com periódicos*, ensinava, prelecionava, convocava meetings; contribuía com avultadas somas quando se faziam coletas; numa palavra, apoiava e segundava, por todos os meios ao seu alcance, os chefes da reforma e suas opiniões. (I: 58, my italics)

> [*Squire Severn read the newspapers to his wife and daughter, and explained to them what they had been unable to understand; he flooded the valley with periodicals*, taught, lectured, called meetings; he contributed with substantial sums when collections took place; in a word, he supported and gave assistance, by all the means within his grasp, to the leaders of the reform and their opinions.]

Maria's father thus took care to politicize the women closest to him (his wife and daughter) as well as the locals. As Francisca noted, the dissemination of radical ideas for the many who were illiterate took place through news being read aloud:

> O sacristão, que era o fanqueiro e capitalista da aldeia, *lia, apoiado no seu balcão, as notícias aos seus fregueses*; o *Catecismo de falácias* do coronel Thompson foi introduzido no vale, lido e discutido e explicado; numa palavra, as grandes medidas parlamentares eram analisadas nos campos, à medida que as sementes caíam na terra. (I: 57, my italics)

> [The sexton, who was the haberdasher and capitalist of the village, *read, leaning on his counter, the news to his parishioners; the Catechism of Colonel Thompson's fallacies* was introduced into the valley, read and discussed and explained; in a word, the great parliamentary measures were analysed in the fields, while the seeds fell on to the ground.]

This is a reference to the famous pamphlet, *Catechism on the Corn Laws* (1827), written by the radical reformer Thomas Perronet Thompson (1783–1869). He went on to enjoy a distinguished career as liberal MP for Bradford (1847–52 and

1857–59).[21] As will be discussed in the second part of this chapter, William Wood shared his political outlook.

There are allusions to two specific newspapers in *Maria Severn* itself. The first concerns an announcement in *The Times*, endowed with a pivotal role in the plot. The second is a reference to *Punch*, or *The London Charivari* (I: 147). Insofar as the novel is set in the period following the great Bill of 1832 (although the exact timing is not specified), the latter allusion appears somewhat anachronistic, given that this weekly satirical magazine was only established in 1841. Nevertheless, it shows that Francisca was in tune with the British humour of *Punch*. In fact, it is likely that the magazine was the source for a further anachronistic citation in the novel, relating to an infamous story about the Duke of Norfolk's insensitive treatment of his tenants in the 1840s, when he advocated 'caril com água para o estômago vazio' (I: 100) [curry with water for the empty stomach]. The story circulated widely at the time and Francisca explained the reference to her Portuguese readership in a footnote: 'Alusão a um discurso feito pelo duque de Norfolk recomendando pós de caril com água para o estômago que carecia de pão' (I: 100)[22] [Allusion to a speech made by the Duke of Norfolk recommending curry powder with water for the stomach that lacked bread].

Maria Severn openly contrasts the backwardness of the 1830s with improvements made in the intervening period. One such example is when the reduction of journey times to the provinces is emphasized through the explicit contrast between the 1830s and the narrative present: 'o trajeto de Londres a Hampshire, que agora [in the 1860s when the novel was written] se faz em duas horas, naquele tempo com as melhores mudas de cavalos não se podia fazer em menos de oito' (II: 173) [the journey from London to Hampshire, which now is made in two hours, in those days with the best changes of horse could not be done in less than eight]. But one particular marker of progress that her novel wishes to foreground to her readers is how far England had advanced in terms of one issue dear to her heart — the status of women and women's rights. *Maria Severn* features one instance of wife-selling, something that would famously provide the opening scene of Thomas Hardy's novel, *The Mayor of Casterbridge* (1886), also set in the early part of the nineteenth century. As Francisca reminds her readers in the periodical, the barbaric practice of allowing 'o marido a lançar uma corda ao pescoço da mulher e levá-la à venda no mercado' (*VF*, 58: 3) [the husband to throw a rope around his wife's neck and to take her to be sold in the market] was a reality about which she had some knowledge: 'Duas foram assim ignominiosamente vendidas entre os anos de 1830, e 1850 em diferentes datas, estando eu então em Inglaterra' (*VF*, 58: 3) [Two women were thus ignominiously sold between the years of 1830 and 1850 on different dates, when I was in England]. This prompted her to regard the Matrimonial Act (which she calls Divorce Act) of 28 August 1857 as a watershed moment for Victorian women, 'para sempre memorável' (*VF*, 58: 3) [forever memorable].

In fact, during her prolonged residence in England, Francisca must have repeatedly read in the press about women's rights, especially from the early 1850s onwards, with the first stirrings of women's movements, including the 1851 publication of Harriet Taylor Mill's 'The Enfranchisement of Women' in the *Westminster Review*, originally anonymously and widely ascribed at the time to John Stuart Mill.[23] The Assistant Editor of the *Westminster Review* was George Eliot, and there is good reason to suspect that Francisca would have been familiar with this periodical at that particular point in time, given that it published favourable reviews of William's musical compositions, as the next section uncovers.

In the pages of *A Voz Feminina*, she alludes to women's achievements in the most varied fields of knowledge, including the scientist Mary Somerville and the political analyst Harriet Martineau (who was also a published novelist). Although she does not mention any women novelists by name in *A Voz Feminina*, the public success and recognition of their works cannot have failed to impress her — following in the footsteps of Jane Austen, major names included the three Brontës, Elizabeth Gaskell and George Eliot.

Relocation to Portugal

The Woods' relationship appears to have been predicated upon a meeting of minds, in the mould of George Eliot and Lewes's partnership. Judging by her writings, Francisca must have been a fascinating, cultured and witty woman for William chose to marry a foreigner who does not appear to have been wealthy and who was, moreover, significantly older than him. It is not entirely clear whether he realized exactly how old Francisca was, but he certainly knew that she was already in her forties. As such, he must have appreciated that her age made her unlikely to be the future mother of his children. Last but not least, the fact that he was willing to move with her to Portugal, leaving his family behind, is a further indication of the close bond they shared.

Evidence that the couple belonged to a privileged elite can be inferred from the 1858 electoral roll, where there is a record of William Thorold Wood living at 48 Cambridge Street, in the parish of St George Hanover Square. Presumably his wife was living there too, but her name did not feature on any roll, since women did not have the vote. The central London domicile conveys rather more financial comfort than the earlier, more peripheral, Clapham address, supporting the hypothesis that William had come into money after his father's death. According to the City of Westminster, 'The largest and most opulent houses were built along St George's Drive and Belgrave Road, the two principal streets, and in Eccleston, Warwick and St George's Squares'.[24]

Little is known about the circumstances and exact timing of the Woods' move to Portugal. On current evidence, it was probably 1858, for while the electoral roll indicated that William Thorold Wood was in London, the aforementioned article on theatre-going indicated that Francisca had attended a performance in Lisbon on 13 July 1858 ('O Teatro D. Maria II', *VF*, 68: 3). One possibility is that she travelled back ahead of her husband to smooth the transition. But, given that neither of the Woods appears in the 1861 census, it certainly seems that by then both were living in Portugal. This suspicion was duly confirmed by an advertisement in English, published in the liberal-leaning newspaper *Jornal do Comércio*:

MUSICAL INSTITUTE, and college for young ladies, n.°s 29 and 31, rua de S. Domingos (à Lapa).

A complete education; including the english, french, and portuguese languages (which are so taught as to enable the pupils to *speack* [sic] as well as write with correctness and elegance); history, both sacred and profane; geography, writing, and arithmetic; embroidery, etc.[25]

It is not difficult to recognize the Woods as the people behind the Musical Institute and College, even though the names of those in charge are not disclosed in the advertisement: not only because of the promotion of a wide-ranging education, but above all because of the location of the establishment in question. We know that numbers 29 and 31, Rua de S. Domingos, was their residence, for it is the correspondence address given for *A Voz Feminina*.

The location that the Woods chose implies that they remained comfortably off. In *Monumentos e edifícios notáveis do distrito de Lisboa*, one can read the following about this neighbourhood:

Beneficiando dum ambiente calmo, nele predominam as moradias individuais, que remontam aos finais do século XVIII, ou inícios do século XIX, emergindo de entre tufos de verdura. É este, na realidade, o tipo mais frequente de moradias apalaçadas das ruas do Sacramento, São Caetano, Pau de Bandeira, Rua do Prior e Rua de São Domingos, esta aristocratizada a partir de finais do século XVIII, apesar da sua origem popular.[26]

[Benefitting from a calm atmosphere, in it predominate individual dwellings, that date back to the beginning of the XVIII, or beginning of the XIX century, emerging from among tufts of green. This is in fact the most usual kind of palatial home in the streets of the Sacramento neighbourhood, São Caetano, Pau de Bandeira, Rua do Prior and Rua de São Domingos, the latter becoming gentrified from the end of the XVIII century, notwithstanding its popular origins.]

An 1853 description confirms that 'A Lapa, Buenos Aires são sítios muito da paixão dos estrangeiros, principalmente dos ingleses: o ar é mais saudável do que o da Baixa, há mais quintais, e pouco sussuro de povo e de carruagens'[27] [Lapa, Buenos Aires are places that appeal greatly to foreigners, mainly to the English: the air is healthier than that of the Baixa, there are more gardens, and less background noise from people and carriages]. Tellingly, this neighbourhood is precisely the one that, a couple of decades later, Eça de Queirós chose for his markedly Anglophile Maia family, as the incipit to his 1888 novel foregrounds: 'A casa que os Maias vieram habitar em Lisboa, no outono de 1875, era conhecida na vizinhança da rua de S. Francisco de Paula, e em todo o bairro das Janelas Verdes, pela casa do Ramalhete' [The house in Lisbon to which the Maias moved in the autumn of 1875 was known in Rua de Sao Francisco de Paula and surrounding area of Janelas Verdes, as the Casa do Ramalhete].[28]

This neighbourhood, of course, was the one in which Francisca had grown up. After more than forty years in a country that Eça de Queirós would later describe as 'probably the first among thinking nations',[29] she was returning to her homeland, steeped in Victorian liberal values. As a 'Teacher of Languages', her accomplishments included not only English, Portuguese and French, but also German.[30] In Lisbon, the Woods set up a private school, and we are briefly privy to the kind of education that may have been on offer in the Rua de S. Domingos, through a letter published in *A Voz Feminina* by Sofia Nesbitt Cunha, one of Francisca's pupils. The letter made reference to rehearsals of *Macbeth* which suggests that Francisca galvanized her charges into activities such as amateur dramatics (Cunha, *VF*, 41: 2). William was involved in this particular performance too, as can be surmised from an examination of the 1872 *Catalogue of the Musical Compositions by William Thorold Wood* held in the National Library of Portugal. It proves that he composed music for several scenes from *Macbeth*.[31] The catalogue does not include any scores, only the words, but it is enough to give us a glimpse of the extent to which the Woods worked as a team. And it is to William that we now turn, in order to understand more fully the family background of the man who became Francisca's lifelong partner, both in a romantic and in a business sense.

Picturing a Victorian Gentleman

The previous section sought to build a more complete picture of Francisca Wood than has previously been attempted. As things stand, there are still many lacunae and one such gap is the fact that there is no known portrait of her. By contrast, it was a likeness of William Wood as a child that first sparked my curiosity about his family background. Even if a picture does not always speak a thousand words, the double portrait of William and his younger brother, Charles Thorold Wood, as children, produced by the society painter Sir Henry Raeburn, and auctioned by Christie's in 1995, certainly suggests that William was born into a privileged milieu.[32]

The sales catalogue of another double portrait, claiming to be a likeness of Willoughby Wood and Arthur Thorold Wood, supplies several invaluable leads:

> The sitters are the first and fourth sons of Charles Thorold Wood of Thoresby, Lincolnshire, a Captain in the Royal Horse Guards. On 1 January 1812 he married Jane Thorold, daughter of Sir John Thorold, 9th Bt., of Syston Park, Lincolnshire. The picture and its pendant (sold at Christie's in 1995) are referred to in a letter written by the sitters' mother in Edinburgh, in which she records that her children had been painted by 'Mr. Henry Raeburn'.[33]

This blurb about the pendant picture enable us to reconstitute the Wood family tree. William's parents, Charles Thorold Wood (1777–1852) and Jane Thorold (1783–1861) were married in 1812. The latter's father, Sir John Thorold (1734–1815), had been an MP and was a bibliophile, so William's interest in politics and culture ran in the family.[34]

A 1911 biography of Raeburn lists a third portrait featuring yet another Wood. It was described as follows: 'Wood, Neville, when a child. Seated in a landscape,

FIG. 1.2. Portrait of William and Charles Thorold Wood
by Sir Henry Raeburn

looking at a spectator, clad in white shirt, a fox terrier lying by his side; his right hand resting on its back, full length; 29 x 24'.[35] Could this have been another sibling of William? If so, how many of them were there in total? A combination of christening certificates and various censuses identified five boys: Willoughby (b. 1813); William (b. 1816); Charles (C. T. Wood Jr, b. 1817); Neville (b. 1818); and Arthur (b. 1821). In addition, searches indicated there were three girls: Emily (b. 1819); Caroline (b. 1824); and Camilla (b. 1825).

According to baptismal records, the Wood children appear to have been born in different locations up and down the country. The eldest, Willoughby, was born in Bramham, West Yorkshire; William and Charles in Cumberland; Neville and Emily in Scotland;[36] Arthur in Sidmouth, Devonshire; and finally Caroline and Camilla in Yorkshire. This implies that the Wood family moved around several times, no doubt because William's father was stationed in various places. By the beginning of 1836, however, Charles Thorold Wood and his large family were based in Foston Hall, in Derbyshire. We know this much because *The Spectator* reported that a fire nearly destroyed their home:

> The first alarm was given by a crackling near the sleeping-room of the second son; who escaped, though nearly suffocated by the smoke in the passages. Mr. and Mrs. Wood, five of the children, and the servants, reached the garden in safety, when they missed two of their younger sons. To rescue them seemed impossible; when the missing boys appeared — having tied sheets and blankets together, and, fastening one end to the bed-post, let themselves down through the window. The eldest of these boys is only fourteen. The property destroyed is very great.[37]

According to the article, then, the alarm was raised by William (the second son) and one can only admire the resourcefulness and presence of mind of the two teenage boys, presumably Neville and Arthur, in the face of looming tragedy.[38]

The family was thus unexpectedly forced to relocate and they moved to Campsall Hall, seven miles to the north west of Doncaster. One of their neighbours, Lady Barbara Tasburgh Charlton, recalled disapprovingly that the Woods were 'reclused and returned no calls'; moreover 'they were strongly turned to education and carried out their bent in a peculiar and very expensive manner'.[39] The boys, unlike their father and paternal grandfather, both educated at Oxford (and a great-grandfather who was a Fellow of Lincoln), do not seem to have followed in these illustrious footsteps.[40] Nor was there any need to, since the family employed several private tutors. According to Lady Charlton, they employed 'Professors of French, German, Spanish, and a music-master besides'.[41]

It also appears that their mother, Jane Wood, an early adherent of homoeopathy,[42] insisted that her sons receive a thorough and dissident scientific training. Jane and Charles Wood's staunch belief in learning meant that the tutors they chose for their brood were of the highest intellectual calibre. One such tutor was Edwin Lankester (1814–1874), who went on to become an important scientist. His biographer indicates that:

Through Lindley, Lankester obtained the post of resident medical attendant and science tutor to the family of Charles Wood of Campsall Hall, near Doncaster, where, with his colleague Dr Leonard Schmitz and his two pupils, he was able to broaden his own scientific knowledge while playing an active part in the Doncaster Lyceum.[43]

Another teacher who spent time at Campsall Hall at the service of the Woods, then, was the German-born Leonhard Schmitz (1807–1890), who went on to become a distinguished Classics scholar and teacher.[44] We know from Lankester's notes that the Wood family were 'indifferent to religion and fervent Owenites' and that Robert Owen (1771–1858), a Welsh social reformer and one of the founders of utopian socialism and the cooperative movement,[45] actually visited Campsall Hall. Lankester described the event in his diary: 'on Monday last, Robert Owen the Socialist arrived at Campsall Hall and I was invited to meet him [...]. It is curious to see with what earnestness the family of the Woods receive his statements'.[46] Owen's visit can be dated to between 1837 and 1839, the period during which Lankester was employed by the Woods. In other words, it would have taken place shortly after the publication of the first volume of his multivolume work, *The Book of the New Moral World* of 1836.

The Woods' 'eccentric' views had practical results. Following the passing of the Great Bill of 1832, which ushered in the philanthropic outlook that came to be associated with the Victorian era, efforts were made up and down the country to improve local education, setting up Sunday schools and lectures. Doncaster itself enjoyed academic activities thanks to the Doncaster Lyceum, documented for the year 1836. But the Lyceum was not the only such endeavour in this part of South Yorkshire, for Campsall Hall itself also provided the backdrop for what today might be classified as community education. William's father, Charles Thorold Wood, was involved in this enterprise, through the creation of The Campsall Society for the Acquisition of Knowledge. As a result, the private tutors employed by the Woods had an active role in disseminating knowledge beyond the confines of the family from the manor house itself, something not noted by Lankester's biographer.

The Society seems to have been particularly active between 1837 and 1839. Several members of the household were involved in the project, including William himself, who would have been twenty at the time. Unusually enough, the activities of the Society are documented through three complementary perspectives: a detailed summary under the heading 'Proceeding of Societies' in a learned journal; the notebooks and diaries of one of the teachers involved (Lankester); and the diary of one of its young pupils, posted online by one of his descendants.

The launch of the Society in June 1837 and its initial weekly meetings are recorded in *The Analyst: A Quarterly Journal of Science, Literature, Natural History and the Fine Arts*:

The society of which we have just given the title is established for the benefit an improvement of the *labouring classes*. At the inaugural meeting, the chair spoke followed by Mr Lankester, who declared to the Chair: 'You have established a society for the acquisition of knowledge, not in this *city*, not in this *town*, but in this *village*, and, so far as I am aware, it is the first society of the kind that has sprung up in so small and secluded spot'.[47]

The Chair was Charles Thorold Wood senior. Honorary members belonging the Wood family were listed as Charles Thorold Wood, Esq., Willoughby Wood, Esq., Neville Wood, Esq., C. T. Wood, jun., Esq, William Thorold Wood, and Master A. Thorold Wood. The name of the Society echoed that of Lord Henry Brougham's Society for the Diffusion of Useful Knowledge founded in 1826. Indeed his *Penny Magazine* was mentioned in *The Analyst*'s summary.

A different perspective on the Society comes from a young local labourer, David Knowles, who benefitted first-hand from the lectures and tuition on offer at Campsall Hall. His diary, which covers a fifteen-month period between 28 November 1837 and 3 March 1939, was posted online by Chris Waltham, David Knowles' great-great-grandson.[48] Knowles's diary entries are short, but they offer a fascinating glimpse into the kind of education that was offered at Campsall Hall. There were regular lectures, sometimes several a week, on topics like phrenology; natural philosophy; lightning and electricity; the wealth of England; political economy (delivered by William Wood); the results of machinery; astronomy; morals (delivered by William Wood); the history of mankind; insects and animals; the human frame. Of particular note among the lectures delivered at Campsall Hall is perhaps the one by Mr Chiosso on universal suffrage on 25 September 1938.[49]

All in all, the topics covered by the various speakers showcase the spread of radical teaching and thinking that was on offer. In other words, The Campsall Society for the Acquisition of Knowledge was a collective effort to democratize knowledge, as a group of individuals influenced by the utopian socialism of Robert Owen came together and took action to try and make a difference. Arguably, it provided a blueprint for William Wood's lifelong commitment to enlightenment of the mind through education, a commitment wholeheartedly shared by his wife.

William Thorold Wood: from Campsall Hall to London

We can follow the trajectories of the male members of the Wood family after they left Campsall Hall: in a pattern familiar in upper-class Victorian families, one middle child trained as a doctor while the youngest boy, Arthur, became a clergyman.[50] The medical career was followed by Neville, who published *A Brief View of Homœopathy* in 1846, but not before he had expounded unorthodox ideas about ornithology, generating a lively scientific debate.[51] As for Charles, he became a utopian socialist, judging by his 1842 translation into English of Madame G. de Gamond's *Fourier and His System*, a book he also prefaced. Such publications bear witness to the unconventional ideas of the two siblings born either side of William. By contrast, as often happens with Victorian women, little is known about William's three younger sisters, though we can surmise that Emily never married from the fact that she still had her maiden name when she died.

As for William, Knowles's diary documents William's involvement not just as an occasional lecturer but moreover as his regular music teacher. Lessons started with the violin, and then moved on to the flute at David's own request. David Knowles (b. 1818), who was only a couple of years younger than William Wood (b. 1816), may well have been one of his first pupils. Simultaneously, the latter's musical disposition meant that he had already made his debut as a composer of drawing-room music, an occupation which reveals an element of upper-class sociability far removed from the more serious educational purposes of The Campsall Society. An early review in *The Analyst* in 1836 praised two pieces: one with words by Mary Russell Mitford, 'Sweet is the balmy evening hour', 'inscribed to his mother', and another, 'Go gently Zephyr', with words translated from Metastasio, 'dedicated, at her request, to the opera singer Madame Malibran de Bériot'.[52] The latter may well have been one of the first Hispanic women he met; like Francisca, she was older than him and, judging by the wording of the dedication, she seems to have made an impression on him. The following year, by contrast, the 'Review' section of the weekly magazine *The Musical World* offered a far from glowing appraisal of several pieces by William, published by Boosey, including four sets of waltzes, as well as light music such as canzonets and a cavatina. The review referred to Mr Wood as an amateur musician who should 'be more selective and fastidious in committing his thoughts to the public'. But it added as a sweetener that 'In all the above pieces there are indications of negligence, accompanied by promises of the capability to produce better things'.[53]

By the early 1840s, evidence suggests that William had relocated to London, probably in order to follow a conventional path for a second child from a well-to-do upper-class family, as he was admitted to Gray's Inn Chambers in 1841. An entry in *Register of Admissions to Gray's Inn* reads 'William Thorold Wood, aged 25, second son of Charles Thorold W., of Campsall Hall, near Doncaster, Esq'.[54] He does not appear to have been called to the Bar, however. Instead, undeterred by his distinctly lukewarm early reviews, he continued to compose music. And of course he may have undertaken a Grand Tour at some point, an interest that may have been sparked by close contact with the continental tutors while employed at Campsall Hall. Certainly the 1872 *Catalogue of the Musical Compositions* lists musical arrangements for German poems by the likes of Heine, composed after leaving Yorkshire.

By 1850, having opted out of the security of a career in law, there is mounting evidence of William's long-standing interest in music. In fact, an advertisement placed on Monday 17 June 1850 in the *Daily News* intimates that he was trying to secure an income from his creative endeavours.[55] Three scores of his musical compositions survive in the British Library, dating from 1840, 1846 and 1848, respectively. The first two are light music, but the third set to music an overtly revolutionary poem, 'The People's Anthem', written by Ebenezer Elliott, an anti-Corn Law poet.[56] This piece seems to indicate a turning-point in William's outlook, following the 1848 Revolution in France and possibly taking his cue from his brother's translation of the utopian socialist Fourier. Indeed it provides evidence that his earlier involvement in a radical political agenda during his Campsall Hall days now influenced his choice of musical subject matter.

Elliott's poem was first published in *Tait's Edinburgh Magazine* in June 1848.[57] But it was then significantly revised 'written for music, at the request of W. T. Wood Esq.', according to the version published in book-form two years later. For this reason, it is worth transcribing here:

The People's Anthem

When wilt thou save the people?
Oh God of Mercy! when?
Not kings and lords, but nations!
Not thrones and crowns, but men!
Flowers of thy heart, oh, God, are they!
Let them not pass, like weeds, away!
Their heritage a sunless day!
God, save the people!

Shall crime bring crime for ever,
Strength aiding still the strong?
Is it thy will, oh Father,
That man shall toil for wrong?
'No!' say thy mountains; 'No!' thy skies:
'Man's clouded sun shall brightly rise,
And songs be heard, instead of sighs.'
God, save the people!

When wilt thou save the people?
Oh God of Mercy! when?
The people, Lord, the people!
Not thrones and crowns, but men!
God! save the people! Thine they are,
Thy children, as thy angels fair:
Save them from bondage, and despair!
God! save the people![58]

Wood's musical composition earned him glowing reviews from a number of quarters. The most significant endorsement came in 1851, when the *Westminster Review* reviewed it, alongside two other compositions. The review heaped super-lative praise on William:

> These pieces of music afford a most convincing proof that musical genius of high order is not wanting amongst us. 'The People's Anthem' consists of a quartette, semi-chorus, and chorus, and has been performed at large meetings at the London Tavern and elsewhere, with admirable effect. The words are very grand and striking, and were written expressly for Mr Wood by the people's poet, Ebenezer Elliott, with the hope of stimulating a lofty tone of patriotic feeling. We cannot doubt that, before long, this truly noble piece will be heard all over the kingdom. It is the Marseillaise Hymn of that peaceful progress to which the efforts of our best minds and hearts are directed, and will be received with enthusiasm wherever a right English feeling prevails.[59]

Lest it should be forgotten, George Eliot was Assistant Editor of the *Westminster Review* precisely at that point in time (1851–54). The review then moves on to discuss other compositions:

The 'Song of the Electric Telegraph' with words by Leeman Blanchard and the 'Meeting of the Nations', with words by Charlotte Young, alluding to the Great Exhibition, are admirable pieces, and show by their treatment that Mr Wood has the true inspiration of the poet, as well as the genius of the musician.[60]

'The Meeting of the Nations', too, was a topical piece, as transpires from its subtitle 'A Song for the Great Exhibition of Industry in 1851'.[61] Young was the author of *The World's Complaint, and Other Poems*, 1847, but this particular poem set to music by William did not feature in her collection.

The existence of the 1872 *Catalogue of the Musical Compositions* helps us to identify other poems he set to music.[62] What is immediately striking is that several were authored by women. These included:

— Mary Russell Mitford, Sweet is the balmy evening hour, 1835–1867;
— Louisa Anne Twamley, Softly Glimmers, 1835, The Christmas Wreath, 1837, Fairy song, 1837–1867;
— Mary Howitt, Little Waves, 1838;
— Mrs Radcliffe, Pour the Rich Libation, 1839;
— Charlotte Young, Love and the Cuckoo, 1850, The Life is What We Make of, 1850, The Worker, 1851, The Meeting of the Nations, 1851;
— Mrs Judson, Maternal Love, 1851.

The famous Ann Radcliffe (1764–1823), the Lusophile Mary Russell Mitford (1787–1855), author of the play *Inez de Castro* (1826–27), and Mary Howitt (1799–1888) all belonged to older generations. But Louisa Anne Twamley, known as Louisa Anne Meredith (1812–1895), and the afore-mentioned Charlotte Young were contemporaries of William.

Still in the turbulent period of 1848–50, William's radical political leanings are documented by more than just the fact that he had set to music 'The People's Anthem'. Indeed, an online periodical search reveals that he took part in meetings of The National Reform Association.[63] For instance, the *Morning Advertiser* indicates that, at an April 1850 gathering, attended by the most high-profile anti-Corn Law political activists such as Colonel Thompson and Richard Cobden, William Thorold Wood represented Stockwell and Clapham jointly with Henry James Stack.[64] It is worth pointing out that alongside well-known radical MPs, the paper reports that there were several ladies present. Could Francisca perhaps have been one of them? We shall never know, since none of their names appear. But we know that some of the meetings took place at the London Tavern where, according to the *Westminster Review*, William Wood's 'The Peoples' Anthem' was 'performed at large meetings [...] with admirable effect'.[65]

This brief overview allows us to build a picture of the gentleman who, only two years later, was to walk down the aisle with the Portuguese Francisca de Assis Martins and who eventually moved with her to the country of her birth.

The Woods' Twilight Years

Lopes speculates that the Woods' relocation to Portugal was motivated by religious reasons, though she did not find evidence of their playing any formal role in evangelical churches.[66] Nor is there any reference to the Woods in English sources. What we do know is they had already been residing in Portugal for several years when the movement towards the creation of the Lusitanian Church took off in the years of 1867–68, before the Church was formalized in 1875.[67] That said, one cannot fail to notice that the Tipografia Luso-Britânica sponsored numerous publications implying evangelical sympathies, as well as two editions of the Bible (see Appendix 1). And, furthermore, in 1877 William Wood was listed as a subscriber to the British Protestant School, which was connected to St George's Chapel.[68]

The last known publications printed in Tipografia Luso-Britânica date from 1877. They include the periodical *O Zoofilo*, where Francisca Wood may have been the anonymous translator of Charlotte Brontë's famous novel *Jane Eyre* under the title *Joana Eyre*, a speculation to which we will return in Chapter 6. Among other items, that year also saw the printing of a curious pamphlet, *As Farpas e John Bull* (1877). The title is eye-catching since it places the Woods in direct dialogue with the celebrated satirical monthly, edited by Ramalho Ortigão. There was, however, already earlier evidence of links to the *Geração de 70*: in 1870 Tipografia Luso-Britânica had printed of two items by F. A. Coelho, one year before Francisco Adolfo Coelho delivered the lecture on education that famously prompted the closure of the Casino Lectures.[69]

Although the 1877 pamphlet is unsigned, William must surely have been its author, given it was written in English. After praising the style of *As Farpas* — 'a veritable oasis of pleasant and entertaining reading in the vast desert of dreary, worrisome, unprofitable Portuguese periodical literature' — Wood moves on to take exception to one article in particular, 'A Mr John Bull', where Ortigão had had a dig at the Prince of Wales.[70] Wood professed himself to be disappointed to see England equated with the figure of the heir apparent, before outlining the main purpose of his letter:

> I propose to show you that you have much to learn from English institutions, customs, and manners that might become the basis of your country's future prosperity and her future greatness; and very much to unlearn from France before you can eradicate, exterminate, stamp out that undercurrent of frivolity, irreligion, and immorality that laid low the national honour and greatness of France in the Franco-Prussian War.[71]

Since this is the only known published open letter of what William Wood presents as a planned series, we can only take an educated guess at what he might have had to say about social, political and intellectual advances in Victorian England. One wonders, however, how Ortigão reacted to this lecture of sorts. It was one thing for a Portuguese intellectual like Ortigão or Eça de Queirós to denigrate his own country, and quite another for an Englishman to conclude that Portugal was 'doomed to remain untaught, uninterested, unenlightened by the great social reforms and advancement going on in other civilized nations, owing to the criminal neglect, indolence, selfishness and egotism of her legislators and public men'.[72] In this respect, it may not be a coincidence that, one decade later, Ortigão chose to entitle his 1887 book about England *John Bull: depoimento de uma testemunha acerca de alguns aspectos da vida e da civilização inglesa*, thereby indirectly answering William Wood. For Ortigão's book showcases not only the greatness of British civilization but also the poverty that could be seen in London.

And what about Eça de Queirós, who was then living in Newcastle? Did he ever come across William Wood's short pamphlet? It is possible that Eça would have been aware of the Woods, for the simple practical reason that in 1880 his close friend the Conde de Arnoso started to build a house in the Rua de São Domingos, the very same street where the Woods resided.[73] Certainly the sentiment about the need to unlearn from France and learn from English institutions, customs and manners, is very much something that Eça himself would advocate throughout the 1880s.

The fact that William Wood's planned series of letters about England does not seem to have materialized and that the serialized version of *Jane Eyre* remained incomplete may be simply an indication of failing health, rather than loss of heart. But as they approached their twilight years, perhaps the Woods were ready to let the younger generation fight for the values that they had upheld in *A Voz Feminina* and *O Progresso*, first and foremost as we shall see, justice, science, reason, freedom of thought, education, temperance and equality between the sexes. After the Tipografia Luso-Britânica closed down, the only trace we currently have of the Woods is as paid-up members of the Society for the Protection of Animals until 1882, thanks to listings in *O Zoofilo*.[74]

William Thorold Wood died in Lisbon. His birth and death dates do not feature on the couple's joint tombstone, but Church records indicate that he passed away on 22 April 1888. Instead, the tombstone was inscribed with a moving tribute from his widow:

> Here lies my darling husband William Thorold Wood
>
> Desatai-vos, correi ó minhas lágrimas
> Flores, velai-lhe o derradeiro sono!
> Passai de leve sobre a campa gélida
> Aragens frias do ceifeiro outono!
>
> [Burst forth, flow, oh my tears,
> Flowers, watch over his last sleep!
> Cold winds of the devastating Autumn
> Blow gently over the frozen grave!]

Curiously, even though William died in the Spring, the bleak image of the cold Autumn winds takes over to convey poetically the symbolic chill of death, which left Francisca bereft.

Notwithstanding the fact that William had been residing in Portugal for nearly three decades, and was buried in Lisbon, in good Victorian mode a death announcement was published in *The Morning Post* on 28 April 1888. Highlighting his three most important family connections, as well as praising his learning and moral virtues, it read as follows: 'cousin to the Bishop of Rochester, to Sir John

Thorold, of Syston Park, and brother to the rector of Widmerpool, Nottingham. He was a man of great mental endowments and exemplary conduct'.[75] The first two were his cousins on his mother's side. Anthony Wilson Thorold (1826–1895) had become Bishop of Rochester in 1877, and would later go on to become Bishop of Winchester.[76] His brother was the aforementioned clergyman Rev. Arthur Wood. On the first anniversary of William's death, an 'In Memoriam' was published in *The Morning Post*, with the following wording: 'on 22 April 1888, at Lisbon. William Thorold Wood, the beloved husband of F. Wood. In loving memory'.[77]

It was perhaps lucky for William that he died two years before the British Ultimatum. Francisca, on the other hand, survived him by more than a decade, and would therefore have been aware of the waves of anti-British feeling it aroused in the Portuguese press.[78] Her tombstone inscription, as previously mentioned, was rather laconic, sticking to the barest facts: 'nasceu em 1802 / faleceu em 1900' [born in 1802 / died in 1900]. By then, her beloved nephew Clarimundo Martins had already been dead for a decade. Nonetheless we can surmise that neither of the Woods died in poverty. One last piece of evidence, the *Probate Calendars of England & Wales, 1858–1959*, helps us to confirm that they remained comfortably off to the end: the personal estate of William Thorold Wood amounted to £5639.[79] Twelve years later, when Francisca died, the *Probate Calendar* for 1901 registered that her effects amounted to the handsome sum of £4152. The earlier of the two probates indicated that the Woods had moved from 31 Rua de S. Domingos to 9 Rua das Janelas Verdes, where Francisca also died, in 1900.[80]

Their financial circumstances explain why they were able to afford to keep *A Voz Feminina* and *O Progresso* going for more than one hundred issues. Clearly, their primary concern was not profit, but rather an educational and necessarily political commitment, as they set themselves the goal of contributing to women's learning. Chapter 2 examines in more detail the changing intellectual background during the period 1848–67, with particular reference to Portuguese women's involvement in print culture. Such an overview will not only give us a better sense of the publishing landscape in the two decades leading up to the launch of *A Voz Feminina* but also subsequently enable a more informed appraisal of historical continuities and discontinuities as Francisca Wood came onto the scene: ready to press for change, she fashioned herself as an unapologetically combative intellectual through her provocative editorials.

Notes to Chapter 1

1. Ana Maria Costa Lopes, 'Religião e género como formas de discriminação no século XIX: o casal Wood, um study case', *Gaudium Sciendi*, 2 (2012), 51–65 (p. 56).
2. Roeckell, L., 'Bollaert, William (1807–1876)', *Oxford Dictionary of National Biography* <http://www.oxforddnb.com>. For this service he received the Portuguese War Medal and was made a Knight of the Order of the Tower and Sword. William Bollaert subsequently published *The Wars of Succession of Portugal and Spain from 1826 to 1840: With Résumé of the Political History of Portugal and Spain to the Present Time* (London: E. Stanford, 1870).
3. See Jennifer Uglow, *George Eliot* (London: Virago, 1987).
4. See Cláudia Pazos Alonso, 'Judith Teixeira: um caso modernista insólito', in *Obras de Judith*

Teixeira: poesia e prosa, ed. by Cláudia Pazos Alonso and Fábio Mário da Silva (Lisbon: Dom Quixote, 2015), pp. 21–38.

5. Anne Marie Colling, 'Precursor do voto feminino no ocidente é um brasileiro: Domingos Borges de Barros nas Cortes Gerais portuguesas em 1822', *Anais do XXVII Simpósio Nacional de História* <http://www.snh2013.anpuh.org/resources/anais/27/1370097714_ARQUIVO_textoanpuh2013.pdf>.

6. p. 113.

7. Ibid., pp. 114–15.

8. Maria Helena C. dos Santos, 'Imprensa periódica clandestina no século XIX: "O Portuguez" e a Constituição', *Análise Social*, 61–62 (1980), 429–45 (pp. 443–44).

9. William Leavitt, 'History of the Essex Lodge of Freemasons', in *The Historical Collections of the Essex Institute*, 4 vols (Salem: G. M. Whipple & A. A. Smith, 1859–62), III (1861), 37–47, 84–95, 121–33, 174–86, 207–18, 253–72 (p. 272) <http://dbooks.bodleian.ox.ac.uk/books/PDFs/555028439.pdf>.

10. Thomson, P., 'Kemble, John Philip (1757–1823)', *Oxford Dictionary of National Biography* <http://www.oxforddnb.com >.

11. Francisca de Assis Martins Wood, *Maria Severn*, 2 vols (Lisbon: Tipografia da Voz Feminina, 1869), I, 276. Henceforth all references to *Maria Severn* will be given in the text, by volume and page number.

12. Charles Edward Horsley, 'Reminiscences of Mendelssohn by his English Pupil', in *Mendelssohn and his World*, ed. by R. Larry Todd (Princeton, NJ: Princeton University Press, 1991), pp. 237–51, pp. 243–44.

13. Gabriela Gândara Terenas, 'Diagnoses especulares: imagens da Grã-Bretanha na imprensa periódica portuguesa (1865–1890)', 3 vols (unpublished doctoral thesis, Universidade Nova de Lisboa, 2004), II, 466.

14. Robert Harrison, 'Banting, William (1796/7–1878)', in *Oxford Dictionary of National Biography*.

15. There was an earlier inconsistency in Chapter 5, where events were described as taking place before 1832: 'Isto não era assim na época de que data esta história, a qual é antecedente à grande reforma parlamentar de 1832' (I: 45) [This was not so in the period from which this story dates, which preceded the great parliamentary reform of 1832].

16. Anon, 'Isabel Fry', *O Amigo da Infância* (Lisbon: Tip. Luso-Britânica), pp. 12–13 & 21–23. There is no indication of year or month of publication, but it was probably 1874.

17. F. de Haan, 'Fry [née Gurney], Elizabeth (1780–1845)', *Oxford Dictionary of National Biography*. Domestication of first names was a common translation practice in the nineteenth century.

18. Cited by Haan.

19. See Jorge Pedro Sousa, Elsa Simões Lucas Freitas and Sandra Gonçalves Tuna, 'Diffusing Political Knowledge in Illustrated Magazines: A Comparison between the Portuguese *O Panorama* and the British *The Penny Magazine* in 1837–1844', in *Diachronic Developments in English News Discourse*, ed. by Minna Palander-Collin, Maura Ratia and Irma Taavitsainen (Amsterdam and Philadelphia: John Benjamins, 2017), pp. 157–73.

20. D. W. Bebbington, 'Miall, Edward (1809–1881)', in *Oxford Dictionary of National Biography*.

21. Michael J. Turner, 'Thompson, Thomas Perronet (1783–1869)', in *Oxford Dictionary of National Biography*.

22. A 1925 article in *The Spectator* briefly contextualizes the allusion: 'It seems an established fact that Norfolk's thirteenth Duke advised his tenants to try curry powder in hot water as an antidote to hunger. [...] The pages of the contemporary numbers of Punch are full of references to the grim suggestion. At the end of 1846 there is a notice of the "Duke of Norfolk's Cookery." In January, 1846, a poem entitled "Ye Peasantry of England," and dedicated to the Duke, recommends: — "When hunger rages fierce and strong To the curry powder go"'. F. M. Collet, 'A Pinch of Curry Powder', *The Spectator*, 15 May 1925, p. 17. <http://archive.spectator.co.uk/page/16th-may-1925/17>.

23. [Harriet Taylor Mill], 'The Enfranchisement of Women', *Westminster Review*, 109 (1851), 289–311.

24. 'Pimlico: Conservation Area — General Information Leaflet', City of Westminster, May 2004 <http://www3.westminster.gov.uk/docstores/publications_store/27%20Pimlico.pdf> (para. 2).

25. Italics in the original. [Musical institute], *Jornal do Comércio*, 23 March 1861, p. 4.
26. *Monumentos e edifícios notáveis do distrito de Lisboa*, ed. by Maia Ataíde and António Manuel Gonçalves, 5 vols (Lisbon: Junta Distrital, 1962–2007), III (1963).
27. *Novo guia do viajante em Lisboa e seus arredores, Cintra, Collares, e Mafra: ornado com algumas vistas dos principaes monumentos de Lisboa* (Lisbon: J. J. Bordalo, 1853), pp. 106–07.
28. Eça de Queirós, *Os Maias* (Lisbon: Livros do Brasil, 1969) p. 5; *The Maias*, trans. by Margaret Jull Costa (Sawtry: Dedalus, 2016), p. 13. Incidentally, for most of the twentieth century the British Embassy was located there as well.
29. Cited by Coelho, *Eça de Queirós and the Victorian Press*, p. 6, foonote 1.
30. One of her chronicles suggests that Francisca gave German lessons (*VF*, 26: 3). Moreover, according to Cortez, her translations of Grimm's tales were directly from German.
31. William Thorold Wood, *Catalogue of the Musical Compositions* (Lisbon: Anglo-Portuguese Printing Office, 1872), pp. 23–24.
32. <http://www.artnet.com/artists/sir-henry-raeburn/17>.
33. This picture was sold in 2012. 'Item lot number: 383', *Tennants Auctioneers* <https://bid.tennants.co.uk/m/lot-details/index/catalog/69/lot/57176?url=%2Fm%2Fview-auctions%2Fcatalog%2Fid%2F69%3Fpage%3D8> (para. 2).
34. See Mark Purcell, 'Thorold, Sir John, ninth baronet (1734–1815)', in *Oxford Dictionary of National Biography*.
35. James Greig, *Sir Henry Raeburn, R.A.: His Life and Works, With a Catalogue of His Pictures* (London: The Connoisseur, 1911), p. 62 <https://archive.org/stream/sirhenryraeburnroogreiuoft/sirhenryraeburnroogreiuoft_djvu.txt>.
36. This means that the toddler in the likeness sold by Tennants in 2012, if executed in Edinburgh, must be Emily since Arthur was not yet born.
37. 'The Country', *The Spectator*, 27 February 1836, p. 9 <http://archive.spectator.co.uk/article/27th-february-1836/9/foston-hall-in-derbyshire-the-residence-of-mr-char>.
38. Although *The Spectator* refers to the elder of the two younger boys as being fourteen, it was the younger boy, Arthur, who would have been fourteen at the time.
39. *The Recollections of a Northumbrian Lady, 1815–1866: Being the Memoirs of Barbara Charlton (Née Tasburgh)*, ed. by L. E. O. Charlton (London: J. Cape, 1949), p. 86.
40. See *Alumni Oxonienses: the Members of the University of Oxford, 1715–1886: Their Parentage, Birthplace and Year of Birth, With a Record of Their Degrees: Being the Matriculation Register of the University*, ed. by Joseph Foster, 4 vols (Oxford: Parker and Co, 1887–88), IV (1888), 1597–99.
41. Charlton, p. 86.
42. 'Obituary of Mrs Jane Wood', *Monthly Homeopathic Review*, 5 (1865), 192.
43. Mary P. English, 'Lankester, Edwin (1814–1874)', in *Oxford Dictionary of National Biography*.
44. Rosemary Ashton, 'Schmitz, Leonhard (1807–1890)', in *Oxford Dictionary of National Biography*.
45. Gregory Claeys, 'Owen, Robert (1771–1858)', in *Oxford Dictionary of National Biography*.
46. Joseph Lester, *E. Ray Lankester and the Making of Modern British Biology* ([n.p.]: British Society for the History of Science, 1995), pp. 6–37.
47. Italics in the original. 'Proceedings of Societies', in *The Analyst: A Quarterly Journal of Science, Literature, Natural History and the Fine Arts*, ed. by William Holl, Neville Wood and Edward Mammatt, 10 vols (London: Simpkin & Marshall, 1834–40), VII (1837), 91–102 (p. 99) <http://dbooks.bodleian.ox.ac.uk/books/PDFs/555020721.pdf>.
48. Chris Waltham, 'David Knowles' Diary 1837–1839', Chris Waltham's Family History <http://chris-waltham-family-history.blogspot.co.uk/2016/05/david-knowles-diary-1837-1839.html> (para. 1). As becomes apparent from the diary entries, as well as giving a range of lectures, William taught French to David Knowles.
49. According to Chris Waltham's introductory paragraph to the diary, James Chiosso (1789–1864) later became 'professor of gymnastics at University College London and inventor of the polymachinon (forerunner of the modern exercise machine)'.
50. Arthur was mentioned by Francisca in the pages of her periodical, when she alluded to charitable Christmas dinners. By way of example, she mentions that twelve years previously (i.e. around 1856) she attended one such dinner at Camp's Mount, which all the children from Campsall

village attended. One of the tables was presided over by the wife of the Reverend Arthur Wood, her brother-in-law (*VF*, 57: 3).

51. These are examined in Gordon R. McOuat, 'Species, Rules and Meaning: The Politics of Language and the Ends of Definitions in 19th Century Natural History', *Studies in History and Philosophy of Science*, 4 (1996), 473–519 and T. R. Birkhead and R. Montgomerie, 'A Vile Passion For Altering Names: The Contributions of Charles Thorold Wood Jun. and Neville Wood to Ornithology in the 1830s', *Archives of Natural History*, 2 (2016), 221–36. Birkhead and Montgomerie argue that it was Charles Thorold Wood jun. rather than his father who published on ornithology.

52. 'Fines Arts — Music', in *The Analyst, A Quarterly Journal of Science, Literature, Natural History and the Fine Arts*, ed. by William Holl, Neville Wood and Edward Mammatt, 10 vols (London: Simpkin & Marshall, 1834–40), V (1836), 343–44 (p. 343).

53. [Review], in *The Musical World, a Weekly Record of Musical Science, Literature, and Intelligence*, ed. by J. Alfred Novello, 70 vols (London: J. Alfred Novello, 1836–90), VI (1837), 108–09. Other reviews include 'New Music by William Thorold Wood', *The Spectator*, 6 May 1837, p. 22. <http://archive.spectator.co.uk/page/6th-may-1837/22>.

54. Joseph Foster, *Register of Admissions to Gray's Inn, 1521–1889: Together With the Register of Marriages in Gray's Inn Chapel, 1695–1754* ([n.p.]: Hansard Publishing Union, 1889).

55. [Advertisements & Notices], *Daily News*, 17 June 1850.

56. See Angela M. Leonard, 'Elliott, Ebenezer (1781–1849)', in *Oxford Dictionary of National Biography*.

57. Ebenezer Elliott, 'The People's Anthem', *Tait's Edinburgh Magazine*, 15 (1848), 403.

58. Ebenezer Elliott, *More Verse and Prose by The Cornlaw Rhymer*, 2 vols (London: C. Fox, 1850), I, 80–81.

59. 'Critical and Miscellaneous Notices', *Westminster Review*, 108 (1851), 130–48 (p. 140).

60. Ibid., p. 140.

61. See '*The Meeting of the Nations — A Song for the Great Exhibition of Industry in 1851* — words by Charlotte Young, music by Wm. Thorold Wood, 1851', *Victorian Sheet Music Covers Collection*, Box 3, Item 81, Special Collections and Archives, Oviatt Library, California State University, Northridge.

62. Given that the focus of this chapter is not to establish William Wood's worth as a composer, but rather the intellectual profile of Francisca's lifetime companion, it is irrelevant for our purposes that the catalogue published the poems but not their scores.

63. See Robert Saunders, *Democracy and the Vote in British Politics, 1848–1867: The Making of the Second Reform Act* (Farnham: Ashgate, 2011), pp. 29–38.

64. See 'National Reform Conference', *The Morning Advertiser*, 24 April 1850, p. 3. Several other meetings were held throughout 1850, according to *The Morning Advertiser*.

65. 'Critical and Miscellaneous Notices', *Westminster Review*, p. 140.

66. See Lopes, 'Religião e género', pp. 58–59.

67. See Henry Edward Noyes, *Church Reform in Spain and Portugal: A Short History of the Reformed Episcopal Churches of Spain and Portugal* (London: Cassell, 1897).

68. *The fortieth annual report of the British Protestant School in connexion with St. George's Chapel Lisbon... with a list of subscribers and accounts of receipts and expenditure* (Lisbon: Anglo-Portuguese Printing Office, 1877), p. 14. Available at <http://purl.pt/30848>.

69. More tangentially, Tipografia Luso-Britânica had brought out *O Cozinheiro dos cozinheiros*, to which Ramalho Ortigão contributed a recipe.

70. William Thorold Wood, *As Farpas e John Bull* ([n.p.]: Tipografia Luso-Britânica, 1877), pp. 5–13. Prince Albert Edward, Queen Victoria's eldest son, was visiting Portugal on his way back from his tour of India.

71. Ibid., pp. 11–12.

72. Ibid., p. 13.

73. See 'São Domingos, Rua de', in *Dicionário de Eça de Queiroz*, ed. by Campos Matos, p. 864.

74. See for instance ['Lista dos subscritores até esta data...'], *O Zoofilo*, 10 May 1877, p. 4.

75. 'Births, Marriages & Deaths', *The Morning Post*, 28 April 1888, p. 1.

76. See A. R. Buckland, 'Thorold, Anthony Wilson (1825–1895)', in *Oxford Dictionary of National Biography*.

77. 'Births, Marriages & Deaths', p. 1.

78. See Maria Teresa Pinto Coelho, ' "Pérfida Albion" and "Little Portugal": The Role of the Press in British and Portuguese National Perceptions of the 1890 Ultimatum', *Portuguese Studies*, 6 (1990), 173–90.

79. 'Probate Calendars of England & Wales, 1858–1959', Find my past, p. 353 <https://search.findmypast.co.uk/search-world-Records/probate-calendars-of-england-and-wales-1858–1959>.

80. Ibid., p. 224. The probate was to Gertrudes Duarte Ferreira. Further investigation suggests she may have been the daughter of one of Clarimundo Augusto Ferreira Martins's brothers, and thus Francisca's great-niece.

CHAPTER 2

In the Public Eye:
Women in Print Culture (1848–1867)

Chapter 1 examined the family background of Francisca Wood and the English gentleman who became her husband, William Thorold Wood, uncovering the historical and cultural contexts that shaped their views. Among several significant findings, it seems that a young Francisca visited Newgate in the company of the early prison reformer Elizabeth Fry, enabling us to postulate that her practical involvement in humanitarian causes dated back to the early years of her time in England. Moreover, the links of the Wood family with radical thinkers like Owen and Fourier, and William's presence at the same political meetings as Colonel Thompson and Richard Cobden, as well as his collaboration with the poet of the people, Ebenezer Elliott, speak volumes for the progressive agenda that was to run through *A Voz Feminina* and *O Progresso*. In order to contextualize properly the originality of Francisca Wood's intervention in a Portuguese context, however, it is necessary to turn our attention to the intellectual climate that she encountered on her return to Portugal, particularly in respect of the presence of women in print culture.

As an alternative to an uncritical reproduction of the conventional paradigm of literary history, according to which the 1860s are book-ended by Camilo Castelo Branco (1825–1890) and Júlio Dinis (1839–1871), this chapter continues to embrace a broader cultural studies perspective. If from the vantage point of literary historiography the 1860s signal the transition from romanticism to realism, once we eschew conventional labels,[1] evidence of the participation of women in public discursive practices becomes equally worthy of note. As Cristo observes, 'todos os grandes nomes da nossa Literatura dos séculos XIX e [início do] XX estão ligados à imprensa do seu tempo' [all the big names of our nineteenth (and beginning of the twentieth) century Literature are linked to the press of their time].[2] And while Castelo Branco and Dinis are no exception, less commonly stated, however, is that both of them resorted to female pseudonyms early in their careers, as will be discussed later. Suffice it to say that the relative longevity of Diana de Avelada, aka Júlio Dinis (itself the pseudonym of Joaquim Guilherme Gomes Coelho), extending between 1862 and 1867, should give us pause for thought: at the most superficial level, it suggests that there must have been enough women active in periodical culture for this presence not to cause undue surprise.

Tellingly, from the broader perspective of the history of ideas, the shift towards greater women's agency during this decade is encapsulated in two memorable symbolic landmarks: at the beginning, in 1860–61, the scandal of Plácido's adultery, imprisonment, trial and release without charge, closely followed by the book that her tribulations engendered, *Luz coada por ferros* (1863); and at its close, Francisca Wood's periodical in 1868–69, which vocally articulated the case for female political rights. Curiously, Plácido and Wood are not usually considered *together*, as symptomatic of the evolution of women's intellectual practices in the 1860s. Plácido's interface with periodical media is seldom scrutinized at length, while *A Voz Feminina* has not yet been properly examined as an interactive literary space, even though two of its serialized novels were subsequently published in book-form in 1869 — Guiomar Torresão's *Uma Alma de Mulher* and Wood's own *Maria Severn* — as well as several other *folhetins* [serials]. Nor have Wood's editorials been systematically analysed yet for their rhetorical and discursive strategies, something which will be addressed in some detail in Chapters 4 and 5.

The present chapter therefore provides an overview of the significance of women's interventions in the 1860s as a continuum, predicated on the interrelation between journalism and literature already visible in earlier decades.[3] The two categories, nowadays often perceived as distinct, were inextricably linked in the public consciousness, and considerably inflected the politics of authorship and marketing. Given the sizable presence of women in the media during the 1860s, the following analysis will focus primarily on four representative female writers. Building on previous scholarship, we first highlight Antónia Gertrudes Pusich and Maria Peregrina de Sousa: active from the 1840s onwards, they had achieved a significant public profile by the early 1860s. While Pusich and Peregrina were fêted as epitomes of *feminine* learning and virtue, other women starting out in the early 1860s swiftly rose to fame, propelled partly by controversy. Of those, we focus on Ana Augusta Plácido and Josephina Neuville.[4] Neuville in particular enjoyed a short-lived *succès de scandale*. Notwithstanding her almost complete erasure from subsequent literary history, we argue that her life-writing may have provided a source for Eça de Queirós's portrayal of women in *Os Maias*. In an attempt to be avoid 're-mediation', and bearing in mind that 'women are not just outside cultural traditions. They structure the spaces that lie between the bold lines picked out by previous generations of art critics and literary critics',[5] we have deliberately chosen one of the few prominent names of the period (Plácido), as well as earlier examples of two writers recognizable at least to specialists (Pusich and Peregrina), together with another name that has remained almost entirely overlooked until recently (Neuville).[6]

As will become apparent, the recovery of information, facts and primary sources is an essential starting-point for the proper understanding of the Portuguese context in the run-up to the launch of Wood's periodical. It is important to consider the flourishing of women in 1860s periodical culture, against which the *Geração de 70* strongly reacted, not least because, as Ana Paula Ferreira perceptively argues, the modern (re)-construction of the Portuguese nation-state entailed, especially from the 1870s onwards, a variety of national(ist) discourses that attempted to pre-empt contamination by the New Woman, of which Francisca Wood was the clearest example.[7] At stake was the domestication of female otherness present 'within the margins of the nation in the figure of a wild, uncivilized [...] and, hence, foreign feminine body'.[8]

Asymmetrical Positions

The effects of the de-authorization of female intellectuals by the *Geração de 70* and a markedly androcentric intellectual culture up to the twilight years of the nineteenth century undoubtedly led to the neglect of the body of works produced by 1860s women, with devastating and long-lasting consequences. An ongoing frustration for anyone who researches nineteenth-century Portuguese women writers is the sometimes fruitless search for copies of primary sources. Items are frequently extant only in one or two libraries and not necessarily, as one might presume, in a copyright library like the BNP (Biblioteca Nacional de Portugal). The practical difficulties in identifying the location of scattered material highlights the issue of cultural amnesia. The woeful neglect of sources means that, to the best of our knowledge, only one of the women discussed in this chapter, Plácido, has had any material republished, at the time of writing. In the 1990s, she enjoyed a limited revival: firstly, in a pioneering anthology which showcased fragments of her works in an accessible modernized form; and secondly in a luxury edition that maintained nineteenth-century spelling, as such inviting readers to view her as a museum curiosity, rather than seeking to promote her literary relevance.[9] It is therefore a matter for rejoicing that Sibila, the bold and unashamedly woman-centric imprint recently launched by Inês Pedrosa and Gilson Lopes, has just brought out in full a modern version of her novel *Herança de Lágrimas*.[10]

Crucially, even if re-editions are seldom forthcoming, there is an unprecedented opportunity to reopen archives because digitization opens up access. To illustrate, on the basis of our sample, works available on open access include:

— through the BNP site: Pusich's journals, *Assembleia Literária*, and *A Beneficência*, which give us access to a range of Pusich's literary works serialized therein; also Plácido's 1871 novel *Herança de Lágrimas*;
— through the Hemeroteca site: one of Peregrina de Sousa's novels *Maria Isabel* can be read in its serialized version in *A Esperança*;
— through the Bodleian library site in Oxford: Neuville's memoirs, *Memórias da Minha Vida*, were digitized in 2009.

For scholarly purposes at least, the digital age can belatedly grant a new lease of life to previously relatively rare and/or unread books and periodicals, even if the old-fashioned spelling is likely to deter consumption by a wider readership. Digitization, then, facilitates access, provided one knows where to look. That said, only a fraction of our corpus is actually available online, so it remains crucial that librarians pay heed to unconscious bias when digitizing materials. More generally speaking, there is not yet a search facility on periodicals, unlike what happens in the English-speaking world, so it is likely that further contributions by these and a host of other women lie buried in periodicals, awaiting recovery.

Women were far less likely than men to have their writings published in book-form. Since all the women considered in this chapter managed to publish in book-form, a tangible symbol of lasting achievement, it suggests how seriously they took authorship. If they were contrary enough to swim against the tide, we owe it to them to understand the constraints under which they were operating. As Muzart writes, 'Lendo-as, sem contextualizá-las convenientemente no período da História em que viveram [...] e, sobretudo, sem se procurar compreender as injunções sociais e políticas que sofreram como mulheres, arriscamo-nos a cometer muitas injustiças' [Reading them, without contextualizing them appropriately in the historical period in which they lived [...] and, above all, without seeking to understand the social and political restrictions they suffered as women, we risk committing many injustices].[11]

Two Mid-Century Pioneers

Antónia Gertrudes Pusich (1805–1883)

It seems fitting to begin in 1848, because the year held the promise of sweeping change in Europe, as exemplified by William Thorold Wood's musical arrangement for 'The People's Anthem' discussed in the preceding chapter.[12] The times were certainly changing and one sign of this, in an unexpected quarter from the point of view of today's reader, is the fact that António Feliciano de Castilho (1800–1875), subsequently so infamously targeted and ridiculed by the *Geração de 70*, used the periodical press to write in favour of female suffrage in 1848.[13] But women themselves were ready to become involved in the political sphere, as demonstrated by Antónia Gertrudes Pusich through her 1848 pamphlet 'Galeria das senhoras na Câmara dos senhores deputados' [Ladies' Gallery in the Chamber of Deputies].[14]

The pamphlet revealed that she was on the receiving end of a campaign of slander, because of a departure from appropriately feminine conduct: an interest in politics which led her to attend Parliamentary sessions. Although at the time women were allowed to sit in on parliamentary debates in a special Ladies' Gallery, it must have been an uncommon sight, judging by the crude reactions it elicited. She was caricatured as a Maria da Fonte figure, in a disobliging comparison.[15] Nearly twenty years later, in *A Queda de um Anjo*, Camilo Castelo Branco continued to dismiss the presence of women in the Ladies' Gallery, with another political comparison, this time to the French Cormenin, one of the authors of the 1848 decree on universal suffrage: 'algumas senhoras doutas enfrascadas em política, amoráveis Cormenins, que aquilatavam o mérito dos oradores com incontrastável retidão de juízo e apurado gosto' [some scholarly ladies inebriated with politics, adorable little imitators of Cormenin, who weighed up the merits of orators, with indisputable right-mindedness in their judgements and refined taste]. The adjectives (enfrascadas, amoráveis, incontrastável) betray Camilo's ironic intentions and he further asserted with comic exaggeration, no doubt playing up to the gallery: 'Lisboa tem dezenas destas senhoras Cormenins' [Lisbon has dozens of such Lady Cormenins].[16]

By contrast, in 1848, the sheer abnormality of Pusich's presence in Parliament must have seemed profoundly 'unhomely' and thus threatened male hegemony. Aside from being ridiculed, the accusations levelled against her were twofold: firstly being a neglectful mother, and secondly entering this male public space par excellence merely to try and find a new husband (the latter can be presumably interpreted as de-authorization on the grounds of self-interest, with suggestions of an unseemly financial and/or sexual appetite). Compounding this campaign of intimidation, Pusich claims to have received anonymous hate mail. However, rather than being cowed into silence by what can be regarded as the equivalent of today's internet trolling, she retaliated publicly by exposing in print the behaviour of her detractors, in a powerful feminist symbolic gesture.

It seems that this experience made her all the more determined to embrace activism, since the following year saw the launch of her first periodicals, the pioneer *Assembleia Literária*, subtitled *jornal de instrução* [Literary Assembly: educational journal] (1849–51). It was followed by *Beneficência*, subtitled *jornal dedicado à Associação consoladora dos aflitos*, [Charity: journal dedicated to the Association for the consolation of tribulations] (1852–55) and the short-lived *A Cruzada*, subtitled *jornal religioso e literário* [The Crusade; religious and literary journal] (1858). Coming from a privileged social milieu, Pusich was not only highly educated and well-connected, but also had a cosmopolitan family background: she was born in Cape Verde to a Portuguese mother and a Croatian father. It seems the family moved to Brazil for a time before returning to Cape Verde, where in 1818 her father became Governor of the islands. She also spent a period of time in Italy with her second husband for political reasons.[17] It is not unreasonable to speculate that her geographical mobility across continents and exposure to different cultures might have enhanced her self-reliance and resilience, as well as her ability to think outside the box. In that sense her profile has some points in common with the well-travelled Francisca Wood.

Kathryn Bishop-Sanchez draws attention to the prologue to her verse narrative 'Olinda, ou a Abadia de Cumnor-Place' (1848), where Pusich alludes to the fact that motherhood curtailed her freedom of activity: 'a cada instante interrompidas as [suas] ideias com o despertar da mais pequenina de [suas] três filhas'[18] [her ideas being interrupted at every moment when the youngest of her three daughters woke up]. Of course, this was a way of demonstrating that she was in fact a caring mother, especially since she also references her impoverished material circumstances (which would justify trying to make a living through writing). She thanks various people 'sem cujo auxílio esta obra morreria na escuridão, como muitas outras que tenho criado, e não tenho podido publicar' [without whose help this work would die in darkness, like many others I have created, and been unable to publish]. The surface humility should not fool us, for she was confident in her abilities, as is confirmed by the fact that she goes so far as to claim the lofty desire of serving her country, notwithstanding a perfunctory acknowledgment of female weakness: 'prestar a sua pátria todos aqueles serviços que uma débil pena feminil pode ofertar, em honra da moral e futuro progresso das letras!' [render to her native land all the services that a weak female pen may offer, in honour of morality and the future progress of letters!].[19]

Pusich's public profile meant that when her play *Constança ou o amor maternal* was staged, in September 1849, it enjoyed great success. Classified by Talan as a comedy,[20] the play contains many autobiographical elements, and 'No fim da representação apareceu no palco com as duas filhas mais novas, tendo sido muito aplaudida'[21] [At the end of the performance she appeared on stage with her two youngest daughters, and was greatly applauded]. This ovation illustrates the importance of 'feminine' self-fashioning, at intersection between the private and public spheres: by focusing on the maternal function, the credentials of Pusich, a widow and a mother of six, were thus confirmed as those of an unassailably virtuous lady.[22] This emphasis on her inherent respectability counters the vilification she had experienced for attending parliamentary sessions only the previous year.

The BNP has a digitized copy of *Assembleia Literária* (although the inaugural issue is missing), but not *Constança ou o amor maternal*. A hardcopy of the latter, as it turns out, is available at the Biblioteca Geral da Universidade de Coimbra. But other forms of cultural memory loss may be more difficult to reverse. In particular, there is speculation that Pusich's long-standing interest in politics led her to become a Freemason around 1864. Oliveira Marques's dictionary lists 'Direito e Razão' as the first adoptive lodge in Portugal, established in Lisbon in the first semester of 1864, with nineteen members.[23] Fernando Marques da Costa's recent book discusses a manuscript source which proves that this lodge did exist, although he seems somewhat doubtful as to whether it was headed by Pusich, since the only contemporary record of her name appears in a satirical article.[24] His healthy scepticism opens up the possibility that Pusich may have been wrongly named. But if it wasn't her, who was it? And who were the other nineteen women or so involved? We will return to this question in Chapter 5.

Maria Peregrina de Sousa (1809–1894)

While the writings of the Lisbon-based Pusich tackled a variety of literary genres,[25] and provided a springboard for some real-life activism, simultaneously the periodical press enabled Maria Peregrina de Sousa to forge a literary career in 1840s and 1850s Porto: her first *folhetim* [serial], *Roberta ou a Força da Simpatia*, was released in *O Periódico dos Pobres* in 1848; *Henriqueta* was published also in instalments in *O Pirata* in 1850 (and only belatedly released in book-form, in 1876, with a preface by Castilho).

Her first novel to appear in book-form was *Retalho do Mundo* (1859).[26] Its opening chapter is absolutely superb, dealing as it does with the interaction between a working-class spinner, Ti Ana, and her twelve-year-old son, who by the end of the chapter has disappeared to enlist as a soldier. It reproduces their colourful northern regional accents phonetically, showcasing Peregrina's interest in ethnography. It also displays an acute awareness of class differences, which Ti Ana attempts to decode for her rebellious son: 'Lebas jeito de seres um mandrião e borracho como foi teu pai! Os fedalgos, tolo, fê-los Deus pra darem ismolas aos probes; não pra comer e dromir' [You look set to turn out just like your father, a drunk and an idler. You daft ha'p'orth, God made the nobility to give alms to the poor; not to eat and sleep].[27] By opening her novel with voices from a working-class family, Peregrina is not only spotlighting their experiences, but also criticizing existing structures. The rest of the novel, however, considers more closely the heavy cost of departing from prescribed conduct for middle-class women, such as the main character, Amélia, who marries well beneath her station and meets a tragic death. Ultimately the tensions between individual aspirations to freedom and the social injunctions to conform are played out in her work. The need for compromise — bearing in mind that the trade-off for commercial success would have been financial gain, potentially a non-negligible consideration for a single woman — leads her to articulate for her middle-class female readers the trope of 'virtue rewarded' in a later novel like *Maria Isabel* (1866).

For the first Portuguese female producer of *folhetins*, the path to public recognition was strewn with pitfalls. Most notably, Camilo Castelo Branco (1825–1890) swiftly dismissed her as too prolific, as the dedication of the satirical poem 'Elógio Fúnebre' [Funeral Eulogy] published in 1854 shows: 'a uma dama, prodígio de fecundidade, que dá à luz três romances, por semana, nos jornais do Porto' [to a lady, prodigiously fecund, who gives birth to three novels per week in the Porto press].[28] The opening and closing stanzas read as follows:

> Atafona de romances,
> És um carril a vapor!
> Romantizas quanto achas,
> E nos folhetins encaixas
> Com satânico furor.
> [...]
> Faz-me dó, pois tu bem podes
> Bordar lenços de cambraia
> Com bonito petit-point;
> E, não sendo aqui ninguém,
> Podes, ser tudo na Maia. (741–42)

> [A mill grinding out novels,
> You're a steam engine!
> Romanticizing everything,
> You roll out novelettes
> With devilish fervour.
> [...]
> I pity you, for you're perfectly able
> To embroider cambric handkerchiefs
> With pretty petit-point;
> And not being anyone here,
> You can be everything in the Maia]

Maia, where Peregrina resided, was located about ten miles from Porto, a fair distance at the time, so Camilo's intention here is probably to highlight the fact that she belonged to the geographical and cultural periphery. Equally interesting for our purposes here is the seventh stanza where Camilo, after repeatedly insisting that the vocation of women was to darn underwear and other clothes, claimed that he believed in female emancipation and even raised the possibility that one day a woman might become 'regedora | escrivã e contadora | eleitora e deputada' [governor | clerk and accountant | voter and deputy]. This is all the better to denigrate Peregrina, however, with the argument that, even in a remote future where more roles might be open to women, including the vote and parliament, she would remain no more than a 'cabo de polícia' [corporal].

In the same year, another satirical poem by Camilo, 'As literatas' (731–34), extended his criticism to all learned women.[29] He caricatured such women in the alliterative line 'Sentada num sofá, Safo saloia' [Sitting on a sofa, rustic Sappho] (p. 732), thereby dismissing female intellectuals as country lasses attempting to look sophisticated. He further addressed 'pais de família' [heads of families] and even at one point 'maridos imbecis' [idiotic husbands] to argue that too much education led women to abandon their domestic duties, such as darning socks and preparing breakfast. His advice to fathers, repeated five times over the course of the poem, was that they should exercise parental authority: 'Dai-lhes para baixo, como eu dou nas minhas!' [Chastise them as I chastise my womenfolk].

However, still in 1854, Camilo's preface to *A Filha do Arcediago* offers an ambiguously self-reflexive moment, as he disclosed the extent to which his stories actually depended on female oral contributions:

> Tudo isto que eu sei, e muito mais que espero saber, é-me contado por uma respeitável senhora, que não vai ao teatro, nem aos cavalinhos, e que tem necessidades orgânicas, mas todas honestas, e, entre muitas, é predominada pela necessidade de falar onze horas em cada dez. Desde que tive a ventura de conhecê-la, não invejo a sorte de ninguém, porque vivo debaixo das mesmas telhas com esta boa senhora, e posso satisfazer a mais imperiosa necessidade da minha organização, que é estar calado. é que não podemos falar ambos ao mesmo tempo.[30]

> [All this that I know, and much more that I hope to know, is told to me by a respectable lady who doesn't go to the theatre or to the horses, and who has organic needs but all honest ones, and among many, is dominated by the need to talk eleven hours out of every ten. Since I had the good fortune to meet her, I do not envy anyone's lot, because I live under the same roof with this good lady, and can satisfy the most pressing need of my organization, which is to be silent. It is because we cannot both speak at the same time.]

It may be hazardous to try and discern the identity of the unnamed 'lady'. She may been a household servant living under his roof but, given the reference shortly after to 'um nome, hoje obscuro' [a name, today obscure], this character may arguably constitute an oblique reference to Peregrina, who wrote under the pseudonym 'Obscura Portuense'. Be that as it may, Camilo is depicting the stereotype of the gossipy woman. While he claims to value her as an informant, he instrumentalizes her and seems unable to envisage women as talented writers in their own right:

> No momento infausto em que os selos do túmulo me fecharem este livro do passado, obliterar-se-á *a fecunda veia de romancista*, donde o público, maravilhado da minha esterilidade, dirá então que os meus romances eram dela; e um nome, hoje obscuro, será exumado do esquecimento para quinhoar da glória dos escritores-fêmeas desta nossa terra tão escassa — ainda bem — desse contra-senso.[31]

[At the sad moment when the seals of the tomb shut me off from this book of the past, the *rich vein of the novelist* will be obliterated, whereupon the public, wondering at my infertility, will then say that my novels were hers; and a name, today obscure, will be exhumed from forgetfulness to share the glory of authoresses in our land, so lacking — thank goodness — such nonsense]

There is little doubt about the value judgement — uttered with almost palpable relief — that in Portugal women writers are mercifully few and far between. The subtext to his disparaging compound noun 'escritores-fêmeas' [biologically female writers] successfully encapsulates his worldview: men are writers, and as such cultivated minds, whereas women are defined by their biological body and its reproductive function. On that basis, since only men have the gift of genius, women writers go against common sense ('contra-senso'). Yet, laced with romantic ambiguity, Camilo seemed aware that the days of masculine hegemony were numbered, and thus prophesied that more women writers would in future partake in literary glory.

Although jibes like these may have been confidence-sapping for Peregrina, she must have taken some comfort in the fact that she had already found a staunch supporter in Castilho by then, and moreover that since 1848 she had built a transnational following in Brazil thanks to the periodical *Iris*, through novellas like 'Pepa'.[32] In the early 1860s she disclosed, piecemeal in private letters addressed to Castilho, some of her biographical circumstances. Based on these, he sought to trace her profile in the 1861 *Revista Contemporânea de Portugal e Brasil*, drawing on her own words but without having previously obtained her consent to do so, as he himself stated.[33] Her account hinged significantly on her feminine modesty and tropes of spontaneity. By sharing details of an apparently squeaky-clean private life, Peregrina could easily be promoted as a professional woman and indeed was framed as such by Castilho. Printed in a periodical that circulated in Brazil, these biographical notes may have further propelled her writing career.

Her transnational profile meant that shortly afterwards, in 1863, she secured sponsorship for her next novel,[34] 'sujeita ao caraterístico e hoje comico título *Radamanto ou A Mana do Conde*' [subject to the characteristic and nowadays comic title *Rhadamanthus or the Count's Sister*], as Leitão de Barros puts it.[35] There is no question that her novels, designed to entertain, were governed by a 'to be continued' narrative logic. Simultaneously, the fact that this *folhetim* was financed by the Brazilian-based Madrepora Society should give a measure of the esteem in which her narratives were held, given that around the same time this philanthropic society was funding paintings of King Pedro V and the distinguished liberal Alexandre Herculano, and moreover supporting the publication of *Arquivo Pitoresco*.[36]

One of the stated aims of the society was to 'Auxiliar a impressão de livros de reconhecido merecimento' [support the publication of books of demonstrable merit].[37] The popularity of serialized fiction, and the virtuosity of Peregrina within the genre, justified sponsorship. The Society duly arranged for the publication of 'dois mil volumes das obras da Sra D. Maria Peregrina de Sousa, dos quais a sociedade recebeu mil, e mandou entregar à mesma senhora as restantes mil' [two thousand volumes of the Works of Mrs Maria Peregrina de Sousa, of which the Society received one thousand and delivered to the said lady the remaining thousand].[38] Leaving aside the vexed question of gauging any so-called aesthetic merit, it is fascinating to identify how a female author was promoted in her lifetime and circulated in a transnational literary-market. The sponsorship presumably co-opted Peregrina into the task of 'socializing' her readership, mainly aspirational middle-class women, in the dominant forms of (trans)national belonging. In the simplest terms, such belonging was predicated upon a common class understanding, as much as nation *per se*. Such a supranational middle-class dimension may have contributed to the transnational circulation of novels in the mid-nineteenth century, and hers in particular.

If success breeds success, the popularity of Peregrina was at its peak when in 1865 the periodical *A Esperança*, subtitled *semanário de recreio literário dedicado às damas* [Hope: weekly journal of literary recreation dedicated to the ladies] (1865–66), a Porto-based periodical, serialized her next novel, *Maria Isabel*. It is worth dwelling on the information supplied on the cover page of *A Esperança* which features, below the image of a woman, two separate lists of contributors, one of women and the other of men. Peregrina was the first named female contributor. They were listed in the following order: Maria Peregrina de Sousa; Maria Adelaide Fernandes Prata; Efigénia do Carvalhal Sousa Telles; Henriqueta Elisa (Pereira de Sousa); Branca de Carvalho; Adelaide Safira de Sampaio e Silva.[39] Since the list was not alphabetical, there is no doubt that she was deemed to be a star attraction. By then, Peregrina was in her fifties and had an established track record. For purposes of comparison, the first named man was Camilo, billed as another selling point. Being ranked on a par with Camilo would no doubt have been especially gratifying for her after he had ridiculed her in his satirical poetry one decade earlier.

Maria Isabel commences in the inaugural number — but not as a *rodapé*, as this is a literary magazine. The novel elaborates on the well-worn trope of virtue rewarded, although, within this conventional framework, it criticizes masculine domination, as perceptively analysed by Mariano's thesis. On the back of what was presumably deemed another success in terms of serialized fiction, the publication of *Maria Isabel* in book form in 1866 features a curious paratext, where the publisher dedicated the book to the Viscount of Vilar de Allen, a well-known Porto businessman, elevated to the nobility only a couple of months earlier, in January 1866. A page-long dedication waxes lyrical about the intertwining of art and business, both 'fathered' by talent.[40] This suggests that Vilar de Allen was being courted and/or rewarded for financial sponsorship. Given a British background on his father's side, it is just possible that this businessman's interest in promoting culture may have been linked to awareness of the success of women novelists in Britain, bearing in mind the ever-growing popularity of the likes of Jane Austen, the Brontës, Elizabeth Gaskell, and George Eliot.

'A Esperança'

It would be tempting to see the weekly *A Esperança* as an heir to the journals of the formidable Pusich and a precursor of the radical ones sponsored by Francisca Wood, but this would be misleading. The main similarity was that *A Esperança* boasted a sizeable cast of female contributors. A major difference, however, lies in the fact that *A Esperança* was primarily a literary magazine. Each issue was filled with a selection of poetry and prose fiction and featured very few opinion articles, despite being eight pages long (twice the size of *A Voz Feminina*). The very few exceptions, however, were highly significant. In a rare opinion piece in defence of female learning, Henriqueta Elisa (1843–unknown) positions herself against women's emancipation:

> Não proclamo o fantasma da emancipação feminina; essa risonha e feiticeira utopia nunca encontrou em minha alma o calor do entusiasmo com que muitas a saudam [...] seria uma grande desgraça para ambos os sexos! Faria no globo uma completa revolução, com todas as suas funestíssimas consequências.[41]

> [I do not proclaim the phantasm of female emancipation; that smiling, enchanting utopia has never found in my soul the warm enthusiasm with which many women welcome it [...] it would be a great misfortune for both the sexes! It would bring about a revolution throughout the world, with all of its absolutely dire consequences]

Although the adjectives 'risonha e feiticeira' [smiling, enchanting] dwell on the allure of utopia, the fear of revolution, in a country that had just emerged from several decades of political turmoil, seemed enough to pre-empt further debate.

Peregrina does not intervene at any point, not even when invited to speak up in favour of female intellectuals by Maria Adelaide Fernandes Prata (1826–1881). Her answer to Prata's *cri de coeur* in an open letter, 'Anime-nos, minha amiga, diga que escrevamos' [Encourage us, my friend, tell us to write], was a resounding silence.[42] One male contributor, however, a rash and brash sixteen-year-old, Alberto Pimentel (1849–1925), was less than encouraging: he declared that men were ready to welcome female talent but that their current offerings, generally speaking, were somewhat lacking. His conclusion was that more study and application was required on the part of women.[43] To quote Mary Beard's comments about the interaction between Telemachus and Penelope in the *Odyssey*, in an essay reflecting on the historical constraints on 'The Public Voice of Women': 'there is something faintly ridiculous about this wet-behind-the-ears lad shutting up the savvy, middle-aged Penelope'.[44]

Francisco Marques de Sousa Viterbo (1845–1910) swiftly sprang to the defence of Adelaide Prata, and women intellectuals generally, in an article entitled 'Estímulo' [Incentive], where he professed to believe in female talent and illustration.[45] In the end, Alberto Pimentel was forced to backtrack, claiming that his words had been misunderstood and that he valued Prata's poetry. Yet, to add insult to injury, he not only confidently proclaimed that there weren't any great past Portuguese woman writers, but furthermore dismissed the notion of lack of opportunities altogether.[46] Adelaide Prata accepted the apology with what, given the curtness of her reply — 'Muito bem, Senhor Pimentel' [Very well, Mr Pimentel] — seems like an ironic tone.[47] Her closing lines ruefully predict a brilliant future for him. She was right: he would go on to become a prolific journalist and writer, who remains known today as Camilo's first biographer.[48]

It is telling that no other woman intervened in the debate, perhaps not wishing to turn it into a polarized gender controversy. Even more telling is that when Maria Adelaide Fernandes Prata published the first Portuguese translation of *Fingal*, in 1867, her version was prefaced by two letters, one them by Sousa Viterbo. Given that he was only twenty-two at the time and therefore young enough to be her son, this goes to show how quickly the talent of men was nurtured and led to their opinions being invested with cultural authority. As we shall see in the next chapter, Prata seems to be the only female contributor to *A Esperança* who reached out to the Lisbon-based *A Voz Feminina*, pledging support with a couple of enthusiastic letters.

Riding the Wave

The mid-nineteenth-century literary marketplace was undergoing rapid change, with more modern forms of marketing from which Peregrina benefited. There is no denying that significant literary and cultural occurrences were increasingly mediated and played out in the press, and that women, as well as their supporters or detractors, were becoming adept at using this shifting landscape to their advantage. By the 1860s both Pusich and Peregrina had enjoyed significant public accolades in their respective cities: Pusich's 1849 play was applauded, republished in her own paper, and a book version was subsequently printed in 1863; meanwhile, Peregrina's seniority was prominently on display in *A Esperança*, on a par with Camilo.

In this context, what does it say that, early on in their respective careers, both Camilo and Júlio Dinis opted for female pseudonyms? In Camilo's case, the entry 'pseudónimos' [pseudonyms] in the *Dicionário de Camilo Castelo Branco* refers to Carolina da Veiga Castelo Branco in 1850–51; to the more obviously satirical name Dona Rosária dos Cogumelos [Lady Rosary of Mushrooms], in 1855; and to Ermelinda Pereira da Costa in 1859.[49] The use of a female pseudonym by Júlio Dinis was arguably even more extensive and significant. For a start, it was with the pseudonym Diana de Aveleda that his first short stories 'Os novelos da tia Filomena' and 'O espólio do senhor Cipriano' were published in the *Jornal do Porto* in 1862 and 1863 respectively. Even more interesting for our purposes was the fact that Diana de Aveleda published several letters to a fictional female friend, Cecília, discussing what 'she' saw as women's place in the world, and advancing the thesis that women's learning would help them to fulfil their mission as educators of the next generation — an argument that was rehearsed in *A Esperança* by Henriqueta Elisa a couple of years later, as we have seen.

Amongst these open letters, one in particular deserves to be mentioned, because it was addressed to Ramalho Ortigão in response to an article he had published in the same paper under the title 'Coisas Inocentes, a Filosofia e a Mulher — sistemas empregados para descobrir a verdade' [Innocent Things, Philosophy and the Woman — Systems used to uncover the truth] (on 21 January). Diana's response, under the heading 'Coisas Verdadeiras' [True Things], published on 25 February 1863, takes issue with Ortigão's misogyny, and prompts a further debate without Ortigão suspecting that Diana is a man.[50] Although Júlio Dinis's ideas were vastly more advanced than Ortigão's, his idea of women's intellectual emancipation was still predicated on the idea that instruction was desirable because it would ultimately help women to better discharge their maternal responsibilities. Be that as it may, what does the public exchange between Ortigão and Diana de Aveleda reveal about the fact that a man was willing to impersonate a woman's voice, and moreover that it was actually credible? Aside from Dinis's skill in carrying it off, it suggests that the possibility of a female signature was no longer such an oddity. In fact, as Outeirinho reminds us, several other men also used female pseudonyms.[51] And as she details, there were certainly dozens of women active in the press in the 1860s and the 1870s. Of those, the most familiar name in nineteenth-century literary historiography probably remains that of Ana Plácido.

Ana Augusta Plácido (1831–1895)

In 1860, at the dawn of the decade, Ana Plácido and Camilo's adultery scandalized Porto and the country at large. Both served time in prison. Since in those days deportation was still seen as a proportionate punishment, the fact that they were released without charge in 1861 signals an opening of mentalities. Eça de Queirós's father was the judge, in absentia as it turns out.

At the time, the court case also ensured notoriety for Ana Plácido, who capitalized on the opportunity to make her mark as a writer. Camilo, a seasoned and well-connected a writer, was astute enough to help her to publish her first book. Plácido's *Luz coada por ferros* (1863) is arguably a watershed moment in terms of modernity and women, in multiple ways. Firstly, since it was, to a large degree, a compilation of prose previously published in a range of periodicals, it highlights the inroads that women were making into the press, and supported the notion that a journalistic profile was the natural first step to publication in book format.[52] Secondly, it enjoyed a preface by the well-known man of letters, Júlio César Machado (who had made his debut as a teenager in Pusich's periodical and that very same year released his well-received *Recordações de Paris e Londres*).[53] It also reprinted endorsements by Camilo's friend, Vieira de Castro, and the today unidentifiable AL. These provide plentiful evidence that a new generation of men was willing to promote women's intellectual endeavours, albeit with what might seem retrospectively as condescending benevolence. Thirdly, it showcased marketing acumen: it is likely that the publisher thought that the volume would sell, because of the scandal with which Plácido was associated and, moreover, the novelty of a subjective female perspective. The relevance of female authorship as a determining factor is confirmed by the fact that the publisher asked her go-between, Camilo, for a photograph of Plácido. For this reason the work had a generous print run: 1000 copies.

If Plácido swiftly became a minor celebrity, her notoriety cannot be solely attributed to either her male promoters or the quality of her writing. Other women would have paved the way. In 'Meditação IV', she herself acknowledged the celebrated Mme Staël and George Sand, the latter still very much alive then, only to state that Portuguese women (a group with whom she identified herself through the use of pronoun 'nós' [we]) fell considerably short of the distinction of these two Frenchwomen.[54] But in the sentence immediately after, Plácido indicates that the 'grandeza do génio' [greatness of genius] which she ascribes to them had in fact been available in Portugal within living memory: 'a Marquesa de Alorna e Catarina Balsemão passaram sem herdeiras' (*Luz coada*: 92) [the Marchioness of Alorna and Catarina Balsemão left no heirs].[55] In other words, by paying tribute to her local predecessors (and their gift of genius), she tentatively envisaged the possibility of a Portuguese female genealogy based on past creative achievements. It logically followed that, given that Portugal had produced gifted women writers in the recent past, there was no reason why there could not be more of the same calibre in the near future. This leads Plácido to rehearse the idea that there could be a new generation of Portuguese female writers and, moreover, that she might lead the way: 'É, afagando esta ideia, que me arrojo primeira no exemplo, e com a esperança de ser imitada e seguida' (*Luz coada*: 92) [Embracing this idea, I myself lead by example, and with the hope of being imitated and followed]. Her statement points to a tentative female tradition, albeit a truncated one. Yet, retrospectively at least, the lacunae are perhaps best seen as missing links, awaiting retrieval. For the fact is that, with the benefit of hindsight, Plácido's statements must be taken with a pinch of salt, bearing in mind that she may have had her own agenda. Were there really no Portuguese women of talent writing at the time?

For personal reasons, she was unlikely to acknowledge Maria Browne (1797–1861), rumoured to have been Camilo's lover.[56] And, in truth, while it may have been genuinely difficult for her to rate any other living female author as 'great', it was more likely that it was convenient to see herself as the exception in the creation of her own myth. Certainly, it seems surprising that Plácido didn't mention Peregrina. She would have known of Peregrina via the *Revista Contemporânea de Portugal e Brasil*, since the periodical was also publishing her own work, either side of Peregrina's afore-mentioned 1861 biographical sketch.[57] Of course her silence may have been justified by the fact that Camilo didn't rate Peregrina. Nonetheless, another woman from the previous generation whom Plácido fails to mention is Antónia Gertrudes Pusich, with whom Camilo had socialized over dinner in the company of other men of letters in 1859, and at the theatre.[58] It is surprising, and perhaps disingenuous, that Plácido effectively chooses to ignore her predecessor's manifold contributions to periodical culture.

Yet, the significance that Plácido attached to the press is self-evident. Following in the footsteps of Peregrina de Sousa, her transatlantic circulation led to the publication of two short-stories in the Brazilian periodical *O Futuro*.[59] And around the same time, possibly taking her cue from Pusich, Plácido even conceived an ambitious project in her quest for financial independence: the publication of a magazine called *Esperança*.[60] Even though she didn't manage to get it off the ground, the library in the Casa-Museu de Camilo holds a flyer for potential subscribers, with the announcement that the paper would come out on 1 January (the year is not specified, but it was possibly 1862).[61] Some critics suggest that this then morphed into the 1865 *A Esperança*;[62] there is however no objective evidence

to substantiate this hypothesis. The most striking characteristic of this pamphlet is
the prominent position of Plácido on the header, as a symbolic mother (redactor
and proprietor) especially given the marked contrast with an all-male cast, featuring
a number of well-regarded contributors. By contrast, as discussed, the 1865 *A
Esperança* had a much better gender balance. In fact, the launch of *A Esperança*
must have been a double blow to Plácido, since it was Peregrina, not her, who was
named as the first female contributor, thereby occupying a symmetrical position
to Camilo. Plácido had the good grace — or good sense — to contribute a couple
of pieces to the inaugural issue.[63] Peregrina's public consecration may also explain
Plácido's eagerness to have her name recorded for posterity in a commemorative
stone, alongside the names of several *homens de letras* who visited São Miguel de
Ceide the following year, in July 1866, thereby placing herself on their level as an
artist, possibly in a bid to outdo Peregina's notoriety.

Josephina Neuville (1826?–unknown)[64]

Competing models were therefore available to Portuguese women of letters: one
relying on the performance of 'proper' femininity (Pusich and Peregrina), and
another capitalizing on a sexually rebellious life-story (Plácido), for which there
was nevertheless an increasing consumer appetite. Plácido's 1863 meditations and
short stories voiced the changing nature of women's own perception regarding their
right to sexual (and textual) self-determination. Neuville would further this strand
with her *Memórias da Minha Vida: recordações das minhas viagens* [Memoirs of My Life:
recollections of my journeys] (1864).[65]

The memoirs appear to have sold out quickly, according to Inocêncio da Silva's
entry: 'obra que, por compreender alguns trechos de ruído e escândalo, obteve logo
rápida extração' [a work which, owing to the inclusion of some passages involving
rumour and scandal, sold very quickly].[66] The presence of multiple copies in the
Biblioteca Nacional de Portugal certainly attests to its popularity. One element
stoking the *succès de scandale* derived from Neuville's unflattering account of one
of her lovers, Jacinto Augusto de Santana e Vasconcelos, an MP. Bulhão Pato's
memoirs confirm that Santana was known in his youth for his womanizing and
quick temper.[67] But while Santana went on to have a respectable career,[68] Neuville
became, to recall the Duke of Wellington's dismissal of his former lover's memoirs,
a case of 'publish and be damned' as her taboo-breaking life-writing resulted in a
dramatic erasure from cultural memory.

Mindful of the desirability of re-opening cultural archives, it is useful to consider
a critical review by Teixeira de Vasconcelos, the Editor of *Gazeta de Portugal*, where
Eça de Queirós was to make his literary debut two years later. Vasconcelos indicated
that *Memórias da Minha Vida* was the talk of the town.[69] In his view, although
Neuville was bound to be punished by reputational damage, not to mention her
own conscience, the ultimate blame had to lie squarely with the publishers, who
should be held to account. In other words, he sees the author as moved by emotions,
while the publishers were, he implies, acting in cold blood — for financial gain,
one imagines. To rub salt in the wound, the imprint implicated in the affair was

that of the celebrated periodical *O Panorama*, initially launched by Alexandre Herculano in 1837, and relaunched in 1846 by the publisher and bookseller António José Fernandes Lopes. Although Vasconcelos does not mention him by name, by then A. J. F. Lopes had nearly twenty years' experience of the Portuguese literary marketplace under his belt and was also the owner of the immensely popular *A Ilustração Luso-brasileira* (1856 and 1858–59). According to the list featured at the back of *Memórias*, the Panorama imprint seems to have issued multiple works by an assortment of 'romantic' staples, today mainly minor authors.[70] A cursory BNP search by publishing house, under 'Tipografia do Panorama', suggests that it brought out approximately 157 titles. It is certainly significant that Josephina Neuville appears to be the only female author listed among them. What might have prompted a shrewd and experienced bookseller to think that there was a market for the life-story of an unconventional and rebellious woman? The answer may lie in the sensational nature of her revelations, but it may not be the only reason.

Neuville's autobiography had been announced as forthcoming as early as 31 March 1858, in a favourable *folhetim* in the liberal daily *A Revolução de Setembro* titled 'Sobre as Memórias de uma Senhora' [About the Memoirs of a Lady].[71] And it seems the book was ready to come out by January 1859, judging by another *folhetim*, published on 21 January 1859.[72] *Memórias da Minha Vida* opens with the transcription of this later *folhetim*, which offers an explanation and includes a 'teaser' in the form of the introduction to the work itself. Although the identity of the Lady in question was initially a mystery, Josephina was eventually tracked down as the author. As a result, she claims to have received threatening anonymous letters to dissuade her from publishing her account in full (I: iv). This campaign of intimidation recalls the experience of Antónia Pusich in 1848, thereby graphically demonstrating what a radical move it was for a woman to plan to publish her memoirs in nineteenth-century Portugal, in breach of feminine propriety.

In the event, there was a six-year gap before the autobiography was eventually released, in 1864. It is of course quite possible that either Neuville or her publisher had flinched at the likely scandal. If so, what might have been sufficiently different just a few years later to have prompted a change of heart? One suspects it was the perfect timing, hot on the heels of the runaway success of the afore-mentioned Ana Plácido's *Luz coada por ferros* in 1863, in the aftermath of her scandalous affair with Camilo. In other words, by 1864, the boundary between private and public spheres had been significantly eroded, as women's private lives were entering the public domain. Sale expectations must have been high since unusually enough, on opening *Memórias da Minha Vida*, readers were faced with the statement that 'A autora reserva o direito de traduzir esta obra em francês e em inglês' [the author asserts her right to translate this work into French and English], as well as a threat to sue pirate copies 'em virtude da lei da propriedade literária' (I: n.p.) [by the law of literary property]. In short, publisher and writer were mindful of the possibility of a transnational market.

Neuville's tendency to be rather liberal with the truth is part of her melodramatic strategy to elicit the sympathy of her readers. In her bid for material and emotional survival, she mobilizes French culture and narrative modes to author(ize) her life experiences. These mediate her frank portrayal of womanhood, sexual scandal and economic hardship in ways previously unheard in the Portuguese bourgeois context of the period.

After losing her mother when she was barely five, Neuville was sent from Brazil to Europe by her womanizing father, lured by the prospect of her inheriting from her childless aunt, Clementina Levaillant, a well-known dressmaker to Lisbon high society. During the long transatlantic sea voyage, the loss of Josephina's doll, which fell into the water, becomes a poignant symbol of her separation from her alleged 'motherland'; it also foreshadows the premature loss of innocence. In Lisbon, her education included a stint in a 'colégio inglês' [British school] in Rua da Horta Seca until, deemed to be a handful by Mme Levaillant, she was moved to other relatives in France to board at the Sacré-Coeur convent school at Conflans, on the outskirts of Paris. After her education was completed, or cut short (supposedly around the age of thirteen), Josephina travelled back to Portugal, then Brazil, where she was reunited with her father and siblings. Crucially, as a teenager, she was again forced to leave Brazil and return to Portugal, on account of a secret which she claimed was not hers to reveal, as mentioned again in the penultimate chapter (II: 250–51). Suffering at the hands of her now jealous and abusive aunt, she married (supposedly before turning fifteen).

Neuville tells us that the couple spent time travelling through countries like France, Germany, Austria, Holland and Hungary (I: 118–90), a fact which justifies the subtitle recordações das minhas viagens [memories of my journeys]. The title resonates with the work published only the previous year by César Machado, recounting his travels in Paris and London, Recordações de Paris e Londres [Memories of Paris and London] (1863). Neuville was arguably tapping into another genre that would enable her to market her text, since the sharing of cultural insights and sightseeing experiences pertaining to relatively little-known lands would likely be another selling-point for her potential readership. It also gave her cultural authority. After demanding a separation from her husband, prompted by her volatile ('exaltada') temperament, repeatedly attributed to her Brazilian birth, and now alone with a baby girl, Clementina, born in Brussels, Neuville comes back to Portugal via Britain, having hired a maid for the journey back. Finding a room of her own, both literally and figuratively, not to mention five hundred a year, would prove a monumental challenge in the years ahead.

Her love story and ensuing relationship with Henrique Pires is at the heart of the narrative. She deploys romantic tropes for (melo)dramatic effect, notably: the buena dicha predictions of a fortune-teller in Bohemia, which justify her leaving her first husband; a depiction of her 'marriage' to Henrique with God as their only witness, as a way to legitimize her de facto union; the enforced separation of the lovers by his family and their subsequent dramatic reunion; and finally the ominous stopping of a clock that foreshadows Henrique's premature demise. After his untimely death, she would have been a scandalous presence in polite Lisbon society. In fact, although she nursed him, she was prevented by his family from keeping him company in his final moments, and later from tending to his grave. Subsequently, while grieving her partner's loss, she had to survive in a socially hostile milieu, in the full knowledge that, plagued by the stigma of two children by different fathers — the second one outside wedlock, since Henrique never married her — her prospects of re-marriage must have been non-existent. In fact, her memoirs also show that her material survival entailed the protection of a wealthy 'benefactor', the notorious former slave-trader Manuel Pinto da Fonseca, known as Monte Cristo, in an unholy alliance with blood-tainted money that, especially for today's reader, further highlights her social unacceptability.[73]

The second volume portrays her relationship with her second lover, the afore-mentioned MP Jacinto Santana de Vasconcelos. Santana (as she mostly refers to him) is presented as selfish and controlling, as well as verbally abusive. In one scene shortly before she summoned the courage to leave him for good, he helped himself to the money she had gathered by cashing in some assets in order to pay her creditors, and squandered it. Yet despite his put-downs, she indirectly claimed some intellectual equality, which spilt into transgressive political discussion as she declared herself a supporter of the Partido Regenerador — significantly not the Partido Histórico that would select Santana as MP for the first time soon after.[74] Furthermore, she recounted how she spent a day with Antónia Pusich canvassing influential men for votes, thereby implying she was independently well-connected with the male political elite (II: 152–57).[75] Neuville's confident claim of her entitlement to be a thinking woman is mediated by her transnational mindset, as she tells her readers that any objections from Santana could be countered with Staël's famous reply to Napoleon: 'Genius has no sex' (II: 157).

Although later parts of Neuville's memoirs falter and at times smack of desperation, they foreground her survival skills as she navigates her precarious position. The motivation to write her life story may have been psychological, a cathartic coping mechanism to bolster her self-esteem. Unable or unwilling to abide by bourgeois social expectations, her emotional sufferings ring true, not least her suicidal episode in Paris early on in her marriage (I: chap. XXVI). And, at key moments, prolonged periods of prostration point to untreated mental illness, such as depression. Simultaneously, the publication of her narrative may have been sparked by financial considerations, since the book may have provided some income at a time of need. In so doing, she would have been fully aware of implicating several people and alienating her own relatives even further. Yet, following the death of her lover Henrique, and her break-up with Santana in 1857, she must have felt that the alternative was destitution.

The controversial *Memórias da Minha Vida* elicited moral outrage, being too much in breach of decorum to survive in the Portuguese collective memory. One of the few to break the silence surrounding these memoirs is Cláudia de Campos, in a pioneering 1895 study that showcased six women writers.[76] Campos's critical assessment displayed a mix of fascination and disapproval towards Josephina's impulsive life-choices and financial profligacy, calling her a 'self-deceiver' (in English in the original). Nonetheless, the contribution of women including to purportedly minor genres such as life-writing — in the case of Neuville, a flexible matrix endowed with sociological documentary value, psychological depth and aesthetic value — ought to prompt us to interrogate afresh cultural and intellectual nineteenth-century history, as well as its economic infrastructure, in relation to women's discursive absences from the canon. At a time when women had such scant cultural legitimacy in the Portuguese literary field, Neuville's autobiographical account offers a dissident voice from the margins — one that not only clamoured for recognition, but also damningly exposed prevailing double standards, underpinned by glaring financial inequality and lack of opportunities for women outside marriage.

A putative afterlife: from 'Memórias da Minha Vida' to Eça de Queirós's 'Os Maias'

Neuville disturbed the semblance of a well-organized functioning country and as such became the abject stain that had to be eradicated. Yet my contention is that she resurfaced in a fictional reincarnation, through Maria de Monforte and her daughter, Maria Eduarda, in *Os Maias* (1888). In the novel, the unruly Maria de Monforte stands for the elite's tainted historical association with the transatlantic slave-trade. Though scapegoated, she is shown to be part and parcel of the fabric of society. Maria de Monforte's father, an ex-slave-trader, was assigned the name of Manuel, which seems to echo that of Neuville's wealthy protector, Manuel Pinto da Fonseca. Neuville's relationship with the real-life Fonseca (who is remembered today as the owner of Quinta do Relógio, in Sintra) may well have fed into the depiction of Maria de Monforte and her father. Moreover, it is probably not a coincidence that Pedro da Maia set eyes on his future wife for the first time 'à porta de Mme. Levaillant' [outside Madame Levaillant's door].[77] As we saw, this well-known dressmaker to Lisbon high society, whose clients included Queen Maria II, was Neuville's aunt and brought her up. Ultimately, after her affair with Tancredo, Maria de Monforte 'a doida fugira com um certo Catanni, acrobata do Circo de Inverno nos Campos Elíseos' [the mad creature had run away with a certain Catanni, an acrobat in the Cirque d'hiver, encamped in the Champs-Élysées].[78] This detail too may have been inspired by Neuville, whose husband was apparently a circus owner.[79]

Furthermore, Eça may have been partly inspired by the colourful real-life story of Josephina Neuville, not only in the creation of Maria de Monforte, but also of her daughter Maria Eduarda. Neuville's French education (she was convent-educated in Paris) gave her what Bourdieu famously identified as precious 'cultural capital'. Far from being just another pretty face, she had the intellectual credentials to entertain the friends that Santana brought to dinner, *homens de letras* such as Bulhão Pato and Lopes de Mendonça, in her house on the outskirts of Lisbon.[80] In this way, she may have been the prototype for the also convent-educated Maria Eduarda, who similarly entertains Carlos's friends in her rural love-nest, A Toca. It is worth recalling that Maria Eduarda, like Josephina, was well-travelled: born in Portugal, she was taken to Italy, Vienna, Paris and subsequently London, where, like Josephina, she experienced considerable financial hardship.

Maria Eduarda's ambiguous position as a 'kept' woman, who has to pawn her jewellery in a bid for self-reliance, echoes that of numerous characters in nineteenth-century literature, ranging from Marguerite Gautier to Emma Bovary, and including Neuville herself. Significantly, Maria Eduarda's convoluted life-story is disclosed in an eminently private setting, A Toca, and moreover to just one privileged interlocutor: her lover Carlos, who, it will soon transpire, is her brother. In so doing, she is adopting the confessional mode of Josephina's memoirs. In Eça's national saga, the subjectivity of the kept woman becomes only a stage in the unravelling of the family-as-nation — foreshadowed early on by the stunning alliterative description of Afonso's armchair, with its proliferation of symbolic meaning, impossible to render in English, an armchair 'cuja tapeçaria mostrava ainda as armas dos Maias no desmaio da trama de seda',[81] [whose woven tapestry still bore the Maia coat of arms fading among silk-threads (my translation)].

From a twenty-first-century perspective, Neuville's fascinating life-story offers a counterpoint that compels us to rethink the central place occupied by *Os Maias* in the collective Portuguese imagination as representative national saga, but also its message. Reading this canonical novel through the prism of *Memórias da Minha Vida* makes visible the silences of history. For instance, the pervasive commodification of women as sex objects stands out in *Os Maias* in what may read like an uncanny *mise en abyme*, at least for those readers in the know, when at the races Dâmaso Salcedo pursues 'a Josefina do Salazar' [Salazar's Josephina, (my translation)], subsequently qualified as 'uma gaja divina, a Josefina do Salazar',[82] [a divine girl, Salazar's Josephina, (my translation)]. No wonder then that this fleeting Josefina, 'belongs' to a man whose surname begins with the same initial as Santana, the real-life lover of Neuville. Arguably this detail betrays Eça's appropriation of Neuville's life-story yet simultaneously encapsulates the unhomely return of the repressed.

As such, insofar as *Os Maias* narrates a history of haunting on a wider scale, Eça's plotline warns of the dangers of Portugal's denial of its own colonial past. When Maria Eduarda returns to Portugal, seemingly as the wife of Castro Gomes — a 'Brazilian' (i.e. a Portuguese man who went to Brazil to make his fortune) and therefore inextricably linked with a time when the former colony had yet to abolish slavery — she is presented as a superior lady. Her surface superiority is enhanced through her cosmopolitan aura and performative sartorial choices: tellingly, she wears a white velvet coat, an ostentatious embodiment not only of luxury but also of absolute whiteness, emphasized by contrast to her entourage which includes a black male servant. On a symbolic level, then, Maria Eduarda comes back to haunt post-imperial Portugal, showing that the white-washing of colonial history can only backfire with tragic consequences. Indeed, ultimately it is not only she, but her brother Carlos, who are in equal measure the grandchildren of the slave-trading Monforte, a point seldom made by critics.

And it is worth adding that, although Maria Eduarda is perceived as a fraud and falls from her pedestal, it is only the upper-class Carlos da Maia who knowingly commits the prohibited act of incest, in a self-destructive moment of hubris. At first sight, the fact that he survives, albeit emotionally blunted, may seemingly enshrine the survival of male privilege in contrast to Maria Eduarda's metaphorical narrative death. Except that, unlike her female predecessors in Eça's fiction (Luisa and Amélia), Maria Eduarda, together with her illegitimate daughter Rosa, does actually escape the ruins of the patriarchal home; in reality her final letter to Carlos shows that she has moved on in a dignified way towards the admittedly conventional reward of marriage. Compared to previous novels, then, the plot of *Os Maias* paradoxically would seem to offer a slightly more hopeful outcome for the main female character, albeit only possible in a non-Portuguese space and for an educated and worldly woman of independent means. It is tempting to think that this may have been a subliminal recognition on Eça's part that, against all odds, even when effectively consigned to the margins, women's voices and life-stories could, to some extent, gesture towards an escape from male domination to survive in an alternative space.

Conclusion

Neuville showcases the importance of exhuming an obscure name from forgetfulness, to paraphrase Camilo's prescient comment about 'authoresses'. Activating the potential of works that circulated but were then neglected by literary history pays dividends: as soon as we allow *Memórias da Minha Vida* to re-emerge as the shadow face of *Os Maias*, it explodes existing accounts of the nineteenth century. As such, we need to make room for the contributions of women to nineteenth-century Portuguese culture, which have been overlooked for too long, leaving the canon almost exclusively populated by a few towering *homens de letras*. Today, this lack of diversity offers a stark contrast to the landscape of Brazil, where scholars such as Zahidé Lupinacci Muzart have recovered and made available hundreds of women. We concur with her about the political importance of recuperation, in order to

> Mostrar que, apesar da ausência desses nomes nas histórias literárias do século XX, elas existiram e foram atuantes, a seu modo, em sua época. O nosso propósito é exatamente este: o se mostrar que elas existiram, que se rebelaram contra o papel 'natural' que lhes foi sempre assinalado — o do confinamento à vida doméstica — e desejaram ter suas vozes ouvidas.[83]
>
> [Show that, despite the absence of those names in the literary histories of the twentieth century, these women did exist and were active, in their own way, in their era. Our intention is precisely this: to show that they existed, that they rebelled against the 'natural' role that was always attributed to them — that of being confined to domestic life — and they wanted to have their voices heard]

In the Portuguese context, the few women whose names are remembered are seldom considered in depth on their own terms or indeed together as a critical mass. First and foremost, this chapter has demonstrated that middle-class women were far from absent in periodical and print culture. As such, contrary to what is frequently asserted, far from being passive and powerless, not only were women active contributors to periodical culture, on several occasions their behaviour was even seen as dangerous enough to be attacked, be it through anonymous letters or satirical poetry. They retaliated through words and deeds, by continuing to prove themselves as cultural agents. Needless to say, through careful navigation of codes of femininity, some writers quickly became more consensual than others.

The case of Peregrina de Sousa is especially striking because of the transnational popularity that her serialized novels enjoyed and the financial backing that ensued in the 1860s. Secondly, as Bishop-Sanchez has noted, women who were linked to an influential man had a better chance of survival.[84] The epitome of this was Ana Plácido. Conversely, this explains why Peregrina came to be doubly discredited and marginalized from literary histories: as a producer of easily dismissed serialized fiction and, circumstantially, for being promoted by Castilho, himself disqualified by the *Geração de 70*.

Simultaneously, this chapter has brought to light that the women mentioned or preserved in literary history are not necessarily the most thought-provoking ones from today's perspective. Edfeldt, in her discussion of individual twentieth-century writers, postulates that more radical and/or subversive writings were often silenced, ignored or suppressed. In a nineteenth-century context, Neuville is the most extreme example of such suppression. Following her breach of decorum, her exclusion is evident and, worse still, self-perpetuating, even down to symbolic details: for instance, unlike the other writers considered in this chapter, there are no known portraits of her, an unfortunate side effect of her swift relegation to the literal — and figurative — margins. Sadly, the same applies to Francisca Wood.

António Costa's 1892 survey *A Mulher em Portugal*, published in Wood's own lifetime, did not allude to either Neuville or Wood.[85] In 1927, Teresa Leitão de Barros mentioned them both, but only in footnotes, a telling sign of literal relegation to the margins.[86] This (mis)treatment is surely not a coincidence since both, in different ways, were freethinking women, whose cosmopolitan upbringing translated into controversial behaviour. Neuville courted sexual scandal: she was the overtly (hetero)sexual Judith Teixeira of the 1860s, a fact that may have preyed on Leitão de Barros's mind in the aftermath of the 1923 'literatura de sodoma' [literature of sodom] censorship.[87] By contrast, for the respectably married Wood (for no one would have known about the unusual 'visiting' arrangement recorded in the 1851 census), the burning issue was not untoward sexual behaviour, but rather intellectual transgression, not least in the form of religious dissidence. Her unorthodox thinking threatened structural male privilege, all the more so because her visions for collective female empowerment and reflections on women's agency were carried out in the public space through the press, as Chapters 3 and 4 will discuss.

Finally, it is worth underlining that several of the women discussed here (Peregrina de Sousa, Plácido; Neuville) appear to have been too isolated to form mutually supportive and meaningful female networks. It cannot have helped that Peregrina lived, as Camilo satirically reminded her, in Maia, or that from 1863 onwards Plácido was based in São Miguel de Seide, an even more remote rural location. Neuville was Lisbon-based, but her silencing in the aftermath of her memoirs means that little is known about her, not even the date of her death. Against this background of geographical and/or intellectual marginalization, nineteenth-century periodicals had the potential to act as the equivalent of today's internet, linking people to each other virtually and generating an imagined community. In practice, between 1848 and 1859, Pusich's periodicals played a significant part in promoting an imagined female community.

Both *Assembleia Literária*, and later in the mid-1860s *A Esperança*, seem to have functioned as hubs. Originating from Lisbon and Porto respectively, they were magnets that afforded women a window of opportunity to participate in the cultural life of the two main cities of the kingdom. Even a fairly cursory look at the format of the male-led *A Esperança*, however, shows that it was essentially a gathering of literary writings: this literary magazine was not conceived to provide a forum for discussion. From that perspective, two years later, Wood's periodical was quite different in both conception and execution. As the next chapter discusses, Wood was a skilled Editor and moreover unafraid of fostering lively dialogue, promoting the sense of a diverse yet inclusive community of contributors and readers. Furthermore, unlike its predecessors, *A Voz Feminina* quickly built enough momentum to aspire to nationwide coverage and, as Chapter 6 will reveal, even had the unusual privilege of being acknowledged in other European periodicals for what it was: as an unquestionable milestone in the Portuguese context.

Notes to Chapter 2

1. In a short and punchy article, Vanda Anastácio challenges us to 'Pensar para além das etiquetas' [Think beyond labels], because labels 'condition the gaze cast over the facts, and introduce distortions in the way they are apprended'. Vanda Anastácio, 'Pensar para além das etiquetas', *Veredas: Revista da Associação Internacional de Lusitanistas*, 10 (2008), 287–94 (pp. 293–94) <https://digitalis-dsp.uc.pt/jspui/bitstream/10316.2/34484/1/Veredas10_artigo16.pdf>.
2. Cristo, *A Epistolaridade*, p. 193.
3. See Biguelini, 'Tenho escrevinhado muito', for details about female authorship during the period 1800–1850.
4. The nineteenth-century spelling of Josephina has been retained, in preference to Josefina, in order to draw attention to a nineteenth-century positionality informed by a French-speaking and Portuguese-speaking dual cultural heritage.
5. Battersby cited in Hilary Owen and Cláudia Pazos Alonso, *Antigone's Daughters? Gender, Genealogy, and the Politics of Authorship in Twentieth-Century Portuguese Women's Writing* (Lewisburg, PA: Bucknell University Press, 2011), p. 208.
6. For instance, Plácido, Peregrina de Sousa and Pusich feature in Buescu's dictionary, but Neuville is absent.
7. Ana Paula Ferreira, 'Nationalism and Feminism at the Turn of the Nineteenth Century: Constructing the "Other" (Woman) of Portugal', *Santa Barbara Portuguese Studies*, 3 (1996), 120–42.
8. Ibid., p. 129.
9. *Ana Plácido: estudo, cronologia, antologia*, ed. by Fernanda Damas Cabral (Lisbon: Caminho, 1991); Ana Plácido, *Luz coada por ferros: escriptos originaes* (Lisbon: Livraria de A. M. Pereira, 1863; repr. V. N. de Famalicão: Lello & Irmão; C. M. V. N. de Famalicão, 1995) and Ana Plácido, *Herança de lágrimas: romance original* (Guimarães: Vimaranense Editora, 1871; repr. V. N. de Famalicão: Lello & Irmão; C. M. V. N. de Famalicão, 1995).
10. Ana Plácido, *Herança de Lágrimas* (Lisbon: Sibila, 2019).
11. Muzart, Zahidé Lupinacci, ed, *Escritoras brasileiras do século XIX* (Florianópolis: Mulheres, 1999), p. 19.
12. As the effects of the French Revolution rippled through the Old Continent, they prompted a flourishing of Christian socialism in the Portuguese press too. See Maria Manuela Tavares Ribeiro, 'The Press: A Political Gospel', *Portuguese Literary & Cultural Studies*, 12 (2007), 265–73.

13. António Feliciano de Castilho, *Felicidade pela agricultura* (Ponta Delgada: Tipografia da Rua das Artes, 1849) <http://purl.pt/106/4>. Castilho was a long-standing promoter of women in words as well as deeds. See for instance Eduardo da Cruz, 'Um "brilhante congresso": escritoras portuguesas no projeto de António Feliciano de Castilho para sua versão d' *Os Fastos* ovidianos', *Soletras*, 34 (2017), pp. 141–65.

14. The full text is available online, transcribed in Ana Costa Lopes, 'Atitude e documento invulgar: a intervenção de uma prestigiada oitocentista, Antónia Pusich, na Câmara dos Deputados', *Povos e Culturas*, 8 (2003), 207–28 (pp. 220–28). <http://icm.fch.lisboa.ucp.pt/resources/Documentos/CEPCEP/POVOS%20E%20CULTURAS_8.pdf >, under the title 'Documento'.

15. A famous instance of female activism, the conservative popular uprising known as Maria da Fonte took place in 1846.

16. Branco, *Obras completas*, ed. by Justino Mendes de Almeida, 18 vols (Porto: Lello & Irmão, 1982–2002), V, 915.

17. Nikica Talan, '*In memoriam* à esquecida Antónia Gertrudes Pusich', *Studia Romanica et Anglica Zagrabiensia*, 50 (2005), 145–92. The most recent website with information on Pusich is <http://www.lirecapvert.org/antonia-gertrudes-pusich1805–1883.html>.

18. Kathryn Bishop-Sanchez, 'Mulheres invisíveis: a escrita no silêncio', *Portuguese Literary & Cultural Studies*, 12 (2007), 169–82 (pp. 179, 178).

19. Ibid., p. 179.

20. Ibid., pp. 176–78.

21. António da Costa, *A Mulher em Portugal* (1892), cited by Talan, *Antónia Pusich*, p. 63.

22. Ibid., p. 58.

23. António Henrique R. de Oliveira Marques, *Dicionário de Maçonaria Portuguesa*, 2 vols (Lisbon: Editorial Delta, 1986), I, 476–77.

24. Fernando Marques da Costa, *As Mulheres na Maçonaria: Portugal, 1864–1950* (Lisbon: Âncora Editora, 2016), pp. 53–57.

25. Pusich's only known novel, *Dois Mistérios*, was serialized in *Assembleia Literária*, nos. 3–21. Although it didn't make it into book form, as far as we know, it was so popular that the author was compelled to reprint it, with modifications, in *Beneficência*.

26. Maria Peregrina de Sousa, *Retalho do mundo* (Porto: E. P. Barbosa, 1859). The novel is not available in the BNP, but can be found in the Gulbenkian library and, curiously, the British library too.

27. Ibid., p. 8. In standard Portuguese, the passage would read 'Levas jeito de seres um mandrião e borracho como foi teu pai! Os fidalgos, tolo, fê-los Deus para darem esmolas aos pobres; não para comer e dormir'.

28. Camilo Castelo Branco, *Folhas caídas, apanhadas na lama* [1854], in *Obras completas*, X, 741–42.

29. Both these poems are cited in Mariano, 'A Personagem feminina', pp. 26–27 and 37 respectively.

30. *Obras*, I, 939.

31. Ibid., I, 940.

32. Mariano's thesis includes an edition and analysis of 'Pepa', a 1848 novella that had remained buried in the periodical *Íris*.

33. António Feliciano de Castilho, 'D. Maria Peregrina de Sousa', *Revista Contemporânea de Portugal e Brasil*, 6 (1861), 272–312 <http://hemerotecadigital.cm-lisboa.pt/Periodicos/RevistaContemporanea/VolIII_1861/No6/No6_master/RevistaContemporaneadePortugaleBrasil_VolIII_1861_No6.pdf>.

34. Done with the help of Castilho, as his correspondence confirmed: 'Vivam e revivam os da Madrépora! Se o meu artigo biographico foi o motor de tão boa resolução viva e reviva tambem o meu artigo biografico; isto é viva e reviva V. Ex a que foi o assumpto; a inspiradora, e quasi que a authora d'elle' [Long life and prosperity to the people of Madrepora! If my biographical article was the driving force for such a good decision, long live my biographical article; that is, long life to Your Excellency who was the topic; the inspiration, and almost the author of it]. Cited in Ana Cristina Comandulli, 'Presença de A. F. de Castilho nas letras oitocentistas portuguesas: sociabilidades e difusão da escrita feminina' (unpublished doctoral thesis, Universidade Federal Fluminense, Niterói, 2014), p. 325.

35. Teresa Leitão de Barros, *Escritoras de Portugal*, 2 vols (Lisbon: Tipografia Artur, 1924), ii, 379–80.
36. See Eurico Dias, 'O Archivo Pittoresco (1857–1868): subsídios para sua história' <http://hemerotecadigital.cm-lisboa.pt/RecursosInformativos/ActasdeColoquiosConferencias/textos/ConfArqPit.pdf>.
37. <http://legis.senado.gov.br/legislacao/ListaTextoIntegral.action?id=60433&norma=76303> — Artigo 2&2.
38. António Manuel Ribeiro, *O Museu de Imagens na Imprensa do Romantismo: património arquitectónico e artístico nas ilustrações e textos do Archivo Pittoresco (1857–1868)* (Coimbra: Imprensa da Universidade de Coimbra, 2014), p. 42.
39. See Helena Roldão, [A Esperança: semanário de recreio literário dedicado às damas], [Ficha histórica], p. 1 <http://hemerotecadigital.cm-lisboa.pt/FichasHistoricas/AEsperanca.pdf>. Male contributors are listed as: 'Camilo Castelo Branco — Ernesto Biester — J. D. Ramalho Ortigão — A. B. Cerqueira Lobo — Alfredo de Carvalho — Augusto Luso — A. Correia — Teófilo Braga — A. Pinheiro Caldas — A. Moutinho de Sousa — Ernesto Pinto d'Almeida — Eduardo Augusto Salgado — Guilherme Braga — Alexandre da Conceição — Pedro Augusto de Lima — Agostinho Albano — Henrique Marinho, e outros' (p. 1).
40. Maria Peregrina de Souza, *Maria Isabel* (Porto: J. P. da Silva, 1866), n.p.
41. *A Esperança: semanário de recreio literário dedicado às damas*, ed. by R. D. César Rey and A. Pereira da Silva, 2 vols (Porto: Tipografia de Rodrigo José d'Oliveira Guimarães, 1865–66), i (1865), 49.
42. Lopes also comments on this silence in *Imagens da mulher*, p. 344.
43. *A Esperança*, i, 96, 104.
44. Mary Beard, *Women & Power: A Manifesto* (London: Profile Books, 2017), p. 4.
45. *A Esperança*, i, 107–09. For further information, see Rita Correia, [Sousa Viterbo, Francisco Marques], [Ficha histórica] <http://hemerotecadigital.cm-lisboa.pt/RecursosInformativos/Biografias/Textos/SousaViterbo.pdf>.
46. *A Esperança*, i, 116–17.
47. Ibid., p. 121.
48. For further information see *Alberto Pimentel (1849–1925): tal é, em resumo, a história do rei e do seu reinado*, ed. by Angelo Gabriel Uehara Ardonde, Isadora Cardoso and Giovanni Rodrigues Bernicchi (Campinas: Instituto de Estudos da Linguagem, 2005), Joomag ebook <https://view.joomag.com/alberto-pimentel-dossiê-com-pesquisa-historiográfica-sobre-o-autor-13-de-novembro-de-2015/0150062001445947694>. Neither Pimentel nor Sousa Viterbo had appeared in the initial list of names of male contributors, no doubt because they were young beginners. But their rising reputation means that they were later named in the table of contents of the second volume of *A Esperança*.
49. 'Pseudónimos', in Alexandre Cabral, *Dicionário de Camilo Castelo Branco*, 2nd edn (Lisbon: Caminho, 2003), pp. 528–29. Camilo's sister was called Carolina.
50. See Ana Rita Soveral Padeira Navarro, 'Da personagem romanesca à personagem fílmica: *As Pupilas do Senhor Reitor*' (unpublished doctoral thesis, Universidade Aberta, 1999), pp. 91–99.
51. Outeirinho reminds us that other men used female pseudonyms in the 1860s: Manuel Pinheiro Chagas used the pseudonym Margarida de Ataíde and, more briefly, Clotilde Z. As for Teixeira de Vasconcelos, he signed as Cristina de Avelar Calheiros, and under this pseudonym corresponded with Margarida de Ataíde, pseudonym of Manuel Pinheiro Chagas, about fashions. Teixeira de Vasconcelos also signed as Izabel de Grosbois. Outeirinho also speculates that Berta de Medeiros, who wrote *crónicas* in the *Diário de Notícias* in 1868, may have been a pseudonym for a male. In 1874 Cesário Verde signed a poem, addressed to João de Deus, as Margarida ('Cadências Tristes'). See 'O Folhetim em Portugal', p. 180, n. 193 and 195; p. 262, n. 132; and p. 312, n. 305.
52. See Cláudia Pazos Alonso, 'Assimetrias de Género: a trajetória de Ana Plácido e o papel de Camilo', in *Representações do feminino em Camilo Castelo Branco*, ed. by Sérgio Guimarães de Sousa (Braga: Centro de Estudos Camilianos, 2014), pp. 39–63.
53. He contributed to the *Assembleia Literária* aged thirteen. See Leal, *Um século*, p. 58.
54. Staël and Sand were indeed the main foreign female role models throughout the nineteenth century, in Portugal as elsewhere. Outeirinho makes the valid point that the emergence of

women's writing in France, given that this country was the main cultural reference for Portugal at the time, helped to fuel the desire for a similar phenomenon in Portugal, or at least for it to be accepted with greater naturality ('O Folhetim', p. 364). Indeed, Portuguese nineteenth-century women writers are repeatedly compared to Alorna, Staël and George Sand (p. 334). There seem to be no models invoked from the English-speaking tradition until much later. This dovetails with the general paucity of translations from English, though a topical work like *Uncle Tom's Cabin* was translated and serialized in *A Revolução de Setembro*, from March 1853 to January 1854 ('O Folhetim', pp. 377–78).

55. Camilo dedicated a study to Alorna, published in 1858 and in all likelihood Plácido would have been familiar with it. See *Obras*, XVI (1993), 1141–47. Balsemão had translated Staël into Portuguese.

56. See entry in *Dicionário do romantismo*, ed. by Buescu.

57. See for instance, 'Horas de luz nas trevas dum cárcere', *Revista Contemporânea de Portugal e Brasil*, 9 (1860), 422–24; Ana Plácido, 'Meditação', *Revista Contemporânea de Portugal e Brasil*, 2 (1862–63), 65–69, and Ana Plácido, 'Meditação', *Revista Contemporânea de Portugal e Brasil*, 4 (1862–63), 197–200.

58. As he recalls in an 1879 letter to his friend Palmeirim, *Obras*, XVI (1993), 959.

59. For a brief discussion of Plácido's offerings in *O Futuro*, see Pazos Alonso, 'Assimetrias de Género'.

60. Maria Amélia Campos, *Ana, a lúcida*, p. 176.

61. See Ana Plácido, ['Folha avulsa para recolha de assinaturas de Esperança'], Archive of Alexandre Cabral, Casa de Camilo Castelo Branco, Folder XXVIII, 94.

62. Fernanda Cabral, p. 27 and Maria Amélia Campos, p. 233.

63. The poem 'A Uns Anos', 15 April 1862; and the poetic prose work 'Num Album'. See *A Esperança*, I, 5–6.

64. To this day, Neuville's dates remain uncertain. According to a conference paper recently uploaded online by Elen Biguelini, she was born in 1826. See Elen Biguelini, 'As memórias de Josefina de Neuville (1826-após 1864): lembranças de uma transgressora', *Academia* <http://www.academia.edu/35738040/as_memórias_de_josefina_de_neuville_1826-após_1864_lembranças_de_uma_transgressora>.

65. Josephina Neuville, *Memórias da minha vida: recordações das minhas viagens*, 2 vols (Lisbon: Tipografia do panorama, 1864) <http://dbooks.bodleian.ox.ac.uk/books/PDFs/590716508.pdf>; <http://dbooks.bodleian.ox.ac.uk/books/PDFs/555057227.pdf>. Further references to these memoirs will be given in the main body of the text.

66. Inocêncio Francisco da Silva, *Dicionário bibliográfico português: estudos aplicáveis a Portugal e ao Brasil* 24 vols (Lisbon: Imprensa Nacional, 1858–1923), XIII, 247.

67. Raimundo António Bulhão Pato, *Memórias*, 3 vols (Lisbon: Tipografia da Academia Real das Ciências, 1894–1907), II (1894), 271–78 <http://purl.pt/248/4/l-78877-p/l-78877-p_item4/index.html>.

68. Jacinto Augusto de Santana e Vasconcelos Moniz de Bettencourt (1824–1888). See *Dicionário biográfico parlamentar, 1834–1910*, ed. by Maria Filomena Mónica, 3 vols (Lisbon: Assembleia da República–Imprensa de Ciências Sociais, 2004–06), I, 379–82.

69. Artur de Vasconcelos, 'Memórias da Minha Vida', *Gazeta de Portugal*, 17 August 1864, n.p.

70. They include Palmeirim; Biester; Júlio Cesar Machado; Bulhão Pato; Rebelo da Silva; Tomás de Carvalho; Rodrigues Sampaio; Latino Coelho; Casal Ribeiro; António de Serpa; Mendes Leal.

71. Fernando Serra, 'Sobre as Memórias de uma Senhora', *Revolução de Setembro*, 31 March 1858, p. 1 <http://purl.pt/14345/1/j-4157-g_1858–03–31/j-4157-g_1858–03–31_item2/j-4157-g_1858–03–31_PDF/j-4157-g_1858–03–31_PDF_24-C-R0150/j-4157-g_1858–03–31_0000_1–4_t24-C-R0150.pdf >.

72. Josephina Neuville, 'Explicação sobre umas memórias', *Revolução de Setembro*, 21 January 1859, pp. 1–2 <http://purl.pt/14345/1/j-4157-g_1858–03–31/j-4157-g_1858–03–31_item2/j-4157-g_1858–03–31_PDF/j-4157-g_1858–03–31_PDF_24-C-R0150/j-4157-g_1858–03–31_0000_1–4_t24-C-R0150.pdf>.

73. The unsavoury activities of Manuel Pinto da Fonseca are documented in Leonardo Marques,

The United States and the Transatlantic Slave Trade to the Americas, 1776–1867 (New Haven, CT: Yale University Press, 2016), especially pp. 148–74.

74. *Dicionário biográfico parlamentar*, ed. by Mónica, I, 380.

75. The memoirs reveal, however, that Pusich and Neuville later fell out.

76. Cláudia de Campos, *Mulheres: ensaios de psicologia feminina* (Lisbon: M. Gomes Editor, 1895), pp. 251–308. Since Josephina Neuville was the only Portuguese considered — alongside chapters on Charlotte Brontë, Mme de Staël, Mme de Lafayette, Esther [*sic*] Stanhope and the Romanian Carmen Sylva — this move suggests the need to place her in a transnational context. See Cláudia Pazos Alonso, 'Publish and be Damned: *Memórias da Minha Vida* and the Politics of Exclusion in Nineteenth-Century Portugal', in *Transnational Portuguese Studies*, ed. by Hilary Owen and Claire Williams (Liverpool: University of Liverpool Press, forthcoming 2020).

77. *Os Maias*, p. 22; *The Maias*, p. 30.

78. *Os Maias*, p. 84; *The Maias*, p. 92.

79. According to Cláudia de Campos, p. 275. This detail would have significantly undermined Neuville's carefully curated image as a respectable lady, so is absent from the memoirs.

80. Neuville, *Memórias*, II, chap. VI.

81. *Os Maias*, p. 9.

82. *Os Maias*, p. 327 and p. 337 respectively.

83. Zahidé Lupinacci Muzart, *Escritoras brasileiras do século XIX: antologia* (Florianópolis: Mulheres; Santa Cruz do Sul; UNISC, 1999), p. 19.

84. 'Mulheres invisíveis', p. 175.

85. António da Costa, *A Mulher em Portugal* (Lisbon: Tipografia da Companhia Nacional, 1892). Instead it praised Pusich's womanly decorum.

86. Barros, II, 379–80. Her comment that Cláudia de Campos was unduly harsh in her judgements about Neuville shows that she had read her memoirs.

87. On the invisibility of Judith Teixeira, see Pazos Alonso 'Judith Teixeira: um caso modernista insólito'.

CHAPTER 3

The Editor and her Team

> Numa terra que estabelece no seio da mesma mãe pátria duas nações de seres diferentes que não têm as mesmas crenças religiosas, nem o mesmo nível de cultura intelectual, nem o mesmo código moral; o que verdadeira e realmente me surpreende e me maravilha é que uma menina [...] tente isolada fazer a sua sorte.[1]

> [In a land that establishes at the heart of the same mother country two nations of different beings that do not have the same religious beliefs, or the same level of intellectual culture, or the same moral code; what really surprises and astonishes me is that a girl [...] should try, on her own, to make her own destiny.]

This is how the well-known journalist and man of letters Júlio César Machado (1835–1890) commented on Guiomar Torresão's debut novel, *Uma Alma de Mulher* [A Woman's Soul] (1869) in his preface.[2] Machado convincingly stressed the intellectual gulf between men and women, as well as the differing religious and ethical codes by which the latter were expected to conduct themselves. By casting light on the prevalence of structural double standards, his intention was no doubt to throw into relief the merit of Torresão's achievement. But in doing so, he was also obscuring the crucial fact that she was in fact far from 'isolated'. In reality, her work did not spring forth out of nowhere: *Uma Alma de Mulher* had initially been serialized in *A Voz Feminina* in 1868, where a collective ethos of nurturing female talent was much in evidence, as this chapter discusses.

Wood's periodical was a weekly which claimed to be 'exclusivamente colaborado por senhoras' [contributed to exclusively by ladies] in its first three issues, but quickly dropped the claim, opting instead for the more generic 'dedicado à ilustração das Senhoras' [dedicated to the enlightenment of Ladies]. It carried on uninterrupted for 102 issues until the end of 1869 — albeit with a change of title to *O Progresso* in the last six months, when Francisca Wood began to share the role of Editor with her British husband William Thorold Wood. This relative longevity may be linked to the sense of urgency experienced by Francisca and her team: they were on a mission. As Cortez rightly remarks, 'a modernidade d' *A Voz Feminina* torna-se flagrante quando se estabelece um confronto com os periódicos femininos que saíram a lume na década de 60' [the modernity of *A Voz Feminina* becomes obvious when it is compared with the women's periodicals published in the 1860s], adding 'mesmo *A Esperança* [...] tinha uma orientação muito conservadora' [even *A Esperança* [...] had a very conservative stance].[3]

The present chapter briefly introduces Wood as the driving force behind the multifaceted *A Voz Feminina* and its successor, *O Progresso*, and characterizes the emerging female community generated from within their pages, in order to bring out her role as *de facto* mentor to a younger generation of women with literary aspirations. Male contributors will also be briefly considered.

A Distinctive Editorial Vision

The project of *A Voz Feminina* was not originally Francisca's brainchild,[4] and this explains why she only became named as 'Redatora Principal' from no. 4 onwards. She was, however, deeply involved with the first three issues. Crucially, her initial contributions set the tone: the opening editorial bears her signature — even though this had been done without her consent, as she subsequently explains to her readers ('Declaração' *VF*, 35: 1–2). As for no. 2, it contains a letter, signed with a simple initial 'W' in a belated bid to protect her anonymity, but whose content nevertheless identifies her ([n.a.], *VF*, 2: 3). This letter puts forward a number of suggestions which will shape her vision for the periodical once she is officially in place as Principal Editor. They include providing an objective summary of the week's political events — something not quite implemented, not least because the periodical would gradually become more politicized, to the extent that the change of title to *O Progresso* simultaneously prompted a change of subtitle from 'revista semanal, científica, literária e noticiosa' [weekly, scientific, literary and news review] to 'jornal semanal, político, literário e noticioso' [weekly, political, literary and news journal], the word 'political' thus superseding the word 'scientific'. Other items on her list included reviews of newly published works 'como há em Inglaterra em grande número' ([n.a.], *VF*, 2: 3) [as there are in England in great numbers], and articles on a variety of subjects such as geography, history, physics and other branches of science. Most of these suggestions would be followed through over the next two years.

Curiously, no. 3 featured a letter addressed to the 'Sra Redatora da *Voz Feminina*' [Lady Editor], again signed merely with the initial W ([n.a.], *VF*, 3: 3). If W, who congratulates the Lady Editor on the noble enterprise she is heading, concealed Francisca, then who exactly was she meant to be addressing? Herself? In any event, W placed the emphasis on women's progress in England (at length), with shorter allusions to America, France, Switzerland and Sweden, in order to argue that Portuguese women too should aspire to become known in Europe for their achievements. The wider transnational background, an ongoing feature throughout the lifespan of the periodical, was certainly one of its unique selling points: 'É admirável a permanente actualização que Francisca Wood [...] revela na divulgação das vitórias que a mulher vai somando nas várias nações europeias' [The constant updating that Francisca Wood [...] reveals in disseminating the victories that woman are accumulating in the different European nations is remarkable].[5]

By no. 4 Francisca had accepted the impossibility of retaining her anonymity and from then on she became identified in the header as 'Redatora Principal'. Soon after, in no. 6, in the rubric named 'Expediente' [Pending Business], she advertised an open-door policy: 'as nossas Ex.mas colaboradoras poderão tratar pessoalmente qualquer assunto literário com a Ex.ma Redatora Principal D. Francisca Wood para cujo fim desde já tem o gosto de lhes oferecer a sua casa Rua de São Domingos à Lapa n. 29 e 31' ([n.a.], *VF*, 6: 4) [our esteemed collaborators may deal personally on any literary matter with the Principal Editor D. Francisca Wood, to which end from now on she has the pleasure of offering them her house at nos. 29 and 31 Rua de São Domingos à Lapa]. This was reiterated in no. 7 ([n.a.], *VF*, 7: 4). In short, once publicly linked to the project, she immediately sought to welcome potential contributors through a personal touch — something that, as we shall see, would pay dividends in terms of their loyalty.

Wood's inaugural contributions give a good idea of the core values underpinning her conception of women's advancement. In terms of the overarching mission of *A Voz Feminina*, she was able to make her mark in other ways too: for instance, comparatively little space was devoted to fashion, possibly in order not to compete with the *Jornal das Senhoras*, launched in 1867, but ultimately because it was not a priority for the Editor, entirely in keeping with the periodical's stated aim of furthering the 'ilustração das Senhoras'. The already sporadic section 'Modas' [Fashions] was completely discontinued in *O Progresso*. In the meantime, the inaugural emphasis on learning and breadth of knowledge soon led to closer engagement with what in England had by then become widely known as 'The Woman Question'.

As a whole, then, *A Voz Feminina* quickly acquired a distinctive ethos, within the readily recognizable generic format of a four-page weekly.[6] Moreover, the cover page retained a fairly standard layout: the weekly editorial in the top half, and the *folhetim* [commentary column or serialized fiction] in the bottom half, a location known as the *rodapé*. One or both items would often spill over on to subsequent pages, where a mixture of articles, *faits divers*, correspondence, as well as further serialized fiction and poetry, could be found. The publication of poems sent in by readers was common practice at the time and a way of fostering active involvement on their part. Susan Kirkpatrick's discussion of 'the special place of poetry in women's emergence as producers of print culture' in the Spanish context is broadly applicable to the Portuguese context too:

> Women who had no formal education but possessed a feeling heart and enthusiastic imagination were authorised to think of themselves as poets by a Romantic aesthetic that viewed art as primarily the expression of emotion and imagination rather than the product of intimate knowledge of the classical tradition.[7]

As for serialized fiction, it remained a reliable staple throughout the periodical's life, as the genre continued to have wide appeal. While many offerings seem stylistically and thematically close to the romantic school that was still enduring, there were examples of a modern style, most notably Francisca's very own *Maria Severn* — the magazine's jewel in the crown in literary terms. It occupied the *rodapé* between numbers 27 and 59, before being relegated to the inside pages, possibly in order to provide greater variety with a quick turnaround of shorter *folhetins* designed to maintain readers' curiosity.

In her monograph on Pusich, Talan estimates that Pusich was responsible for around 50% of the content of her journals and Francisca Wood's involvement may be statistically comparable to that of her predecessor, for she too played a variety of roles within the periodical. Not content with the onerous task of the building of a core team of trusted contributors while being single-handedly chief Editor until her husband came on board three quarters of the way through, she produced the following:

— the lion's share of editorials (see Tables 1 and 2).

TABLE 1. Summary of Editorial Contributions in *A Voz Feminina* (number per person)

Editorials (listed alphabetically by surname)	Number of Editorials
Andrade, Mariana Angélica	7
Costa, Amália Cândida Isabel da	1
Marques, F. de Abreu	5
Matos, Francisco A. de,	3
P., Carlota A., (male pseudonym)	4
Torresão, Guiomar	5
Viana, João Luís da Silva	1 (letter)
Wood, Francisca	26
Wood, William Thorold	6
Unsigned but claimed by Francisca Wood	18 (+ 1 ? in issue no.10 missing from BNP)
Unsigned brief note to frame transcription	1 article from *A Voz do Povo* (Funchal)

TABLE 2. Summary of Editorial Contributions in *O Progresso* (number per person)

Editorials (listed alphabetically by surname)	Number of Editorials
Araújo, João de Sousa	1 (letter addressed to Francisca Wood)
Coelho, J. C. Teixeira	1
Farol, F.	1 (letter addressed to Francisca Wood)
Goegg, Marie	1 (transcription of speech)
Wood, Francisca	8
Wood, William Thorold	1
Unsigned	13

Just under one third of the editorials bear her signature (32 out of 102) but in no. 35 she declared that *all* articles published anonymously up to then were in fact authored by her ('Declaração' *VF*, 35: 1). This declaration enables us to ascribe another nineteen early editorials to her, thereby raising the proportion to a whopping 50% of the total (51 out of 102).[8] A full list is included in Appendix 2;

— furthermore, there are thirteen unsigned editorials in *O Progresso* and, with two Editors at the helm, it is often far from straightforward to ascribe authorship, so we have not attempted to do so here. There is, however, an argument for considering the possibility of co-authorship since, given that William Wood was not a native speaker of Portuguese, it seems likely that Francisca translated or at least revised her husband's texts. A full list is included in Appendix 3;
— several series of articles such as 'Educação física e moral' [Physical and moral education];[9] 'Cartas a Luísa' [Letters to Luísa], which covered theological topics and later scientific ones; 'As Mulheres inglesas e o direito eleitoral' [English women and the right to vote];
— an abridged version of an article from *The Englishwoman's Review*;
— snippets of news about what was happening abroad (including the rubric 'O que se faz lá fora' [What is Happening Abroad]), sometimes translated from English sources;
— replies to readers who had written in;
— a novel, *Maria Severn*, serialized between nos. 27 and 101;
— translations from German (Grimm's tales).

Under the enlightened leadership of Francisca Wood, *A Voz Feminina* became a collaborative space and the poetry and correspondence sent in by eager readers, which often afforded glimpses of geographical provenance, attests to its nationwide circulation. As one might expect, those readers were predominantly from the three main cities, Lisbon and environs, Porto and Coimbra, but occasionally from more remote provincial locations such as Viana, Guiães (Vila Real),[10] and even S. Miguel (Azores). At a time when the building of the railways and the modernization of other distribution networks was enabling faster links between the provinces and the capital, the paper fostered a sense of a female community.[11]

In no. 6, in 'Expediente' [Pending business], among other things, Wood claims that there had been requests for copies of the periodical from abroad and that the print-run had reached 2000 copies (p. 4).[12] The unexpectedly large size of the print-run may give us pause for thought. The earlier *O Panorama* had achieved a record 5000, so a circulation of 2000 indicates the timeliness of *A Voz Feminina*. Moreover, we can be reasonably confident that the paper reached Brazil and Cape Verde, from correspondence received, and because there was a specific price for Brazil quoted on the header from no. 22 onwards.[13]

As well as filling a gap in the market and focusing on community-building, the popularity of the paper in the initial six weeks stemmed from the fact that it avoided controversial content that might have alienated potential readers. Editorials in issues 2–5, all signed by Carlota A. P.,[14] placed the emphasis on the need for female education, a conviction universally shared among the readership. By contrast, once Wood took up editorial space again, even though theological concerns were regarded as a male domain in Catholic countries, she did not shy away from discussing Christianity in an unsigned lead article ([n.a.], ['O Cristianismo...'] *VF*, 7: 1–2).

By the time Francisca took stock of the first six months, in July 1868, there had been six reviews, four offering praise and two expressing condemnation ([n.a], ['Domingo último...'] *VF*, 26: 1). Positive reviews stemmed from *Aurora do Cávado* (Barcelos); *Correio dos Dois Mundos* (Lisbon); *Gazeta da Beira*; and the influential *A Revolução de Setembro*. Later favourable responses, reproduced within the pages of *A Voz Feminina*, originated from a broad range of newspapers across Portugal, including *Eco do Algarve*; *O Egiptaniense* (Guarda); *A Folha de Coimbra*; *O Jornal de Setúbal*; *País de Coimbra*; and the *Voz do Povo* (Funchal). Brito, Robalo and Guimarães, noting the preponderance of provincial papers among these titles, suggest that, although the influence of the Church would have been significant everywhere and more so in small towns, it is conceivable that local Editors may have had a certain amount of intellectual freedom, especially if they were also the actual owners of the newspaper. Furthermore, the majority had liberal leanings, which may account for their receptivity to an editorial line that soon turned out to be anticlerical.

The fact that some quarters were appalled by the mounting anticlerical tone of *A Voz Feminina* is evidenced by the two adverse papers 'enunciando sentimentos hostis, aviltando-se um dos dois por um estilo antipodal ao cavalheirismo, pois atacou grosseiramente a redatora' (*VF*, 26: 1) [expressing hostile sentiments, one of the two debasing itself with an unchivalrous style, for it crudely attacked the Editor]. Although Wood did not name her vitriolic antagonist at this juncture, she would do so indirectly a year later in the editorial where she announced her 'resignation' as Editor (['Aos Il.mos e às Ex.mas assinantes da Voz Feminina'] *VF*, 74: 1–2), by singling out the Editor of *Bem Público*. This periodical was headed by the Marquês de Valada. As we will see in Chapters 4 and 5, blanket opposition to the often radical and therefore contentious ideas espoused in *A Voz Feminina* was to be regularly found in his visceral responses. Suffice to say that he greeted the changeover to *O Progresso* with a racist comment: '*A Voz Feminina* servia aos seus fregueses língua bunda com molho à portuguesa' [The *Voz Feminina* dished out to its customers a barbarian language with a Portuguese dressing].[15] It is a tribute to Francisca's determination that by then she had kept going single-handedly at the helm for nearly eighteen months, though she occasionally confessed her despondency: 'tenho chorado a obscuridade e seclusão em que até então vivi, e que tão grata e genial me era' (*VF*, 35: 1) [I have wept over the obscurity and seclusion I lived in until then, and which was so pleasing and congenial to me]. The ongoing persecution must have taken its toll and may thus help to explain her planned resignation as figurehead. In the event, she was dissuaded from leaving by a cluster of faithful readers. Instead, her husband joined her at the helm as Co-Editor of *O Progresso* in July 1869 (William Wood, *P*, 77: 111–12). His unwavering support was crucial to the maintenance of the project.

The timing of the announcement of the change of title is curious, since it occurs only one week after the periodical had printed a letter in English by William Wood, answering Theodore Stanton at 'the *Revolution* New York' (*VF*, 73: 4).[16] After outlining to his transatlantic addressee the guiding principles of *A Voz Feminina* (equality between the sexes and religious tolerance) William Wood went on to state that readers who 'were earnest in the cause of progress may be counted on the ten fingers', adding 'we are content, accordingly, with acting as pioneers, and cannot flatter ourselves that in the *Voz Feminina* we possess an organ of public opinion already formed'. William Wood also noted that 'the receipts of our journal have never equalled its expenses, and I fancy we have rather more than the usual proportion of readers who neglect to pay their subscriptions' (*VF*, 73: 4).

Surprisingly, however, the price of O *Progresso* was boldly set at half of that of *A Voz Feminina*, selling at 20 *reis* as opposed to 40 *reis* per issue. In so doing, the Woods probably thought they would enlarge the pool of potential readers, but must have realized this still might not suffice to break even. Furthermore, while the rebranding emphasized the ethos of a periodical 'earnest in the cause of progress', *A Voz Feminina* lost some female readers after the change of title. And, numerically speaking, women contributors lost ground, especially in terms of editorials, Francisca being the only woman from the original team to retain a leading profile in O *Progresso* (see Table 2). Equally importantly, the unique selling point of *A Voz Feminina* was diluted, since there were already other papers in circulation called O *Progresso*, a buzzword that may well have had resonances of the positivism of Auguste Comte. Certainly, in terms of market share, the paper became more obviously in competition with a huge array of periodicals with liberal leanings.

In short, it is likely that the campaign mounted by *Bem Público* contributed to the rebranding as O *Progresso*. And although after William Wood became Co-Editor the gender-based vitriol abated somewhat, in keeping with the fact that Valada thought anticlericalism was 'menos indecente na pena de um homem' [less indecent coming from the pen of a man],[17] his fierce opposition must have been a determining factor in the eventual demise of the paper, through underground mobilization of Church hostility. But not before readers had been treated to another six-month period of intense engagement with a range of progressive ideas, which will warrant closer scrutiny in subsequent chapters.

The Female Cast at the Heart of *A Voz Feminina*

There was profound disquiet among detractors, notably *Bem Público*, that women could operate a successful journalistic operation. The use of female pseudonyms by two male contributors early on (Carlota A. P. and Leonor A. P. G.) did not help matters, propagating the belief that the paper was not produced by women, but in truth the paper enjoyed the participation of many women. Among those with established credentials who pledged their early support, one finds Maria Adelaide Fernandes Prata (1826–1881),[18] a contributor to the 1865 periodical A *Esperança*, as the previous chapter indicated. However, Prata, though present in every issue of *A Voz Feminina* from no. 2 until no. 8, seems to have ceased her involvement after the first couple of months. The Coimbra-based poet Amélia Janny (1842–1914) also participated, in no. 19, having been chased up, as is clear from correspondence (*VF*, 15: 3), though she was admittedly a reluctant contributor. There were, however, some significant absences, most notably perhaps the veteran Antónia Gertrudes Pusich and the promising newcomer Maria Amália Vaz de Carvalho. We know that at least Vaz de Carvalho was approached, for she was cited as having declined on the grounds that writing for the press was a male endeavour, 'o jornal, enfim, deve ser masculino' [the newspaper should, after all, be masculine], an attitude scolded by Francisca ([n.a.], *VF*, 25: 4).

Vaz de Carvalho was being disingenuous, as she had already published the occasional literary piece in the ephemeral press by then, but this was an early sign that intellectual women fell into two distinct camps: more radical ones like Wood were kept at an arm's length by more conservative ones, of which Vaz de Carvalho remained for decades the most obvious exemplar. At the time, however, this ideological rift was concealed by the fact that Wood had secured the enthusiastic adhesion of another equally promising and energetic newcomer from very early on. Her name was Guiomar Torresão.

One third of the way in, Francisca Wood felt compelled to issue a 'Declaração' [Declaration] to counter head-on the slander from *Bem Público* that her journal might not be primarily written by women. She quite reasonably pointed out that:

> As Sras Maia, Andrade e Torresão, assim como várias outras senhoras que hão honrado esta publicação, já eram escritoras bem conhecidas antes da existência da *Voz Feminina*. As meninas Caron, Lília Torres e Sofia Cunha, vivem cercadas por numerosas pessoas respeitáveis e com seus pais, nenhum dos quais se prestaria a uma impostura tão vil. (*VF*, 35: 1)

> [Mesdames Maia, Andrade and Torresão, as well as several other ladies who have honoured this publication, were already well-known writers before *Voz Feminina* existed. Misses Caron, Lília Torres and Sofia Cunha live surrounded by numerous respectable people and with their parents, none of whom would lend themselves to such an unworthy deception.]

It is reasonable to suppose that the six female names she singled out on this occasion were those that most readily sprang to mind, and as such refer to the people she regarded as her closest contributors. For this reason, they deserve special scrutiny. In addition, we should note that Wood discriminates between three who were already known to the public, Guiomar Torresão (1844–1898), Mariana Angélica de Andrade (1840–1882) and Emília da Maia (1848–1912), and a group of less experienced younger 'girls' ('as meninas [Anne-Marie] Caron, Lília Torres and Sofia Cunha'). As far as we know, the latter were making their debut in her periodical.

Emília da Maia (1848–1912)

The first contributor mentioned by Francisca in her 'Declaração' as being already known to the readership of the paper was Emília da Maia. She had a transatlantic background, having been brought up in Brazil until the age of fifteen, and only moving to Portugal in 1863.[19] Maia was certainly precocious, with a poem published at the age of fifteen in a Brazilian magazine. She would have been barely twenty when she started contributing to *A Voz Feminina*. Of the six names mentioned by Wood, she was the only one to be married and by November 1868 we have evidence that she was a mother too, because she dedicated a poem to her daughter (*VF*, 43: 4). A recent article by Póvoas lists and analyses seventeen of her poems. He rightly points out that 'A vertente predominante será a romântica, com temas como a evasão, a infância, a pátria e a religiosidade dando o tom à lírica. [...] [T]ambém se observa a glosa de dois autores canónicos do Romantismo brasileiro, Casimiro de Abreu e Gonçalves Dias'[20] [The predominant strand is the romantic one, with topics like escape, childhood, the native land and religiosity lending a lyric tone. [...] One also observes the gloss on two canonical authors of Brazilian Romanticism, Casimiro de Abreu and Gonçalves Dias]. As Póvoas intimates, the very title of a poem like 'Canção do exílio' [Song of exile] (VF, 34: 4) self-consciously foregrounds itself as a rewriting of Gonçalves Dias. Poetically authorized by her predecessor, Maia's longing for the greater sensuality of her native country spreads over ten stanzas, and is furthermore underscored by the anaphora of the verbal form 'quero' [I want]. As such it foregrounds the subjectivity of a female desiring self, transgressive for the context of the period.

Emília da Maia's poetry elicits interest for a twenty-first-century reader primarily for its rewriting of canonical Brazilian authors. While her poetic compositions exceed in number her prose contributions, a handful of opinion articles nonetheless suggest an incipient awareness of women's issues: for instance, she picks up on a theme initially developed by Mariana de Andrade and writes an article on 'Mais Algumas Portuguesas Distintas' (VF, 32: 1–2) [Some More Distinguished Portuguese Women].[21] Subsequent offerings include a reflection on women such as the heroic Mme de Sombreuil (VF, 57: 3–4). Another example is an article where she writes about the imminent launch of a new French periodical (Gazeta das Damas) in order to defend the desirability of female erudition, with the winning argument that since Portuguese ladies copied French fashions they should likewise imitate French intellectual fashions (VF, 63: 4).[22]

Emília da Maia continued to produce lyrical compositions until the final issue of O Progresso. After the demise of the periodical, she went on to contribute to Torresão's Almanaque das Senhoras, and published poetry in book-form.[23] She was in many ways representative of an educated middle-class woman of the period, who sought to reconcile aesthetic ambitions with the socially acceptable role as angel in the house.

Mariana Angélica de Andrade (1840–1882)

Setúbal-based Mariana Angélica de Andrade had a good literary pedigree, since one of her ancestors was the poet Curvo Semedo and she was the daughter of the writer and Diário de Notícias journalist Joaquim António Serrano.[24] At the grand age of nearly twenty-eight, she was the oldest of the three main contributors mentioned by name in Francisca's 'Declaração'. In 1874, after she had honed her skills for several years as a woman of letters, she went on to marry the philologist and writer António Cândido de Figueiredo, himself a contributor to A Voz Feminina, and perhaps best known today for his 1899 Novo Dicionário da Língua Portuguesa.

Andrade's first contribution is the poem 'A criança adormecida' (VF, 8: 4) [Sleeping child], but she soon revealed a more unexpected turn of mind: no. 11 sees a piece on Molière, a topical theme as Castilho had just translated Le Tartuffe, yet daring in its allusion to the religious controversy over the burial of the anticlerical seventeenth-century French playwright (*VF*, 11: 3). In the same issue, the seven-stanza poem 'Liberdade', with an epigraph by the liberal Herculano, 'céu livre, pátria livre e livre a mente' [open air, free country and free minded] drawn from *Poesias* (1850),[25] featured a middle stanza that revealed awareness of wider contemporary European politics, by giving a passing reference to Russian-occupied Poland (*VF*, 11: 4).

Andrade wrote seven editorials in total. The first one cited Ana Plácido's seminal 'Meditação IV' from *Luz Coada por Ferros* (*VF*, 16: 1). An article spanning several issues about 'O Vestuário das senhoras' [Ladies' attire] (*VF*, 24: 2–3; *VF*, 25: 3; *VF*, 26: 2) offered a cogent historical reflection on fashion.[26] Her commitment to recovering past female intellectuals was then made visible in the article 'Portuguesas distintas' [Distinguished Portuguese Women] (*VF*, 27: 2; *VF*, 28: 1–2; *VF*, 29: 2–3), which eloquently foregrounds the names of many earlier learned women: Balsemão, Alorna, Luisa Sigueia; [Públia] Hortênsia de Castro; Joana de Meneses; Isabel de Castro e Andrade; Soror Violante do Céu; Ignácia Xavier; Rosa Soares; Sebastiana de Magalhães; Francisca Possolo da Costa (translator of Staël); Bernarda de Lacerda; and the painter Luísa Maria Rosa. Curiously, the Frenchwoman George Sand creeps into her list. Subsequent offerings include articles such 'Pintoras notáveis' [Notable painters] (*VF*, 37: 3), devoted to Portuguese female painters, as well as biographical sketches of the likes of Milton (*VF*, 46: 3–4), Byron (*VF*, 52: 2; *VF*, 53: 4) and Lamartine (*VF*, 66: 2).

Andrade would have endeared herself to Wood for her staunch support of women's education (*VF*, 23: 1) and her interest in animal protection, visible in her editorial 'Brado a favor dos animais' [A cry in favour of animals] (*VF*, 57: 1–2). She also took upon herself to comment on the 'Questão Ibérica' [Iberian Question], a political hot potato following the deposition of Queen Isabella II in neighbouring Spain in September 1868 (*VF*, 43: 2–3).[27] No doubt she was emboldened by the fact that an article signed by 'Uma colaboradora' [possibly Wood herself?] had appeared a fortnight earlier, where women's so-called lack of interest in politics was attributed in an ironic tone to 'razões mui cogentes' [very cogent reasons] among them the fact that 'esta ciência, de todas a mais emaranhada, é vedada a cabeças femininas, talvez por ser incompatível com a magnitude das cuias' [this science, the most confusing of them all, is forbidden to female heads, perhaps because it is incompatible with the size of their hair pieces] ([n.a.], *VF*, 41: 2). Where Andrade parted company with Wood's radical opinions, however, was in her diffidence concerning women's pursuit of political rights: 'mulher política! Deus me livre de tal' [political woman! God preserve me from the like] (*VF*, 30: 1). Given Andrade's dislike of politics, it follows that her last contribution took the form of two poems in no. 74 ('Saudades da infância' and 'A Uns olhos azuis (sem serem os meus)' *VF*, 74: 4). This was precisely the issue where Wood announced the imminent transition from *A Voz Feminina* to *O Progresso*. Her 'desertion' must have been a blow for Wood.

After the demise of the magazine, Andrade's first collection of poetry, *Murmúrios do Sado* (1870) brought together pieces that had first circulated in Francisca's periodical. The very title *Murmúrios do Sado* foregrounded the question of audibility as well as a peripheral location. It is perhaps unsurprising then that, in an attempt to offset her marginality, the majority of Andrade's poems bore epigraphs by Portuguese male writers, an exception being Ana Plácido. In a public acknowledgement of a woman-centred solidarity, however, the collection was dedicated to her godmother and also featured poems addressed to female friends, including a poem to Caron, another of the long-standing contributors to *A Voz Feminina* cited by Wood.[28] As had been the case with Plácido and Prata before her, Andrade had to rely on the cultural authority of a male-authored preface to validate her literary debut: in the event she turned to her near contemporary Cândido de Figueiredo. Her husband-to-be used his 'Proémio' to emphasize the legitimacy of female intellectual pursuits, while ruling out women's demands for political equality. As a contributor to *A Voz Feminina* himself, he would have been fully aware of the heated debate about female suffrage that had in the meantime taken centre-stage in the periodical, to be discussed in Chapter 6.

The fact that in the aftermath of *A Voz Feminina* its regular female contributors had acquired increased prestige can be demonstrated with one example: *A Aristocracia do Génio e da Beleza Feminil na Antiguidade* [The Aristocracy of Genius and Female Beauty in Antiquity] by José Palmela. Initially published in 1871, in Coimbra, Palmela's study went through several editions, attesting to its popularity. From 1872 onwards the original preface by Júlio César Machado was joined, as stated on the front-cover, by 'juízos' [appraisals] from Victor Hugo, the Spanish Ambassador D. Angel F. de los Rios, Mariana Angélica de Andrade and Guiomar Torresão.[29] In other words, women were prominently showcased there on a par with men — in fact not any man, but someone of the calibre of Hugo — and endowed with the cultural authority to proffer critical evaluations. Moreover, it is worth pointing out that one particular paragraph in Palmela's chapter on Sappho also underwent a small but significant tweak. The original first edition had stated that, not unlike Sappho, contemporary women in Portugal were still fighting against 'calúmias e inimizades' [calumnies and enmities] of both men and other women. The names of contemporaries adduced were those of Antónia Pusich; Francisca Wood; Guiomar Torresão; Mariana de Andrade; the Brazilian Maria Ribeiro; and the Coimbra-based Amélia Janny. The reference to Francisca Wood, who Palmela qualified as a 'romancista distinta e de grande erudição' [a distinguished novelist of great erudition], implies that he was aware of her novel and consequently almost certainly of *A Voz Feminina* too.[30]

Interestingly, after the demise of *O Progresso* some of Andrade's subsequent poetry engages with broader political motifs that suggest republican sympathies. One such example is a poem first published in the *Grinalda Literária*, on 10 June 1874 entitled 'À Liberdade', where the names of Victor Hugo and Emilio Castelar were invoked in the closing lines of the poem:

> Há dois nomes que a memória
> Reverente há de guardar;
> Inscreve-os a liberdade
> No seu formoso estandarte,
> Repetindo em toda a parte:
> Victor Hugo, e Castelar![31]

[There are two names that
Reverent memory must preserve;
Freedom inscribes them
On its beautiful banner,
Repeating everywhere:
Victor Hugo, and Castelar!]

One cannot fail to notice that both Hugo and Castelar's names had featured in Wood's periodical; Hugo was cited several times. As for Castelar, the periodical reacted at various points to democratic developments in neighbouring Spain and Andrade herself had done so. Moreover, she could not have failed to be aware that Wood herself went so far as to write an open letter to Castelar (*VF*, 72: 1–2), to be examined in Chapter 5.

Until her premature death Andrade continued to write poetry, posthumously gathered in *Revérberos do Poente* (1883). Particularly salient in that collection is her poem entitled 'Camões'. In the context of the tri-centenary of his death — a commemoration closely linked with Republican ideals — Andrade adds her voice to the national commemorations. Her opening statement is that her gender should not matter since she aspires to share in the celebration:

A festa é nacional; venho também a ela
Que importa ser mulher, se tenho aspirações?'

[It's a national celebration; I am joining in
What does being a woman matter, if I have aspirations?]

Although she was cleverly asserting her right to be a writer, without ever explicitly stating it, insofar as her form of words couched the statement as a question, the rhetorical question also left open the possibility that being a woman *did* in fact matter, given the systemic inequalities so clearly outlined in César Machado's comments at the start of this chapter. Andrade's poem concludes:

Eu trago a minha oferta, embora a mais singela,
E junto a voz humilde às grandes ovações
Se a festa é nacional, venho também a ela
porque nasci na terra em que nasceu Camões![32]

I bring my offering, though the simplest,
And add my humble voice to the great ovations
If it's a national celebration, I am joining in
Because I was born in the land where Camões was born!

In so doing, under the cloak of performative modesty, she was claiming her intellectual equality on the basis of a shared belonging to the nation. Hers is a more political move than might seem at first sight: Camões became a pretext to assert her entitlement to be a cultural player. In so doing she was in fact countering the fact that, as the Spanish author Carolina Coronado had famously intimated in her 1840s poem 'Libertad' [Freedom]:'Ni hay nación para este sexo' [Nor is there is a nation for this sex].[33] Significantly, other women too availed themselves of the opportunity generated by Camões's tri-centenary celebrations to highlight their shared belonging to the nation.[34]

Guiomar Torresão (1844–1898)

Today, the best-known of the names cited by Wood remains that of the versatile Guiomar Torresão, who had spent part of her early life in the Cape Verde Islands. In 1868, although still in her early twenties, Torresão had already made her mark with a comedy staged in the D. Maria II theatre (1867) as well as a handful of shorter literary pieces scattered in the press.[35] She was in the fortunate position of having the lawyer and playwright António Joaquim da Silva Abranches (author of the 1840 *O Cativo de Fez*) as her godfather; in a male-dominated world, his support would have been crucial in order to clinch her lucky break at the D. Maria II. Even so, she was unquestionably a spirited woman, who would go on to have a long and prolific journalistic and writing career and remained in the public eye for the next three decades. Although Torresão was not a complete novice, it is my contention that *A Voz Feminina* constituted her most sustained apprenticeship, a point that, rather surprisingly, has been overlooked up to now.[36]

The first contribution of the feisty Guiomar Torresão, in the *folhetim* [commentary column], with the title 'Saudação' [Greeting], occurs in no. 4. There, while highly complimentary about the purpose of the paper, she expressed reservations about the practice of publishing translated fiction, in evidence in the *rodapé* of the first three issues. Instead she suggested that an original novel in Portuguese, even if only passable, would usually be preferable to a translation, however good: 'de ordinário, prefere-se um original sofrível a uma versão boa' (*VF*, 4: 1). Up to then, from the inaugural issue onwards, the periodical had been publishing two fairly unremarkable stories, without identification of source but probably translated from French.[37] To her credit, Wood immediately acted on Torresão's suggestion: since conveniently the first tale concluded in no. 3 and the second in no. 4, from no. 5 onwards *A Voz Feminina* started to run as a serial Torresão's own original novel *Uma Alma de Mulher* [A Woman's Soul]. Torresão had perhaps not been expecting to be approached so quickly, for it certainly looks as though she was writing from week to week, rather than having readily available material: every so often there is no weekly instalment (for instance the *folhetim* rubric in no. 11 is taken up with a piece in English by Bulwer-Lytton, 'Love Stronger Than Death', *VF*, 11: 1–2). Even so, *Uma Alma de Mulher* ran from no. 5 to no. 26 to its natural conclusion.

On the literary front, even though Torresão's initial 'Saudação' had expressed misgivings about women's poetry, she did in fact supply the occasional poem. She also re-emerged as the author of a series of short stories, 'Contos morais' [Moral tales]. In a short prologue, she explained their gestation to her 'querida redatora' [dear editor]:

> Surgiu-me esta ideia à sombra da frondosa acácia do seu jardim, ouvindo gorjear as avezinhas, confundindo os seus arrulhos melodiosos com as vozes infantis que me deliciavam os ouvidos. [...] Esta ideia nasceu, e ficou como flor por desabrochar, oculta na estufa do meu peito; caiu, porém, sobre ela um raio de sol, a palavra de V. Exa, e a flor tremeu na haste, abrindo afinal as pétalas! (*VF*, 34: 2)

> [This idea occurred to me under the shade of the leafy acacia tree in your garden, hearing the little birds twitter, their tuneful cooing mingling with the

children's voices that delighted my ears. [...] This idea was born, and remained like a flower about to bloom, hidden in the greenhouse of my breast; however, like a ray of sunshine, your words fell upon it, and the flower trembled on its stem, finally opening its petals!]

While the background sound of 'vozes infantis' reminds us that Wood's home doubled up as a school, this extract confirms the support that she provided her young team and the positive impact she had on their confidence. In practice her open door policy, advertised in no. 6 as we saw, encouraged the kind of sociability that seems to have generated opportunities for informal mentoring and networking.

Torresão stated her intention to dedicate each tale to a different friend. Indeed it was characteristic of her to dedicate her work to other women; the earlier *Uma Alma de Mulher* had been dedicated 'A minha boa mãe' (*VF*, 5: 1) [To my good mother]. But it was also a generalized trend: there were frequent protestations of female friendship inside the pages of the periodical, whether among the collaborators themselves or to other female friends and relatives, for example through the dedication of poems, stories and even articles.[38] These heightened the sense of belonging to a female-centred community. The first short story, 'Amor de Filha' [A Daughter's Love], is dedicated to Anne Marie Caron, one of the younger contributors to *A Voz Feminina*, a choice that reflected their *esprit de corps* (*VF*, 34: 2).

In the meantime, another aspect of Torresão's pivotal and multifaceted role is her appetite for undertaking signed book reviews, something that Wood had outlined in her initial vision for the periodical. This is noteworthy because it places Torresão in a position of authority as she takes on the daunting task of evaluating a range of contemporary male writers while still at a relatively early stage of her career: Júlio Dinis (no. 16); João de Deus (no. 60), Sousa Carvalho (no. 63), Guilherme de Azevedo (no. 64), Araújo Assis (no. 68). To this we can add an editorial on drama, in which she cites Shakespeare, Hugo and Garrett and concludes with a reference to *A Morgadinha de Valflor* [The Heiress of Valflor] by Pinheiro Chagas (*VF*, 73: 1–2); as well as an early *folhetim* [commentary column] on the play *A Doida de Montmayour* [The madwoman of Montmayour] (*VF*, 6: 1–2). Of particular interest is a later *folhetim* that provides a bio-bibliographical overview of the contemporary Cuban-born Gertrudis Gómez de Avellaneda (1814–1873) (*P*, 79: 119–21).[39] At least part of Torresão's interest in Avellaneda may have been fuelled by a biographical coincidence, since both were born on remote colonial islands.

Torresão did not shy away from avant-garde ideas concerning female suffrage. In fact, the first of her five editorials (*VF*, 42: 1–2) provides a cogent response, rebutting of Andrade's more moderate position, as we shall see in Chapter 6. Torresão remained active as a valued contributor until her final contribution, on 8 August 1869, consisting of a translation of an article from the French periodical *Le Droit des Femmes* bearing her signature, which was inserted within the unsigned article 'Uma Senhora portuguesa médico [*sic*]' ([n.a.], *P*, 82: 134). How can we account for her early departure? One explanation is that, as someone who was determined to live by the pen, she had to be financially self-supporting; her priority therefore would have been to be paid for her labour. As far as we know, Wood did not seem to have taken on board the desirability of doing so, certainly not in the first year, where she alludes to the fact that all contributors were unpaid ([n.a.], *VF*, 33: 1). But perhaps more importantly, in order to achieve financial independence, Torresão could not afford to alienate the majority of her potential readership, be they men or women. Strategic choices had to be made. In all likelihood she had realized (or been advised?) that being linked to the Woods would not stand her in good stead in the long run.

The details concerning the publication of her novel *Uma Alma de Mulher* [A Woman's Soul], in 1869, certainly display an acute awareness of the functioning of the Portuguese literary marketplace. Initially advertised as about to be published by Tip. da Voz Feminina, her novel was instead released by a more established publisher, Tip. de J. G. de Sousa Neves. Torresão may have been swayed by the fact that the latter had published Camilo Castelo Branco's novel *O Sangue* [Blood] (1868) only the previous year, and had printed some of his other novels for the publisher Campos Junior.[40] In addition to an introductory letter penned by her godfather, she also secured a preface by Júlio César Machado, cited at the beginning of this chapter. Machado was an excellent choice in marketing terms, given that he had prefaced Ana Plácido's collection six years earlier. Another proof of marketing acumen was that when Torresão's second volume of prose fiction, *Rosas Pálidas* [Pale Roses] (1873), came out, the dedication of 'Amor de Filha' was no longer to the fairly obscure Anne Marie Caron but to a rising star: Maria Amália Vaz de Carvalho.[41]

Probably emboldened after closely shadowing the formidable female Editor of *A Voz Feminina* over a nineteen-month period, Torresão launched the yearly *Almanaque das Senhoras* in 1870. Significantly, the contacts made while working in Francisca Wood's periodical meant that over the years Torresão was able to draw on colleagues who had previously contributed to *A Voz Feminina* such as Mariana de Andrade, Emília da Maia, Maria Adelaide Fernandes Prata, Catarina Máxima de Figueiredo and Delfina Caldas Vieira. Impressively, Torresão was also able to cajole a number of established high-profile intellectuals not previously associated with *A Voz Feminina* to feature in her *Almanaque*: Pusich; Peregrina de Sousa, Canuto; and Chiape Cadet.[42] Disappointingly, but perhaps not surprisingly, Wood was nowhere to be seen.

Like *A Esperança*, *Almanaque das Senhoras* listed female and male contributors separately and it is telling that the 'Senhoras' listings started with Maria Amália Vaz de Carvalho, whom Torresão was keen to court.[43] In the first year alone, the list of male contributors to the *Almanaque* included heavyweights such as António Feliciano de Castilho, Bulhão Pato, Brito Aranha, João de Deus, João de Lemos, Júlio César Machado, Júlio Dinis, Pinheiro Chagas and Tomás Ribeiro.[44] This list, like the female one:

> Atesta a capacidade de negociação de Guiomar. Atrair nomes representativos das letras nacionais, bem como simpatias em favor das causas femininas, poderia significar mais capacidade financeira para garantir que o anuário tivesse longevidade [...]. Certamente a aceitação da presença masculina no jornal também está relacionada à necessidade de conquistar respeitabilidade junto à sociedade.[45]

[Attests to Guiomar's negotiating skills. Attracting representative names from national letters, as well as sympathy for female causes, might mean greater financial capacity to guarantee the longevity of the annual [...]. Certainly acceptance of the masculine presence in the annual is also related to the need to achieve respectability vis-à-vis society.]

The operative word here has to be respectability: after the closure of *O Progresso*, Torresão fully understood the need for a wide appeal and, crucially, for male patronage. She therefore nurtured some influential men of letters, known to be willing to champion women as intellectuals:

De acordo com pesquisas de Ernesto Rodrigues, a casa de Guiomar Torrezão era um local de leitura pública. Entre as senhoras que frequentavam o espaço estavam D. Júlia de Gusmão e D. Emília da Maia que, após as leituras, recitavam poesias juntamente com Guiomar, no seu salão à Rua Formosa, em Lisboa. Entre os homens, destacam-se Castilho, Júlio Machado, D. António da Costa, Sousa Viterbo.[46]

[According to Ernesto Rodrigues's research, Guiomar Torrezão's home was a place for public readings. Among the ladies who frequented the place were D. Júlia de Gusmão and D. Emília da Maia who, after the readings, recited poetry along with Guiomar, in her salon in the Rua Formosa, in Lisbon. Among the men, Castilho, Júlio Machado, D. António da Costa and Sousa Vitero stand out.]

Still in the context of *Almanaque das Senhoras*, Lopes highlights that Torresão uses male self-publicizing strategies, promoting 'a sua própria imagem junto do público no seu *Almanaque* através da publicidade de cartas de louvor, de poesias, de outros textos encomiásticos e de reconhecimento que lhe eram endereçados por correspondentes de ambos os sexos'[47] [her own image with the public in her *Almanaque* through the publication of letters of praise, poetry, other encomiastic texts and recognition that they were addressed to her by correspondents of both sexes]. It is worth adding, however, that self-promotion was not an exclusively male strategy: Wood regularly transcribed in *A Voz Feminina* positive reviews from a range of other newspapers in order to generate a buzz.

Torresão, like Mariana de Andrade and Emília da Maia before her in *A Voz Feminina*, was committed to disseminating knowledge of the achievements of Portuguese women virtually from the inception of the *Almanaque*, for instance through the article 'Portuguesas célebres' (1871: 46–51) [Famous Portuguese Women] or through reviews of contemporaries such as Amélia Janny (1874: 1–7) and Ana Maria Ribeiro de Sá (1875: 1–7).[48] Foregrounding the visibility of past and contemporary writers was a much needed tactic, in order to offset the refusal of the leading men of the *Geração de 70* to countenance growing evidence of female authorship. As is widely known, the *Almanaque das Senhoras* was (in)famously ridiculed by Ortigão in 1877.

His position with regard to female intellectuals was patronizing at best, and downright dismissive at worst, as evidenced by his misogynistic aphorism in *As Farpas* that women should produce 'menos odes e mais caldo' [fewer odes and more broth].[49] Had Torresão been a novice, his indictment may have brought her to a grinding halt. Instead, his reductive conflation of 'literatas' with poetry backfired badly: it elicited two swift and spirited female responses.[50] One of them was from Torresão herself, in a fitting demonstration that he had underestimated the fact that she was his intellectual match: her article was steeped in finely judged irony, reminiscent of Wood's responses through open letters to be discussed in more detail in Chapter 5. But Ortigão's barb was not the only setback: Torresão also had to contend with cartoons by Rafael Bordalo Pinheiro, between 1879 and 1884 in particular.[51] And other members of the *Geração de 70* too remained deeply misogynistic. For instance, in 1884 Oliveira Martins declined to contribute to *Almanaque das Senhoras*, on the grounds that the role of women 'salvo as excepções privilegiadas, como v. Ex.a — é cozinharem bem a panela a seus maridos, saberem lavar os filhos e remendar-lhes os calções' [with the exception of privileged cases like yours — is to cook meals well for their husbands, know how to wash their children and darn their underwear].[52]

Undeterred, Torresão continued to position herself strategically: in 1880, she became one of the founding members of the Association of Portuguese Journalists and Writers.[53] The yearly *Almanaque das Senhoras* continued to run successfully until her death in 1898, and indeed thereafter. One survival tactic may have been the deployment as ammunition of a string of contributions by living female intellectuals from abroad. Wood too had turned to transnational connections to counter the narrow-mindedness of her male opponents, as Chapters 5 and 6 will discuss in greater depth. In addition, throughout the 1880s Torresão herself penned short biographies of Maria Leticia Rattazi (1879; pp. 3–15); the British painter Maria Carpenter (1880: 3–8); the Spanish Concepción Gimeno de Flaquer (1881: 3–9); the French Julieta Lamber otherwise known as Mme Adam (1881: 3–20); the Spanish Faustina Sáez de Melgar (1883: v–xii) and Emilia Pardo Bazán (1885: 3–12); the French Georges de Peyrebrune (1890: 3–14); the Brazilian Júlia Lopes de Almeida (1898: 3–11).[54] In fact, this interest in profiling women from other nations had begun in *A Voz Feminina* with her aforementioned *folhetim* showcasing the Cuban-born Gertrudis Gómez de Avallaneda.[55] Lopes raises the pertinent possibility that the presence of foreign voices in the *Almanaque das Senhoras* may have been a clever subterfuge to voice positions that Portuguese women were reluctant to articulate openly, thereby indirectly keeping the pro-feminist debate alive after the demise of *O Progresso*.[56]

While not being overtly controversial was an imperative for Torresão in order to secure financial success, her first-hand contacts in Paris — where she spent two months in 1885, and was in touch with the likes of Peyrebrune, Ratchilde and Mme Adam — must have brought home to her how out of kilter Portugal was with the growing intellectual and sexual freedom visible elsewhere. Furthermore, it is worth mentioning the little-known fact that in 1896 Torresão prefaced a collection of articles by the American suffragist Tennessee Claflin (Lady Cook), translated into Portuguese in a volume titled *Estudos*.[57] Back in 1870 Claflin was the first woman to open a Wall Street brokerage firm, along with her sister Victoria Woodhull, who later became the first woman to run for President of the United States. By belatedly linking her name again to that of a radical suffragist, Torresão had come full circle — even if admittedly Claflin had secured social respectability in later life by marrying the Sir Francis Cook, Viscount of Monserrate. This may explain why, more than two and a half decades after the demise of *A Voz Feminina*, Torresão remembered her former mentor and belatedly decided to pen 'Apontamentos acerca da escritora Francisca de Assis Martins Wood' [Notes on the writer Francisca de Assis Martins Wood], dated 13 July 1896, according to the *Catálogo da livraria do falecido distinto bibliógrafo e bibliófilo José Maria Nepomuceno*.[58] What might Torresão have had to say about Francisca? Did she know that her former Editor was in fact still alive in 1896? Were these notes ever published or did they remain in manuscript form? Sadly, unless such a document resurfaces, it is yet another instance of cultural memory loss surrounding Francisca Wood. In the event, it was too little and too late to redress the silence that had already surrounded Francisca's name for a quarter of a century.

The novices: bringing on younger contributors

This chapter would not be complete without a brief examination of the names, today unknown, of the three 'beginners' cited by Francisca in her aforementioned 'Declaração', 'As meninas Caron, Lília Torres, e Sofia Cunha', and their early attempts at writing for public consumption. Lília Torres only had a fleeting presence in *A Voz Feminina*, with several travel sketches across Portuguese locations (nos. 17–24). Her style earned her the praise of a male reader who wrote a letter transcribed by the Editor. Wood did not disclose his identity referring to him simply as a 'literato de Coimbra' ([n.a.], ['Publicamos os seguintes extratos...'] *VF*, 26: 4).

By contrast Anne Marie Caron and Sofia Nesbitt Cunha became long-standing contributors. A sequential examination reveals how Francisca was able to nurture them, thereby encouraging both to maintain an ongoing presence in the periodical. Furthermore, one of Caron's letters is especially interesting in respect of her insertion into an empowering female-led network. Not only because it was addressed to Mariana de Andrade, thereby emphasizing the bonds generated within the communal space of the periodical, but also because it provides us with further evidence that Francisca served as a role model and intellectual mentor, when Caron discloses how much she enjoyed spending time with her: 'delicio-me às vezes horas e horas a ouvi-la conversar, não é assim que se forma o pensamento? Que a inteligência se robustece?' (*VF*, 37: 4) [I sometimes enjoy myself for hours on end listening to her conversation, isn't this how thought is shaped? How intelligence grows?].

Caron's first signed piece was serialized fiction in French: *Aurélie et Eliska ou les deux amies*, dedicated 'A Mlle Elvira Augusta Andrade' (nos. 17–45), an offering that signalled significant literary ambition. The Editor's decision was to publish it in the inside pages, possibly because it was written in French, but this was also in keeping with the fact that Caron, unlike Torresão, was unknown to the readership. Immediately after her serialized novel came to an end, Caron took on the fashion rubric (nos. 46, 47, 51, 56, 61, 64, 69, 74, where she signs as Anna Caron). This was interspersed with pieces such as 'Victor Hugo e os inocentes' (*VF*, 57: 3) [Victor Hugo and the innocents], about charity work, or Mina Auck (*VF*, 63: 2), as well as a letter to the Editor about the fact that in France important cultural icons such as Alexandre Dumas were promoting opportunities for women to further their learning (*VF*, 66: 4). Caron remained a presence almost to the end, and in later issues there were also translations: an anecdote by Fénelon (*P*, 91: 169), and serialized fiction 'A Americana' (nos. 97–100). The diversity of her range suggests that Francisca wished to keep her on board and help her to find her voice, but the fact that only her translated fiction was published on the front page arguably indicates a lesser profile.

Perhaps the most curious case is that of Sofia Nesbitt Cunha, who again would not be tasked with any editorials, a fact that can be easily understood once we realize that she was introduced by Francisca as being a 'menina de quinze anos' [fifteen-year old girl] (['Damos a seguinte carta...'] *VF*, 17: 4). Her first contribution took the form of a letter written in English. This endearing piece revealed Cunha's eager interest in the novels by Torresão and Caron, serialized within the pages of the magazine. As well as Portuguese and English, Sofia read French fluently, and her missive disclosed that she was in the process of reading *Les Aventures de Télémaque* [The Adventures of Telemachus] by Fénelon. Since it transpired later that Sofia was one of Francisca's pupils (*VF*, 41: 2) this choice is perhaps revealing, above all, of Francisca's didactics intentions, for the latter could surely not have failed to notice that Telemachus's tutor, Mentor, turned out at the end of the tale to be a female entity, Minerva, goddess of wisdom.

Sofia Nesbitt Cunha translated *faits divers* from English into Portuguese: 'Terramoto nas ilhas de Sandwich' ([n.a.], *VF*, 30: 3–4) [Earthquake in the Sandwich Islands], 'O Espiritualismo' (*VF*, 32: 2) [Spiritualism].[59] From French she translated texts such as 'A Cuia' (*VF*, 37: 2–3) [The hair piece], 'Crueldade para com os animais' (*VF*, 39: 3) [Cruelty to animals]; both these topics were close to Francisca's heart: female vanity and the protection of animals. Given Sofia's youth, one suspects Francisca must have guided her choices and asked her to try her hand at translating specific self-contained pieces. By the time the periodical drew to a close, Sofia had graduated to a literary translation from English, sustained over three issues: 'Romance numa carruagem a vapor' [Romance in a steam-driven carriage] (nos. 100–02).

Both Caron and Cunha were thus valuable for ensuring a semblance of continuity after the untimely departure of Andrade and, eight weeks later, Torresão. In a similar vein, we can perhaps briefly allude to the case of Eliza Elliott (whose name, like that of Sofia Nesbitt Cunha, suggests a distinctly British background). Although she was not one of the six names mentioned in Francisca's 'Declaração', her presence as a latecomer gives us a telling indication of Francisca's *modus operandi* in terms of promoting young female voices and nurturing their talents. In an open letter to be further discussed in Chapter 5, Wood had rebuked a male reader, João A. Elliott, for believing that he was entitled to determine how far his younger sister's intellectual aspirations were allowed to go: he deemed culture to be fine but not politics (*P*, 78: 117). The name of his younger sibling was not disclosed at that point, but it seems reasonable to speculate that it was Eliza Elliott, whose translation from English of a novella, *Cecília*, was serialized soon after (nos. 84–89). In effect, Wood was offering this young woman an intellectual opening, presumably in a bid to counter the prevailing limitations of her milieu.

Male Champions

Wood strongly believed that men could be pro-women and one of her strategies was to enlist as many potential allies as possible. While she found a staunch supporter in her husband from the start, a number of radical young men rallied around her in the pages of *A Voz Feminina* and *O Progresso*. Her early editorials, in the first year of the periodical's life, privileged dialogue with forward-thinking male journalists. The way that Wood engages with such journalists was designed to make them feel good about supporting the cause of women. For instance, she addressed J. C. de Freitas Jacome, who had published a piece in *Diario de Noticias*, as follows:

> A redatora desta folha agradece ao Sr. J. C. de Freitas Jacome, em nome das suas Colegas e de todas as escravas brancas, escuras e pretas, espargidas sobre a face da terra, o apoio que ele presta à causa do sexo feminino. ([n.a.], *VF*, 21: 1)

> [The editor of this paper thanks Mr. J. C. de Freitas Jacome, in the name of her Colleagues and all the white, dark and black slaves, scattered across the face of the earth, for the support he lends to the cause of the female sex.]

The formulation is striking, implicitly equating the status of all women, irrespective of race, to that of slaves. In so doing, Wood may be taking her cue from of Mary Wollstonecraft, who asked in her 1792 *A Vindication of the Rights of Women*: 'Is one half of the human species, like the poor African slaves, to be subject to prejudices that brutalize them?'. It must be noted that the conflation of race and gender, from today's perspective, is overly simplistic: women of colour were far more likely to be living in actual slavery.

Wood's lead article closed with a comment from the afore-mentioned journalist Júlio César Machado. On closer inspection, the paraphrase turns out to have been taken from his preface to Ana Plácido's *Luz coada por ferros* (1863).[60] Why did Wood cite from Machado rather than from Plácido herself, since she was clearly familiar with her predecessor's work? 'Meditation IV', for instance, would have been very effective, and was in fact quoted by Mariana de Andrade in one of her early editorials, as we saw. One possible explanation is that Wood did not wish to scandalize her readership by invoking the authority of a controversial woman. A more likely reason, however, is that Plácido was far less influential than Machado at the time — even though, with the benefit of hindsight, it is clear that her work can be regarded as a watershed moment in Portuguese literature.

Eight weeks later, in the front page, Wood transcribes a critical review by Júlio C. Machado published in *A Revolução de Setembro*, where he had complimented *A Voz Feminina*, singling out Delfina Vieira Caldas,[61] Anne Marie Caron and Torresão in particular, while also drawing attention to the earlier journalistic projects of Antónia Gertrudes Pusich ([n.a.], *VF*, 29: 1–2).[62] In a later editorial,

Wood continued to regard Machado as a male champion, citing from two sections of his preamble to Plácido's *Luz Coada por Ferros*:

> — Não perdoam facilmente, diz o nosso elegante escritor J. C. Machado, essas a que os jornais do género chamam no dia imediato ao baile — rainhas das festas — que uma entre elas, tão formosa como elas, como elas tão senhora, se permita, além de conversar, sorrir, amar, dançar, — pensar! As mães indicam-na às meninas como perigosa; os burgueses evitam olhá-la; os noivos temem-se; e os tolos, que andam em maioria, dizem consigo que uma senhora que tem espírito é uma senhora que se afasta do seu fim, e que eles não se acham preparados, de um dia para o outro, a conversar num baile com uma senhora que pensa, porque vão a um baile para se distraírem e não para terem trabalho. (*VF*, 36: 1)

> ['They don't forgive easily', says our elegant author J. C. Machado, 'those ladies that certain kinds of newspaper call "queens of the party" on the day immediately after the ball, that one among them, just as beautiful as they are, a lady just like them, should allow herself not only to talk, to smile, to dance — but to think! Mothers point her out to the girls as dangerous; the bourgeoisie avoid looking at her; engaged couples fear for one another; and the fools, who constitute the majority, tell themselves that a spirited lady is a lady who turns away from her purpose, and that they do not feel prepared, from one day to the next, to interact at a ball with a lady who thinks, because they go to the ball in order to amuse themselves, not to have to work'.]

Machado thus lamented that thinking women had yet to become socially acceptable, all the more so since foolish men (which according to him were abundant) were simply not equipped to deal with them as intellectually equal companions. The indelible stain on Placido's name is that, as a learned woman, she would have been widely regarded as 'uma senhora que se afasta do seu fim', the purpose of women generally agreed to be decorative while single — and, presumably, breed plentifully once married.

The second extract from Machado's preface can be held up as a benchmark of male support for learned women, in his dismissal of physical beauty as only superficially attractive:

> Existe entre nós, 'já não um núcleo, mas uma vasta classe de homens altamente instruídos e talentosos; homens que pela condição do seu moral não podem apreciar a sociedade de figurinos; homens que sentem um friozinho quando contemplam a mulher puramente linda como se afagassem estátuas de pedra'. (*VF*, 36: 1)

> [There exist among us, 'not only a nucleus, but a vast class of highly educated and talented men; men who through the disposition of their character are unable to appreciate the company of clothes-horses; men who feel a chill when they contemplate the merely beautiful woman as if they were caressing statues made of stone'.]

By then in his thirties, J. C. Machado was a well-established journalist, influential but ultimately still fairly middle-of-the-road. In practice, it was a younger male generation that was more likely to champion woman's full emancipation. Wood welcomed them, for she realized that an exclusively female space was probably neither viable nor indeed desirable. In the pages of *A Voz Feminina* several young men in their twenties embraced her feminist cause. Culturally speaking, they had more clout to do so then their female counterparts (as the example of Adelaide Prata in Chapter 2 underlined). They were, however, conceivably open to the cultural authority of an older woman endowed with a cosmopolitan aura — a model pertaining to salon culture in elite circles, where the earlier example of the influential Marquesa de Alorna springs to mind.

Several of these radical young contributors, whose names are largely forgotten today, were entrusted with editorials. Francisco António de Matos (1845–1902) and Francisco de Paula Abreu Marques (1847–1921) penned three and five editorials respectively.[63] An open letter from João Luís Silva Viana to Wood featured as a lead article (*VF*, 65: 1–2). Viana was Editor of *O Correio dos Dois Mundos* until it folded in February 1869, and his glowing endorsement of *A Voz Feminina* in his own periodical had been transcribed earlier in no. 27 ([n.a.], ['Com a devida vénia...'] 27: 1). Equally significantly, he translated into Portuguese, from an unnamed source, a biography of Toussaint L'Ouverture (1743–1803), the leader of the Haitian Revolution, serialized in nos. 60–64.

In *O Progresso*, editorial space was occupied with the transcription of letters by António Fernandes de Figueiredo Ferrer Farol (1839–1893) (*P*, 81: 127–28)) and João de Sousa Araújo (1848–1931) (*P*, 98: 195–96). The latter, soon to become the fiancé of Cesário Verde's sister, had previously contributed an article 'A Mulher e os seus direitos' (*P*, 96: 188). And the Republican J. C. Teixeira Coelho had a rousing article about female emancipation (['Mais um Brado', *P*, 95: 183–84), which led Wood to thank him and proclaim that she 'ufana-se de o contar no número dos seus generosos e disinteressados campeões' [she was proud to count him among the number of her generous and disinterested champions] ([n.a.], *P*, 95: 184).

Other contributors, even though they did not produce editorials, were equally vital to the liberal image cultivated by the periodical. António José de Carvalho signed the poems 'A Victor Hugo' (*VF*, 38: 4), and 'Um Brado patriótico: a Portugal' (*VF*, 39: 4) [A Patriotic shout: to Portugal], and pledged his support when the periodical was rebranded *O Progresso* (*P*, 77: 112).[64] The fact that the journal provided a platform for heterodox thinkers, some attracted by its manifest anticlericalism, is perhaps most visibly attested by the contributions of José Cipriano da Costa Goodolfim (1842–1910) on religion, in particular 'Deus e o homem' (*VF*, 59: 2–3; *VF*, 69: 3; *VF*, 70: 4). He went on to pen the pamphlets *A Religião dos Padres: A Propósito do Sermão Anti-Evangélico do Padre Serrano* (1870) [The Religion of the Fathers: On the Anti-Evangelical Sermon of Father Serrano] and *O Celibato Clerical* (1872) [Clerical Celibacy].

As in the case of women, there were other less overtly politically minded contributors such as António Cândido de Figueiredo (1846–1925), who would go on to marry Mariana de Andrade and become a distinguished scholar, with poems under his own name and the series 'Cartas de Coimbra' [Letters from Coimbra] as Luís de Lencastre.[65] In addition, there was a sprinkling of poetic offerings by

João de Deus (*VF*, 59: 4; *P*, 90: 166). The periodical also transcribed poetry by the Brazilian Tomás Antônio Gonzaga (*P*, 82: 134). The publication of the occasional poem in later issues of *O Progresso* seems mostly a space-filling strategy, although the choice was often not innocent: the liberal Alexandre Herculano was a public intellectual with a record of controversial anticlerical writings, and in the case of Gonzaga there is a political point, to be discussed in Chapter 4.

Conclusion

As Machado's eye-catching formulation cited at the beginning of this chapter reminds us, women in 1860s Portugal had to contend with such entrenched systemic obstacles that it wouldn't be too far-fetched to imagine 'no seio da mesma mãe pátria duas nações de seres diferentes' [at the heart of the same mother country two nations of different beings]. To offset this damaging cultural segregation, Francisca was able to facilitate and nurture the greater participation of women in what was, after all, one of the few public spaces available to them. By surrounding herself with a team of trusted, loyal core members of both sexes, some naturally more talented and/or experienced than others, Wood sought to promote a mutually reinforcing appreciation of solidarity and develop an inspiring collaborative project — one that launched important debates concerning female expectations in a shifting cultural landscape. Under her leadership, *A Voz Feminina* and its successor *O Progresso* engendered an enlightened group dynamic.

For the most part, we do not know what became of the contributors identified as novices in Francisca's 'Declaração'. The *Dicionário no Feminino (séculos XIX–XX)* features additional material only about Anne-Marie Caron, indicating that subsequently she continued to move in first-wave feminist circles, most notably by collaborating in Castro Osório's *A Semeadora* between 1915 and 1918 as a war correspondent from Paris.[66] Of the more experienced contributors, the combative Torresão went on to have a long and productive career, and can be regarded in many ways as Wood's intellectual heir, not least in the way she went on to cultivate transnational connections by virtue of necessity. She travelled to France, made connections in Spain, and saw her work circulate in Brazil. Credited as one of the first nineteenth-century women to support herself through writing, Torresão managed to navigate skilfully a largely hostile milieu. She adopted strategies similar to Wood's on several occasions, but also learnt from her mentor's mistakes as she strove to maintain a wide appeal, crucial to her own economic survival as a single woman.

In the late 1860s, however, in terms of the sophistication of her feminist thinking, Wood was miles ahead compared to her young female cast and other Portuguese contemporaries. Thus, since the Woods could not flatter themselves that in *A Voz Feminina* they possessed an organ of public opinion already formed, as William Wood put it, the only way forward was to act as pioneers — which was tantamount to *forming* opinion. Arguably Francisca Wood's revolutionary critical thinking on gender would not be emulated for decades until the Setúbal-born Ana de Castro

Osório launched the periodical *Sociedade Futura* [Future Society] in 1902 and published the compilation *As Mulheres Portuguesas* [Portuguese Women] in 1905.[67] It is to the modernity underpinning the thought of Wood's lead articles, in which she rehearsed first-wave arguments a full three decades before Castro Osório, that we now turn in Chapter 4.

Notes to Chapter 3

1. Guiomar Torresão, *Uma Alma de Mulher: romance original* (Lisbon: Tipografia J. G. de Sousa Neves, 1869), p. 9.
2. See entries on both Machado and Torresão in *Dicionário do Romantismo*, ed. by Buescu. It is worth noting that Machado was the youngest of the intellectuals considered by Santos in her monograph.
3. Cortez, *Os Contos de Grimm em Portugal*, p. 93, footnote.
4. In no. 64 we find out retrospectively the names of the people initially involved: the owners were Mr. Gameiro and Mr. Macedo, and for the first month the Editor was Mr. Pinto Almeida (Francisca Wood, *VF*, 64: 3).
5. Cortez, p. 92, footnote n. 103.
6. All previous researchers have assumed that the format does not vary. There were however two six-page-long issues (nos. 55 and 56), which will be discussed in Chapter 6.
7. Susan Kirkpatrick, 'Women as Cultural Agents in *Spanish Modernity*', in *A Companion to Spanish Women's Studies*, ed. by Xon de Ros and Geraldine Hazbun (London: Boydell & Brewer, 2011), pp. 227–42 (p. 230).
8. The BNP run of *A Voz Feminina* is missing no. 10, so our calculation assumes that Wood was in charge of the editorial for this issue, as occurs in the four weeks before and after. On the other hand, we have not factored into this calculation a later unsigned editorial (no. 44) because, although framed by what is clearly the voice of Wood in her role as Editor, it consists primarily of the transcription of an article.
9. These were not signed, but the signed editorial in no. 43 ('Escrito dedicado' *VF*, 43: 1–2) indicates that she was their author.
10. The poet writing from Guiães was Catarina Máxima de Figueiredo de Abreu Castelo-Branco (1829–[?]). See *As Senhoras do almanaque*, ed. by Lousada, Chaves and Abreu. According to Cardoso she was the mother of the first-wave feminist Maria Feio (Maria Figueiredo Feio Rebelo Castelo Branco) (1870–1939). See Nuno Catarino Cardoso, *Poetisas portuguesas: antologia contendo dados bibliográficos e biográficos acerca de cento e seis poetisas* (Lisbon: N. C. Cardoso, 1917), p. 98. <https://archive.org/details/poetisasportugueoocarduoft/page/n13>. In a literary context, Guiães is more commonly associated today with the provenance of Zé Fernandes, the wayward first-person narrator of Eça de Queirós's *A Cidade e as Serras*.
11. The 'Expediente' in no. 39 ([n.a.], *VF*, 39: 1), where subscribers from eleven different locations were urged to pay their dues, confirms circulation in places like Braga, Covilhã, Faro and Guarda, at the time remote from Lisbon.
12. The 'Expediente' also welcomes Luís de Almeida de Melo e Castro as the manager, until his withdrawal in no. 21. His profile was rather incongruous for the lofty purpose of the paper, since he was a 'boémio alfacinha' [Lisbon bohemian] and a 'cantador de fado, amador tauromáquico, figura imprescindível em todas as tabernas' [singer of fado, amateur bullfighter, indispensable figure in all the taverns]. See Marina Tavares Dias, *Lisboa desaparecida*, 9 vols (Lisbon: Quimera, 1987–2007), III (1992), 23–24.
13. Between nos. 23 and 31, the bottom right hand corner on p. 4 indicates there is an agent in London: 'H Ballière, 219, Regent Street'.
14. It would transpire later that Carlota A. P. was in fact a man (Francisca Wood, *VF*, 64: 3). Wood acknowledged that Carlota A. P. and Leonor A. P. G were two men writing under female pseudonyms, but she insisted that all other participants were female. The accusation shows how unusual the significant female make-up of the magazine was at the time.

15. [Marquês de Valada], ['Lemos as despedidas da *Voz Feminina*...'], *Bem Público*, 24 July 1869, pp. 19–20 (p. 19). Although all articles are unsigned, Wood ascribes the attacks to him, and so we will assume that Marquês de Valada was their author.

16. *The Revolution* was a radical periodical launched in 1868, by Elizabeth Caddy Stanton and Susan B. Anthony. See Chapter 6.

17. 'Veritas Odium Parit', *O Bem Público*, p. 399.

18. Prata was the acclaimed translator of *Fingal: poema em seis cantos* (1867). See *The Reception of Ossian in Europe*, ed. by Howard Gaskill (London and New York: Thoemmes Continuum, 2004).

19. 'Emília Adelaide Moniz da Maia', in *Dicionário no feminino (séculos XIX–XX)*, ed. by Zília Osório de Castro and others (Lisbon: Horizonte, 2005), pp. 303–04.

20. Mauro Nicola Póvoas, 'Fontes primárias e redescobertas: o caso de Emília da Maia', in *Língua portuguesa: ultrapassar fronteiras, juntar culturas*, ed. by Maria João Marçalo and others (Évora: Universidade de Évora, 2010), pp. 1–21 <http://www.simelp2009.uevora.pt/pdf/slt56/04.pdf>.

21. She listed several pre-modern names: Agustinha Barbosa da Silva; Rosa Soares; D. Maria de Castro; D. Joana Margarida de Castro; Paula de Sá.

22. See also Lopes, *Imagens da mulher*, pp. 411–12.

23. *Fleurs* (1878), *Penas* (1912) and the posthumous *As Palavras de Nosso Senhor Jesus Cristo* (1916). None of these are available in the National Library of Portugal, but Maria features in Nuno Catarino Cardoso's 1917 anthology, *Poetisas Portuguesas*, suggesting he had had access to at least some of her works. See Cardoso, p. 171. Cardoso is careful to recall that she was a contributor to *A Voz Feminina*, alongside Torresão and Andrade.

24. See *Mariana Angélica de Andrade: a poetisa do Sado*, ed. by Anita Vilar (Setúbal: Centro de Estudos Bocageanos, 2009).

25. From the poem 'A Arrábida', stanza 11. Alexandre Herculano, *Poesias*, 2nd edn (Lisbon: Viúva Bertrand e Filhos, 1850), p. 51 <http://purl.pt/167/3>.

26. See the section 'A abordagem antropológica e sociológica da moda' [The anthropological and sociological approach to fashion] in Lopes, *Imagens da mulher*, pp. 483–90.

27. See Maria da Conceição Meireles Pereira, 'A Questão Ibérica: imprensa e opinião 1850–1870' (unpublished doctoral thesis, Universidade do Porto, 1995) <https://repositorio-aberto.up.pt/handle/10216/55312?locale=pt>, especially pp. 242–43.

28. Mariana Angélica Andrade, *Murmúrios do Sado* (Setúbal: Tipografia José Augusto Rocha, 1870), p. 63. Previously, within the pages of the periodical itself, Torresão had transcribed a poem that Andrade had written for her in her album (*VF*, 38: 2). For more about the tradition of albums, see Ernesto Rodrigues, *Cultura literária oitocentista* (Porto: Lello, 1999), pp. 42–55.

29. José Palmela, *A Aristocracia do Génio e da Beleza Feminil na Antiguidade*, 4th edn (Coimbra: Imprensa da Universidade, 1872).

30. José Palmela, *A Aristocracia do Génio e da Beleza Feminil na Antiguidade* (Coimbra: Imprensa da Universidade, 1871), pp. 52–53. By the time the fifth edition was reprinted, Palmela had added three names: Maria Amália Vaz de Carvalho and the Brazilians Narcisa Amália de Oliveira Campos and Amália dos Passos Figueiroa. The presence of the latter two stresses the importance of the transatlantic connection. As for Vaz de Carvalho, her marriage to the Brazilian-born Coimbra graduate Gonçalves Crespo in 1874 may have put her on Palmela's radar, but there is no doubt that she was on the rise. José Palmela, *A Aristocracia do Génio e da Beleza Feminil na Antiguidade*, 5th edn (Coimbra: Imprensa da Universidade, 1876), p. 156.

31. Mariana Angélica Andrade, 'À Liberdade', *Grinalda Literária*, 10 June 1874. Transcribed in Vilar, p. 38.

32. See *Mariana Angélica de Andrade*, ed. by Vilar, pp. 64–65.

33. Cited by Maryellen Bieder, 'Women Authors in the Romantic Tradition (1841–1884) and Early Feminist Thought (1861–1893)', in *A New History of Iberian Feminisms*, ed. by Silvia Bermúdez and Roberta Johnson (Toronto: University Press of Toronto, 2018), pp. 127–46 (p. 133).

34. For instance, Pusich published *Homenagem a Luiz de Camões* in 1880.

35. 'Guiomar Torresão', *Escritoras: Women Writers in Portuguese before 1900* <http://www.escritoras-em-portugues.eu/1417106880-Cent-XIX/2015-0531-Guiomar-Torreso>. Furthermore, '*As Dez da noite*: comédia em dois atos: tradução, 1868', was announced in the pages of *A Voz Feminina*.

36. Andrea Germano de Oliveira Romariz suggests that Torresão's *Almanaque das Senhoras* may have been influenced by her early contributions to *Almanaque de Lembranças Luso-Brasileiro*, but is silent on the extent to which her skills were perfected as a trusted contributor of *A Voz Feminina* through almost weekly practice over a nineteen-month period. See Andrea Germano de Oliveira Romariz, 'O Almanaque de Lembranças Luso-Brasileiro: um ensaio para um projecto maior?' (unpublished master's thesis, Universidade de Lisboa–Faculdade de Letras, 2011) <http://repositorio.ul.pt/bitstream/10451/5145/6/ulfl106395_tm.pdf>.

37. 'Uma lenda' [A legend] translated by Ana Amélia de Figueiredo (nos. 1–3) and 'Lago das lágrimas' [Lake of tears] translated by Henriqueta de Figueiredo (nos. 1–4).

38. In addition, one serialized novella, 'Reminiscências do Passado' [Reminiscences of the Past] by Pulquéria R. D. F, possibly a pseudonym, might be read as the story of an unrequited love between two women (nos. 66–69).

39. This piece was reproduced in *Meteóros*, with a small change to the closing paragraph as Avellaneda had died in the meantime. See Guiomar Torresão, *Meteóros* (Lisbon: Tipografia Christovão A. Rodrigues, 1875), pp. 66–73. *Meteóros* has been digitized by the Bodleian Library <http://purl.ox.ac.uk/uuid/907521b054ab41fab49113a69d4f5c7d>.

40. For more information on Sousa Neves, see João Luís Lisboa, 'From Publishing to the Publisher: Portugal and Changes in the World of Print in the Nineteenth Century', in Márcia Abreu and Ana Cláudia Suriani da Silva, eds, *The Cultural Revolution of the Nineteenth Century: Theatre, the Book Trade, and Reading in the Transatlantic World* (London: I. B. Tauris, 2016), pp. 69–86 (p. 79).

41. Torresão, *Rosas pálidas: narrativas originais* (Lisbon: Roland & Semiond, 1873), p. 155.

42. See Maria da Conceição Pinheiro Araújo, 'Tramas femininas na imprensa do século XIX: tessituras de Ignez Sabino e Délia' (unpublished doctoral thesis, Pontifícia Universidade Católica, 2008), p. 143 <http://tede2.pucrs.br/tede2/handle/tede/1894>.

43. Torresão had published a poem praising Vaz de Carvalho in 1869 in *Almanaque de Lembranças Luso-Brasileiro* (Araújo, p. 265). Two decades later, in 1896, she sketched her 'biography' in *Almanaque das Senhoras*. Guiomar Torresão, *Almanaque das senhoras para 1896* (Lisbon: Sousa & Filho, 1895), pp. (3–16). Vaz de Carvalho did not reciprocate Torresão's goodwill, however, for she refused to contribute to a posthumous collection gathered by Torresão's sister. See *Trechos literários de Alexandre Herculano e cartas do mesmo e de outros escritores ilustres a Guiomar Torresão*, ed. by Felismina Torresão (Lisbon: [n.pub.], 1910), pp. 100–02.

44. In subsequent years, it included Alexandre Herculano, Antero de Quental, Alberto Pimentel, Camilo Castelo Branco, Eça de Queirós, Gonçalves Crespo (Araújo, p. 142). See also letters to Júlio Dinis and Gonçalves Crespo in Mauro Nicola Póvoas and Louise Farias da Silveira, 'Guiomar Torresão e as "Cartas Póstumas" do Periódico Feminino O Mundo Elegante (1887)', *Navegações*, 5 (2012), 101–05.

45. Araújo, p. 143.

46. Ernesto Rodrigues (1999), cited by Araújo, p. 140. The news items transcribed by Rodrigues as his source dates from 1872.

47. Lopes, *Imagens da mulher*, p. 513.

48. Araújo, p. 270.

49. Ramalho Ortigão, *As Farpas*, 15 vols (Lisbon: Livraria Clássica Editora, 1943–46), X, 33.

50. For an analysis of Torresão's rebuttal, see Lopes, *Imagens da Mulher*, pp. 511–31. See also the indignant response, under the pseudonym of Irmã de Caridade, in *Diário da Manhã*, transcribed in Ortigão, XI, 2–26. Its author demonstrated keen awareness of Ortigão's lack of sensitivity in relation to questions not only of access to education but also of class. This *polémica* [controversy] is still awaiting a more extensive analysis, not least since Ortigão, wounded in his pride, replied in January 1878 (XI, 27–44).

51. José-Augusto França, *Rafael Bordalo Pinheiro: o português tal e qual*, 3rd edn (Lisbon: Livros Horizonte, 2007), p. 112.

52. Cited in Ana Maria Costa Lopes, 'Alguns Aspectos da Luta de Guiomar Torrezão pela Igualdade', *Povos e Culturas*, 9 (2004), 455–70 <http://icm.fch.lisboa.ucp.pt/resources/Documentos/CEPCEP/POVOS%20E%20CULTURAS_9.pdf>.

53. Esteves, p. 104.

54. Listed in Araújo, pp. 270–71.

55. According to the list in Araújo, p. 270, Camilo Castelo Branco is one of the few Portuguese men about whom she writes a biography. Guiomar Torresão, *Almanaque das senhoras para 1884* (Lisbon: Sousa & Filho, 1883), pp. 3–14. He had publicly shown his support for Torresão, when he prefaced the 1881 compilation *No Teatro e na Sala* in which her rebuke of Ortigão was printed (or possibly reprinted, if so without indication of provenance).

56. Lopes, *Imagens da mulher*, p. 519.

57. Guiomar Torresão, 'Biografia da Autora', in Viscondessa de Monserrate, *Estudos* (Lisbon: Tipografia do Comércio de Portugal, 1896), pp. v–xix.

58. Luís Trindade, *Catalogo da livraria do falecido distinto bibliógrafo e bibliófilo José Maria Nepomuceno* (Lisbon: Empresa Editora de Francisco Artur da Silva, 1897). Entry 2668, p. 386.

59. This is an unexpected translation for 'spiritism'. The links between Spiritism and feminism in the Iberian Peninsula are later embodied by the feminists Maria Veleda (1871–1955) and Maria O'Neill (1873–1932). For a discussion of the Spanish context, see Christine Arkinstall, *Spanish Female Writers and the Freethinking Press* (Toronto: University of Toronto Press, 2014).

60. 'Eu, diz o Sr. Júlio C. Machado, em se me falando de alguma mulher só como bonita, sinto um friozinho como se fizesse festas a uma estátua! — Não queremos que os nossos generosos amigos sintam esse friozinho' ([n.a.], *VF*, 21: 1) [For me, says Mr. Júlio C. Machado, when they talk to me about some woman simply as pretty, I feel a cold chill as if I were stroking a statue! — We don't want our generous friends to feel that chill].

61. Delfina Vieira Caldas wrote in no. 24 (*VF*, 24: 3–4), and went on to publish short translations (*VF*, 27: 3) and two autobiographical pieces both titled 'A Amizade' [Friendship] (*VF*, 50: 3; and *P*, 92: 174). The value placed on female friendship fits in with the ethos of the magazine which was keen to promote an informal support network.

62. Wood does not mention Pusich in any of her editorials, but she cites Maria José da Silva Canuto: 'Diz a Sra Canuto: "A mulher viu ao longe a luz, há-de acercar-se-lhe"' (*VF*, 35: 2) [Mrs Canuto says: 'Woman has seen the light in the distance, she will draw near to it']. Canuto's assertion dovetailed neatly with Plácido's title. Both women were determined to find enlightenment (*luz*), however many obstacles (*ferros*) stood in their way. Canuto was a contributor to *Gazeta Pedagógica*, with which Wood was familiar since it was cited in *O Progresso* ('Educação das Mulheres nos Estados Unidos', *P*, 81: 129).

63. For details about Francisco de Paula Abreu Marques, see Adriano da Guerra Andrade, *Dicionário de pseudónimos e iniciais de escritores portugueses* (Lisbon: Biblioteca Nacional, 1999), p. 389.

64. He was the Editor of *O Egitaniense* (Guarda), 1868. See *Jornais e revistas portugueses do século XIX*, ed. by Gina Guedes Rafael and Manuela Santos, 2 vols (Lisbon: Biblioteca Nacional, 1998–2002), I, 286.

65. For the identification of Luís de Lencastre as a pseudonym of Cândido de Figueiredo, see Adriano Andrade, p. 171.

66. 'Anne-Marie Caron', in *Dicionário no Feminino (séculos XIX–XX)*, ed. by Zília Osório de Castro and João Esteves (Lisbon: Horizonte, 2005), p. 124.

67. For overviews of a range of turn-of-the-century feminist writers, see Maria Regina Tavares da Silva, *Feminismo em Portugal na voz de mulheres escritoras do início do século XX* (Lisbon: Comissão da Condição Feminina, 1982) and the articles by Esteves and by Madden in *A New History of Iberian Feminisms*. All commendably signpost Francisca Wood as a precursor. On *Sociedade Futura* see Bezari.

CHAPTER 4

Questioning Subordi/Nation

Chapter 3 introduced *A Voz Feminina* and *O Progresso*, shedding new light on their network of contributors, and Wood's ongoing role in nurturing and mentoring the next generation. Nonetheless, even though scholars agree on the symbolic significance of Francisca as a female figurehead in her role as Editor, what has yet to be undertaken is a more systematic analysis of her own actual editorials. As Janice Hamlet asserts, 'the editorial page is the intellectual focal point of any newspaper. Editorials serve to provoke, debate, set agendas, crusade for change, persuade, and often challenge'.[1] A highly prized genre particularly in the nineteenth century, the editorial 'initially defined itself clearly as an extension of the freedom of expression of the owner of a partisan media. In this context, the editorial had a clear goal: to state a position in public debate'.[2] Aside from communicating opinion through authorial presence, one of the more subtle functions often expected of the editorial mode was 'that of voicing the identity of the newspaper and reaffirming it in the historical continuity of its brand'.[3] This chapter, then, analyses the historical continuity of Wood's extraordinarily combative thinking through close textual analysis, showcasing how her lead articles over a two-year period provided a discursive platform that she used to examine and deconstruct gendered behaviour. It demonstrates that her periodicals were a milestone, in terms of a modern conceptualization of religion and politics.

In Portuguese cultural historiography, such modernity has long since become routinely associated with the all-male *Geração de 70*. Yet, by and large, their analyses left existing structural gendered biases unexamined. By contrast, Wood tackles gender asymmetries head-on. Her commitment to these pressing issues will be considered with reference to some of the key themes highlighted by Paletschek and Pietrow-Ennker, in their analysis of European feminist movements in the nineteenth century, namely: debate on gender relations; improvement of women's education; better employment opportunities for women; political rights for women; the social purity movement.[4] To these, we will add Wood's own incisive insights into the damaging impact of unchecked hegemonic masculinity, a concept defined by R. W. Connell as a 'configuration of gender practice [...] which guarantees (or is taken to guarantee) the dominant position of men and the subordination of women'.[5] Among the many institutions that have enshrined and perpetuated male privilege, one particular all-male institution stands out for allowing hegemonic masculinity to flourish in the Portuguese context: the Catholic Church. Wood targets it relentlessly.

Cultivating the Thinking Woman

Wood's opening editorial for the newly launched *A Voz Feminina* is unambivalent about her intention of being involved in the construction of a modern nation:

> Bem-vindo sejas ano novo de 1868. Bem-vindo sejas a este pitoresco e lindo Portugal! Muitas outras nações — algumas ricas e extensas — não te podem festejar com aclamações jubilosas, como nós, os pigmeus da Europa [...].
>
> Não te podem, meu ano bom, sorrir como o nosso Portugal, onde pulula o progresso da civilização racional, onde a cultura intelectual de seus jovens filhos começa a luzir com esse brilho deslumbrador. (*VF*, 1: 1)
>
> [Welcome, New Year of 1868. Welcome to this picturesque and beautiful Portugal! Many other nations — some rich and expansive — cannot celebrate you with such jubilant cheers as us, the pygmies of Europe [...].
>
> They cannot, my good year, smile at you like our own dear Portugal, where the progress of rational civilization pulsates, where the intellectual culture of its youth begins to shine with such dazzling brilliance.]

Francisca strikes an upbeat tone as she chooses to describe, through alliteration, though possibly with more rhetorical flair than accuracy, Portugal as a country 'onde pulula o progresso', only then turning her attention to her female contemporaries: 'Mas nós mulheres — quero dizer Ex.mas Senhoras, que fazemos?' [But we women — I mean, my dear ladies — what are we doing?]. Although women lag behind because they squander their efforts on fashion, her tone is one of encouragement, not least as she is careful to include herself in the group. She exhorts her female readership to join the progress of a rational civilization by rejecting their ongoing status as mere decorative dolls: 'Não queiramos por mais tempo ser, o que até agora temos sido — bonecas!' (p. 1) [Let us no longer be satisfied with being what we have been until now — dolls!].

She deploys the compelling argument that public displays of gallant behaviour on the part of men do not translate into true respect in practice. If, as a child, she easily tired of her dolls, casting them away without a second thought, the editorial pursues the analogy to suggest that men are likewise bound to toss away as mere playthings those women who do not have the erudition to relate to them. This, of course, is exemplified throughout the fiction of Eça de Queirós, whose portrayal of homosocial bonding repeatedly suggests that intellectual companionship between men is generally more satisfying than relationships with the opposite sex.

Wood, however, is more optimistic than Eça and goes on to argue that if the aim of a woman is to earn the lasting interest and respect of a male companion, true learning is a better investment than looks, which unavoidably fade over time. In short, it is ultimately in women's self-interest and self-preservation, she implies, to be more than superficially attractive dolls, patronized by men. Crucially, in her bid to raise women's aspirations, she makes the point that women do not lack innate ability or intelligence:

> Aos atrativos que a natureza nos deu, juntemos a preponderância que dá o saber. Às portuguesas não falta inteligência; falta-lhes o amor do estudo sério, falta-lhes o hábito de análise filosófica, não só sobre assuntos abstratos, mas até sobre os fenómenos mais familiares que nos circundam. (pp. 1–2)

> [To the charms which nature has bestowed upon us, let us add the superiority conferred by knowledge. Portuguese women do not lack intelligence; what they lack is the love of serious study, they lack the habit of philosophical analysis, not only in relation to abstract matters, but even in relation to the more familiar phenomena around us.]

A recurrent theme throughout Wood's editorials is that God created men and women as equals but, as she points out here, intellectual faculties need honing. Critical analysis and philosophical enquiry are an acquired habit: they require commitment to serious study, without which the logical implication is that female intellectual gifts will go to waste.

Wood ends this opening editorial strategically, with a reference to the role that women, as mothers, have in shaping future generations:

> E isto não é tudo. A influência da mulher pensadora; da mulher que observa, que aprende, que tem substituído, por meio de estudo sério, um discorrer lógico e correto aos raciocínios pueris de crianças; é no seu lar doméstico como o sol na floresta, abrange tudo quanto o rodeia. Ainda mais; estende-se às gerações futuras nos filhos que hão de brotar em homens. (p. 2)

> [And that is not all. The influence of the female thinker; of the woman who observes, who learns, who through serious study has replaced the puerile reasoning of a child with a logical and sound discourse; is, in her home, like the sun in the forest, she reaches everything that surrounds her. And there's more; her influence stretches forward to future generations through her sons who will one day grow into men.]

This rousing mission statement was a sure way to unite her readers, given that the role of mothers as educators was one of the strongest arguments for the education of women, deployed by the likes of Júlio Dinis, as we saw in Chapter 2. The otherwise politically conservative Maria Amália Vaz de Carvalho would subsequently have recourse to it. Later first-wave feminists used it as a rallying aim, most famously Ana de Castro Osório in *Às Mulheres Portuguesas*, although it is worth noting that she rounded off her chapter 'A Instrução' [Education] with an addition that explicitly allowed for the diverse roles and ambitions that women might seek to fulfil outside marriage and maternity: namely she foregrounded the urgency of 'educar a mulher para ser a educadora dos filhos' [educating mothers to be the educators of their sons] alongside that of 'educar a mulher em geral para viver de si mesma e para si, quando pertença à enorme legião das que ficam solteiras' [educating woman in general to live by her own means and for herself, should she belong to the huge legion of those who remain single].[6]

Both Wood and Osório were female thinkers ahead of their respective times. In fact, the pursuit of complete intellectual equality and freedom is condensed in Wood's radical freethinking motto 'a mulher livre ao lado do homem livre' [the free woman beside the free man], which was proudly displayed as part of the header of *A Voz Feminina* from January 1869 onwards.[7] For her part, in *As Mulheres Portuguesas*, the number of times that Osório reiterates the word 'livre' [free] and its various cognates amounts to thirty-two, but one sentence in particular seems to echo closely Wood's slogan: 'Torna-se preciso que o homem já educado eduque a sua companheira; que o homem livre escolha a mulher já livre' [It becomes necessary that the man who is already educated should educate his partner; [and] that the free man should choose the woman who is already free].[8] More than thirty-five years earlier, however, Wood's eye-catching slogan vividly captured her desire to rethink the prevailing balance of power not just between the sexes, but more broadly in society at large, since it implied that not all men were free either. In this respect, she breaks new ground by paying particular attention to the consequences of a patriarchal society that was, according to her, fuelled by the Catholic Church.

Critiquing Religious Subordination: Anticlericalism in Action

In her second ever editorial, Wood challenged the assumption of female inferiority that mostly informed the Catholic Church in the long nineteenth century in Portugal, reminding her readers of the fact that, from the outset, the Christian message was highly revolutionary insofar as it preached that 'a mulher era igual ao homem, o pobre igual ao rico, e o vassalo igual ao rei na faculdade de se elevar moral e intelectualmente' [woman was equal to man, pauper equal to rich man, and the vassal equal to the king in the ability to raise themselves morally and intellectually] (['O Cristianismo...'], *VF*, 7: 1–2). It naturally followed that this more generous interpretation of Christianity actually facilitated women's intellectual emancipation.

Unlike Catholics, Protestants of both sexes were invited to contribute actively to the reading of the Bible. As Lopes points out, this presupposed implicit 'confiança nas competências femininas na interpretação da Bíblia, o que as foi habilitando, ao longo do tempo, a comportamentos, em muitos casos tidos em países católicos, como "masculinos"' [confidence in female competence to interpret the Bible, which, down the ages, enabled them to behave in ways often held in Catholic countries to be 'male'].[9] Moreover, several researchers highlight the pivotal role of at least one woman in Lisbon from 1860 onwards: Ellen Roughton (also known as Helena Roughton).[10] She opened a free primary school in Cruz do Tabuado, today Praça José Fontana. And in Porto, Frederica Smith became active from 1869 onwards. It seems that these women took a leading role in Bible readings and worship, becoming actively engaged in preaching and what would be known today as community outreach actions. For her part, Francisca Wood illustrates the positive impact of religion in the early Church, by naming several learned women:

> Um grande número das mulheres agora canonizadas foram notáveis pelos seus talentos e pela sua ilustração. Lioba, amada de S. Bonifácio pela sua *eruditionis sapientia*; Hipácia, preceptora de Clemente, Bispo de Alexandria; Catarina, que explicava a filosofia cristã nas escolas de Alexandria, confundindo os filósofos pagãos; Perpétua, que escrevia ela mesma os autos do seu martírio e daquele

dos seus companheiros, eram todas mulheres eruditas e algumas delas poetisas. (['O Cristianismo...'], *VF*, 7: 1, italics in the original)

[A great number of the women now canonized were notable for their talents and their learning. Leoba, loved by St. Boniface for her *eruditionis sapientia*; Hypathia, teacher of Clement, Bishop of Alexandria; Catherine, who taught Christian philosophy in the schools of Alexandria, confounding the pagan philosophers; Perpetua, who herself recorded her martyrdom and that of her companions, they were all learned women and some of them were poets.]

Needless to say, the radical ideas so vocally espoused in the periodical triggered a reaction. Researchers of Church History in nineteenth-century Portugal, such as Afonso (2009), trace various moments of backlash against Protestants, which entailed expulsion or imprisonment, among others.[11] Salient events include the 1840s crackdown on Robert Reid Kalley in Madeira; the 1852 Penal Code which enshrined greater intolerance towards alternative religions; and parliamentary speeches such as that of Marquês de Valada, who protested against the excesses of Protestant propaganda in 1855. Two years later, in 1857, the Marquis would launch *Bem Público* [The Public Good], precisely the periodical that mounted an offensive against *A Voz Feminina* for the best part of two years.

This hate campaign, which has been so far completely overlooked, took issue with the perceived unfemininity of *A Voz Feminina* from its first unsigned article (probably penned by the Marquês de Valada himself), published on 7 March 1868: 'a verdade é que se não acha a suavidade, o mimo, a fragrância que do coração da mulher católica se comunica a tudo o que sai da sua pena' [the truth is one does not find the gentleness, the tenderness, the fragrance which is communicated from the heart of the Catholic woman to everything that comes from her pen].[12] The author goes as far as to state that:

A *Voz Feminina* só tem de feminino o seu nome. Não a escrevem penas femininas [...]. Quer se fazer crer que há em Portugal um grupo de senhoras que pedem o que as mulheres estrangeiras de uma reputação equivoca, e algumas ainda menos que isso, chamam a *mulher livre*, e isso não pode ser: por honra da mulher católica, seja qual for a nação a que pertença, não podemos crê-lo. (p. 276, Italics in the original)

[The only feminine thing about *A Voz Feminina* is its name. It isn't written by feminine pens [...]. They want us to believe there is a group of ladies in Portugal who are asking for what foreign women of dubious reputation, and some even less than this, call the *free woman*, and this cannot be: for the honour of the Catholic woman, no matter which nation she belongs to, we cannot believe it.]

By implying that most of the contributors must be men, the Marquis is deploying heavy-handed irony to stress that Portuguese women could not possibly be so unwomanly. His assumption, be it genuine or feigned, underlines how unusual Wood's feisty voice was. He sought to de-authorize her ideas on the grounds of inadequacies of both form and content: 'são tantos os erros de linguagem, como os de história, principalmente de doutrina' [there are as many errors of language as of history, mainly of doctrine].[13] Despite her wide-ranging learning, enthusiasm had certainly got the better of Wood in the case of Hypathia in the afore-mentioned article: Hypathia could not have been canonized since she was not a Christian, a factual mistake gleefully pointed out by Valada. Nor could she have taught Clement, Bishop of Alexandria, who had lived one century and a half before her (in fact she taught Synesius, the future Bishop of Ptolemais).

Wood refused to be cowed, however, and her discursive arguments in *A Voz Feminina* suggest that she felt entirely comfortable with her entitlement to deploy her considerable intellectual gifts. Four months later, another of her editorials denounces the dominant Jesuit paradigm of controlling women as a manipulative and cynical attempt to minimize female intellectual power. Wood's strongest argument is that, far from denying the reality of women's intellectual gifts, the Church acknowledged them but saw them as dangerous. As a result, it preached that they must be kept in check:

> Consultai o jesuitismo, consultai as sagazes autoridades de França, e de Itália. Lá não se diz à mulher que não tem inteligência; pelo contrário, diz-se-lhe que tem muita; que tem grandes e ricos dotes espirituais; mas que se não deve servir deles: que os deve guardar numa boceta, bem canforados para que lhe não dê a traça. (*VF*, 21: 1)

> [Consult the tenets of Jesuitism, consult the wise authorities of France and of Italy. There they do not say that woman lacks intelligence; on the contrary, they say she has a great deal; that she has huge and copious spiritual gifts; but that she must not make use of them: that she should keep them in a casket with mothballs, so they don't attract moths.]

Certainly, despite occasional errors of detail, Wood's voice conveys authority. This leads her to formulate the reply 'A Uma Assinante da Voz Feminina' (*VF*, 53: 1–2) [To a female subscriber of A Voz Feminina] in which she advised her reader to have nothing to do with the Jesuits, citing by name Rademaker (1828–1885), the priest responsible for the restoration of the Society of Jesus in Portugal in 1858.[14] According to Wood, women indoctrinated by priests were unable to think for themselves. Her counter-arguments, founded on the biblical word itself, imbue her with unquestionable authority, by drawing on the Bible to prove that female enslavement is entirely cultural rather than natural or God-willed. Her courage in speaking openly against the Society seems astonishing. Unsurprisingly, there was retaliation from *Bem Público*, where Francisca was labelled as 'um Salomão-fêmea, de cujo boca brotam os conceitos como a água de uma bica' [a female Solomon, from whose mouth concepts spring like water from a spout] before the article proceeded to a counter-attack by citing the 'inquisição protestante contra os católicos durante os reinados de Henrique VIII *o polígamo*, de Eduardo VI, e de Isabel *a poliandra*' [Protestant inquisition against Catholics during the reigns of Henry VIII, *the polygamist*, Edward VI, and Elizabeth I *who practised polyandry*].[15] Valada's coup de grace was to lament Wood's lack of 'consideração e respeito à Religião Católica, que é a do país onde se acha' [consideration and respect for the Catholic Religion, which is that of the country in which she finds herself].[16] This reads like a veiled threat, given that as a Portuguese national, and moreover as a woman, she would have been more vulnerable than a foreigner to religious persecution.

Given how daring her anti-Jesuitic stance was, it is no exaggeration to consider Wood one of the first openly anticlerical women in Portugal, and possibly even the very first, in an intellectual lineage that would later intensify with Angelina Vidal. In fact, in a chapter on 'Anticlericalismo', Luís de Abreu Machado highlights the fight against Jesuitism as one of the main themes of anticlerical discourse.[17] In another of the headings listed in his overview, 'A mulher', Machado briefly discusses depictions of women in anticlerical literature, noting how at the opposite end of the spectrum from images of either seduced or fanatical women, a positive appraisal of the 'mulher *propagandista*' [propagandist woman] can be found. He concludes that 'o espírito laicista e livre-pensador' [the secular and free-thinking spirit] that animated the nascent feminist movement in Portugal logically led to a rejection of the clergy's oversight of consciences.[18] Although he does not cite any names, it is clear that Wood was one such feminist *avant la lettre* and that her proselytizing discourse already bears the hallmarks of turn-of-the-century feminism.

Exposing the Naturalization of Male Privilege

Wood sought to question historically sedimented cultural inequalities and her open letter to 'A uma assinante da Voz Feminina' [To a subscriber of A Voz Feminina] was only one of her many attempts to encourage women to think for themselves. A couple of early editorials, prompted by two poems sent in by 'Uma Assinante da Capital' presented the argument that male adultery ought to be deemed as serious an offence as female adultery, even though public opinion implicitly condoned or turned a blind eye to the former:

> A *opinião pública* é uma quimera inventada pelo homem para melhor ampliar a sua vontade de operar; é um fantasma com que os homens têm conseguido assustar as mulheres antes que elas se tivessem dado ao trabalho de pensar, e de analisar; antes de estarem em estado de distinguir o falaz do positivo. (*VF*, 13: 1, italics in the original)

> [*Public opinion* is a chimera invented by men to better extend their field of operations; it is a phantasm with which they have succeeded in frightening women before the latter have taken the trouble to think, and to analyse; before they are in a fit state to distinguish the fallacious from the positive.]

Wood argues that public opinion is man-made and, as such, designed to allow men to satisfy their passions (as opposed to reason). It is based firstly on historically sanctioned male entitlement and secondly on generalized ignorance (which the Church was keen to maintain, especially for women):

> Qual é a origem da opinião pública; donde procede; em que se baseia? A opinião pública tem a sua origem, assim como a sua base, em primeiro lugar nas prerrogativas que o homem em todos os tempos se tem arrogado para com Imunidade satisfazer as suas paixões, as quais em nenhum tempo a generalidade tem tido a força de dominar, e em segundo lugar, na ignorância da multidão, prestes sempre a meter-se debaixo dos pés do poder irresponsável. (p. 1.)

> [What is the origin of public opinion; whence does it come, on what is it based? Public opinion has its origin, as well as its basis, in the first place in the

prerogatives that man throughout time has arrogated to himself so that he may satisfy with Immunity his passions, which the majority have at no time had the strength to dominate, and, in the second place, in the ignorance of the masses, always ready to place themselves beneath the feet of irresponsible power]

The capitalized word, 'Immunity', draws attention to the systemic pervasiveness of male privilege, underlining the fact that men are effectively above the law. Although Francisca does not cite the Civil Code of 1867 here, the widespread prevalence of double standards regarding sexual morality led her to call for legal redress, so that seducers should be held to account legally for dishonouring women:

> É indispensável que a legislação venha ao socorro do sexo chamado *fraco*, o qual, desamparado pelas leis, se vê absolutamente entregue aos alvitres repreensíveis e pecaminosos do sexo chamado *forte*; uma considerável parte do qual consiste dessa classe de vadios viciosos, cujo principal objeto é procurarem-se *conquistas*. (*VF*, 38: 1, italics in the original)[19]

> [legislation must unquestionably come to the aid of the so-called *weak* sex, which, unprotected by the laws, is left completely open to the reprehensible and sinful suggestions of the so-called *strong* sex, a considerable part of which consists of that class of depraved idlers whose main purpose is to seek out *conquests*.]

Ana de Castro Osório would later tackle the naturalization of male privilege enshrined in the Civil Code, in the ante-penultimate and penultimate chapters of her *Às Mulheres Portuguesas*, where she highlighted the sexual double standards implicit in the legal protection afforded to men who fathered illegitimate offspring. Her analysis of the law is pioneering, as is her solution to male sexual misconduct: rather than arguing for the law to stamp out male seducers by increasing penalties, as Wood had, she suggested that a change of mindsets might offer a way forward to solve the problem. In other words, society should accept single mothers without moral condemnation and ensure that they had adequate opportunities to support themselves. The modernity of Osório's standpoint is all the more remarkable because she was aware that such an essentially matriarchal arrangement might spell the dissolution of the existing configuration of the family and by extension of social order.[20] On this point, then, her arguments are more imaginative than her predecessor, daring to envisage the demise of patriarchy.

The Structural Inequality of Access to Education

Wood's editorials, however, were particularly persuasive in outlining the insidious effects of 'naturalized' double standards with regard to access to education. As well as maintaining that women were intellectually equal to men and that structural inequality was thus man-made rather than willed by God, Wood identifies as a root cause the wide gulf between the resources made available to men and those available to women, with regard to the material conditions that supported their respective intellectual developments.

In one of her most remarkable editorials, she cogently reasons: 'O que seria o homem se a sua educação se limitasse ao estudo *puramente manual* do piano, a

escrever, a ler duas ou três línguas e a falá-las pessimamente, aos primeiros rudi-
mentos de geografia, a coser, bordar crochet' (*P*, 93: 175, italics in the original)
[what would become of man if his education was limited to the *purely manual* study
of the pianoforte, writing, reading two or three languages and speaking them badly,
to the basic rudiments of geography, sewing, embroidering, crochet]. She wittily
critiques persistent double standards through a *reductio ad absurdum*, citing the dis-
couraging comments that young girls must hear a regular basis:

> Suponhamos que era costume entre o sexo masculino, como tem sempre sido
> entre o outro, bradar ao jovem que por acaso abria um livro de estudos abstratos
> ou clássicos, 'menino feche esse livro; isso não lhe pertence. Vá estudar o seu
> piano ou vá fazer a sua costura'; a que ficaria reduzida a inteligência de um
> Cuvier, de um Herschel, de um Morgan, ou enfim de qualquer desses espíritos
> eleitos que tanta honra fazem à humanidade? A tocar um poucochinho de piano
> sem saber um ceitil de teoria, a estropiar as línguas que *tinha aprendido*, enfim, a
> ser fátuo e banal. A ilação é lógica. (*P*, 93: 175, italics in the original)

> [Let us suppose that it was the habit among the male sex, as it has always been
> among the other one, to shout out to the young man who ventures to open
> a book of abstract or classical studies, 'Close that book, child; it isn't for you.
> Go and study your piano or go and do your needlework', to what would the
> intelligence of a Cuvier, a Herschel, a Morgan be reduced, or in fact any
> of those especially favoured spirits who do such great honour to humanity?
> Playing the piano just a tiny little bit without knowing an iota of theory,
> making a mess of the languages he *had learned*, in short, being fatuous and banal.
> It's a logical conclusion.]

In addition, the lack of opportunities compounds in practice the adverse effect of
cultural assumptions that curtail women's path to self-improvement:

> Faltam os meios para a mulher se instruir. Os homens vão a Coimbra, viajam,
> têm acesso às bibliotecas nacionais onde se acham arquivados preciosíssimos
> tesouros de literatura, e há para os pobres escolas nocturnas, *clubs*, e associações
> onde se podem enriquecer mentalmente, muito além das aspirações da sua
> classe.
> Para as mulheres o que há? Nada absolutamente onde possam adquirir
> saber sério e sólido, [o] único que as pode arrancar às alucinações fátuas do
> pedantismo. (*VF*, 36: 1, Italics in the original).

> [There are no resources for a woman to learn. Men go to Coimbra, they
> travel, they have access to the national libraries, storehouses of precious literary
> treasures, while for the poor there are night schools, clubs, and associations
> where they can obtain intellectual enrichment, far beyond the aspirations of
> their class.
> What is there for women? Absolutely nothing where they can acquire
> serious and solid knowledge, (the) only kind that can tear them away from the
> fatuous delusions of pedantry]

Here, one of Wood's tactics is to expand at length on the multiple ways in which,
in other countries, bourgeois and upper-class ladies (as underlined by the use of
the word 'senhoras') had at their disposal institutions that were, according to her,
women-friendly, with open-door policies. Such institutions of learning, together

with multiple printed resources, consequently enabled them to cultivate their minds, and nurture scientific knowledge as well as artistic skills:

> Noutros países as senhoras frequentam as bibliotecas nacionais; há escolas grátis de desenho; há livrarias donde, por uma pequena soma anual, lhes trazem a casa as melhores biografias; excelentes e divertidíssimos livros de viagens; descrições de diferentes países; romances históricos de grande mérito, e por fim obras nas quais, sem se enfastiarem, se podem pôr ao facto de utilíssimas descobertas da ciência moderna; obras escritas, não para homens científicos, mas para o leitor de todas as classes.
>
> Há, a mais, por módico preço, livros elementares sobre química e astronomia, onde se pode aprender, em casa, a teoria de numerosos fenómenos, e há instituições, onde pela soma de 200 réis se passa o dia inteiro vendo aqueles mesmos fenómenos elucidados pela prática; assim como inúmeros outros experimentos da mais alta utilidade.
>
> Há jardins zoológicos, salas de estatuaria, galerias de pintura frequentadas por milhares de senhoras; e agora há no Havre um maravilhoso aquário com quarenta e dois tanques supridos por cem mil litros de água que se renova três vezes por dia, onde, tanto o homem como a mulher, pode aprender os segredos dessa existência, até agora desconhecida, que se passa no fundo dos mares, começando pela *anemona marinha* que é o primeiro elo entre a vida vegetal e animal. (pp. 1–2, italics in the original).

> [In other countries ladies frequent the national libraries, there are free art schools, there are bookshops where, for a modest annual subscription, they have delivered to their home the best biographies, excellent and extremely entertaining travel books; descriptions of different countries, historical novels of great merit, and finally, works through which, without becoming bored, they can keep up to date with the latest discoveries of modern science; works written not for the man of science but for the reader of all social classes.
>
> There are, furthermore, for a reasonable price, elementary books on chemistry and astronomy, where one can learn, at home, the theory of numerous phenomena, and there are institutions where for the sum of 200 'réis' one can spend the whole day seeing those same phenomena elucidated in practice; as well as innumerable other experiments of the highest utility.
>
> There are zoological gardens, rooms full of statues, art galleries frequented by thousands of ladies, and now in Le Havre there is a marvellous aquarium with forty-two tanks fed with one hundred thousand litres of water that is renewed three times a day, where both men and women can learn the secrets of the existence, hitherto unknown, which takes place at the bottom of the sea, beginning with the *sea anemone* that is the first link between vegetal and animal life.]

The enumeration over three paragraphs with the anaphoric 'there are' emphasizes the availability of libraries, art galleries, zoos, aquariums, and the proliferation of books on subjects ranging from geography to astronomy, in stark contrast with the prevailing narrowness of the Portuguese milieu. In terms of libraries, Wood may have been thinking of the British Library, inaugurated in May 1857, when she was still residing in Britain, while the reference to the aquarium in Le Havre proves that she was keeping abreast of developments in other countries, probably through the press, since it was only inaugurated in 1869.[21]

In order to drive the contrast home, when Wood turns to a description of what is available in Portugal, she only offers a concise one-sentence list, consisting of four pedestrian items. These contrast comically with the abundance of riches available elsewhere in Europe:

> Mas entre nós, desgraçadas, de tudo se carece, exceto modistas, janelas, cuias e escândalo. (p. 2).

> [But among us, poor wretched females, everything is lacking, except for dressmakers, windows, false ringlets and scandal.]

Her implication is that the sphere of action of Portuguese women is confined to fashion (dressmakers, false ringlets) and gossip (windows, scandal). The last item on the list, 'scandal', a generic abstract noun, alludes to immorality, which Francisca, rightly or wrongly, regularly attributed to a lack of education and intellectual training. Her pithy statement, relying on zeugma, if written a few years later by a man, would surely have become vintage Eça by now.

This thread is picked up in the following editorial, where Wood refines her thinking further, in order to draw attention to the fact that, even if women were suddenly presented with plentiful opportunities, mindsets would have to change dramatically before they found themselves in a position to take advantage of any enhanced cultural provision:

> Mas suponhamos que um governo menos espavorido pela carantonha do *deficit*; um governo extremamente liberal, e altamente filosófico, dava providências contra este mal: suponhamos a nossa Lisboa enriquecida e embelezada com a posse de quanto agora lhe falta — bibliotecas públicas; galerias de pintura, e de escultura, com todos os aparelhos e requisitos para o estudo daquelas artes; (falo segundo o que tenho visto noutros países) laboratórios de ciências práticas, e de experimentos ilustrativos; tudo muito asseado; com prelectores, lentes, e atendentes; e, tudo isto — *GRÁTIS*. ('Os Satélites' *VF*, 37: 1)

> [But let us suppose that a government less scared by the ugly face of the *deficit*; an extremely liberal, and highly philosophical government, were to take measures against this ill: let us suppose our Lisbon enriched and enhanced by the possession of everything it currently lacks — public libraries, galleries filled with paintings and sculptures, with all the equipment and requisites for the study of those arts; (I speak from what I have seen in other countries) practical science laboratories and laboratories with illustrative experiments; everything impeccably clean; with lecturers, professors and assistants, and all of this — *FREE*]

At this point, the contrast between an abundance of places geared towards learning, intended to facilitate knowledge, and their inexplicable lack of use is emphasized through unanswered rhetorical questions:

> O que sucede? Naqueles aposentos reina o silêncio e o quietismo da morte. O estrangeiro que os visita pergunta de que servem, porque se acham assim abandonados? (p. 1.)

> [What happens? In those rooms, silence and the stillness of death reign. The foreigner who visits them asks: what they are for, why are they so abandoned?]

The conciseness of this paragraph generates a pause for effect, in order to create suspense. As we are led to adopt the disbelief of a foreigner's gaze, we can only speculate that women are unwilling to embrace erudition. Only in the next paragraph is an explanation supplied. It turns out that the main obstacle stems from a deeply ingrained cultural tradition:

> Noutros países, enxames de senhoras se aproveitam com avidez, com júbilo, com ufania mesmo, de tão preciosas vantagens. Entre nós um *alvitre rotineiro*; um absurdo ignóbil e degradante nulificaria estas grandes medidas civilizadoras. Aqui as senhoras não podem sair sem um rabo-leva, ou, como este é um termo de entrudo, diremos, sem um satélite. A criada, o criado, o mano, a mana, a avó, a tia, devem sempre acompanhar a senhora a quem algum dever ou algum negócio urge a sair de sua casa. (p. 1, italics in the original)

> [In other countries, swarms of ladies take advantage of such precious advantages avidly, with jubilation, with pride even. Among us a *routine opinion*; an ignoble and degrading absurdity would nullify these great civilizing measures. Here the ladies cannot go out without a 'donkey's tail' pinned on them, a Carnival term that can also mean a chaperone. The maid, the manservant, the brother, the sister, the grandmother, the aunt, must always accompany the lady who is forced by some duty or business to leave her house.]

The reluctance or inability of Portuguese women to leave their homes unsupervised is condemned as a degrading and insulting form of surveillance, which hinders their freedom and intellectual development. As British travellers to Portugal often stressed, Portuguese women, especially those belonging to the higher classes, were unable to circulate in public spaces and were mostly confined to the home.[22] Wood does not mince her words: as far as she is concerned, it is an absurdity.

Biology is not Destiny

In addition to revealing how the cultural prohibition of autonomy and mobility in public spaces has a deleterious effect on women's intellectual freedom, one of the most unexpected aspects of the irresistible modernity of Wood's conceptualization of gender is that she decouples the biological function of women (giving birth) from their intellectual aspirations, thereby rejecting any essentialist understanding of their socially determined role. In a striking lead article, she makes the point that a certain type of men consider women exclusively in the light of their breeding capacity:

> Falo meramente da classe que, ou habitualmente depreciando, e por conseguinte vituperando, ou habitualmente insultando com elogios hiperbólicos, a mãe, a esposa, a irmã e a filha, sustentam contudo que a melhor mulher é a que dá maior número de filhos ao mundo. ([n.a.], *VF*, 20: 1)

> [I speak merely of the class which, either habitually disparaging, and therefore vituperating, or habitually insulting with hyperbolic praise, the mother, wife, sister and daughter, nevertheless maintains that the best woman is the one who brings the greatest number of sons into the world.]

According to her, this conception of the purpose of women harks back to more primitive times, when it was necessary for the survival of the species to keep replenishing the stock of men lost in battle:

> Este vetusto e grosseiro aforismo é tolerável procedendo dos lábios do homem que desde o despontar da sua virilidade tinha andado de espada em punho, demolindo a raça humana, buscando-a além dos Alpes, buscando-a nas regiões inóspitas da Rússia para juncar a terra com frios cadáveres. Naturalmente apreciava quem repovoasse; quem preparasse novos banquetes ao afiado gume da sua espada. (p. 1)

> [This ancient and crude aphorism is tolerable when it issues forth from the lips of the man who from manhood onwards had gone sword in hand, demolishing the human race, seeking it beyond the Alps, seeking it in the inhospitable regions of Russia to strew the earth with cold corpses. Naturally he appreciated whoever might repopulate; whoever might prepare new banquets for the sharp blade of his sword]

Even in a civilized nineteenth-century context, some men seem to have kept their primitive mindset. Their prejudices continue to essentialize and objectify women as mere breeding animals, as Wood caustically shows through the use of increasingly graphic language:

> Mas que haja ainda homens no século XIX que possam encarar a mãe que lhe deu o ser, e a companheira do seu lar doméstico, depois de terem aventado tal conceito, é o que realmente surpreende; porque equivale a dizer-lhes: — Vós, minha mãe, e tu minha esposa, sois duas gatas, ou duas cadelas, ou duas ratazanas, ou duas coelhas; ou enfim duas de qualquer das brutas que só vivem para comer, dormir e multiplicar a sua raça. (p. 1)

> [But that there should still be men in the nineteenth century who can face the mother who gave them life, and the companion of home and hearth, after having voiced such a notion, is what is really surprising; because it is the equivalent of telling them: You, my mother, and you, my wife, are two cats, or two bitches, or two rats, or two doe-rabbits; or indeed two of any of the brute beasts that live only to eat, sleep and multiply their race.]

The incongruous juxtaposition of the symbols of sacred femininity *par excellence*, mother and wife, with the polysyndeton using animal imagery (where the word 'bitches' is perhaps loaded) drives the point home. The *Bem Público*'s shocked reaction in respect of this line of argument probably reflected a majority view of the period: 'Aqui o seu fanatismo ultrapassou todos os limites' [Here her fanaticism has gone beyond all the limits].[23]

But she doesn't stop here: in the apostrophe that follows, what may initially appear to be a respectful, perhaps even excessive, acknowledgement of the superiority of her male interlocutors turns out to be sarcastic. The two superlatives ('sapientíssimas' and 'privilegiadíssimas') [most wise and most privileged] are the first hint that Wood's subservience is a send-up, confirmed when she cites an overtly revolutionary Spanish song:

> Ah, meus senhores, tem por acaso alguma de vossas sapientíssimas privilegiadíssimas senhorias ouvido certa canção espanhola:

'Trágala, trágala, trágala, narigón
Trágala, traga la [*sic*] constitución'
[...] Hão-de tragá-la, meu senhores. (p. 1)

[Ah, my lords, by chance has one of your most wise privileged lordships heard a certain Spanish song:

'Swallow it, swallow it, swallow it, big nose
Swallow it, swallow the constitution'
[...] You will swallow it, my lords.]

These lines allude to a song popularized at the time of the 1820 Spanish Constitution.[24] Her contemporary readership, however, would surely also have in mind the rather more recent events that had led to the dethronement of Isabel II and the proclamation of the Republic in Spain in September 1868. She is in effect ridiculing such 'lords' for their utter inability to move with the times. It is of course likely that she had the aristocratic Marquês de Valada directly in mind in the first instance.

While Wood ridicules the retrograde mindset of some men on the subject of gender, she strategically plays down their number by limiting them to a 'class', so as to give herself a fighting chance. Yet, if truth be told, they were probably the vast majority of the male population at the time in Portugal, as well as the rest of Europe. It is hardly surprising, then, that following their lead, women too were guilty of conservative views. Wood concludes this editorial by contrasting once more the ongoing backwardness of Portugal with the giant strides being taken abroad, with a reminder that women's intelligence is a God-given gift:

Ah! Nesta querida terra, onde meus pais viram a luz do dia, e dormem o sono da morte, respiram entre cardumes de rosas, cardumes de mulheres que desprezam o precioso dom da inteligência com que o Omnipotente as doou; que condenam também nas irmãs conterrâneas qualquer prova de apreciação daquela incomparável dádiva. (p. 2)

[Ah! In this our beloved land, where my parents saw the light of day, and sleep the sleep of death, there breathe among shoals of roses, shoals of women who scorn the precious gift of intelligence with which the Omnipotent has endowed them; and who also condemn in their fellow countrywomen any proof of appreciation of that incomparable gift.]

Wood indicates that the reproductive function keeps women enchained, in the Dark Ages, with their eyes resolutely closed to the possibility of the light ('luz') that would signify enlightenment:

Escravas que abraçadas às suas cadeias fecham os olhos para não ver a luz resplandecente da auréola que lhes poderia coroar a fronte. Dignas companheiras na verdade dos vândalos, que em presença de factos históricos incontrastáveis continuam a calcular o valor intrínseco da mulher pelo número da sua progénie. (p. 2)

[Slave girls embracing their chains, who close their eyes so as not to see the resplendent light of the aureola that might crown their brow. Worthy companions in truth of the vandals, who in the presence of irrefutable historical facts continue to gauge the intrinsic value of the woman by the number of her offspring.]

The insistence on decoupling women from their biological function, by asserting that woman is not only merely a product of nature, is extraordinarily radical for the period.

Political and Economic Emancipation: 'a mulher livre'

Towards the end of 1868, Francisca contrasted 'antediluvian' ideas with liberal and progressive ones, in a lead article entitled 'As Damas em Londres' [The Ladies in London], where she also alluded to progress in Spain, probably emboldened by the recent revolution in Spain and ongoing advances in Britain. She concluded by heaping praise on those Portuguese men who spontaneously encouraged women to raise their expectations and supported their aspirations to political enfranchisement:

> O homem que, sem apreender que a mulher livre degenere em padre, ou deputado, ou em ministro de estado, ou em orangotango, lhe brada: 'Ergue-te desse marasmo moral em que jazes; nós somos pela completa igualdade política dos dois géneros da humanidade', homens enfim que sem temerem as vituperações da multidão mesquinha, levantam a voz e dizem: 'queremos a mulher livre ao lado do homem livre'. (*VF*, 45: 1)

> [The man who, without surmising that the free woman will degenerate into a priest, or deputy, or minister of state, or an orang-utan, shouts out to her: 'Climb up out of that moral stagnation in which you wallow; we are all for complete political equality of the two sexes of humankind', men, in fact, who without fear of the vituperation of the petty mob, raise their voice and say: 'we want the free woman beside the free man'.]

At this juncture it would have been difficult for Wood to envisage a chain of cause and effect between 'completa igualdade política' [complete political equality], and a dramatic overhaul of women's roles, enabling them to occupy positions of authority, be it in religious or politic contexts. The scaremongering implicit in the fear of such sweeping social change is thus captured in the humorous fear that she might 'degenere em padre, ou deputado, ou em ministro de estado, ou em orangotango' [degenerate into a priest, or member of parliament, or minister of state, or an orang-utan]. Accordingly, Wood concludes by articulating what would officially become the rallying cry of the periodical one month later, in what constitutes a positive turning on its head of the negative associations of 'mulher livre' [free woman] (i.e. a sexually loose woman), with which the Marquês de Valada had repeatedly attempted to denigrate her project.

Nearly one year later, Wood returns to the topic of women's political rights with what is one of her most shrewd and entertaining editorials:

> Desde que o direito da mulher a regalias políticas e sociais iguais às do homem tem assumido o vulto de *facto*, nos países onde este direito se tem discutido seriamente pelos dois sexos, certa classe de homens a quem repugna ver a escrava levantada do lodaçal em que jaz, mas que ao mesmo tempo se envergonham de votar abertamente pela escravidão, concedem tudo à mulher com a mais

magnânima magnanimidade; querem que a mulher seja tudo menos... política! (*P*, 84: 139, italics in the original)

[Since the right of women to political and social prerogatives equal to those of men has become a matter of *fact*, in the countries where this right had been seriously discussed by the two sexes, a certain class of men who are opposed to seeing the slave girl raised out of the quagmire in which she lies, but who are at the same time ashamed to vote openly for slavery, grant everything to women with the most magnanimous magnanimity; they want women to be everything but... political!]

The language is hard-hitting, as she once more compares the current condition of women to that of slaves. Simultaneously she ridicules the irrational fears that lead to the continuation of oppression:

Estremecem ao imaginar a distante possibilidade de verem as suas caras esposas, e mimosas filhinhas, deputadas a Cortes, ministras de Estado, juízas de todas as varas, e generalas de exército; e — fatal circunstância! — a mulher política há-de *nolens volens*, ir ao parlamento ser Ministra de Estado, Juíza de todas as varas e Generala do exército! No almirantado ainda não nos meteram; lá chegaremos, sem dúvida. (p. 139, italics in the original)

[They shudder on imagining the remote possibility of seeing their dear wives, and delicate daughters as deputies in the Cortes, ministers of State, judges in all branches of the law, and generals in the army; and — fatal circumstance! — the political woman, whether one likes it or not, must go to parliament to be Minister of State, Judge in all branches of the law and General of the army! They haven't foisted on us the admiralty yet, but no doubt we'll get there.]

The effectiveness of the satire partly relies on her feminization of job-titles (deputadas, ministras, juízas and generalas), in a way that would have been inconceivable at the time, quite simply because politics, the law, and the army, were entirely out of the reach of women. In a context of hegemonic masculinity, any job in these fields, let alone a top job, was completely unattainable.

The argument that it would be statistically almost impossible for a woman to step into any position of political influence had already been cogently rehearsed in no. 39. Here, Wood pursues a slightly different tack by humorously qualifying the choice of examples as 'undeniably poetic':

Entretanto, há na selecção já mencionada dos nossos empregos futuros, uma provisão inegavelmente poética. Ainda nenhum destes certos senhores nos fez soldados rasos, ou mesmo cabos de esquadra, carpinteiras, serralheiras, ou porteiras das Cortes; nada, é sempre deputados, ministros, juízes e generais que havemos de ser! (p. 139)

[However, there is in above mentioned selection of our future jobs, an undeniably poetic provision. None of these particular gentlemen has made us common soldiers, or even police corporals, carpenters, locksmiths, or doorwomen of the Cortes; absolutely not, we're always bound to be members of parliament, ministers, judges and generals.]

As she astutely points out, women do not even have a foothold in the lower ranks of the military or the police. As for Parliament, they were unlikely to get a foot through the door, even as unskilled labour [*porteiras*].

Still in the same paragraph, she goes on to underscore that the kind of employment already held down by women is in fact unglamorous, low-paid, and precarious: they are typically washerwomen or dressmakers. Moreover, she subtly draws attention to the unsavoury fact that one of the most readily available female professions is prostitution and that it is, moreover, condoned by those in power:

> Mas isso pode-se entender também de um modo nada poético, e é que os tais *certos* senhores que objetam a que exerçamos as primeiras dignidades da nação, não *objetam* a que sejamos serralheiras, carpinteiras, lavadeiras, costureiras pela maior parte arcando com a miséria, ou mesmo a que nos matriculemos para nos abrirmos essa carreira brilhante e generosamente autorizada pelos governos cristãos da Europa que inevitavelmente conduz aos acúleos da situação da Pária, e geralmente às honras dos hospitais, e das valas dos Prazeres e de S. João. (p. 139, italics in the original)

> [But this can also be understood in a way that is not in the least poetic, and it is that those *fine* gentlemen who object to our exercising the first dignities of the nation, do not *object* to our being locksmiths, carpenters, washerwomen, seamstresses, most of us struggling with poverty, or even to our matriculating in order to open that brilliant career generously authorized by the Christian governments of Europe that inevitably leads to the thorny situation of the Pariah, and generally to the honours of the hospitals, and the common graves in the Prazeres and S. João cemeteries.]

Here she highlights economic inequality, wryly foregrounding the fact that the only 'graduation' available to women, prostitution, far from paving the way to a brilliant career, actually inevitably leads to poverty, illness and premature death. She disparages the self-interest that motivates certain gentlemen to keep women in a state of servitude:

> Sim, desembioquemo-nos; é o medo de serem privados dessas deleitosas *bonnes-bouches* que conduz estes certos senhores a objetarem a que a mulher seja política; é o medo de que ela se lhes equipare; é o egoísmo das almas pequenas. Tais homens objetam igualmente a que a mulher seja independente pela sua indústria; querem-na o que tem sempre sido, sua criada e seu joguete. (p. 139, italics in the original)

> [Yes, let us call a spade a spade: it is the fear of being deprived of those delightful little morsels that leads these fine gentlemen to object to women being political; it is the fear that she may equal them; it is the egoism of small minds. Such men also object to women being independent through their own work; they want them to be what they have always been: their maid and their plaything.]

Wood's argument is that the 'egoísmo das almas pequenas' [the egoism of small minds] has often had an deleterious effect on the governance of nations, as history shows:

> Agastam-se com a possibilidade imaginária de que a mulher seja elevada às dignidades do estado que os homens hão até agora ocupado, — as mais das vezes com desdoiro seu, e ruína para a pátria, como o prova a história em geral,

e em particular o nosso estado atual de pobreza e de degeneração; mas não se agastam de ver a mulher arrastada nesse lamaçal de atos ignominiosos; de a ver expirar na miséria e nos hospitais! 'Oh que sábios protetores! Que dignos timoneiros! Quanto lhes devemos!' (p. 139)

[They become vexed just imagining the possibility that woman is raised to the dignities of the state that men have occupied until now — most times leading to their discredit, and ruin for the country, as history generally demonstrates, and in particular our current state of poverty and degeneration; but they are not vexed on seeing woman dragged through the mire of ignominious acts; seeing her die destitute, in the hospital! 'Oh what wise protectors! What worthy helmsmen! How much we owe them!']

At the close of this paragraph, the emotional tricolon underscores, in a rueful and perhaps bitter outburst, that such self-serving men are anything but wise protectors of women or the nation.

This particular editorial was prompted by a news item that some German male typographers had protested against the employment of women in their printing-business because the latter undercut them, as they received lower salaries. Wood's response to this news is astonishingly modern, as she contends that these men should have rebelled against this state of affairs and stood up for the principle of equal pay for equal work: 'em tal caso deveriam sublevar-se para que os salários das mulheres fossem equiparados aos dos homens: é a medida mais lógica, e teria achado eco nas simpatias dos espíritos nobres' (p. 140) [in such a case they should have protested so that the women's salaries equalled the men's: it is the most logical measure, and would have found echoes in the sympathy of noble minds].

The remainder of Wood's analysis is equally penetrating, as she explains how the men who prevent women from thinking for themselves, in order to maintain them in a tyrannical and abject dependence, are usually the same ones who wield the power of words to seduce them and take advantage of what they see as their playthings (*joguetes*), before cynically discarding them without being accountable for their subsequent 'ruin' (financial and metaphorical):

Mas arguir é inútil. Estes meus senhores que não querem a mulher tipógrafa pertencem à mesma *espécie* do género *homo* que não quer a mulher política, nem escritora, nem pensadora; que não a quer em nenhuma outra condição que a de uma dependência abjecta. São estes os homens que cantam os dotes e as fascinações da mulher em estrofes hiperbólicas; que lhe chamam estrela do céu, aura de perfumes inebriantes, bonina dos campos, antes de a arruinarem, e que zombam dela e lhe chamam fraca depois de a arruinarem; que com um sorriso triunfante vêm o seu joguete ir de queda em queda até por fim se atascar no lodaçal do vício. Infelizmente não se acha esta espécie de homens limitada a uma ou outra camada da sociedade; está disseminada por todas, desde a sala de S. Bento até aos botequins janotas, e destes aos botequins *cabarets*. (p. 140, italics in the original)

[But argument is pointless. These fine gentlemen who do not want female printers belong to the same *species* of *homo* that does not want woman to be political, or a writer, or a thinker; who don't want her in any condition other than abject dependence. These are the men who celebrate the gifts and charms of woman in hyperbolic verses; who call her a heavenly star, aura of heady perfume, daisy of the fields, before they ruin her, and mock her and call her weak, after ruining her; who with a triumphant smile see their plaything sink lower and lower until she is finally mired in the morass. Unfortunately, this species of man is not limited to one level of society or another; it is spread throughout the social classes, from the chamber in São Bento to the dandies' cafés, and from these to the *cabarets*.]

This is one of Wood's longest editorials, which suggests the strength of her feelings on matters of economic, political and symbolic inequality. Unusually enough, the analysis is then followed by a humorous sketch focusing on the interactions between an imaginary character and his wife: 'Vou descrever um dos *habitués* do botequim janota. É o sr. Sinfrónio' (p. 140, italics in the original) [I am going to describe one of the habitués of the dandies' bar. Mr. Sinfrónio]. What transpires from this micro-narrative is the arrogance of Sinfrónio's entitled behaviour, which means that he treats his wife no better than his servant — a parallel further brought out because Wood ascribed the name of Sinfrónia to the household servant, while his wife remains nameless.

The contrast between Sinfrónio's freedom of movement and the limited domestic routine of his spouse is stark. Although we are told that he occasionally writes *folhetins* [commentary columns] for the press, when he returns home to find her reading a newspaper, an act which emphasizes her ability to exercise a modicum of choice, he immediately clamps down on her unseemly behaviour, horrified she might be, or indeed become, a 'mulher política' [political woman]. The news item that she was reading was, non-coincidentally, about the Bishop of Viseu. This is an allusion to D. António Alves Martins, who in 1867 in Rome famously refused to sign a declaration recognizing the secular power and the infallibility of the Pope.[25] Sinfrónio blows out of all proportion his spouse's intellectual transgression, insofar as it is perceived to challenge the division of gender roles and therefore his marital authority. Despite her otherwise tame behaviour at home, he comically jumps to the conclusion of imminent social disorder: 'Aí está o que é ser mulher política; mulher que passa o tempo lendo os jornais! Daqui a nada quer ser deputado a Cortes, ministro, juiz ou general!' (p. 140) [There you have it, the political woman, the woman who spends her time reading newspapers! In no time at all she'll want to be a member of parliament, a minister, a judge or even a general!].

Rethinking Hegemonic Masculinity: 'o homem livre'

If this sketch vividly illustrates through caricature the overbearing attitude of a typical middle-class Portuguese male, it is because Wood is insightful enough to zoom in on dominant masculinity and see it for what it is: a construct. In this respect, another of her later editorials (*P*, 93: 175–76) is remarkable for its analysis. The fact that it is self-consciously couched as an essay — 'hoje levanto a voz para provar logicamente a *não-superioridade* dessa metade do género humano' (p. 175, italics in the original) [today I speak up in order to prove logically the non-superiority of that half of the human species] — is significant for, as Arkinstall sustains:

Because reason has conventionally been identified with the masculine, and emotion and empathy with the feminine, nineteenth-century female writers who appropriated the essay to advance feminist claims positioned themselves in the realms of reason and an Enlightenment culture that premised the equality of all human beings due to their innate capacity for reason.[26]

Wood's first move is to argue that men do not have sufficient evidence of female inferiority because, up to the present moment, equality of opportunities had been sorely lacking:

Mas os homens não podem *provar* que a mulher lhes seja moralmente inferior; não podem porque ignoram o que a mulher é moralmente. A mulher nunca se tem achado numa posição social que favorecesse o desenvolvimento das suas faculdades intelectuais. E se não, que digam os apologistas da inferioridade da mulher qual tem sido a instrução que se tem permitido ao sexo desde que o mundo *histórico* é mundo até ao século bendito em que vivemos? Que escolas, que universidades, que ciências se lhe hão franqueado? (p. 175, italics in the original)

[But men cannot *prove* that woman is morally inferior to them; they cannot because they don't know what woman morally is. Woman has never found herself in a social position that favours the development of her intellectual faculties. And if not, let the apologists for woman's inferiority say what instruction the fair sex has been allowed since the *historical* world has existed up to the blessed century we live in? What schools, what universities, what sciences have been opened up to them?]

Her second argument is that so-called male superiority does not stand to close scrutiny because history provides plentiful evidence of mismanagement:

Por agora as suas asserções são gratuitas e infundadas; enquanto que nós, mulheres, possuímos dados incontrovertíveis para negar e pronunciar *irrisória* a pretensão do homem à superioridade. Esta asserção não é gratuita, é baseada em *factos* e elucidada por *factos*. Abra-se o livro da história dessa metade da humanidade que desde que os séculos são séculos tem timonado os destinos do género humano! Oh, livro fatalíssimo para a vaidade do homem! (p. 175, italics in the original)

[For the moment their assertions are gratuitous and unfounded; whereas we, women, possess incontrovertible data to deny and pronounce man's pretension to superiority *laughable*. This assertion is not gratuitous, it is based on *facts* and elucidated by *facts*. Open up the history book of that half of humanity that has steered the destinies of humankind since time began! What an extraordinarily fatal book for man's vanity!]

She adduces the authority of an 'ilustre escritor' [illustrious writer] Professor F. W. Newman, to prove historical mismanagement by men.[27] Citing Newman would inevitably have lent gravitas to her argument in the minds of her contemporary audience, whether they were aware or not that he was the younger sibling of the famous Catholic convert, John Henry Newman, later made a Cardinal. On further investigation, Francis Newman's quotation turns out to be from 'A Lecture on Women's Suffrage', delivered in the Bristol Athenæum on 24 February 1869, although it is difficult to determine whether Francisca had had access to the full text, or just reports in the press about its contents.[28] She then expands on the evidence:

> E na verdade o que nos apresentam essa páginas sangrentas, essas páginas de desvarios incríveis, de paixões infrenes? Guerras de ambição, guerras de opiniões políticas, guerras de opiniões religiosas, o grande oprimindo o humilde, os ricos e poderosos atropelando-se mutuamente; por toda a parte doestos e vinganças, por toda a parte os homens atascando-se em marnéis dos vícios mais hediondos. [...] Em que consiste essa superioridade? Os efeitos indigitam as causas.
>
> [...] Logo, a superioridade é dos poucos; é excecional; não geral; não um atributo do sexo. (pp. 175–76)
>
> [And what, in fact, do these bloody pages, these pages of incredible folly, of unbridled passions show us? Wars of ambition, wars of political opinions, wars of religious opinions, the great oppressing the humble, the rich and powerful trampling all over each other; everywhere insults and revenge, everywhere men getting bogged down in the morass of the most foul vices. [...] Where is the superiority in that? The results point the finger at the causes.
>
> [...] So then, the superiority is of the few; it is exceptional; not general; not an attribute of sex.]

Here she dissociates hegemonic masculinity from biological maleness, indicating that the former is not innate. Still in the same lead article, her challenge to hegemonic masculinity closes with a particularly interesting deconstruction of the notion of (male) heroism, in which heroism becomes equated with violence and predicated upon subjugation of fellow human beings: 'Também nos fala a história de *heróis*. Ah, sim, heróis! Mas o que são eles? Homens que hauriam constantemente a eflúvia do sangue humano por eles derramado; que erguiam a sua glória sobre a ruína do seu próximo!' (p. 176) [History also speaks to us of *heroes*. Oh yes, heroes. But just what are they? Men who constantly breathed in the effluvium of human blood they shed; who raised their glory on the ruin of their fellow man!].

To this gloom-ridden definition, she juxtaposes her own idea of heroism: 'Vou dar a minha ideia do *herói* nas palavras inspiradas do poeta Gonzaga' (p. 176, italics in the original) [I shall give my own notion of the *hero* in inspired words of the poet Gonzaga]. Once more, she is citing a male writer to invest her declaration with greater authority, this time the canonical Brazilian poet Tomás Antônio Gonzaga (1744–1807), author of *Marília de Dirceu* (1792), in order to open up the possibility of cultivating a more attractive brand of (non-hegemonic) masculinity. In the first three stanzas of his poem 'Lira XXVII', Gonzaga argued that two of the great heroes of classical Antiquity (Alexander and Caesar) were in fact no better than a lucky pirate in the case of the former, while only a thin dividing line separated the latter's success from vile treachery:

> Alexandre, Marília, qual o rio,
> Que engrossando no Inverno tudo arrasa,
> Na frente das coortes
> Cerca, vence, abrasa
> As Cidades mais fortes.

Foi na glória das armas o primeiro;
Morreu na flor dos anos, e já tinha
Vencido o mundo inteiro.

Mas este bom Soldado, cujo nome
Não há poder algum que não abata
Foi, Marília, somente
Um ditoso pirata,
Um salteador valente.
Se não tem uma fama baixa e escura,
Foi por se pôr ao lado da injustiça
A insolente ventura.

O grande César, cujo nome voa,
À sua mesma Pátria a fé quebranta;
Na mão a espada toma,
Oprime-lhe a garganta,
Dá Senhores a Roma.
Consegue ser herói por um delito;
Se acaso não vencesse, então seria
Um vil traidor proscrito.[29]

[Alexander, Marília, like the river
That swelling in winter destroys all,
Before the cohorts
He approaches, conquers, burns
The strongest cities.
In the glory of arms he was first;
He died in the flower of his years, and had already
Conquered the whole world.

But this good soldier, whose name
No power can destroy
Was, Marília, merely
A lucky pirate
A bold highway man.
If he does not have a low and dark repute,
It was because impudent fortune
Went to stand by injustice.

The great Caesar, whose name flies,
With his own Land breaks the faith;
His hand takes up the sword,
By making its throat choke,
He gives rulers to Rome.
He manages to be a hero through wrongdoing;
If he hadn't conquered, then he would be
A vile, proscribed traitor.]

Her idea of heroism thus challenges its prevailing definition according to
hegemonic masculinity. Her lead article does not quote Gonzaga's next stanza,
which nonetheless is particularly interesting as it provides an alternative definition
of heroism, redefining it as 'viver justo' [leading a just life]:

O ser herói, Marília, não consiste
Em queimar os Impérios: move a guerra,
Espalha o sangue humano,
E despovoa a terra
Também o mau tirano.
Consiste o ser herói em viver justo:
E tanto pode ser herói o pobre,
Como o maior Augusto.[30]

[To be a hero, Marília, does not consist
In burning Empires: he too wages war,
Sheds human blood,
And depopulates the land
Who is an evil tyrant.
Being a hero means leading a just life:
And a poor man may be a hero
Just like the greatest Augustus.]

This particularly confident editorial, couched as an essay, contrasted with the announcement in the following issue that the paper was to fold two months later. After this, there is only one more lead article signed by Wood, the ante-penultimate one. It is nonetheless an astonishing one, for therein she positions herself against celibacy and demonstrates that the hegemonic masculinity of the Church creates casualties within the institution itself ('O Celibato', *P*, 99: 199–200).

Her starting-point is a private letter she claims to have received from a priest, disclosing the desperation of a young man tied 'à fria laje do altar' (p. 200) [to the cold stone of the altar]. She considers his vow of chastity barbaric and goes on to argue that 'O monaquismo e o celibato do século XIX são realmente anomalias' [monastic life and celibacy in the nineteenth century are truly abnormal]. She quotes the Bible's injunction 'Crescei e multiplicai-vos' [Be fruitful and multiply] as proof that God did not intend man to be celibate. And she further points to the ills generated by enforced separation from the world, such as desperation, degeneration and debauchery (p. 199). She rounds off the editorial with a plural apostrophe:

Mártires das alucinações humanas, homens e mulheres que contra a vossa vontade jazeis 'amarrados à fria laje do altar' quebrai os vossos grilhões: os vossos votos são uma profanação da vontade Divina tão claramente expressa em tudo quanto vive e morre. Saí dessa existência desnaturalizada; entrai no mundo para amardes, e para gozardes as delícias de ser amados, e sobretudo para trabalhardes em prol do melhoramento moral da vossa espécie. (p. 200)

[Martyrs to human delusions, men and women who against your will lie 'bound to the cold stone of the altar', break your fetters: your vows profane the Divine will so clearly expressed in everything that lives and dies. Leave that unnatural existence: go out into the world to love one another, and to enjoy the delights of being loved, and above all to work on behalf of the moral improvement of your species.]

This is extraordinarily heretical thinking, insofar as she is presenting vows of chastity as contrary to God's will, adducing the argument that the latter is 'so clearly expressed' in the natural world. In short, celibacy creates martyrs (as well as degenerates or debauched monsters). If we read between the lines, it is clear that Wood is advocating the right to experience pleasure through sexual love, at the other end of the spectrum from what she deems to be a 'existência desnaturalizada' [unnatural existence]. Moreover, the fact that she explicitly addresses her apostrophe to both men and women implies that, in her mind, both sexes are equally entitled to find sexual fulfilment. The expression of a standpoint that readily acknowledges bodily needs and desires was exceptionally radical for its time, coming from the mouth of a lady. Retrospectively at least, it gives a whole new inflection to the motto 'a mulher livre ao lado do homem livre'. It is perhaps unsurprising, then, that Wood only broached such a contentious subject when *O Progresso* was already in the process of winding down.

Conclusion

This chapter hopes to have demonstrated the full scale of Wood's audacity in going against prevailing mores and her courage in sustaining the momentum despite the relentless campaign against her waged by *Bem Público*. As a feminist thinker, she was very clear that the nation needed new women but that, equally, it needed new men. Her cogent critique of hegemonic masculinity showed that the latter was deeply damaging to both men and women, hence the need to free both sexes from the shackles of tradition, in order to construct a more egalitarian society.

Reflecting on the demise of *O Progresso*, the last ever (unsigned) editorial remarked:

> Se as senhoras portuguesas, em geral, observam com indiferença a desaparição de uma folha que tem constantemente advogado os seus direitos sagrados, não sucederá assim com o partido teocrático; partido essencialmente hostil a qualquer empresa cujo fim seja a elevação e a ilustração da mulher; partido que tem horror às palavras — ciência, progresso, liberdade, razão, e educação popular; porque com tais agências nenhuma teocracia pode coexistir. (P, 102: 211)

> [If Portuguese ladies, in general, observe with indifference the disappearance of a news sheet that has constantly advocated their sacred rights, the same will not happen with the theocratic party; a party essentially hostile to any undertaking whose purpose is to elevate and educate women; a party that abhors the words — science, progress, liberty, reason and popular education; because no theocracy can co-exist with such agents.]

The virtually unlimited power wielded by the clergy, contemptuously described here as a 'partido teocrático' [theocratic party], is precisely what her periodical sought to uncover. Her exposure of the obscurantism fostered by the Church represented an enormous threat to the status quo. Foucault comments that 'Power is tolerable only on condition that it masks a substantial part of itself. Its success is proportional to an ability to hide its own mechanisms'.[31] Thus, by exposing Church hegemony and ensuing gender discrimination, Wood showed that unchecked power was intolerable. In practice, however, her voice was one which could be swiftly de-authorized because it was deemed to be deeply distasteful coming from a woman living in a nation where, as César Machado had candidly reminded readers in his 1869 preface to Guiomar Torresão's *Uma Alma de mulher,* cited at the beginning of Chapter 3, women were not expected to have the same intellectual or religious freedom as their menfolk.

By contrast, a few years later, when *O Crime do Padre Amaro* squarely depicted multiple abuses of power arising from the Catholic Church's hegemony, the anti-clerical message of Eça would not fall on deaf ears, as the novel's ample transnational afterlife indicates. Moreover, in his third version of *O Crime,* Eça developed the character of Dr. Gouveia as a mouthpiece for science and reason, in a couple of speeches that exposed and indicted the prevailing Catholic monopoly on thought.[32] These were precisely among the concepts that, as Wood rightly predicted in the above quotation, had the capacity to deal a lethal blow to the Church establishment. In other words, Wood's journalism is in many respects as hard-hitting as Eça's religious libel in *O Crime do Padre Amaro.* It is certainly curious, then, that Eça's pronouncements, even fictional ones, are now generally regarded as having political significance, while those by Wood don't seem to deserve as much as a footnote. Part of her initial silencing was undoubtedly motivated by the fact that her analysis was far more radical from a gendered perspective than any propounded by her male contemporaries, with far-reaching implications in terms of existing social structures. It was an instance of 'too much, too soon', alienating her from a wider support base; but today the case for her contribution to the history of ideas, not least the unprecedented way in which her anticlerical analysis underpins the originality of her avant-garde feminist thought, deserves to be re-opened.

In fact, it is telling that years later, in 1905, when Osório interpellated Portuguese women (and men), unlike Wood she studiously avoided any detailed discussion and analysis of the stronghold of the Church, focusing instead on the need for female education in order for women to fulfil their roles as equal to men and proper mothers, as well as their own potential. Even if Osório does not seem to have been aware of the earlier controversy surrounding Wood, she must have felt that going down the route of criticism of the Church would be too divisive and therefore counter-productive. It may also be for the same reason that her short chapter 'As Mulheres e a Política' sticks to generalities and does not mention the question of female suffrage once,[33] whereas Wood repeatedly uses her editorials to campaign for voting rights, as the next two chapters will demonstrate. In that sense, Wood was more willing than Osório to stick her neck out for her beliefs, even if these quickly placed her on a collision course with the Catholic establishment.

Retrospectively, it seems clear, firstly, that for the Wood 'to expound a theory is also an action... an important political intervention... *to say something is to do something*',[34] and, secondly, that her combative actions posed a threat to historical male supremacy. The insight that '*to say something is to do something*' is particularly relevant in 1860s Portuguese periodical culture, because raising awareness of women's systemic subaltern status was a necessary first step before any collective movement could have a realistic chance of gathering momentum. As the next chapter will pinpoint, intent on *doing something* by the most obvious means at her disposal — the press — Wood becomes ever more forceful in her political intervention through her creative use of open letters, as she opts to engage in dialogue with key figures invested with transnational authority.

Notes to Chapter 4

1. Janice D. Hamlet, 'Editorials', in *Encyclopedia of Journalism*, ed. by Christopher H. Sterling, 6 vols (Los Angeles & London: Sage, 2009) v, 473–77 (p. 478).
2. François Demers, 'The Editorial and Public Debate. Introduction', *Sur Le Journalisme*, 5.2 (2017) pp. 84–86 (p. 85).
3. ibid, p. 85.
4. Sylvia Paletschek and Bianka Pietrow-Ennker, 'Women's Emancipation Movements', p. 318.
5. Raewyn W. Connell, *Masculinities*, 2nd edn (Cambridge: Polity, 2005), p. 77.
6. Osório, *Mulheres Portuguesas*, p. 63.
7. The words were not hers, however, as the slogan had featured as an epigraph in an earlier editorial in favour of women's instruction penned by F. A. de Matos (*VF*, 24: 1), where it was ascribed to another male journalist, Ferreira [*sic*] Farol, also a supporter of women's rights (see for instance Farol, *P*, 81: 127, where he dates his pithy statement to 1865). Wood had adopted it a fortnight later, in July in 1868 (*VF*, 26: 1), then reiterated it in 'Nova medida' (*VF*, 43: 2) [New Measure], as well as in an editorial where she called on progressive men to encourage women to raise their expectations ('As Damas em Londres', *VF*, 45, 1). It is fitting then, that even before the motto was chosen to brand the distinctive collective project of *A Voz Feminina*, it had already circulated and been shared among several contributors. Crucially, it proved the existence of male support for her project.
8. Osório, *Mulheres Portuguesas*, p. 71.
9. Lopes, 'Religião e género', p. 59.
10. See Timóteo Cavaco, 'Ellen Roughton (1802–1883): mãe, educadora, anunciadora do Evangelho', *Refrigério: mulheres na seara*, 161 (2016), 11–21 <https://refrigerio.ciip.pt/2016/04/refrigerio-n-o-161-abr-jun-2016/>. Her son, Francis Roughton, set up the Sociedade da Bíblia [Bible Society] in 1864.
11. José António Martin Moreno Afonso, *Protestantismo e educação: história de um projecto pedagógico alternativo em Portugal na transição do séc. XIX* (Braga: Instituto de Educação e Psicologia da Universidade do Minho, 2009) includes a useful chronological table in Annex 5. See especially pp. 356–61.
12. 'Quem vem lá', *Bem Público*, 7 March 1868, pp. 275–77 (p. 275).
13. Ibid, p. 277.
14. See Francisco Malta Romeiras, 'Jesuit Historiography in Modern Portugal', *Jesuit Historiography Online* <http://dx.doi.org/10.1163/2468-7723_jho_COM_192570>.
15. 'A Voz Feminina', *Bem Público*, 30 January 1869, pp. 236–37 (p. 236).
16. Ibid., p. 237.
17. Luís de Abreu Machado, 'Anticlericalismo', in *Dança dos Demónios: intolerância em Portugal*, ed. by António Marujo and José Eduardo Franco ([Lisbon]: Círculo de Leitores, 2009), pp. 125–202.
18. Ibid., pp. 187–88.
19. Another example: 'sentimos ser de urgente necessidade, que se decretem leis penais contra o vil sedutor que insinuando-se no espírito da mulher com intentos traiçoeiros excita nela as paixões de que ele mesmo é pusilânime escravo, e depois chama-lhe fraca!' (*VF*, 52: 2) [we feel it is a matter of the utmost urgency to pass penal laws against the vile seducer who, insinuating himself into the woman's mind with treacherous intentions, awakens in her the passions to which he himself is a pusillanimous slave, and then he calls her weak!].
20. Osório, *Mulheres Portuguesas*, pp. 265–70.
21. See Adrien Dollfus, 'L'Aquarium du Havre', *Histoire Naturelle* <http://informations-documents.com/environnement/histoire-naturelle/23-111%20l%20aquarium%20du%20Havre.htm>.
22. See Ana Vicente, *As Mulheres portuguesas vistas por viajantes estrangeiros: séculos XVIII, XIX, XX* (Lisbon: Gótica, 2001).

23. 'A Voz Feminina', *Bem Público*, 6 June 1868, pp. 378–79 (p. 378).

24. See Emilio La Parra, 'La Canción del Trágala: cultura y política popular en el inicio de la revolución liberal en España', *Les Travaux du crec en ligne*, 6 (2009), 68–86 <http://crec-paris3.fr/wp-content/uploads/2011/07/actes-03-La-Parra.pdf>.

25. As a result, the Bishop of Viseu was particularly well-regarded in Protestant circles (see Afonso, p. 62 and p. 359). For a recent appraisal, see Maria Máxima Vaz, *A Voz da Liberdade* (Lisbon: Chiado, 2018). A pamphlet by F. de R. Palmeirim, *O Duque de Loulé e Bispo de Viseu ou as velhas e as Novas Aspirações de Portugal*, was publicized in *O Progresso* (no. 94, p. 183).

26. Christine Arkinstall, 'A Feminist Press Gains Ground in Spain, 1822–1866', in *A New History of Iberian Feminisms*, ed. by Silvia Bermúdez and Roberta Johnson (Toronto: University of Toronto, 2014), pp. 111–25 (p. 111).

27. See Timothy C. F. Stunt, 'Newman, Francis William', in *Oxford Dictionary of National Biography* <http://www.oxforddnb.com/>.

28. Francis Newman, *A Lecture on Women's Suffrage: delivered in Bristol Athenaeum, February 24th, 1869* (London: London Society for Women's Suffrage, 1869; repr. [n.a.]: The Francis William Newman Society, 2009) <http://www.fwnewman.org/Library/Works/SPE/LWS_2-24-69.pdf>.

29. Tomás Antônio Gonzaga, *Marília de Dirceu* (Rio de Janeiro: Garnier, 1992), pp. 91–92.

30. Ibid., p. 92.

31. Michel Foucault, *The History of Sexuality*, trans. by Robert Hurley, 3 vols (New York: Pantheon Books, 1978–86), I (1978): *An Introduction*, p. 86.

32. Eça de Queirós, *O Crime do Padre Amaro: 2.ª e 3.ª versões*, ed. by Carlos Reis and Maria do Rosário Cunha (Lisbon: Imprensa Nacional–Casa da Moeda, 2000). See especially pp. 583–91 and pp. 969–77.

33. Osório, *Mulheres Portuguesas*, pp. 65–74.

34. Finlayson, *An Introduction to Feminism*, p. 5.

CHAPTER 5

Activism through Open Letters

Print culture is fundamental to an understanding of nineteenth-century Portugal on multiple counts. By the 1870s periodicals had become a regular fixture in Portuguese middle-class households and realist fiction reflects this trend. For instance, the incipit of Eça's *O Primo Basílio* [*Cousin Basílio*] (1878) situates the main character, Luísa, immersed in the *Diário de Notícias*, while in the epilogue a minor male character, Paula, is seen reading *A Nação*.[1] Neither choice of titles is innocent: *Diário de Notícias* was a daily whose launch in late 1864 heralded a new era for commercial journalism, as the Introduction recalled, while *A Nação* was a Catholic and monarchist paper.[2] As such, it provided an easy target for Paula's bitterness against the status quo, which the narrator describes as leading him towards atheism and the Commune. The reference to the 1871 Paris Commune would have been understood by contemporary readers as shorthand for freethinking ideas.

Furthermore, one third of the way through *O Primo Basílio*, Torresão's *Almanaque das Senhoras* also makes a cameo appearance at a *soirée*, as the source of an ultra-romantic poem put to music, sung by Basílio with Luísa at the piano, shortly before they exchange their first kiss.[3] It is evident that Eça's inclusion of the *Almanaque das Senhoras* as a contributing element to the start of the affair between Basílio and Luísa built on Ramalho Ortigão's skewed and dismissive attitude towards this annual, iterated only the previous year in *As Farpas*, as Chapter 3 highlighted. The message could not be clearer: *O Primo Basílio* portrayed women as passive consumers of the press, and implied that only men (even unsophisticated ones like Paula) were in a position to react against the ideologically backward narrative of the nation reproduced through a significant sector of the press. Nonetheless, Eça's apparently realistic portrayal of women, disseminated and uncritically accepted by subsequent generations of readers, conveniently obscured the fact that, one decade earlier, Francisca Wood had already proved herself to be a shining example of a Portuguese woman who drew on her analytical faculties to enact intellectual dissidence through her editorials and argue for the necessity of structural change, as documented in Chapter 4.

This chapter explores how Francisca Wood, intent on the recognition of women as intellectuals, sets out to reclaim their right to debate on an equal footing with men some of the pressing issues that affected them — and therefore the nation — all the while noting that 'equal footing' is a misleading term, since women were not legally equal by any stretch of the imagination. Since combative newspapers remained a common paradigm in nineteenth-century journalistic practice through the 1860s,[4] what was unusual in the case of *A Voz Feminina* was the female Editor. For this reason, Woods editorials stand as a prime example of resistance to hegemonic masculinity, foregrounding her as a *de facto* public intellectual. Hamlet reminds us that by the early nineteenth century, the Editor was 'the most important (and often the best known) figure at a publication'.[5] In addition, the public-facing nature of the Editor's statements cannot be ignored: 'as editorials are public, mass communicated expressions of public opinion, they are probably the most widely circulated opinion statements in society, regardless of whether they are widely read'.[6]

In the following analysis, we will examine one of the recurrent discursive strategies deployed by Wood in her leaders: open letters, often in the form of petitions, addressed to men in positions of authority. These range from the most contentious topics (anticlericalism and issues of citizenship) to the most unexpected (animal welfare). As she sought to foster debate on controversial religious, political and ethical questions, Wood addressed fellow journalists and readers in editorials couched as open letters, a stratagem used at various times in the first year of the periodical's life. The turning-point came right at the start of the second year with the editorial 'A uma assinante da *Voz Feminina*' (no. 53), discussed in the previous chapter, where her anti-Jesuitic positions were propounded.[7] The effectiveness of the tactic can be gauged by the fact that this piece was transcribed in at least one other paper, as documented by the double character assassination that ensued in *Bem Público*: 'A comadre *Aurora* para agradecer à comadre *Voz Feminina* os elogios que dela recebeu, lambendo os beiços reimprimiu o artigo desta dirigido *a uma assinante*' [The garrulous editor of the *Aurora* in gratitude to the garrulous editor of *Voz Feminina* for the praise he received from his co-religionary, licking his chops, has reprinted the latter's article addressed 'To a Female Subscriber'].[8] Clearly Wood's open letter had touched a raw nerve for Valada, given that this jibe comes after he had already taken her to task at length for her blatant disrespect for Catholicism, the official state religion, as we have seen.

As Cristo highlights in her study *A epistolaridade nos textos de imprensa de Eça de Queirós*:

> Um pouco à semelhança do panfleto, a carta aberta toma geralmente uma estrutura argumentativa e um tom persuasivo e o epistológrafo pretende, neste caso, alcançar o seu público, fazendo com que este tome uma decisão, assuma um pensamento, partilhe uma determinada opinião.[9]

> [A bit like a pamphlet, the open letter generally has an argumentative structure and a persuasive tone, and the letter-writer aims, in this way, to reach the readers so that they take a decision, adopt a position, share a particular opinion.]

Emboldened by the reactions, both positive and negative, that her letter 'A uma assinante' generated, Wood goes one step further: she formally begins to petition men in power. She starts on a relatively modest scale, with a seemingly self-contained and practical issue, by entreating the local authorities in Lisbon to deal with widespread cruelty to animals. Within a matter of weeks, however, two other lead articles broaden her scope to increasingly inflammatory issues: the right of women to education and the thorny question of the vote. In so doing, her public interventions, addressed to figureheads endowed with transnational significance at opposite ends of the spectrum, Pope IX (1792–1878), and the Spanish Republican leader, Emilio Castelar (1832–1899), must necessarily be understood as political interventions at a time when women had limited opportunities to ensure that their voices were heard in the public sphere. In our analysis, then, we consider Wood's choice of interlocutors, mindful that 'o receptor da carta desempenha uma função vital na estratégia textual, constituindo, com o sujeito da enunciação, o segundo termo interlocutivo' [the recipient of the letter has a central function in the textual strategy, holding, after the person who enunciates, the second interlocutory position].[10]

Petitions for the Protection of Animals

To the best of our knowledge, Wood's campaign for animal welfare is the first sustained intervention to occur in nineteenth-century Portugal.[11] Her petition, 'Apelo: à Ex.ma Câmara Municipal de Lisboa' (*VF*, 66: 1–2) [Appeal: to the Honourable City Council of Lisbon] to improve measures for the protection of animals, is the first formal appeal to be made in the periodical, and, as such, provides a stepping-stone for subsequent ones, while modelling debating skills for her readership. It opens as follows:

> *Meus srs.* — V. Ex.as como distintos e dignos constituintes dos senados desta metrópole têm ao seu alvedrio dispensar muito bem, não só a humanidade, mas a todos os viventes que conjuntamente com V. Ex.as respiram as auras na nossa pátria. [...]
> Meus srs., os cães e os gatos, os cavalos, os bois, os burros, e as galinhas, são criaturas sencientes, que sofrem com a falta de alimento suficiente, com o trabalho excessivo, com o desalinho e inconveniência dos lugares em que os abrigam, e com os desapiedados tratos que recebem dos desalmados que os governam. (p. 1)

> [*Dear Sirs* — Good gentlemen, as distinguished and honourable members of the senate of this metropolis, you exercise your will, not only over humankind but over all living creatures who, alongside you, good sirs, breathe the airs of our land. [...]
> Dear Sirs, dogs and cats, horses, oxen, donkeys and hens, are sentient beings, that suffer with under-feeding, with over-working, with the poor up-keep and inadequacy of their shelter, and with the remorseless treatment that they receive at the hands of the soulless individuals who rule over them.]

From the outset, Wood subtly placed the onus on the moral worthiness of her addressees through the alliterative 'distintos e dignos' [distinguished and honourable]. After stressing their standing as official representatives, she appeals to their compassion, emotionally highlighting the ill-treatment of animals through the tricolon 'com... com... com' [with... with... with]. Wood then adduces an argument of a more practical nature, namely that to deal with this wrongdoing would hardly cost any money: 'Ilustres srs. do município de Lisboa, V. Ex.as PODEM, seguramente sem aumentar o *deficit*, sem mesmo pôr dedo nos fundos do município, obstar a tanto e tão grande penar' (p. 1) [Noble sirs of the Council of Lisbon, good gentlemen, you CAN, certainly without increasing the deficit, without even touching the council's funds, prevent such great and terrible suffering]. The power of the Councillors is emphasized through the use of the capitalized verb.

After making four concrete suggestions for preventive measures, and proposing fines for non-compliance, which underscores the clarity of her thinking, she concludes by rhetorically drawing attention to her subaltern status as a woman with the concomitant expectation of gentlemanly conduct: 'Tudo espero do cavalheirismo e bondade de V. Ex.as. De quem sou humilde e respeitosa serva' (p. 2) [I trust in your chivalry and goodness, good sirs. Of whom I am your humble and respectful servant]. By cleverly describing herself as such, she is tactically deploying female weakness as a rhetorical trope, thereby using femininity in a manner most likely to elicit a positive reaction from those in high office. This is not something she will do as blatantly when dealing with other causes, as we shall see.

The next editorial was a follow-up on the same topic, this time a petition to heads of families: 'Apelo: aos chefes de família' [Appeal: to heads of households] (*VF*, 67: 1–2). Although the majority would have been male, she was careful to include women by addressing 'todo o homem e mulher em cujo peito palpita um coração compassivo' (p. 1) [every man and woman in whose breast beats a compassionate heart]. Within the jurisdiction of their own homes, she emphasizes, men and women had the opportunity to lead through both word and deed. By expecting and enforcing a more humane treatment of animals such as horses and cats, all readers could effect change in the behaviour of their domestic servants and children.

More unexpectedly, in her bid to tackle the cruel handling of poultry — described as 'a prática de atar criação pelas pernas, e assim em molhos, levá-la de cabeça para baixo à venda pelas ruas de Lisboa' (p. 1) [the practice of binding chickens by their legs and carrying them upside down in bunches through the streets of Lisbon, offering them for sale] — she offered a striking example of grassroots activism, dating back to the time of the debate surrounding the abolition of slavery in England:

> Posso porém assegurar-lhes que em Londres quando se tratava de resgatar os escravos da Jamaica, medida que, como todo o arrojo de benevolência civilizadora, teve que arcar com poderosa e enérgica oposição, a arraia-miúda *recusava* comprar açúcar fabricado por escravos. A mulher que entrava numa tenda a comprar o seu vintém de açúcar tinha sempre o cuidado de recomendar que lhe não dessem *trabalho de escravos*. Ela pouco entendia da questão, mas o marido que lia os jornais ou os ouvia ler e frequentava os *meetings* públicos ensinava-lhe o recado. (p. 1)

> [I can, however, assure you that in London, when there was a move to free the slaves of Jamaica, a measure which, like any courageous act of civilizing benevolence, meant taking on powerful and energetic opposition, the lower orders *refused* to buy sugar manufactured by slaves. The woman who went into a shop to buy her two ha'p'orth of sugar always made a point of urging them not give her the *fruit of slave labour*. She understood little of the matter, but her husband who read the newspapers or heard them read out and who attended public meetings taught her the message.]

The example of ordinary English housewives, boycotting the purchase of sugar from Jamaica in a protest against slavery, is particularly effective here: it showed that women from all walks of life could be mobilized for a just cause. It moreover emphasizes Wood's long-standing interest in social reform and activism, dating back to her time in England. Her contention was that a similar boycott by Portuguese consumers in connection with the mishandling of poultry would lead vendors to change their ways.

The closing paragraph of this particular editorial was not entirely well-judged, culturally speaking, for she contrasts the (foreign) example of a young schoolboy who went from tormenting and destroying bird nests to protecting them, with the ongoing cruelty of (Portuguese) bullfighting (p. 2). One suspects that, insofar as bullfighting was an entertainment deeply ingrained in national culture, this comment was bound to lead to a loss of credibility for her cause.

Nonetheless, her fight for the protection of animals continued. In no. 84 she transcribed verbatim eight points from the Código de Posturas da Câmara Municipal [City Council By-laws] under the rubric 'do modo de tratar os animais publicamente' [On the public treatment of animals] (P, 84, 140), to put pressure on those responsible. In no. 88, in 'À Ex.ma Câmara Municipal de Lisboa' [To the Esteemed City Council of Lisbon] (P, 88, 155–56), Wood once again used her editorial to address the authorities, citing the by-laws once more, in order to point out the existence of such laws, but the lack of their application in practice. She suggested that, in order to maintain their own self-respect, the authorities should put a stop to the sorry public spectacle of horses drawing heavy loads uphill when injured and exhausted. In this instance, Wood shows herself to be conversant with the law, and her logic is irrefutable. This enables her to go one step further in the following paragraph, where she stubbornly returns to the cruel way in which fowls are routinely carried when being taken to market. This time, her argument hinges on the contrast between everyday Portuguese behaviour and the penalties such behaviour would incur elsewhere in Europe, citing the example of a one-off act of animal cruelty that was immediately fined. The implicit message is that Portugal is backward compared to the rest of Europe.

She rounds off by pre-empting potential objections that compassion towards humans is more urgent than towards animals. Her counter-argument is that there are already institutions to deal with a host of social problems: asylums, hospitals, charitable institutions for orphans, as well as laws against wrongdoing, whereas animals do not have any champions.

In sum, the campaign for animal welfare is unexpected in the periodical, because in Portugal the issue was yet to impinge on the public consciousness. Yet ironically, of all the causes that Wood embraced, it was the one that would yield fruit first, with the creation of the Portuguese Society for the Protection of Animals only a few years later, in late 1875.[12] In 1876 the newly created Society launched a short-lived *Boletim da Sociedade Protetora dos Animais*, and from January 1877 it sponsored a fortnightly magazine, *O Zoofilo* [Zoophile]. The fact that the latter was printed by the Tipografia Luso-Britânica during the first year of its life strongly points to the Woods' involvement, since they owned that press. Certainly, Henriques speculates that the creation of the Sociedade Protetora dos Animais was influenced by British presence in Portugal and linked to Protestant practices, though he seemed entirely unaware of Wood's editorials, which predate the existence of the association.[13]

One decade later, *Os Maias* [*The Maias*] (1888) featured a passing reference to the Society and its members:

> Um dia [Maria Eduarda] viera indignada da Praça da Figueira, quase com ideias de vingança, por ter visto nas tendas dos galinheiros aves e coelhos apinhados em cestos, sofrendo durante dias as torturas da imobilidade e a ansiedade da fome. Carlos levava estas belas cóleras para o Ramalhete, increpava violentamente o Marquês, que era membro da Sociedade Protectora dos Animais. O Marquês, indignado também, jurava justiça, falava em cadeias, em costa de África...
>
> E Carlos, comovido, ficava a pensar quanta larga e distante influência pode ter, mesmo isolado de tudo, um coração que é justo.[14]

> [One day, she [Maria Eduarda] had returned in outrage from the Praça da Figueira, filled almost with ideas of revenge, having seen on the poulterers' stalls baskets crammed with chickens and rabbits that suffered for days on end the torment of confinement and the pain of hunger. Carlos took this fine rage with him to Ramalhete and passionately berated the Marquis, who was a member of the Society for the Protection of Animals. The Marquis, equally indignant, vowed that justice would be done, and even spoke of imprisonment and deportation to the coast of Africa for the perpetrators.
>
> And Carlos, much moved, reflected upon the broad far-reaching influence that a just heart can have, even if that heart lives the most isolated of lives.][15]

Although the vignette might suggest that Eça de Queirós is poking harmless fun at a cause that was very marginal in those days, what is disturbing, on further inspection, is that Carlos is simply unable to envisage the possibility of Maria Eduarda herself taking direct action. Perceived by Carlos (and Eça de Queirós?) as a woman removed from *res publica*, she is effectively bound to the domestic sphere, thus requiring the mediation of her lover to intervene in any public matter, however small. In Eça's worldview, only men could be visualized as members of a pressure group — contrary to what happened in practice, since membership of the Portuguese Society for the Protection of Animals was open to both sexes.[16] Retrospectively, at least, the irony lies in the assumption that even though Maria Eduarda's was a 'just heart', because she was a woman her influence could only be second- (or even third-) hand. Since the ridiculously ineffectual Marquis over-reacts by advocating deportation, a punishment disproportionate to the crime, the just cause embraced by Maria Eduarda is ultimately belittled. By contrast, the real-life (and also transnational) Wood had intervened publicly to campaign for change — and pragmatically so, unlike the Marquis. But rather than acknowledge that women had a voice in the public sphere, it was more expedient for Eça de Queirós to present this particular cause as an irrelevant upper-class hobbyhorse. In fact, he cannot resist another dig at the Society in the chapter that follows, where it is praised as a most useful association by the inept Sousa Neto, a high-ranking civil servant in the Ministry of Education.

Address to the Pope

Ultimately, at the time, the protection of animals could be dismissed as a fairly marginal and self-contained upper-class ideal, whereas other principles embraced by *A Voz Feminina* were certainly highly inflammatory. For instance, throughout the lifespan of the periodical, in her bid to make the case in favour of female education, Francisca assumed the arduous task of exposing the obscurantism fostered by the Catholic Church. Immediately after her first two petitions to the Lisbon City Council, as if emboldened by her own momentum, it is nonetheless arresting to find her addressing no less a person than the Pope himself ([‘O Bispo de Montpellier recebeu...’], *VF*, 68: 1–2).

This untitled editorial stemmed from a recent pronouncement by Pope Pius IX, who had stated in a papal brief his objection to the steps taken by the French Education Minister, Duruy, to facilitate the opening of secondary education to Frenchwomen. He claimed that ‘estão preparando, não boas mães de família, mas mulheres *enfunadas com vã e oca ciência*’ (p. 1) [they are preparing not good mothers, but women *puffed up with vain and empty knowledge*].[17] At this point, Wood challenges the leader of the Catholic Church: ‘Seja-me permitido perguntar a Sua Santidade donde deriva ela esta ilação?’ (p. 1) [Allow me to ask His Holiness how he arrived at such a conclusion?]. She continues in the same vein with a series of other rhetorical questions addressed to him (but by extension her readership too) that underline that he lacks concrete proof that learning is detrimental to women, given that until very recently the number of those taught to read and write has been negligible.

A follow-up argument highlights that academic study had not changed men for the worse, quite the contrary. At this juncture, Wood could not resist the temptation to remind her readers of shameful episodes in Church History, including the Inquisition, using highly charged language, chosen for its rhetorical effect:

> Pergunto mais, meu Senhor, os estudos académicos, os estudos de ciências têm deteriorado os homens? Têm feito deles maus pais de família? Não por certo. Os homens eram maus pais, tirânicos maridos e pseudocristãos, quando não estudavam, ou quando só estudavam teologia e os enigmas da metafísica. Então queimava-se o próximo, frigia-se o próximo, torturava-se o próximo; então a carnificina de S. Bartolomeu, então o império do Santo Tribunal da Inquisição! Agora, que os homens se ocupam de ciências, que estudam e que se *atrevem* a cogitar, já não há desses brinquedos horripilantes. (p. 1)

> [Indeed, let me ask, my Lord, have academic studies and the pursuit of science ruined men? Have they made them bad heads of families? Of course not. Men were bad fathers, tyrannical husbands and pseudo-Christians when they did not study, or when they only studied theology and the mysteries of metaphysics. Then they burned their neighbours, fried their neighbours, tortured their neighbours; then came the Saint Bartholomew’s Day massacre, then came the dominance of the Holy Office of the Inquisition! Now that men explore the sciences, study and *dare* to think, there are no longer such horrific entertainments.]

Wood alternates between addressing the Pope by his title as ‘Sua Santidade’ [Your Holiness] and ‘meu Senhor’. The latter is ambiguous for it can mean both ‘my Lord’ and 'dear Sir'. The apostrophe is used ironically to pay mock religious reverence ('my Lord'), but perhaps also surreptitiously to place herself on an equal footing with the Pope. The daringness of doing so cannot be overstated: it would have been controversial behaviour coming from a man — coming from the pen of a woman, someone in a subordinate position, not only in the eyes of the Church, but also of society as a whole, it was nothing short of revolutionary. After contrasting a past marred by inhuman cruelty with a present characterized by the fact that the study of philosophy and science has immeasurably improved mankind, criticism of the Pope in the second half of her editorial centres on his allegedly deficient understanding of the Christian message of love. This is another extraordinarily provocative move, given that she was writing for a Portuguese audience at a time when, in the absence of separation between Church and State, Catholicism ruled. In fact, the First Vatican Council (1869–70) was soon to enshrine the dogma of papal infallibility. Consequently, to interpellate the Pope, casting aspersions on his lack of charity and love towards others, is almost heretical.

She intimates that his uncharitable stance is responsible for perpetuating the gross injustice of women's lack of access to education. In that vein, she compares upper-class Portuguese women to their Chinese counterparts, in an allusion to the practice of foot-binding. As for lower-class women, she points out that they are entirely at the service of their children and husband, and yet despised by them. A related argument, then, becomes that men themselves are dissatisfied with the current state of affairs as evidenced by their plentiful attacks on women for alleged faults. Here, she wittily piles up in a single sentence, for comic effect, a list of derogatory adjectives, 'vaidosas, frívolas, míopes, débeis, invejosas, traidoras, indolentes... que sei eu!' [vain, frivolous, short-sighted, weak, envious, treacherous, indolent... I don't know what else!], before dismissing it with the succinct statement that she is sick and tired of it: 'O catálogo é longo e a pena está cansada' (p. 1) [The list is long and my pen is exhausted]. She then cleverly turns the argument on its head, remarking that if women are as bad as they are generally painted, not much can be lost by giving them an opportunity. Her profound conviction is that they can only improve. In fact, she suggests that they will be cleansed of their previous flaws, flaws for which men are ultimately responsible according to her: 'limpas de todas as nódoas, de todas as máculas que hão recebido passando pelas mãos dos homens' (p. 2) [cleaned of all the stains, of all the taints with which they have been tarnished upon passing through the hands of men].

This enables her to outline an alternative to the Catholic Church, and wax lyrical about her vision for a church of peace, love, unity and solidarity in 'tempos vindoiros' [days to come], once women have had the full benefit of education. Wood's next argument is somewhat convoluted as, according to her, the French Education Minister, Duruy, was simply retrospectively redressing the injustice against multiple women who had suffered at the hands of men. Although the women alluded to — the ill-fated Marie Antoinette (1755–1793), Princess Lamballe (1749–1792), Madame Roland (1754–1793), Charlotte Corday (1768–1793), who was Marat's assassin, and Marie Sombreuil (1768–1823) — may seem a mixed bag, all were linked with the violent times of the French Revolution and celebrated for their courage and integrity. All, with the exception of the heroic Sombreuil, died at the guillotine. Although the inclusion of Queen Marie Antoinette arguably weakens the argument, by rehabilitating women that she perceived as martyrs among 'tantíssimas outras que foram, por maneiras várias, vítimas do despotismo bárbaro de homens em quem não tinha ainda despontado a luz das ciências positivas e da filosofia moral que agora esclarece as suas decisões' [so many other women who were, in different ways, victims of the barbarous despotism of men on whom the light of the positive sciences and the moral philosophy that now enlightens their decisions had not yet dawned], Wood was urging the Pope, and by extension her readers, to move with the times, as the italicized French assertion '*Le monde marche*', confirms.[18] For good measure, she adds 'e as mulheres com ele' [The world is moving forward, and women with it].

She wraps up the editorial rather more convincingly, asserting that the clock cannot be turned back on the 'great cause' of women's rights:

> As mulheres francesas, meu Senhor, já não recuam, e se recuassem, nos domínios da preclara e virtuosíssima Rainha Vitória está recrutando-se uma coorte de denodadas senhoras que capitaneadas por alguns dos espíritos varonis mais ilustres do nosso século, caminha a glorioso triunfo; e debaixo dos seus estandartes que as brisas dos céus afagam, caminhará, enquanto a sua causa for a da paz e de justiça universal, esta ínfima e humilde portuguesa. (p. 2)

> [French women, my Lord, do not retreat, and even if they were to do so, in the realms of the distinguished and virtuous Queen Victoria, there is a cohort of intrepid women being recruited who, led by some of the most brilliant male minds of our century, are marching towards triumphant glory; and under their banners which the sky's breeze caresses, for as long as their cause be that of peace and universal justice, this insignificant and humble Portuguese woman will march with them.]

Thus, even if French women were to backtrack, British ladies will stand resolute, thanks to the support of their male peers. At this point, having seamlessly moved from educational matters to suffrage, Wood is implicitly contrasting the attitude of British men, described as having brilliant minds, with that of the backward Pope, unflatteringly labelled as an 'ancião belicoso' (p. 2) [pugnacious old man] a couple of paragraphs earlier.[19] The backdrop to her comments would have been self-evident to some of her readers at least: in Britain, in advance of the second Reform Bill in 1867, John Stuart Mill had presented to Parliament a petition in favour of female suffrage. Orchestrated by Barbara Bodichon, it collected 1499 signatures in the space of just a fortnight. Although women did not then win the vote, it was only the beginning of a campaign that would result in the first tranche of British women securing suffrage rights in 1918.

Furthermore, the political enfranchisement of women, presented as the cause of progress (a word never actually used in this editorial), is described as a transnational movement, giving it stronger credibility in practice. Over a rousing five-line long final sentence, Wood employs emotive poetic language ('as brisas dos céus afagam' [the sky's breezes caress]), and the use of the future 'caminhará' [will march] to show her determination to join the transnational movement for female emancipation, even if she, a Portuguese woman, remains isolated for the time being. In practice, in the light of the growing number of women across Europe adhering to the cause, her current insignificance ('ínfima e humilde' [insignificant and humble]) functioned as yet another factor of persuasion to convince her readership of the legitimacy of feminist claims, since it implied that Portugal's intellectual backwardness was in urgent need of remedy. Through a combination of rational argument and rhetoric, then, she clearly hoped to persuade her readers — Portuguese women and men — to support what she held up as the cause of peace and universal justice.

Letter to Emilio Castelar

It is Wood's unwavering belief in the transnational cause of women's rights that leads her, a mere four weeks later, to address an open letter the revolutionary Spanish leader Emilio Castelar ('Carta ao digno deputado a Cortes o Il.mo Sr. D. Emílio Castelar' [Letter to the worthy delegate to Parliament, the Honourable Mr. Emílio Castelar], *VF*, 72: 1–2). The periodical reacted at various points to democratic developments in neighbouring Spain, following the dethronement of Isabel II in September 1868 and the ensuing proclamation of the First Republic. This time, Wood's strategic open letter to a man in high office stems from the conviction that Castelar is a potential ally:

> Eu sei que há de haver no país de V. S.ª, e no meu, quem me censure por causa desta carta, ou mais bem da *quimera* sobre a qual ela versa. Está isso no curso natural do progresso; mas também o está que os séculos façam justiça a quem de um modo ou de outro labuta dedicando-se ao melhoramento da sociedade, e ao esclarecimento da justiça e da verdade. [...] Os séculos [...] hão levantado Espinosa da abjeção em que os homens no seu tempo o haviam lançado. (p. 1)

> [I know that there will be people, in your country as much as in mine, who would criticize me on account of this letter, or rather, on account of the *chimera* it discusses. This is a natural part of the course of progress; but so too it is that the centuries should do justice to whoever has, in one way or another, fought, dedicating themselves to the betterment of society and to the enlightenment of justice and truth. [...] The centuries [...] have raised Spinoza from the abjection into which the men of his own time had cast him.]

Quite apart from the allusion to Spinoza, a symbol of religious dissidence, Wood goes on to refer to other visionaries and/or nonconformists who generated controversy in their lifetime, such as Socrates, Columbus, Molière and Harvey, in order to underscore the fact that the passage of time had vindicated such pioneers. Only then does she fully explain that the *chimera* she dreams of concerns the situation of women:

> Mas sr. D. Emilio Castelar, V. S.ª que é na Europa o verdadeiro campeão da liberdade não sofismada por dogmas e erros vetustos; V. S.ª preclaro filho dessa gloriosa Espanha que surgiu das cinzas da morte política linda como a *fenix* para dar às nações da terra o exemplo sem procedente de uma revolução, na qual (excetuando a clerezia, sempre adversa ao progresso do racionalismo) as paixões e o antagonismo individual hão cedido o predomínio ao sentimento

do bem da pátria; V. S.ª que sabe por experiência própria o que é ser oprimido, menoscabado, vituperado, e perversamente interpretado, não pode deixar de simpatizar com os anelos da alma de uma mulher por ver o seu sexo elevado da abjeção moral em que jaz, à categoria de entes cogitativos e inteligentes, e à fruição de todas as regalias políticas, como uma metade da humanidade, importante pela missão que o criador lhe confiou. (p. 1)

[But you, Mr Emilio Castelar, my good Sir, who, in Europe, are the true champion of a liberty not swathed in sophistry, dogmas and time-worn errors; You, distinguished son of that glorious Spain which rose from the ashes of political death, beautiful as a *phoenix*, to bring the earth's nations an unprecedented example of a revolution in which (with the exception of the clergy, always resistant to the progress of rationalism) passions and individual antagonism have given way to the good of the country; You, knowing from personal experience what it means to be oppressed, slighted, decried and wantonly misunderstood, must surely sympathize with the aspirations lodged in the soul of a woman, to see her sex raised from the moral abjection in which it lies, to the category of thinking and intelligent beings, and to the enjoyment of all political privileges, as half of humanity, important on account of the mission with which its creator entrusted it.]

This highly rhetorical ten-line sentence addresses Castelar as the true champion of freedom in a born-again democratic Spain. She includes keywords like 'progresso do racionalismo' [the progress of rationalism] and 'bem da pátria' [the good of the country] and, in order to win over her interlocutor, reminds him of his own past trials and tribulations, before mentioning women's aspirations to be regarded as 'entes cogitativos e inteligentes' [thinking and intelligent beings] and by the same token to enjoy 'todas as regalias políticas' [all political privileges].

Although Wood is introducing the vexed question of the vote, before pursuing further the topic of women as intellectual equals, her next paragraph expands over a six-line sentence on women's mission as mothers in a bid to enlist the sympathy of her addressee: 'Esta missão, meu senhor, é a de tutelar o desenvolvimento moral da infância' (p. 1) [This mission, good sir, is to guide children's moral development]. Only then does she allude to progress being made elsewhere so that, by the time she broaches the question of equality, it can be couched as a matter of unjustly withheld political rights:

V. S.ª por certo não é daqueles que disputam à mulher o dote da inteligência! Não é possível à vista das provas que as americanas e as inglesas estão dando ao mundo de uma intelectualidade tão vasta e tão rigorosa; à vista dessa lide renhida que as súbditas de Sua Majestade Britânica estão mantendo contra aqueles que lhes negam os seus direitos políticos; à vista desse movimento do sexo, desperto do seu longo sono, que se faz sentir em toda a Europa. (p. 2)

[My Good Sir, you are surely not one of those men who deny women the gift of intelligence! It is not possible, given the proof which American and English women are providing to the world of such vast and rigorous intellectual thinking; given the fierce struggle that the subjects of Her Britannic Majesty are waging against those who deny them their political rights; given that movement of the fair sex which, awoken from a long slumber, is making itself known all across Europe.]

Wood's plea is furthermore shrewdly interspersed with a paragraph that pre-empts potential opposition, with the argument that women's mission as mothers and housewives, while it demands the public elevation of their status, in practice should also serve to allay overblown fears of ensuing social disorder:

> Tão pouco é possível que D. Emilio Castelar seja um desses homens que supõem a mulher ilustrada, a mulher elevada à dignidade que lhe compete, à fruição de regalias civis e de direitos políticos, capaz de abandonar o seu lar doméstico, e os seus deveres de mãe e de dona de casa. (p. 2)

> [Nor could you, Mr Emilio Castelar, be one of those men who think that the enlightened woman, the woman who is raised up to the dignity which befits her, to the enjoyment of civil privileges and political rights, might be capable of abandoning hearth and home, and her responsibilities as a mother and housewife.]

This logically leads her to ask the Republican leader for women to be included in the democratic widening of political rights, evoked here under the banner of the famous French revolutionary slogan, thereby demonstrating that Wood was fully aware that the recent Spanish Constitution of 1869 had enshrined the principle of universal male suffrage:

> Apelo, pois, à grandiosidade do seu espírito, ao seu amor da justiça imparcial e universal; apelo em nome do meu sexo para que sejamos incluídas nesse brado de 'liberdade, fraternidade e igualdade' com que V. S.ª fechou o seu memorável discurso de 12 de abril último. (p. 2)

> [I therefore call on your greatness of spirit, on your love of impartial and universal justice; I call on you, in the name of my sex, that we be included in that cry for 'liberty, fraternity and equality' with which you ended your memorable speech on 12th April past.]

Castelar's famous speech on religious freedom and the separation between Church and State made his name in Spain and further afield and was swiftly reported in the Portuguese press too.[20] What is quite remarkable, however, is that Wood saw it for what it was: a watershed moment in nineteenth-century politics. She concluded by explicitly urging Castelar to make history, by being the first to grant women equal rights: 'levante V. S.ª também a voz como apóstolo da manumissão da mulher, e que seja a nobre Espanha a primeira nação da terra a proclamar um princípio de igualdade sem reserva' (p. 2) [make your voice heard, good sir, as an apostle for the manumission of women, and let noble Spain be the first nation on the Earth to proclaim the principle of equality without reservation]. The use of the term 'manumissão' [manumission] is perhaps not innocent here, since slavery was still operational in Cuba at the time and Castelar was known to be an abolitionist.[21]

Above all, Wood was quick to seize a historically unique opportunity to campaign on behalf of women's political rights, by the most obvious means at her disposal: a petition in the press addressed to an influential and potentially sympathetic interlocutor. Needless to say, the intention was also to draw the attention of her readership to the controversial theme of political equality for women in the Portuguese context as well. Reading between the lines, the aim was to give her readers food for thought when confronted with the gap between 'progressive' Spain and 'backward' Portugal, since this technique of spotlighting backwardness was one that Wood had exploited in her previous open letters. It is not known if Wood's open letter reached Castelar.[22] In a newly republican Spain in the throes of political change, the battle for female suffrage would have been too divisive to be entertained. The Spanish Republic fell in 1874, too soon to see any legal change. Accordingly, Spanish and Portuguese women were only granted the vote half a century later, in 1931, and in the latter case with significant restrictions based on educational level. This timeline demonstrates how exceptionally trail-blazing Wood's activism was in the context of 1860s Portugal.

Backlash in *Bem Público*

Needless to say, the contentious ideas so vocally espoused in *A Voz Feminina* triggered a backlash, in particular in the periodical *Bem Público*. Its campaign against *A Voz Feminina* was sustained over nearly two years: in 1868 it published seven unsigned articles characterized by attacks either on Wood herself or contributions by others; the following year, there were another eleven, also unsigned.[23] Most employed violent and aggressive language, including references to Wood's periodical as a 'folha hermafrodita' [hermaphrodite paper].[24] The reaction to the closure of *O Progresso* in yet another diatribe, on 22 January 1870, may suffice to illustrate the general tone: 'Os seus lábios são apenas órgãos de inépcias, e de prosas rococó, onde o barbarismo dos conceitos está em perfeita harmonia com o barbarismo das palavras' [Its lips are merely an organ for ineptitude, and for extravagant prose in which the barbarity of its concepts is in perfect harmony with the barbarity of its language].[25] Wood's ideas were thus de-authorized on the grounds of both form and content, as Valada poked fun at the foreign turns of phrase that crept in, linking them in the same sentence to heterodox thought ('barbarismo dos conceitos' [barbarity of concepts]).

It is worth delving further into one article in particular, titled 'A Livre pensadora' [The free-thinking woman] in what was clearly intended to be a denunciation. It offers a virulent response to the article that Wood had addressed to the Pope. Indeed, in the main body of the article, the fact that she was openly accused of possessing an 'espírito maçónico' [a spirit of Freemasonry] bears this charge out.[26] The accusation may not have been unfounded since Wood's list included Princess Lamballe, a figure who presided over the Lodge of the Social Contract before becoming Grand Mistress of all of the Lodges of Adoption in France, not to mention her allusion to Pelletan, who was also a Freemason. The unnamed author of 'A Livre pensadora' contemptuously suggests that Wood might wish to read the biographies of the '*matronas* livre-pensadoras que vão acima nomeadas' (p. 363) [aforementioned free-thinking *matrons*], thereby de-authorizing learned women as unfeminine. The women he had listed were Ninon de Lenclos, Mme du Châtelet, Deffand, d'Epinay and Roland. This is, of course, an entirely misguided argument: while the anonymous author enumerates these names to bolster his argument that the Pope was entirely justified in preventing women from gaining access to higher education, today they are remembered as early modern intellectuals and/or forward-thinking activists. For instance, the earlier Ninon de Lenclos (1620–1705), Voltaire's friend Mme du Châtelet (1706–1749), as well as Deffand (1697–1780) and d'Epinay (1726–1783) were all celebrated for their learning, while the eighteenth-century politically active *salonnière* Mme Roland (1754–1793) is linked with the Age of Enlightenment. A victim of the French Revolution, celebrated for her posthumously published memoirs titled *Appel à l'impartiale postérité* [Appeal to impartial posterity], Roland was in fact the only writer on Valada's list also named by Wood in her address to the Pope.

It is worth dwelling briefly on the question of female Freemasonry, for it was highly topical in 1860s Portugal. Oliveira Marques's dictionary lists 'Direito e Razão' as the first adoptive lodge, in Portugal, established in Lisbon in the first semester of 1864, with nineteen 'workers'.[27] It is conceivable that Wood was one of them, bearing in mind at least two documented links with Freemasons, the first of which was her favourite nephew, Clarimundo Martins, to whom she dedicated her novel *Maria Severn* (1869). Indeed, an entry in the *History of the Essex Lodge of Free Masons* by William Leavitt records that he went to Salem (Massachusetts, United States) in 1855 and was admitted to the Lodge on 7 August 1860.[28] The second confirmed contact with Freemasonry was the second Count of Parati, listed in *O Progresso* as having been one of its subscribers from the outset (['Ex.mas Sras e Srs. assinantes...'] *P*, 94: 179). Significantly, he was the Grand Master of Grande Oriente Lusitano between 1859 and 1869. A further reason to suspect Wood's allegiance to Freemasonry is the contents of the editorial she wrote in the immediate aftermath of Valada's article: his 'A Livre pensadora' was published on 22 May 1869, and only one week later, on 30 May 1869, Wood's editorial was the above-mentioned petition to Emilio Castelar. Her appeal to the Spanish leader may therefore be regarded as a covert yet defiant response to Valada, since Castelar was widely known to be a Freemason. In other words, by addressing him at this juncture, Wood was being doubly provocative.

On the other hand, it is perplexing that the putative leader of the first female Freemason lodge, Antónia Gertrudes Pusich,[29] herself a pioneering journalist, did not contribute to *A Voz Feminina* as one might perhaps have expected. In truth, the monarchist and Catholic Pusich was unlikely to have warmed to the anticlerical cause so openly espoused by Wood. By contrast, the latter was closely aligned with the ideological tenets of 'a futura geração de feministas... [que] acrescentará à questão de género a questão do anticlericalismo e do regime político' [the future generation of feminists [... that] will add to the question of gender the question of anticlericalism and the political regime].[30] Costa is here alluding to the next generation of feminist fighters, whose adherence to Freemasonry is well-documented, such as Adelaide Cabete (1867–1935), Ana de Castro Osório (1872–1935) and Carolina Beatriz Ângelo (1878–1911). Could it be that the annals of history may have failed to properly record some of the more controversial activities pursued by mid-nineteenth-century women, and even potentially mixed up the identities of the two most outspoken public intellectuals of the Regeneration, Pusich and Wood? Certainly, irrespective of the absence of Pusich from her paper, Wood's contacts with Portuguese Freemasons, as well as her intellectual engagement with a range of European figures past and present known to be Freemasons, fits in well with the fact that her periodical stands as an early instance of women's transnational political mobilization in Portugal.

Letter to Subscribers about the Closure of *O Progresso*

The unrelenting diatribes by the Marquês de Valada no doubt took their toll on Wood's paper and led to a dwindling readership. Six months after the attack published as 'A Livre pensadora', Wood gave advance notice to her subscribers, in yet another open letter, of the forthcoming demise of the paper. The only other time previously that she had used an editorial to communicate with her audience in such a fashion was also a momentous occasion, when, nearly five months earlier, she had broken the news of the imminent change of title from *A Voz Feminina* to *O Progresso* ('Aos Il.mos e às Ex.mas assinantes da "Voz Feminina"', *VF*, 74, pp. 1–2). In this later address to her subscribers, she does not mince her words:

> As senhoras neste país, salvo uma pequeníssima e honrosa fracção, não sabem e não querem saber que a mulher é, pela sua qualidade de ente racional e cogitativo, intitulada a todas as regalias e privilégios que a outra metade da humanidade se há até agora arrogado como de seu direito exclusivo. Assim pois um assunto calorosamente discutido em França e em Inglaterra, estabelecido como princípio inconvertível na América do Norte, e tacitamente admitido na Alemanha, na Suíça, e mesmo na Rússia, aqui não tem tido outro efeito que o de evocar uma corrente de oposição indireta e clandestina. A discussão aberta e franca é um dos meios mais eficazes de aquilatar o mérito de qualquer assunto. Mas nunca um só lidador se apresentou desassombradamente na arena. (*P*, 94: 179)

> [The ladies in this country, except for a very small and honourable fraction, do not know and do not wish to know that because of her quality of rational and thinking being, woman is entitled to the prerogatives and privileges that the other half of the human race has hitherto arrogated to themselves as their exclusive right. Thus, a matter passionately discussed in France and in England, established as an undeniable principle in North America, and tacitly acknowledged in Germany, Switzerland and even in Russia, has had no effect here other than to elicit a wave of indirect and covert opposition. Frank and open discussion is one of the most effective means of measuring the value of any matter. But not a single fighter has ever stepped openly into the arena.]

She is specific:

> [...]. Um antagonismo cruel e quase incrível, mas à surdina, da parte das senhoras; um silêncio hostil da parte dos literatos; uma oposição acérrima das cabeças tonsuradas são os elementos gélidos e desalentadores que me fazem recuar.

> [A cruel, almost unbelievable antagonism by stealth, on the part of ladies; the hostile silence of the men of letters; the fierce opposition of the tonsured heads; these are the icy and disheartening elements which make me retreat.]

Wood lucidly ascribed the untimely demise of *O Progresso* to a combination of reasons as she points the finger at a range of opponents: firstly, suspicious of progress and unprepared to fight for their rights, women have undermined her efforts by stealth, effectively leaving her *persona non grata* in the capital. Secondly, the indifference or hostility of men of letters ('literatos') has militated against change. Thirdly, and most damagingly, in the absence of support from any influential male public intellectuals or any mobilization on the part of women, the clergy was ultimately able to manipulate public opinion against her. However, she defiantly claimed that the predictable opposition of the Catholic Church would not be able to supress her name in the long run, despite — or precisely because of — its backward agenda, so glaringly out of step with the rest of Europe and North America:

> Não podem [...] impedir que o meu nome se ache arquivado como o da primeira mulher que neste país levantou a voz em prol dos direitos do seu sexo e contra o estado de abjeção moral e jurídica em que se acha metade do género humano. Não podem privar-me da honra, e, permita-se-me a expressão, da ufania de ter há dois anos apostolado esta santa e nobre causa unicamente *pelo amor* da causa.

> [They cannot [...] prevent my name from being recorded as that of the first woman who, in this country, spoke up for the rights of her sex and against the state of moral and legal abjection in which half of the human race lies. They cannot deprive me of the honour, and, let me be permitted the expression, the pride of having for two years preached this holy and noble cause solely *for the love* of the cause.]

Wood may not have been quite the first woman to speak up, but the extent of her engagement through the most public medium at her disposal — the periodical press — was certainly unprecedented in scope, reach, and indeed in longevity. It proved that she had the courage to act as a 'thinking woman'. She was clear not only about her personal convictions but indeed the legitimacy of 'the cause':

> Retiro-me, pois, do público português ... mas não deponho as armas. Vou reunir os meus esforços aos das minhas irmãs francesas e inglesas e com elas apostolizar a causa do meu sexo que não é a deste ou daquele país, mas essencialmente a do século XIX.

> [So I withdraw from the Portuguese public... but I do not lay down my arms. I will join my efforts with those of my French and British sisters and preach with them the cause of my sex, a cause that doesn't belong to this or that country, but is essentially that of the nineteenth century.]

The vocabulary used here is clearly feminist insofar as Wood considers herself part of an international sisterhood that enthusiastically embraced the crusade for 'the cause', a word repeated twice in the course of this editorial.

In the medium term, however, the erasure from cultural history of a formidable feminist thinker like her may have been compounded by the fact that, as Abranches persuasively argues, the ambivalence and deep-seated discomfort often elicited by British 'mestras' [governesses] — who by virtue of their education were in a position of intellectual authority in nineteenth-century Portugal — led to:

A necessidade sentida pelas feministas do período pré-republicano, em busca de legitimação, de estabelecerem uma clara distinção entre um feminismo 'falso' e um 'verdadeiro' [...] em grande parte resultante da importância da associação, no imaginário público, dos ideais feministas com representações de mulheres assexuadas, masculinas, desnaturadas — inglesas.[31]

[The need felt by the feminists of the pre-republican period, in search of legitimation, to establish a clear distinction between a 'false' feminism and a 'true' one [...] deriving largely from the importance of the association, in the public imagination, of feminist ideas with representations of asexual, masculine, unnatural women — Englishwomen.]

Moreover, in the aftermath of the British ultimatum of 1890, republicanism fed on Anglophobia, leaving the next generation of intellectuals and activists, such as Angelina Vidal (1853–1917), unable or unwilling to claim Wood as their foremother. In short, by the time that the likes of Cabete, Castro Osório and Ângelo embarked on the struggle to gain the vote once more, in the early twentieth century, Wood's intervention more than thirty years earlier had been wiped out from collective memory. If, as Owen and Pazos Alonso contend, 'the lack of access to neglected female forebears was clearly a material problem for women writers at the beginning of the [twentieth] century',[32] then perhaps it was even more so for activists, given that Wood's cutting-edge editorials were published in the ephemeral press and never reprinted. By contrast other voices were preserved in book-form, drowning out hers, most famously perhaps that of *As Farpas* as *Uma Campanha Alegre* in 1890–91. In practice then, Wood's contrary opinions were edited out from collective consciousness and therefore the history of ideas.

Conclusion

One hundred and fifty years on, cultural memory loss is worth interrogating, especially in order to probe further the power dynamics and logic surreptitiously at work behind mechanisms of exclusion. As Ana Paula Ferreira perceptively argues, the domestication of female otherness present 'within the margins of the nation in the figure of a wild, uncivilized [...] and, hence, foreign feminine body', entailed a variety of national(ist) discourses that attempted to pre-empt contamination by the New Woman, especially from the 1870s onwards.[33] No wonder then that Wood's 'female otherness' — her unorthodox intellectual dissidence which laid bare structural male privilege — was vilified and de-authorized by Valada as the 'improper' speech of a female 'foreigner' whose thought was deemed to be essentially deficient. A further twist in the tale is that the Marquês de Valada, the Editor in charge of *Bem Público*, was himself ridiculed one decade later for not conforming to the rigid gender norms he so desperately clung to: indeed, he is primarily remembered today for being outed as the protagonist of a homosexual scandal in 1881.[34] Retrospectively, this scandal makes his blanket condemnation of Wood's perceived transgression of gender roles seem at best misplaced, and at worst deeply ironic. But it also alerts us to the rigid enforcement of hetero-normative sexuality and its public policing.

Notwithstanding the disparagement Wood had to contend with, her spirited engagement through open letters with key men in positions of authority amply demonstrates her intellectual confidence in the public arena, as she places herself on an equal footing with them. The examples discussed in this chapter uncover the extent to which she boldly anticipated both the anticlerical stance that would feature on the agenda of the *Geração de 70* and the first-wave transnational feminism that self-evidently would not. Her active defence of animal welfare too suggests that she was well ahead of her time, since nearly two decades later the issue could still be ridiculed by Eça de Queirós in *Os Maias*. Yet, the latter was a cause far less controversial than the vexed question of women's rights, so it is hardly surprising that the Portuguese Society for the Protection of Animals got off the ground more than two decades before the first female-led association, the Portuguese League for Peace came into being, in 1899, headed by Alice Pestana. That Wood revealed herself ready to embrace the collective 'causa [...] da paz e de justiça universal' [cause [...] of peace and universal justice] a full thirty years before Pestana is nothing short of remarkable.

What was it that placed her so far ahead of her contemporaries, a true visionary able to bring into public view the intertwined strands of peace and feminist equality? The answer is that in the face of indifference or downright hostility at home, Wood realized that her most effective strategy in her campaign for women's rights was to showcase validation and support for her ideas from abroad, where the subject matter was being 'calorosamente discutido' [passionately discussed]. As such, the next chapter leaves to one side the anticlerical dimension of her political analysis, in order to focus more closely on how *A Voz Feminina* drew on the transnational circulation of ideas as part and parcel of the early emergence of first-wave feminism amplified by the press.

Notes to Chapter 5

1. Eça de Queirós, *O Primo Basílio* (Lisbon: Livros do Brasil, 1960), p. 11 and p. 450 respectively.
2. *A Nação* had been highly critical of the Casino Lectures, and Eça de Queirós had retaliated with an article in *As Farpas*.
3. *O Primo Basílio*, p. 108.
4. Cristo, *A Epistolaridade*, p. 103.
5. Hamlet, 'Editorials', p. 478.
6. Hamlet, p. 473. The advent of the internet is changing this.
7. In addition, she dialogues with colleagues in other papers. See for instance 'Escrito dedicado ao Il.mo Sr. J. T. Cardona, distinto folhetista da "Gazeta da Beira"' in no. 43, and 'Ao Il.mo Sr. J. T. Cardona' in no. 47, or 'A *Folha* (jornal de Coimbra)' in no. 52.
8. 'Os compadres calumniadores', *Bem Público*, p. 259. The periodical alluded to is likely to have been *A Aurora do Cávado*, from Barcelos.
9. Cristo, p. 77.
10. Cristo, p. 71.
11. Alice Moderno, an early campaigner usually credited as the first female activist in the Azores, was only born in 1867, so Wood's intervention pre-dates the latter's by a couple of decades.
12. According to: 'Quem somos', Sociedade Protectora dos Animais <https://spanimais.wixsite.com/spa-lisboa/quem-somos>.
13. Henriques, João Paulo, 'O pioneirismo protestante na génese de organizações universalistas em

Portugal', *Revista Lusófona de Ciência das Religiões*, 7-8 (2005), 97-107, p.105. <https://revistas. ulusofona.pt/index.php/cienciareligioes/article/view/4141>. Henriques stated that 'Em Lisboa, a SPA assumiria, em 1883, o pioneirismo na luta pela abolição das corridas de touros' [In Lisbon, the Society for the Protection of Animals would take on a pioneering role in the fight for the abolition of bullfighting in 1883'], without taking into account that Wood had forcefully initiated this debate in two of her editorials, nos. 89 and 90 ('As Toiradas', 26 September 1869, pp. 159-60 and 'As Toiradas', 3 October 1869, pp. 163-64). Similarly Afonso's *Protestantismo e educação* does not allude to the earlier pioneer intervention of Francisca Wood, although he highlights that the children's magazine *O Amigo da Infância*, a magazine also printed by Tip Luso-Britânica, fostered respect for animals.

14. *Os Maias*, p. 368.

15. *The Maias*, p. 370.

16. *O Zoophilo* published lists of names of members of the Society. Both Francisca and her husband paid subscriptions until 1882.

17. See Françoise Mayeur, 'Les Évêques français et Victor Duruy: les cours secondaires de jeunes filles', *Revue d'histoire de l'Église de France*, 159 (1971), pp. 267–304 <http://www.persee.fr/doc/ rhef_0300–9505_1971_num_57_159_1872>.

18. *Le monde marche* was the title of a book by the French Republican Eugène Pelletan, published in 1857.

19. The Pope was by then in his late seventies. See Ivor F. Burton and Douglas Woodruff, 'Pius IX: Pope', Encyclopædia Britannica, ed. by Adam Augustyn and others <https://www.britannica. com/biography/Pius-IX>.

20. Emilio Castelar, 'Discurso sobre la libertad religiosa y la separación entre la Iglesia y el Estado: (12-IV-69)', Biblioteca Virtual Miguel de Cervantes <http://www.cervantesvirtual.com/obra-visor/discurso-sobre-la-libertad-religiosa--0/html/feedc9c0–82b1–11df-acc7–002185ce6064_1. html#I_1_>.

21. Castelar would go down in history, among other reasons, for his role in bringing about abolition in Puerto Rico and Cuba, a cause he had first embraced in his 1859 book *La Redención del esclavo*.

22. There is evidence, however, that he wrote a short undated note to Guiomar Torresão, Wood's right-hand woman in *A Voz Feminina*, see *Trechos literários*, ed. by Felismina Torresão, p. 68.

23. In 1868: 275–77, 300–01, 307–09, 325, 331–33, 339–40, 378–79. In 1869: 236–37, 244–45, 259–61, 362–64, 391, 398–99 (first semester) and 19–20, 34–36, 49–50, 74–75, 107–08 (second semester). In addition, in 1868, there was a letter from a reader, J. A. da Graça Barreto, who wished to clarify that he was not the anonymous author of previous articles. See J. A. da Graça Barreto, ['.... sr. e amigo...'], *Bem Público*, 9 May 1868, pp. 348–49.

24. 'A Voz Feminina', *Bem Público*, 6 June 1868, p. 378.

25. ['Perguntam-nos algumas pessoas...'], *Bem Público*, 22 January 1870, p. 230.

26. 'A Livre Pensadora', *Bem Público*, 22 May 1869, pp. 362–64 (p. 363).

27. Marques, *Dicionário da maçonaria portuguesa*, I, 476–77.

28. William Leavitt, 'History of the Essex Lodge of Freemasons', in *The Historical Collections of the Essex Institute*, 4 vols (Salem, MA: G. M. Whipple & A. A. Smith, 1859–62), III (1861), 253–72 (p. 272) <http://dbooks.bodleian.ox.ac.uk/books/PDFs/555028439.pdf>.

29. Fernando Costa, *As Mulheres na maçonaria*, pp. 53–57.

30. Costa, p. 59.

31. Graça Abranches, 'Homens, mulheres e mestras inglesas', in *Entre ser e estar: raízes, percursos e discursos da identidade*, ed. by Maria Irene Ramalho and António Sousa Ribeiro (Porto: Afrontamento, 2002), pp. 255–305 (p. 282).

32. Owen and Pazos Alonso, *Antigone's Daughters?*, p. 208.

33. Ana Paula Ferreira, 'Nationalism and Feminism', p. 129.

34. See Robert Howes, 'Concerning the Eccentricities of the Marquis of Valada: Politics, Culture and Homosexuality in Fin-de-Siècle Portugal', *Sexualities*, 1 (2002), 25–48 and Fernando Curopos, *L'Emergence de l'homosexualité dans la littérature portugaise (1875–1915)* (Paris: L'Harmattan, 2016).

CHAPTER 6

Spreading the Word

The previous chapter detailed how Francisca Wood did not shy away from broaching divisive political issues: on the one hand, she presented a searing critique of the Catholic Church, and on the other, she aligned herself with the emerging Republican mood in neighbouring Spain. Both republicanism and anti-clericalism can be regarded as transnational causes. This chapter turns to a more detailed consideration of the contemporaneous emergence of another transnational movement, feminism, and its growing presence in her periodical.

As Käppeli indicates, across several countries 'la presse féministe trouve son troisième souffle à partir de 1868' [the feminist press finds its third wind from 1868 onwards], building on scattered instances in the 1830s and in the aftermath of 1848.[1] After noting the pioneering case of the *English Women's Journal* in Britain, Käppeli cites for 1868 the examples of Marie Goegg-Pouchoulin in Switzerland, Susan Anthony and Elizabeth Caddy Stanton in the US with *The Revolution*, as well as Anna Maria Mozzoni in Italy with *La Donna*; for the following year, she mentions Léon Ritcher in France with *Le Droit des femmes*.[2] What Käppeli's general overview does not consider is the extent to which the 'échanges d'expériences qui s'opèrent à travers la presse' [the exchange of experiences carried out via the press] also became relevant that the very same time in the Portuguese context, thanks to the launch in January 1868 of *A Voz Feminina*.[3]

Francisca Wood's long residence in England meant that she had been immersed in a culture of change, particularly when the fight for women's rights started to build momentum in Britain, from the 1850s onwards. In 1851 Harriet Taylor Mill published her influential 'Enfranchisement of Women' in the *Westminster Review*, a venue that was familiar to the Woods, as was discussed in Chapter 1.[4] Significantly, Wood was almost certainly still residing in England in 1857, when the Divorce Act, known officially as the Matrimonial Causes Act, was passed. To her mind this represented a landmark for women's rights and thus, when *A Voz Feminina* transcribed a news item sent in by a reader that detailed a real-life account of wife-selling, as reported in the British press, Wood promptly noted that the reader must have seen it in an old newspaper, since such practice had been outlawed in Britain since the Divorce Act of 1857 (G., Leonor, A., P., [pseud], *VF*, 5: 4 and [n.a.], *VF*, 5: 4).

After Wood's return to Portugal, the public visibility of the 'Woman Question' continued to grow in Britain throughout the 1860s. In 1866, Barbara Leigh Smith

Bodichon, who had set up the *English Women's Journal* in 1858 and was responsible for the first Women's Suffrage Committee, collected 1,499 signatures in favour of female suffrage within a fortnight, in advance of the second Reform Bill. The petition was presented to Parliament by John Stuart Mill, Harriet Taylor Mill's husband.[5] The Manchester Suffrage Committee, now often cited as a landmark for the start of the suffrage movement, was founded in February 1867. Its secretary was Lydia Becker, who was caricatured in a *Punch* cartoon on 30 March 1867 and again on 28 May 1870, proving how topical the Woman Question had become.[6]

The latter cartoon was chosen as our front cover in order to reflect the fact that, emboldened by her familiarity with the British context, Wood too pressed for change in pursuit of the elusive cause of emancipation, by aligning herself with leading suffragists across Europe and the US, as this chapter uncovers.

Border Crossings

The momentum building around the Woman Question in Britain may explain why, on Saturday 6 June 1868, an influential periodical, *The Athenaeum*, saw fit to register in its 'Weekly Gossip' column the following event:

> The Female Question is making strange progress. From a city so little likely to be stirred by sentiment as Lisbon we have received several numbers of a paper called *A Voz Feminina*, which is written by ladies and devoted to the cause of woman's emancipation. The chief editor is Madame Francisca De Assis Martins Wood, the Portuguese wife of an English gentleman. Space is given to fiction, poetry, musical history, and fashions; the latter being described in French. *A Voz Feminina* would be useful to persons who are studying Portuguese.[7]

Such a context may help to explain not only what led a high-profile Victorian title to register the appearance of a periodical written in Portuguese, but moreover, why, in the footsteps of the *The Athenaeum*, this news item was widely featured in the regional press in what might be regarded as an early equivalent of modern-day retweeting. As the table below summarizes, within less than ten days, more than a dozen papers across the British Isles, from Bristol to Tipperary in Ireland, had duly transcribed the *Athenaeum* article:

Monday, 8 June 1868
    — *Dundee Courier*, Angus, Scotland
    — *Birmingham Daily Post*, Birmingham
Tuesday, 9 June 1868
    — *Western Daily Press*, Bristol
Wednesday, 10 June 1868
    — *Liverpool Mercury*, Liverpool (repeated on 12 June)
Thursday, 11 June 1868
    — *Hull and Eastern Counties Herald*, Yorkshire
Friday, 12 June 1868
    — *Newcastle Courant*, Tyne and Wear
    — *Tipperary Vindicator*, Tipperary, Ireland
Saturday, 13 June 1868
    — *Sheffield Daily Telegraph*, South Yorkshire

— *Lancaster Gazette*, Lancashire
— *Leicester Chronicle*, Leicestershire
— *Birmingham Journal*, Birmingham
— *Tower Hamlets Independent*, London
— *Kentish Mercury*, London
— *Berkshire Chronicle*, Reading
— *Manchester Times*, Manchester

Saturday, 11 July 1868
— *Pall Mall Gazette*, London

Tuesday, 14 July 1868
— *Southern Reporter and Cork Commercial Courier*, Ireland

Furthermore, the *Athenaeum* snippet was also reproduced in the US less than three weeks later, specifically in the New York feminist weekly *The Revolution*: firstly, under the heading 'What women are doing and have done', on 25 June 1868, citing *The Athenaeum* as its source; and again under the title 'Portugal Reached', on 9 July 1868.[8] A periodical launched in 1868 by the well-known American feminist activists, Susan Anthony and Elizabeth Caddy Stanton (1815–1902), '*The Revolution* considered it important to publicize and document women's entrance into new fields and project a sense of women's history', something that *A Voz Feminina* also attempted on a more modest scale.[9] Indeed, as Kramarae and Rakow go on to explain:

> we can see *The Revolution* not simply in terms of its use as a tool by Anthony and Stanton to advance their own cause of women's suffrage, but also in the web of its interconnections with other periodicals, women's organisations, women's parlour or 'picnic' discussion groups, readers and writers, and other means of communicating used by women.

This 'web of interconnections' was not only national but also international, or rather transnational, crossing and even repudiating national boundaries.[10]

Although *A Voz Feminina* was identified as part of that transnational web, surprisingly, the extent to which Wood's attempt to disseminate progressive ideas concerning the rights of women to a nationwide Portuguese audience may have been informed by a transnational background has not yet been properly examined. This is what this chapter seeks to do, primarily through an analysis of Wood's evolving strategies. In the first year of the periodical's life, she orchestrates a lively debate through editorials, which foreground to her national imagined community of readers echoes of what is going on in other countries. In the second year, her campaign for female emancipation is boosted by the publication of correspondence received from abroad (England, France, Switzerland and even the USA) and dedicated articles such as the series 'As senhoras inglesas e o direito eleitoral' [English women and the right to vote] and a newly created rubric 'O que se faz lá fora' [What is happening abroad]. At various junctures she cleverly played with design and layout, in order to emphasize the overarching message of her crusade for parity, which the motto 'a mulher livre ao lado do homem livre' [the free woman beside the free man] so synthetically encapsulated.

Female Suffrage through Portuguese Eyes

1868 — Discussion through editorials

Familiarity with what *The Athenaeum* referred to as 'the Female Question' in Britain was key to *A Voz Feminina*. A salient aspect of *A Voz Feminina* is that the main contributors addressed each other directly in order to engage in intellectual debate. In this respect, the periodical provided a public yet safe space in which they could formulate their ideological positions, not least with regard to contested progressive ideologies, one of the most topical being whether women should have political rights.

As is often the case in the ephemeral press, many contributors had only a fleeting presence, even though Wood took care to encourage every reader who wrote in. She excelled at gently coaxing contributions out of them, and did so successfully in several cases. A particularly telling instance was that of Amália Cândida Isabel da Costa. The Coimbra-based Costa initially sent in a letter in no. 17 (*VF*, 17: 4) and was encouraged by Wood to share some of her compositions: a poem of hers was duly published in no. 19 ('Nem sempre', *VF*, 19: 4) alongside further correspondence (['Ex.ma Sr.ª Redatora...'] *VF*, 19: 4). Rather more unprecedented is the fact that she was then given the editorial slot in no. 22 (*VF*, 22: 1). In a well-written and forcefully argued opinion article, she revealed her familiarity with John Stuart Mill's progressive ideas but, nonetheless, argued cogently that women should not seek political rights. It is worth recalling that the reference to Stuart Mill must be understood specifically in the context of the 1866 petition in favour of female suffrage, since *The Subjection of Women* would only be published the following year.

Costa's article sparked off a range of responses. Fraser, Green and Johnston comment that the 'journalism of the periodical press was a fundamentally provocative and reactive medium, initiating dialogue on topics of the day, and demanding a response'.[11] This was certainly the case in this instance, as a heated debate on the topic ensued over the next few months. Mariana Angélica de Andrade penned the next editorial (*VF*, 23: 1) where she effectively concurred with Isabel da Costa's position, by defending the right of women to education while remaining silent on the subject of female engagement in the political arena, as was discussed in Chapter 3. In no. 24, a male contributor, F. A. de Matos (*VF*, 24: 1), called for women's emancipation. But since he argued that the courts, parliament and battlefields should remain an exclusively masculine prerogative, what he had in mind was primarily intellectual emancipation.

By contrast, the following week, Francisca's husband, William Wood argued passionately for actual political rights for women in an editorial titled 'Artigo dedicado às Ex.mas Sras D. M. A. de Andrade e D. A. I. da Costa, por um zeloso advogado da causa do sexo feminino' [Article dedicated to the ladies M. A. de Andrade and A. I. da Costa, by a zealous champion of the cause of the female sex] (*VF*, 25: 1–2). He explicitly praised:

> Homens sensatos, tais como Mr Stuart Mill, que creem dever a mulher exercer
> em toda a amplura da esfera pública, a influência a que as suas faculdades inatas

são adaptadas; que desejam vê-la analisar os grandes tópicos do bem e do mal público; enfim, lançar o peso da sua influência moral e intelectual na balança da justiça. (p. 1)

[Sensible men like Mr Stuart Mill who believe that a woman should exercise, in all the breadth of the public sphere, the influence to which her innate faculties are well adapted; who wish to see her analyse the great topics of public good and evil; in short throw the weight of her moral and intellectual influence onto the scales of justice]

This is arguably one of the most significant debates in the pages of the periodical and it is important to read it sequentially as the texts are dialogical: we cannot fail to notice that we do not hear from Isabel da Costa again, even though it had been the publication of her editorial that had brought a highly contentious issue into the open. Over the next few weeks, after Andrade maintained her position — 'mulher política! Deus me livre de tal' [political woman! God preserve me from the like] (*VF*, 30: 1) — the debate shifted to the need for female education, something all the main contributors could agree on: for instance, a piece by F. A. de Matos (*VF*, 32: 1) was followed by several editorials by Francisca Wood on the matter. But the genie was out of the bottle and the subject of women in politics did not go away. In September 1868, Francisca Wood herself brought it back, foregrounding English women's crusades in favour of the vote:

Num distrito ao noroeste de Inglaterra mil e cem senhoras, entre as quais se acham os nomes de Lady Elizabeth Drummond, da Sra. Berkley [*sic*] e de outras pessoas de distinção, requereram ser admitidas na lista de eleitores para Manchester, alegando que se achavam legalmente qualificadas, pois que como donas de casa e proprietárias contribuem para o estado. Noutros condados as senhoras hão reclamado os mesmos direitos, e nalguns já as autoridades civis das paróquias as têm admitido nas listas de eleitores. (*VF*, 35, 'Declaração': 1)[12]

[In an area of north-west England 1100 ladies, among whom one finds the names of Lady Elizabeth Drummond, Mrs Berkley [*sic*] and other distinguished ladies, demanded to be admitted to the electoral roll for Manchester, claiming that they were legally qualified since as heads of house and property owners they contributed to the state. In other counties, women have demanded similar rights, and in some the civil authorities in the parishes have now accepted them on the list of voters.]

Four weeks later, in no. 39, in her first thorough discussion of the thorny question of women's suffrage, in an editorial to which she assigned the extraordinary title 'Delírio Rábido-Político' (*VF*, 39: 1–2) [Rabid-Political Delirium], Francisca Wood presented herself as comparatively moderate, by initially distancing herself from the excesses of a speech in Chicago, where the idea of a new government led by women was mooted, and condemning its 'radicalismo rábido' [rabid radicalism].[13] A *volta*, however, occurs halfway through:

Mas encare-se esta questão com sensatez, e sem os estremecimentos nervosos e contorções espasmódicas que atacam algumas senhoras e senhores quando se fala de mulher política. (*VF*, 39: 1)

[But let us deal sensibly with this matter, without the nervous tremors and muscle spasms that beset some ladies and gentlemen when the political woman is mentioned.]

The irony here is that the hysterical reaction, comically conjured up by the image of nervous tremors and muscle spasms, affects men and women equally. The subtext is that men become irrational whenever women's political rights are discussed. By contrast, Wood fashions herself as the voice of common sense [*sensatez*]:

Entenda-se que a mulher investida com direitos políticos iguais aos do homem, não está por isso obrigada a deixar a sua casa e a sua família aos ratos, para ir exercer cargos que mesmo poucos homens exercem. Dêem-se a pena, minhas senhoras e senhores, de fazer o cálculo seguinte. De três milhões de habitantes que se aninham no seio da nossa pátria, quantos são os senadores; quantos os juízes; quantos os ministros de estado; quantos enfim os homens que exercem esses cargos públicos a que a mulher se crê impelida, arrastada, no momento em que se lhe fala de ser mulher política? Talvez não chegue a mil pessoas. (pp. 1–2)

[Let it be understood that the woman invested with political rights equal to those of men, is not for this reason obliged to leave her house and her family to fall into rack and ruin, in order to go and carry out functions that few men indeed carry out. Take the trouble, my ladies and gentlemen, to make the following calculation. Out of three million inhabitants who nestle in the heart of our country, how many are senators, how many are judges, how many are ministers of state, how many men, in a nutshell, carry out these public duties to which women believe they are driven, dragged, as soon as they hear about being a political woman? It probably does not amount to one thousand people.]

Here she is adducing statistical evidence in order to prove that the likelihood of women taking up political office is entirely negligible (less than 1000 in 3 million). Furthermore, she hypothesizes about the worst case scenario, to show that in practice little would change:

Suponhamos que a gentil leitora que agora tem a nossa folha debaixo dos olhos se achava amanhã, ao despertar, emancipada da sua atual menoridade; que se achava revestida do direito de mandar o seu voto à urna; de agir nos diferentes atos e cenas da vida pública como seu marido, ou como seu irmão. Dedicar-se-ia, a minha leitora, com menos sossego à sua família, ou ao remanso do seu *crochet*? Por certo que não. O *direito* não envolve *obrigação*. Os milheiros de mecânicos, artífices, artistas, negociantes; homens enfim de todas as classes que vivem e morrem sem nunca terem tomado parte nos misteres da vida pública, gozam contudo, direitos políticos como qualquer representante da nação. (p. 2, italics in the original)

[Let us imagine that the gracious lady reader who now has our news sheet beneath her eyes found herself tomorrow, on awakening, emancipated from her current status as a minor; that she found she had acquired the right to cast her vote in the urn; to act in different events and scenes of public life like her husband, or like her brother. Would my dear reader devote herself less calmly to her family, or to the peace and quiet of her *crochet*? Surely not. The *right* does not involve *obligation*. The thousands of mechanics, craftsmen, artists, traders, indeed men of all walks of life that live and die without ever having taken part in the occupations of public life, nevertheless enjoy political rights like any representative of the nation.]

By distinguishing between right and obligation, italicized in the original to throw the difference into relief, Wood is laying to rest fears about women suddenly flooding the public arena. To drive home the point that potential breakdown of social organization is an unlikely scenario, she follows it up with a further paragraph that is even more explicit:

> Repetimos, pois, que queremos a mulher investida com todos os direitos políticos e legais, como membro da humanidade que constitui as nações da terra; mas queremos também que assim resgatada da sua ignominiosa menori-dade; que assim moralmente engrandecida, dê a primeira prova da sua super-ioridade moral, rejeitando com desprezo essas pretensões insensatas da mulher que, não cognoscente da honrosa missão a que o Criador a destinou, do imenso, incalculável bem que pode fazer sem ultrapassar os umbrais da sua morada, quer arrojar-se a arena pública para ali evocar as risadas mofadoras do mundo sensato, ostentando a sua inópia numa órbita a que não é destinada. (p. 2)

> [We repeat, then, that we want woman to be vested with all the political and legal rights, as a member of the humanity that makes up the nations of the earth. But we also want her thus rescued from her ignominious status as a minor, thus morally aggrandized, to give the first proof of her moral superiority, by rejecting with contempt those foolish pretensions of the woman who, unaware of the honourable mission for which the Creator has destined her, of the immense, incalculable good she can do without setting foot over the threshold of her home, wishes to hurl herself into the public arena, there prompting the mocking laughter of the sensible people, by parading her inadequacy in a sphere for which she is not destined.]

On the one hand, Wood is calling for female emancipation from shameful minority (the word 'menoridade' is repeated twice in the course of this piece and may be an allusion to Kant) but on the other hand she contrasts the unwise pretensions of American women cited at the beginning of the article with the proper femininity of Portuguese ones. This is an early iteration of the contrast between 'false' feminism and a 'true' one which would run through Portuguese first-wave feminism. According to Wood, the Portuguese woman will continue to honour the 'missão a que o Criador a destinou' [mission for which the Creator has destined her], rather than join 'uma órbita a que não é destinada' [a sphere for which she is not destined]. The repetition of the word 'destined' is interesting here, as Wood is making the supposition of an ongoing natural difference between male and female roles. According to her, then, women should have the same rights as men, but paradoxically with the reassurance that in practice natural(ized) structures of power would remain unchanged, since they were hardly likely to aspire to political office.

The disagreement continued to occupy the front pages: a further editorial by Andrade (*VF*, 41: 1–2) brought Guiomar Torresão into the debate, as mentioned in Chapter 3, paving the way for further airing of progressive views. Torresão devoted her first editorial, on 1 November 1868, to a forceful defence of women's intellectual ability and their right to equality, citing the ongoing parliamentary debate in England about women's right to vote, specifically in connection with women who were the head of their family (*VF*, 42: 1–2). Torresão followed up on this matter a few weeks later in her editorial of 20 December 1868, where she explicitly alluded to Lydia Becker and her bid to collect signatures to revise the law so as to allow women to vote (*VF*, 49: 1–2). Clearly Torresão had had access to the British press through Wood, as she herself indicated in her article.

In short, the periodical showcases a clever strategy on the part of the Editor, in a bid to keep the 'Woman Question' at the forefront of her readers' minds: she proposes editorials penned by a variety of trusted contributors, including men, to give critical mass and ongoing visibility to the debate. Given the diversity of the positions defended, the periodical showcases not only women's ability to engage in reasoned debate but also their democratic right to disagree with each other.

1869 — Building transnational alliances

Wood's concerted effort to document for her readers what was going on elsewhere in Europe, particularly England, seemed to have become a strategy of choice to legitimize her ongoing commitment to free Portuguese women from the shackles of tradition, by educating them and raising their aspirations. On 31 January 1869, in a radical departure from the usual four-page format of *A Voz Feminina*, the issue was increased to six pages. There is palpable excitement in Guiomar Torresão's editorial, 'A Imprensa', as she waxes lyrical about the circulation of ideas through the press and its civilizational impact, until the reason is finally revealed at the end: Francisca Wood has been contacted by Marie Goegg (1826–1899), an early Swiss feminist, who was the founder of the first-ever international association of women.[14] Wood must have realized straightaway the symbolic importance of the fact that Goegg had reached out to her, since she decided to extend the usual format to a six-page issue (no doubt with associated printing costs) in order to reproduce in full the contents of the letter addressed to her, and more importantly, the speech delivered by Goegg to the Second Congress of the League for Peace and Freedom on 26 September 1868, in her role as President of the newly created International Association of Women (Goegg, *VF*, 55: 2–3).[15] The speech highlighted the League's unanimous support of equal rights for women:

> O Congresso reconhece, como princípio, que todos os direitos humanos, económicos, civis, sociais e políticos, pertencem à mulher, e decide estudar os meios mais apropriados a aproximar a época em que ela possa gozar pleno uso desses direitos. (p. 3)

> [The Congress recognizes, as a principle, that all human rights, be they economic, civic, social or political, belong to women, and decides to study the most appropriate means to bring closer the time where they may enjoy full use of those rights.]

This serendipitous contact was a welcome boost for Wood, fully vindicating the fact that four weeks earlier the motto of her paper, proudly displayed in the header, had become 'a mulher livre ao lado do homem livre' [the free woman beside the free man]. As for the explanation of how Wood's endeavours had come to the attention of the Swiss feminist in the first place, Goegg's letter revealed that she had been given Wood's contacts by Lydia Becker (p. 2) — a fact which therefore suggests that the latter two were already in epistolary contact.

The following month, Wood penned a series of three articles under the title 'As senhoras inglesas e o direito eleitoral' [English women and the right to vote], published in three consecutive issues from 24 February 1869 onwards (nos. 58–60). The first piece began by tracing a dismal portrayal of women's subjugation until the 'forever memorable' Divorce Act of 28 August 1857 (known as the Matrimonial Causes Act). As was mentioned in Chapter 1, mistreatment included lawful wife-beating and wife-selling, as the law authorized 'o marido a lançar uma corda ao pescoço da mulher e levá-la à venda no mercado. Duas foram assim ignominiosamente vendidas entre os anos de 1830 e 1850 em diferentes datas, estando eu então em Inglaterra' [the husband throwing a rope around his wife's neck and taking her to be sold in the market. Two wives were thus ignominiously sold between the years of 1830 and 1850 on different dates, when I was in England] (VF, 58: 3). Although Wood was inaccurate in stating that the Matrimonial Causes Act granted equality between the sexes in matrimonial matters, enthusiasm, compounded by her Anglophilia, may have got the better of her. In her article, Wood describes female mobilization: 'formaram-se comissões de senhoras em cada freguesia e espalharam-se por todo Londres os membros daquelas comissões, solicitando votos em apoio da petição que tencionavam mandar ao parlamento' (p. 3) [committees of ladies were set up in each parish and the members of those committees spread throughout London, asking for votes in support of the petition they intended to send to Parliament].

Wood's second article begins by invoking British women's considerable intellectual achievements in a range of fields, citing distinguished scientists such as Mrs Marcet and Mrs Somerville, as well as Harriet Martineau.[16] She further points out that Martineau, whom she described as a political economist, wrote editorials for Daily News for sixteen years.[17] She also alludes to the fact that in Britain women writers 'ocupam uma posição em nada inferior à dos homens' [occupy a position that is in nothing inferior to that of men] and, to further support her argument, added that Queen Victoria herself was a writer. Wood then clarified that English women were seeking two rights: firstly the vote and secondly for unmarried women to manage their own income. Regarding the second point, she emphasized that there was a sizeable number of women, either rich or in employment, who were ratepayers — 'Só na cidade de Manchester e no concelho de Salford se contam de 13 a 14,000' [just in Manchester and Salford there are 13,000 to 14,000] — and felt short-changed. She told her readers that the popular agitation demanding legal reform had started two years previously; although she did not cite any names, she mentioned committees of ladies in London, Bristol and Manchester. She furthermore explained that, given that in some places the right to vote was recognized while in others it was rejected, a new law was urgently needed (VF, 59: 2).

Her third article brought her readers up to the present. Commenting on the ongoing campaign of women for the vote, she remarks that 'A batalha poderá ser longa e renhida, mas por fim a causa da justiça há de triunfar assim como triunfou a causa do servo contra o poderoso senhor que se arrogava o direito de dispor até da sua vida e da honra de suas filhas' (*VF*, 60: 3) [the battle may be long and ferocious but eventually the cause of justice will triumph, just as the cause of the serf against his powerful Lord, who claimed to have rights over even his life and the honour of his daughters, eventually triumphed]. According to Wood, Harriet Martineau was the earliest voice in the debate, some thirty years previously. She attributed to her the following words:

> Talvez haja quem ria de me ouvir dizer que as mulheres devem ter direito a escolher os seus representantes; mas o que importa isso! Também o Velho Mundo riu, quando ouviu o brado de Washington pela independência do Novo Mundo, e contudo o Novo Mundo é independente. (p. 3)

> [There may be some who laugh on hearing me say that women should have the right to elect their representatives, but what does that matter! The Old World also laughed when it heard the cry of Washington for the independence of the New World, and yet the New World is now independent.]

Wood reports that Lydia Becker had recently become the public face of the movement, as secretary of the Manchester women's group. In fact, Wood informs her readers that Becker had sent to *A Voz Feminina* the report of a meeting held in October 1868, chaired by Mrs Kyllmann as President.[18] Becker had also sent in a photograph of herself in which, according to Wood, she looked about thirty — in reality Becker, who was born in February 1827, was already in her early forties. This personal contact effectively provided a direct source of information about the English context. Wood concludes her article by expressing the hope that there would be a debate concerning women and the right to vote in the next parliamentary session, and stressed that signatures for the petition were being sought far and wide, even in Lisbon itself (p. 3). In other words, as a political commentator, Wood had her finger on the pulse and was well-informed about the progress of the 'Woman Question' in Britain, ensuring that it was closely reported in *A Voz Feminina* as it unfolded.

These were indeed exciting times for the first suffragists: in March 1869, a short unsigned entry titled 'Eleições em Inglaterra' [Elections in England] reported the fact that several women were able to vote in municipal elections because 'os nomes desta senhoras tinham sido registrados antes de que o Supremo Tribunal de Justiça desse a sua decisão contra a reclamação das senhoras para serem admitidas à urna [the names of these ladies had been registered before the Supreme Court of Justice delivered its decision against the demand of women to be allowed to cast their vote]. Accordingly 'Quinze senhoras votaram em Finsbury [...]. Em Manchester nove senhoras votaram e várias em Lancashire' [Fifteen ladies voted in Finsbury [...]. In Manchester nine ladies voted and several in Lancashire]. The author of the article, in all likelihood Wood herself, rejoiced that all but one voted Liberal rather than Conservative (*VF*, 63: 4). In point of fact, the year of 1869 represented a watershed moment in the female suffrage campaign. In the words of Millicent Garrett Fawcett:

That year deserves to be remembered as one in which the most important step was made in the direction of women's complete political enfranchisement. A municipal reform act was passed which conferred upon women householders the right to take part in municipal elections.[19]

The sense that the subject of women's rights was increasingly sweeping not only Britain, but France too (symbolically still the main cultural model for the periodical's Portuguese audience), is conveyed in the same issue on the previous page, where a short news item titled 'Associação das senhoras francesas' [Association of French Ladies] reported the creation of a French group for women's rights in Paris, led by Mrs André Léo (*VF*, 63: 3).[20] These were indeed exciting times of change, as the Woman Question appeared to be making visible strides. One source of information was Goegg, as is shown by a letter addressed to her in English by Wood, in which Wood thanks her correspondent for sending her a copy of *Le Droit des femmes* (['Dear Madame Goegg...'] *VF*, 74: 4).[21] An example of her ongoing connections with French-speaking feminists came in the form of a further open letter from Wood to the French activist, Mrs André Léo, written in French, where she thanked Léo for sending her a copy of the essay she had published that very year, *La Femme et les mœurs* [Women and Customs] (*P*, 81: 128). In practice, then, Wood acted as a cultural mediator, in an attempt to provide up-to-date news on the women's movements gathering momentum in Europe, in order to encourage her readers to feel that the time was ripe for change at home too. It provided a template for Portuguese women to consider, showing how women elsewhere were increasingly coming together to take action and launching associations.

In this context, it is probably no coincidence that a striking serialized biography of Toussaint L'Ouverture (1743–1803), translated into Portuguese from an unnamed source by João Luís da Silva Viana, appeared from 7 March 1869, being published between nos. 60 and 64 (running in tandem with Wood's own articles on 'As senhoras inglesas e o direito eleitoral' [English women and the right to vote]). On the one hand, it was a highly topical offering, since it kicked off on in the immediate aftermath of the passing of the decree abolishing slavery in all Portuguese colonies, signed on 27 February 1869, which *A Voz Feminina* reported, albeit without further comment. The timing of the publication of a serialized biography of Toussaint L'Ouverture arguably speaks volumes about the periodical's awareness that this was a long overdue measure.[22] On the other hand, given the overall thrust of *A Voz Feminina*, there is a case for suggesting that a biography of the leader of the Haitian Revolution, which may at first appear to be an item not directly related to the Woman Question, in fact functions as additional commentary: it subtly complements a series of articles on the march of progress, not least given the analogy repeatedly made by Wood and her cast of contributors about women being akin to slaves in need of emancipation. Moreover, Wood would have been keenly aware not only of the popularity of the analogy in Britain, but also that Harriet Martineau, whom she seems to have regarded as the modern initiator of the fight for women's rights, had published a biography of Toussaint L'Ouverture in 1840.

Hot Off the Press: Ammunition from Abroad

Wood defended her policy of opening up *A Voz Feminina* to both men and women by emphasizing that several foreign periodicals also followed a similar practice (*VF*, 64: 3). The titles that she cited, most of them equally radical in outlook, were listed in Portuguese, but can be translated back into their original language as follows: in Geneva, the *Journal des femmes*; in England, *The Englishwoman's Review*; and in North America six titles, *The Revolution*, *The Sorosis*, *Women's Advocate*, *The New York Women's Advocate*, *Mother and Home*, and *Hearth and Home* — the last of these directed, as she reminded her readers, by the well-known author of *Uncle Tom's Cabin*, Mrs Beecher Stowe. It is worth noting that some of these periodicals had only been recently launched, which provides further proof that Wood was very much *au fait* with what was going on elsewhere in the western world at a time when, as Käppeli contends, feminist journals gathered (transnational) momentum. Like some of her counterparts, Wood regularly publicized, recycled or adapted material pertaining to the Woman Question, all of which were common practices at the time. For instance, she translated and condensed the analysis expounded in one specific article from *The Englishwoman's Review*.[23] Originally titled 'Employment of Women and Children in Agriculture', it was re-named 'Mulheres Lavradoras' (*VF*, 73: 3–4) [Rural Working Women] in Portuguese, thereby demonstrating her sensitivity not just to gender but also to class issues beyond the interest in charitable philanthropy in evidence in the early numbers of *A Voz Feminina*.

We already know the identity of Wood's main contacts in Switzerland (Marie Goegg), England (Lydia Becker) and France (André Léo) but, given how well-informed she seems about print culture in the US, where did her extensive information come from? Nine weeks after *A Voz Feminina* had listed six North American titles, a clue comes in the form of an open letter written in English by William Wood to Theodore Stanton, of *The Revolution* (*VF*, 73: 4). Theodore Stanton (1851–1925) was the son of the feminist activist Elizabeth Caddy Stanton, one of the editors of the progressive periodical *The Revolution*, one of the titles listed.[24] His father was the abolitionist Henry Stanton and in fact, when writing to Theodore, William mistook him for Henry. What is significant is that like-minded revolutionary women and men worldwide were availing themselves of new opportunities afforded by the press to disseminate information and create informal international networks to support each other across national boundaries. In fact, in April 1869 *The Revolution* had published the translation of a one-page article by Marie Goegg in the *Journal des Femmes*, entitled 'Woman's rights in Europe'. The piece mentioned *A Voz Feminina* noting, however, that 'this question [of the vote] has not yet taken deep root in Portugal'.[25]

In his open letter to Theodore, William summarized the Portuguese situation, providing what may simultaneously seem like an indirect justification for Goegg's cautious appraisal:

> Those earnest in the cause of progress may be counted on the ten fingers. We are content, accordingly, with acting as pioneers, and cannot flatter ourselves that in the *Voz Feminina* we possess an organ of public opinion already

formed... the English here [i.e. in Lisbon] are perfectly indifferent, or, to speak more correctly, adverse to the cause we advocate. We have only one English subscriber, and have not succeeded in obtaining a single signature to the petition to [the British] Parliament for the political enfranchisement of women. (p. 4)

The petition must be the one that Francisca had alluded to at the close of her series of articles on 'As senhoras inglesas e o direito eleitoral' [English women and the right to vote] (*VF*, 60: 3).

A subsequent open letter by William Wood, this time printed on the front page and addressed to the Editor of *The Printers' Register*, also dealt with the gradual progress being made in England with regard to female suffrage, rejoicing in 'Mr Jacob Bright's amendment to the Municipal franchise bill' (*P*, 80: 123). It stated that 'the next step will no doubt be the concession of the right of married women to property [...]. After this, the right of women to the parliamentary franchise cannot long remain in abeyance'. The letter also clarified that 'the petition on this subject from English residents in Lisbon, had five signatures, and was presented by Sir Charles Wentworth Dilke'.[26] This suggested the difficulty in mobilizing the British community in Lisbon. It seems reasonable to extrapolate from these paltry numbers that discussions about the female vote would have been equally alien among the Portuguese at this juncture. Indeed William Wood concluded the letter by stressing that 'the public mind remains in an apathetic and unenlightened condition, and the efforts of one or two individuals in advance of the rest of the communities can produce but slight results' (p. 123).

If the Woods' individual activism deserves to be singled out, especially in the light of their lucid recognition that it was merely a drop in the ocean, ahead of its time in a Portuguese context, so too does the reference to Dilke: he was a man who famously boasted when his life was coming to an end that 'I have known everyone worth knowing from 1850 until my death' and whose network of connections was significantly strengthened by the fact that his family owned *The Athenaeum*.[27] The contact with Dilke, however indirect, may provide an explanation as to why the influential Victorian periodical had publicized the appearance of *A Voz Feminina* one year earlier, in the terms quoted at the beginning of this chapter; although it was a newsworthy item in its own right, a personal connection may have helped. Certainly the links between the Woods and Dilke did not stop with the parliamentary petition, for when a few months later Francisca Wood published her serialized novel *Maria Severn* in book-form, she offered a copy to Dilke himself, as can be ascertained from the presence of a handwritten dedication in the copy held by the British Library.[28]

Letter 'Ao Ilmo João A. Elliott'

Mainstream periodicals throughout Europe were closely reporting on the Woman Question, as the re-tweeting of the original news-clip published in *The Athenaeum* discussed at the outset of this chapter confirms. Conversely, evidence of Wood's engagement with (male) British thinkers via the same paper, and possibly other sources too, comes in an open letter to the today unknown João A. Elliott (*P*, 78: 117). Wood chides Elliott for taking for granted his entitlement to determine how far his younger sister's intellectual occupations should be allowed to advance: he deemed politics to be out of bounds.[29] Although his condescending willingness to countenance learning was arguably already a small step in the right direction, it was far from sufficient for the feisty Wood, who takes him to task: 'V. Exa portanto escraviza a mulher porque enquanto ela estiver sujeita ao *quero* e *não quero* do homem é sua escrava' [Dear Sir, you enslave women, because while they continue to be subjected to the will of man, they will remain his slave]. Drawing on Professor F. W. Newman's lecture on women's suffrage, Wood argues that the power that the law bestowed on husbands (and here, by implication, on siblings) was more degrading for the men themselves than for the women concerned.[30] She followed up on this argument by suggesting that in more advanced countries men were becoming increasingly ashamed of treating women as inferiors, a pattern that she was at pains to present as a hangover from more primitive times.

Wood redeploys similar arguments to those mustered in previous and subsequent editorials to underline that there was no incompatibility between women and political activism, before invoking a curious example drawn from the respectable mainstream *Athenaeum*, namely that between 4000 and 5000 women had gathered in Central London to show their support for a Mr Miall. She is silent, however, on the fact that Miall was a campaigner for the disestablishment of the Church, which chimed with her own anticlerical sympathies but would have been explosive at the time in Portugal. The separation of Church and State became one of political objectives of the Republican Party (created in 1876), showing how avant-garde Wood's political sensibilities were. She was careful to add in her letter, moreover, that it didn't follow that women would wish to occupy public office, adducing maternity as the reason in a lengthy paragraph. So, once more, to reassure Elliott — and by extension her wider readership — she was arguing that 'o que a mulher europeia ambiciona é tão-somente igualdade legal [...] é o *direito* e não o *exercício* que a mulher quer, deve, e há de ter' [the European woman only aspires to equality before the law [...] it is the *right* and not the *exercise* that woman wants to have, must have and will have].

In her closing paragraph she concludes her bid to incite Elliott to rethink his overbearing attitude, by recommending authoritative opinions:

> Leia V. Exa o relatório da comissão do parlamento de Massachusetts sobre as vantagens de se dar à mulher direitos eleitorais; leia a preleção do professor F. W. Newman 'on Women's Suffrage', e a revista da obra do Mr Mill no *The Athenaeum* de 19 de junho último. Estou certa da conversão de V.Exa, e que se enlistará nas fileiras dos valentes e generosos soldados desta honrosa cruzada.

> [Please read the report of the committee of the Parliament of Massachusetts about the advantages of giving women electoral rights; read the lecture by F. W. Newman 'on Women's Suffrage', and the review of Mr Mill's work in *The Athenaeum* of 19 June 1869. I am confident about your conversion, good Sir, and that you will join the ranks of the valiant and generous soldiers of this honourable crusade.]

The evidence from the United States is compelling because it does not stem from an individual but from (federal) Parliament itself. As for the two British men she cites as further proof of the support of men for women's rights, John Stuart Mill was highly influential as a politician and his 1869 *The Subjection of Women* quickly became a milestone. Ironically, however, the review of Mill's book in *The Athenaeum* was invoked in vain here: although Wood thought it expedient to cite the authority of *The Athenaeum*, the anonymous reviewer had in fact expressed misgivings at the likely upheaval if women were granted political power.[31] Assuming that Wood had actually had access to the contents of the review, had she misread the thrust of the argument? Or could it be that she was banking on the fact her readers would take her word for it and no one would take the trouble to trace the review itself?

Be that as it may, once more, by tactically resorting to the tried and tested device of the open letter, Wood was making use of ammunition from England and America to persuade one man in particular in the first instance, but by extension her entire readership too, of the fairness of women's demands for equality. She marshalled her strategy of choice, namely demonstrating the gulf between the progress being made elsewhere in Europe, and the backward attitudes in Portugal. That said, the fact that she was, on the evidence of his name, addressing an Anglo-Portuguese man, shows that the crucial division was not between England and Portugal *per se*, but between enlightened men and men in need of enlightenment. Indeed, in her closing sentence, reason blends seamlessly into a more affective style, with three particularly persuasive adjectives (valiant, generous, honourable) intended to win over her interlocutor and readership at large.

Also of particular note here is the redeployment of the religious word 'crusade' in a more secular context. Wood's conviction that the pursuit of women's rights was a crusade confirms her as a precursor to first-wave feminism in Portugal. Although one decade earlier Pusich had been the Editor of *A Cruzada* [The Crusade], her 1858 periodical was primarily a *jornal religioso e literário* [religious and literary journal] as its subtitle indicated. By contrast, the meaning that Wood bestows on the word 'cruzada' aligns her with first-wave mobilization in a transnational nineteenth-century context. In Portugal the word became perhaps most visibly embraced when the country joined World War I, in 1916, since the name chosen for one of the many budding women's organizations, was precisely 'Cruzada das Mulheres Portuguesas' [Crusade of Portuguese Women].[32]

'O que se faz lá fora'

While Wood repeatedly drew on the British press, her knowledge of what was simultaneously going on elsewhere remained firmly in evidence. Occasionally, it even came via a Portuguese source: for instance, she transcribed from the *Gazeta Pedagógica* an article by C. Hippeau about Vassar College in the States, in order to foreground the ongoing importance of women's education. Vassar had been founded in 1861 to further young women's higher education, as the respected French academic and educator Célestin Hippeau, explained ('Educação das Mulheres nos Estados Unidos', *P*, 81: 129–30 (p. 129).[33] This example proves that mobilizing shorter news snippets (primarily gleaned from abroad, whether second- or third-hand) as ammunition in the inside pages of the periodical was an integral strategy, complementing weekly high-impact editorials and/or open letters.

In the last three months of the periodical's life, in particular, from no. 87 onwards, and building on the long-running section of 'Variedades' [Miscelleanous], *O Progresso* started a section entitled 'O que se faz lá fora' [What is happening abroad]. This occasional column, signed by Wood herself, offered particularly compelling information under one eye-catching heading. Unlike the varied thematic spread found in the short news-clips channelled through 'Variedades' virtually since the inception of *A Voz Feminina*, the overwhelming majority of news items were now firmly focused on the Woman Question. For instance, an article transcribed from yet another British source, *The Quarterly Review*, reported that Tennyson, author of *The Princess* (1847) and Poet Laureate, was amongst those who had voted in favour of the foundation of a college for women (*P*, 87: 153). Although not named, the college in question must have been Girton, the first Oxbridge female college, established in Hitchin (Hertfordshire) in 1869 and subsequently transferred to Cambridge.[34] The first reference to the planning of 'uma universidade para senhoras entre Londres e Cambridge' [a university for women between London and Cambridge], under a group led by Mrs Davies, had been made some twenty months earlier, on 8 March 1968 ('Variedades', *VF*, 8: 4). Although the periodical had divulged the news that women were already studying at other universities in England and Scotland some time earlier, in the rubric 'Variedades', the symbolic breaking through of the glass ceiling that the creation of a female Oxbridge College represented cannot have been lost on someone like Wood, who had spent four decades in Britain.

A fortnight later, the financial aspects of supporting women's learning came to the fore as Wood cited from *The Athenaeum* news about scholarships for female medical students, before rejoicing in the creation of a Women's Club and Institute, in Newman Street, London. She explained the desirability of ladies' clubs, giving women access to the comforts routinely available to (gentle)men in the numerous and exclusive all-male clubs. In her view, the availability of a public women's space was particularly attractive given the number of women who could not afford to run their own house and therefore had to rent a room in a lodging-house or a boarding-house. She went into some detail about the prohibitive cost of keeping a home of one's own, so it seems likely that she was speaking from first-hand experience (*P*, 89: 160).[35]

In between these two weeks, the column 'O que se faz lá fora' gave advance notice of the third Congress of the League for Peace and Freedom in Lausanne, stating that thanks to Mme Goegg's intervention, the statutes of the League were woman-friendly. They stipulated that 'As mulheres serão admitidas sob as mesmas condições e com os mesmos direitos que os homens' [Women will be admitted under the same conditions and with the same rights as men]. The League's aim, it was stated, would be the 'formação de uma federação dos povos europeus' [formation of a federation of European states] (*P*, 88: 156).[36] The presence of several such accounts in the periodical, showcasing the intersection of Wood's feminist convictions with pacifist sympathies, both movements unheard of at the time in Portugal, is yet another proof of her exceptionally forward-looking ideals. Indeed, the Liga Portuguesa da Paz [Portuguese League for Peace], which brought together some of the most important Portuguese turn-of-the-century Portuguese feminists, was only founded thirty years later, in 1899, by Alice Pestana (1860–1929), duly credited by Esteves as 'a leading figure [...] associated with the establishment of feminist and pacifist movements in Portugal'.[37]

Given the flourishing mobilization elsewhere, it may come as a shock, then, that just a few weeks later Wood used editorial space to break the news of the imminent closure of *O Progresso* at the end of 1869, through the open letter previously discussed in Chapter 5 (['Ex.mas Sras e Srs. assinantes...'] *P*, 94: 179). For attentive readers, it had been clear that there weren't enough subscriptions to cover the running costs of the enterprise. However, financial considerations were not among the reasons invoked, as Wood lamented instead the covert war waged against her by some Catholic priests, and their indoctrination of Portuguese women. The issue was astutely laid out, since on the next page, in stark contrast to this editorial, the irregular column 'O que se faz lá fora' reappeared, after a five-week hiatus, to feature a longer report on the third Congress of the League for Peace and Freedom in Lausanne. It highlighted the presence of a number of French luminaries, and cited the closing speech, where Victor Hugo stressed that 'O socialismo é vasto, alcança todos os problemas humanos; o todo da concepção social [...]; proclama *o direito da mulher*, — *essa igual do homem* (*P*, 94: 180) [Socialism is vast, it reaches all human problems; the whole of social conception [...]; it proclaims the *rights of woman* — *she who is equal to man*].[38] In other words, the news of the imminent demise of *O Progresso* appeared severely at odds with what was going on elsewhere in Europe.

To emphasize the clash between forward-looking values and the backwardness of the Portuguese majority who rejected them, Wood adopted a similar strategy the following week, only this time in reverse: the upbeat tone of an editorial by Teixeira Coelho in favour of the interlinked causes of democracy and female emancipation ('Mais um Brado', *P*, 95: 183–84) offered a stark juxtaposition with the more downcast open letter she addressed in English to The Printers' Register to communicate the imminent closure (*P*, 95: 184). A subsequent number also continued to play with the layout in the same vein: Wood used editorial space to transcribe (in Portuguese translation) a speech by the President of the International Association of Women, Mme Goegg, delivered at the aforementioned Congress ([n.a.], *P*, 97: 191–92). This exhilarating piece of news contrasted sharply, however, with an open letter printed immediately after, addressed to her French counterpart Mrs André Léo (*P*, 97: 192). Wood announced to her 'Chère Soeur' [Dear Sister] the news of the imminent closure of the periodical at the end of 1869, reiterating in French what she had already explained three weeks earlier to her subscribers in no. 94. One suspects that Wood was again consciously playing with the design of the periodical to foreground the extent to which the prevailing narrow-mindedness of the Portuguese milieu was at odds with the forward-looking international mood of the time. The idea of transnational sisterhood and the gathering of momentum is also particularly striking here as, while Wood acknowledged that only a select number of women in Portugal sympathized with the principles her advocated, she was confident that 'Elles sèmeront et les semences donneront du fruit' [They will sow and the seeds will bear fruit] (*P*, 97: 192). The image of sowing situates her campaign squarely within an intellectual continuum that would flourish, over four decades later, in the title of the feminist periodical, *A Semeadora* (1915–18) headed by Ana de Castro Osório.

As is apparent from the pointed juxtapositions described above, even after the periodical's days were numbered Wood still maintained her fighting spirit and sense of humour. This can be seen equally in the last couple of issues, where she remained determined to showcase the widespread of women's progress in 'O que se faz lá fora'. In no. 101, the column cited periodicals from countries ranging from Italy (*La Donna*, with the names of nine its contributors supplied, including Gualberta Alaide Beccari) to Germany (*Die Neuen Bahen*, with Luise Otto-Peters at the helm). Also published in German was the US journal *Die Neue Zeit*, while in Switzerland the paper *Bund* had offered a series of articles on the rights of women. In addition, there were well-attended meetings in Cassel and Frankfurt. In fact, even Russian women were opening their eyes to the cause of female emancipation (*P*, 101: 208–09).[39] Again, this compelling evidence of mobilization, spilling from the press into real-life gatherings, can be read as a thinly veiled criticism of the short-sightedness of her own fellow countrymen and women. She indicated, by way of conclusion, that she would tackle the British case in the following issue.

Indeed, the last ever 'O que se faz lá fora' presented the progress in England in more detail, although it continued to invoke other countries too, including Germany, where a Congress on 5–6 November had gathered eminent male and female delegates to discuss 'the moral and social advancement of women'. Wood detailed several practical resolutions agreed in Berlin to further the extension of female education at primary, secondary and tertiary level. In the case of Britain, citing as a source *The Athenaeum*, she focused on university access: she named several university professors (of Latin, Physics and Chemistry) who were pushing their very able female disciples, and rejoiced that the University of Edinburgh had opened its lectures to women. Also of particular note are references to John Stuart Mill and his seminal work *The Subjection of Women* (she underlined that it had been translated into several languages, including Russian) and to Professor Newman and his stance in favour of women's suffrage, both previously invoked by Wood.[40] She concluded by urging her readers to subscribe to the French *Le Droit des femmes*, with which we know she was familiar through Mme Goegg. To facilitate action, immediately below Wood's swansong readers could find a description of *Le Droit des femmes*, complete with information about how to subscribe to it (*P*, 102: 212–13). On a more poignant personal note, she also asked her readers to purchase her novel, *Maria Severn*, to serve as a lasting reminder of her friendship.

After the Demise of O *Progresso*

If the radical ideas of *A Voz Feminina* / *O Progresso* created outrage in some quarters, judging by the regular put-downs by Valada in *Bem Público*, thereby blatantly contradicting *The Athenaeum*'s somewhat aloof description of Lisbon as a city 'so little likely to be stirred by sentiment', barely one year after the demise of *O Progresso* Lisbon was again publicly stirred by sentiment. This time, it was with a series of public lectures that subsequently became widely regarded as an era-defining moment in Portuguese cultural history, and went down in the (male) annals of history as synonymous with the start of modernity: the 1871 Casino Lectures. Needless to say, no one spoke up for women's rights: that was a revolution that the *Geração de 70* could not countenance.

One question that arises is what became of Francisca Wood once her periodical folded. Twice in the last few issues of *O Progresso* she alluded to the fact that she intended to join forces with her English and French counterparts. It is therefore conceivable that she may have gone on to write articles for the press elsewhere. The fact that she was considered part of an emerging international network is certainly documented by an immediate display of solidarity in the pages of *Le Droit des femmes* on 22 January 1870, where Goegg duly transcribed snippets of Wood's open letter to André Léo.[41] Furthermore, in 1870, when Lydia Becker launched her periodical *The Female Suffrage*, she listed the Woods as its Portuguese contact.[42] But there seems to be no trace of her in the foreign press thereafter.

Of course, age was not on Francisca's side and this may explain her conspicuous absence one decade later, from the 1884 volume entitled *The Woman Question*, edited by Theodore Stanton — with whom William Wood had corresponded fifteen years earlier in the heady days of *A Voz Feminina*. In that collection, the entry on Portugal stuck out like a sore thumb, for it was the only one to be wholly written by a man, the Republican Rodrigues de Freitas. Stanton provided a justification of sorts in his Editor's Preface, stating that the authoress [*sic*] Maria Amália Vaz de Carvalho had been enlisted but had been unable to carry out the task, owing to illness.[43] It is certainly fair to say that one might have expected Wood, rather than Vaz de Carvalho, to be approached. Assuming that Wood had been passed over in favour of the latter, this seems especially ironic considering that she had made an enemy of the young Vaz de Carvalho, when in 1868 she had chided her for refusing to contribute to *A Voz Feminina* (*VF*, 25: 4). In the intervening period, Vaz de Carvalho — who was broadly in favour of female education but advocated that women should not seek political rights — had gradually built a reputation in literary circles as a journalist and writer. Since her ultimately conservative positions did not present a threat to the men of the *Geração de 70*, her salon, especially from the 1880s onwards, became a meeting-point for the intellectuals of the period. Ramalho Ortigão prefaced her compilation, *Crónicas de Valentina* (1890), confirming her credentials as a leading intellectual — a glaring case of the consecration of a woman deemed exceptional by her male peers, at the expense of many others, like Francisca Wood, who were far more forward-looking.

Although on one level Francisca Wood seemed to have sunk without a trace after the demise of *O Progresso*, on another the fact that Tipografia Luso-Britânica remained active until 1877, as detailed in Appendix 1, shows that this was not the case. In addition, she may have channelled her energies into the translation of Charlotte Brontë's famous novel, *Jane Eyre*, serialized under the title *Joana Eyre* in the pages of the newly founded *O Zoofilo*, a periodical initially printed by the Tipografia Luso-Britânica. A reason to suspect the Woods' involvement with *O Zoofilo* was that its motto consisted of a quotation from Wilkie Collins, featured in Portuguese: 'O padecer de uma criatura fraca, e indefesa na sua mudez, é certamente um dos espectáculos mais aflitivos para a alma compassiva' [The misery of a creature, weak and helpless in his muteness, is surely one of the saddest of all the mournful sights which this world can show].[44] Indeed, only a few years earlier, in 1873, the Tipografia Luso-Britânica had brought out Collins's novel *Armadale* in translation. Another clue that Wood may have been the anonymous translator of the serialized *Jane Eyre* in *O Zoofilo*, is the contents of a short introductory note concerning its forthcoming publication. The brief, unsigned note published at the beginning of 1877 presupposed a fairly detailed knowledge of the contemporary reception of Brontë in 1847 — which only someone in Francisca's position could have acquired at first-hand. It stated that this novel was first published under the pseudonym Currer Bell; that the first edition sold out in two months; and that only then did it become known that the novel had been penned by a woman writer, Carlota (i.e. Charlotte) Brontë, 'com grande surpresa, e não pouco orgulho das damas inglesas'[45] [to the great surprise and not a little pride of English ladies].

In practice, Brontë's novel offered a counterpoint to Queirós's two realist novels: firstly *O Crime do Padre Amaro* [*The Crime of Father Amaro*] (initially serialized in 1875 and subsequently revised twice), and secondly *O Primo Basílio* [*Cousin Basilio*] (1878), where the multiple social constraints affecting middle-class women were portrayed. But while Queirós's fiction chronicled asymmetries in the gendered distribution of power that resulted in the death of his female protagonists at the end of both novels, it failed to offer any concrete solutions to redress the balance. In fact, the culpable men identified in the novels' respective titles ultimately remained unpunished. By contrast, *Jane Eyre* arguably provided an empowering model of womanhood for Portuguese readers, one in which education and paid employment were presented as the way forward to ensure greater female self-determination.

Preliminary close textual analysis leads us to believe that Francisca was indeed the anonymous translator of Brontë's novel, and that she could be relied upon to continue having a mind of her own, since the Portuguese translation emphasizes the feminist content of the original.[46] To illustrate with just one passage, taken from Jane's famous reflections in chapter 12, an examination of the original and its Portuguese translation throws up some small but significant differences:

> Women are supposed to be very calm generally: but women feel just as men feel; they need exercise for their faculties, and a field for their efforts, as much as their brothers do; they suffer from too rigid a restraint, too absolute a stagnation, precisely as men would suffer; and it is narrow-minded in their

more privileged fellow-creatures to say that they ought to confine themselves
to making puddings and knitting stockings, to playing on the piano and
embroidering bags. It is thoughtless to condemn them, or laugh at them, if
they seek to do more or learn more than custom has pronounced necessary for
their sex.[47]

[Supõe-se que as mulheres são geralmente apáticas; mas as mulheres sentem
como os homens; carecem tanto como estes de exercício para as suas faculdades
e de arena para os seus esforços; sofrem os atritos de uma sujeição demasiado
rígida, de uma estagnação absoluta, exatamente como os homens sofreriam;
e aqueles dos nossos mais ditosos próximos que opinam devermo-nos limitar
a fazer meia, tocar piano ou bordar chinelas, manifestam um entendimento
acanhado. Só por falta de raciocínio nos podem condenar, ou escarnecer, por
querermos aprender mais, ou empregar-nos diferentemente do que o costume
prescreve para o nosso sexo.][48]

The rendering of 'they suffer from too rigid a restraint' as 'sofrem os atritos de
uma sujeição demasiado rígida' introduces the concept of subjection, in a way that
immediately calls to mind the title of John Stuart Mill's famous *On the Subjection
of Women*, a book to which Wood had referred in the pages of her periodical. But
this is not the only instance of feminist amplification of meaning. We cannot
help noticing that Brontë's indictment of men as 'thoughtless' is highlighted in
Portuguese via the expression 'falta de raciocínio' [lack of reasoning] and moreover
emphasized with 'só' [It is only because of lack of reasoning]. This phrasing chimes
with Wood's staunch defense of rational thought as a means to foster greater gender
parity. The sequence 'they seek to do more or learn more' is then conveyed as
'querermos aprender mais, ou empregar-nos diferentemente' [our wanting to learn
more or employ ourselves differently]. Quite aside from transforming 'seek' into
the stronger 'want', the reversal of the original word-order of the verbs 'to do' and
'learn' underlines a natural progression from women's quest for knowledge to their
undertaking of useful activity.

Above all, the most striking difference is the fact that Brontë's generalizing
third-person plural formulation is rendered in Portuguese through the first person
plural, thereby bringing to the fore a female collective, further emphasized by the
translation of 'their sex' as 'o nosso sexo' at the close of the sentence. Overall, then,
the *Zoofilo* translation becomes a more directly politicized statement than Brontë's
original, by explicitly engaging a community of female readers through the use of
a first person plural. This is a device that Wood had deployed in *A Voz Feminina*,
not least in her inaugural editorial, where she promoted study by highlighting its
long-term benefits.

Thus, the serialization may have been Francisca Wood's way of continuing,
behind the scenes, to counter prevalent male images of passive and objectified
women. Given that the rebellious Jane had initially shocked many readers in
Britain, its serialization in a periodical committed to animal protection, a cause
that had barely begun to register in Portugal, showed that Wood was determined
to continue to speak up, albeit from a marginalized space. The translation, begun in
the second issue of *O Zoofilo*, carried on for nearly six years, with the last published

instalment appearing in September 1882.[49] Although it promised 'continua' [to be continued] as usual, it appears to have been discontinued thereafter, without a word of explanation about why it failed to reach its proper conclusion. Whatever the reasons behind the decision may have been, it is worth repeating the obvious fact that age was not on Wood's side.

Conclusion

The present chapter has problematized male-centred accounts of nineteenth-century Portuguese cultural history, by demonstrating that *A Voz Feminina* was far ahead of its time, so much so that it can profitably be read as part of a budding network of feminist journals. Indeed, Wood's extensive engagement with the Woman Question was quite unheard of in the Portuguese context and, for that reason, it must be considered from a transnational perspective. Reading *A Voz Feminina* and *O Progresso* transnationally sheds light on the infectious sense of excitement felt by an early Portuguese feminist, determined to act as cultural mediator during the early beginnings of the first international suffrage movements.

As revolutionary women availed themselves of fresh opportunities to create international networks and support each other across national boundaries, the role played by the press in the dissemination of radical ideas in the second half of the nineteenth century becomes central. From 'a city so little likely to be stirred by sentiment as Lisbon', we see resistance to the status quo and change in the making, week after week, in a valiant attempt to counter the prevailing stereotype of Portuguese women as passive as the inspirational Wood embraces a broader transnational movement, alongside her European sisters, Lydia Becker, André Léo, and Marie Goegg. That said, while by the late 1860s the British Becker, the French Léo, and the Swiss Goegg already formed part of collective associations and would go on to contribute to feminist debates in Europe over the next few decades, drawing support from the organized movements they had helped to get off the ground, by contrast the Portuguese Francisca Wood had been a pretty isolated voice from the outset when trying to spread the word in her own country. And after the closure of her paper she became ever more relegated to the margins. Although she subsequently joined the newly created Portuguese Society for the Protection of Animals, and was almost certainly involved in literary translation in *O Zoófilo*, the primary purpose of this particular association was too far removed from 'the Cause' to contribute in any meaningful way to the keeping alive of the Woman Question in Portugal.

In order to grasp the contemporary significance of Wood's intervention, rather than an approach that relies on validation through immediate results and/or legacy, a different mode of evaluation may be required. As M. Sage Milo argues in connection with the radical early twentieth-century *Freewoman* in Britain:

> To appreciate the power of the *Freewoman* — and periodicals in general — as counterculture, we need to think about their context, particularly about what would be considered normative or acceptable and what would have been radical and oppositional in their own time. This challenges us to conceptualise the

impact of periodicals in ways that go beyond sales, subscriptions, or longevity, which often belied the resonance of these publications for their readers.[50]

The positive resonance of Wood's periodicals for her contemporary readership was undeniable, as documented by the correspondence sent in from all corners of Portugal, not to mention the praise lavished in a range of other papers. Moreover, impact can — and in this instance surely must — be measured by the strength of negative feeling, embodied in the venom poured out in *Bem Público*. In that connection, it seems pertinent to remember, as Kramarae and Rakow observe in connection with the periodical *The Revolution*, that the fight for the vote 'was not about getting the women the vote *per se*. It was really about redefining women and men. [...]. To redefine women, men would have to be redefined as well, a revolutionary proposition'.[51]

As such, the ground-breaking vision of the courageous Wood, probably 'a primeira mulher que neste país levantou a voz em prol dos direitos do seu sexo e contra o estado de abjeção moral e jurídica em que se acha metade do género humano' (*P*, 94: 179) [the first woman in this country who spoke up for the rights of her sex and against the state of moral and legal abjection in which half of the human race lies], ought to give us food for thought. Indeed, largely fuelled by Wood's editorial vision, *A Voz Feminina* and *O Progresso* stand as a vocal embodiment of a radical feminist counterculture in the context of 1860s Portugal. The fact that its unique mobilization under the banner of 'a mulher livre ao lado do homem livre' experienced several setbacks, and would take more than one century to become a legal reality in Portugal, is a tribute to the radical nature of the principle that Wood embraced.[52]

Notes to Chapter 6

1. Anne-Marie Käppeli, 'Scènes Feministes', in *Histoire des femmes en occident*, ed. by Georges Duby and Michelle Perrot, 5 vols (Paris: Plon, 1991), vol. iv: *Le XIXe Siècle*, ed. by Geneviève Fraisse and Michelle Perrot, pp. 495–525 (pp. 500–01).
2. Käppeli may have conflated the older and established Anna Maria Mozzoni, author of *La donna in faccia al progetto del nuovo Codice civile italiano* (1864) with Gualberta Alaide Beccari, editor of *La Donna*.
3. ibid., p. 504. The fact that her account overlooks Wood's periodical is unsurprising given that existing analyses of Wood at the time (one article by Leal in 1981 and one by Brito et al. in 1886) were both in Portuguese.
4. [Harriet Taylor Mill], 'The Enfranchisement of Women', *Westminster Review*, 109 (1851), 289–311.
5. See Harold L. Smith, *The British Women's Suffrage Campaign, 1866–1928* (2nd rev. edn) (Harlow: Longman, 2010); and Martin Pugh, *The March of the Women: A Revisionist Analysis of the Campaign for Women's Suffrage, 1866–1914* (Oxford: Oxford University Press, 2000). See also 'Votes for Women: The 1866 Suffrage Petition', Commons Select Committee, Parliament, 31 May 2016 <https://www.parliament.uk/business/committees/committees-a-z/commons-select/petitions-committee/petition-of-the-month/votes-for-women-the-1866-suffrage-petition/>.
6. Lydia Becker would also launch a periodical, *The Female Suffrage* in 1870. See Linda Walker, 'Becker, Lydia Ernestine (1827–1890)', in *Oxford Dictionary of National Biography* <http://www.oxforddnb.com/>.

7. 'Our Weekly Gossip', *The Athenaeum*, 6 June 1868, p. 799. This was duly noted in *A Voz Feminina* a fortnight later, on 21 June 1868 ([n.a.], ['A redacção da *Voz Feminina...*'] *VF*, 23: 1).
8. 'What women are doing and have done', *The Revolution* [New York], 25 June 1868, pp. 395–96 (p. 396), which cited *The Athenaeum* as its source, and secondly under the title 'Portugal Reached' [New York], 9 July 1868, p. 11.
9. Cheris Kramarae and Lana F. Rakow, eds, *The Revolution in Words: Righting Women, 1868–1871* (London: Routledge, 1990), p. xxviii.
10. ibid, p. xxx.
11. Cited in Linda Hughes, 'Sideways!: Navigating the Material(ity) of Print Culture', *Victorian Periodicals Review*, 47 (2014), 1–30 (p. 4).
12. It is just about conceivable that the Mrs Berkley she alluded was in fact Miss Lydia Becker.
13. The name of the feminist speaker is unfortunately impossible make out.
14. On Goegg see Helen Rappaport, *Encyclopedia of Women Social Reformers*, 2 vols (Santa Barbara, CA, and Oxford: ABC-CLIO, 2001), I, 259–61.
15. It is probable that Goegg had written to Wood in French. Although most educated Portuguese women at the time would have been able to read French fluently, the decision to publish Goegg's letter and speech in a Portuguese translation reflects the fact that Wood thought it important enough that it should reach the widest possible audience.
16. See Elizabeth J. Morse, 'Marcet, Jane Haldimand (1769–1858)'; R. K. Webb, 'Martineau, Harriet (1802–1876)'; and Mary R. S. Creese, 'Somerville, Mary (1780–1872)', all in *Oxford Dictionary of National Biography*.
17. According to Webb, in fact for fourteen years, between 1852 and 1866.
18. See the entry on Philippine Kyllmann (1834–1916) in Rappaport, I, 329–30, which clarifies that she resigned from the committee soon afterwards, over a disagreement with Lydia Becker.
19. Millicent Garrett Fawcett, 'The Women's Suffrage Movement', in *The Woman Question in Europe: A Series of Original Essays*, ed. by Theodore Stanton (New York: G. P. Putnam's Sons, 1884), pp. 1–29 (p. 16).
20. See Léo (1824–1900) in *Les Vies d'André Léo: romancière, féministe et communarde*, ed. by Frédéric Chauvaud and others (Rennes: Presses universitaires de Rennes, 2015).
21. The French periodical, co-directed by Léon Ritcher and Marie Desraimes, started in 1869. See Alison Finch, *Women's Writing in 19th-Century France* (Cambridge: Cambridge University Press, 2000), p. 247.
22. The decree was signed on 27 February 1869. The serialized biography of Toussaint L'Ouverture commenced on 7 March 1869 ('Toussaint L'Ouverture', trans. by João Luís da Silva Viana, *VF*, 60: 3–4) while the news of the publication of the decree was reported on 14 March 1869 ('Variedades', *VF*, 61: 4). The last instalment was dated 'Belém, 16 December 1867' ('Toussaint L'Ouverture', trans. by João Luís da Silva Viana, *VF*, 64: 2–3).
23. 'Employment of Women and Children in Agriculture', *The Englishwoman's Review of Social and Industrial Questions*, 11 (1869), pp. 155–76. *Englishwoman's Review* was the successor to the *English Women's Journal*, set up in 1858 by Barbara Bodichon.
24. See Kramarae and Rakow.
25. Marie Goegg, 'Woman's Rights in Europe', *The Revolution* [New York], 15 April 1869, pp. 228–29.
26. Charles Wentworth Dilke (1843–1911) was elected Liberal MP for Chelsea in 1868, at the age of 25, and went on to become a major Victorian figure. See Roy Jenkins, 'Dilke, Sir Charles Wentworth, second baronet (1843–1911)', in *Oxford Dictionary of National Biography*. According to Crawford, 'Dilke, a Radical Liberal, closely associated with J. S. Mill [...] had in July 1869 spoken at the first public meeting of the London Society for women's suffrage'; Elizabeth Crawford, *The Women's Suffrage Movement: A Reference Guide, 1866–1928* (London: Routledge, 2001), p. 169.
27. Jenkins.
28. Wood's offering may have been primarily a gesture of courtesy since, although Dilke had studied Classics, there is no indication that he could read Portuguese. Alternatively, it may also have been prompted by the hope of generating publicity for her novel which, as far as we can ascertain, did not occur.

29. His sibling was presumably Eliza Elliott, one of Wood's young protégées, discussed in Chapter 3.
30. See Chapter 4 for more information about Newman and his lecture, in the context of her later editorial (no. 93).
31. 'Literary Review of John Stuart Mill, The Subjection of Women', *The Athenaeum*, 19 June 1869, pp. 819–20.
32. Irene Flunser Pimentel and Helena Pereira de Melo, *Mulheres Portuguesas* (Lisbon: Clube do autor, 2015), pp. 178–79.
33. The theme of female higher education would be taken up in the next issue, with an unsigned article celebrating the forthcoming graduation of the first Portuguese woman doctor, 'Uma senhora portuguesa médico' [sic] [A Portuguese lady doctor]. It underlined that several other countries already boasted qualified female doctors ([n.a.], *P*, 82: 134). The unsigned article, possibly authored by Wood herself, is curious: if the information is correct, it places a question-mark over the prevailing consensus that the first woman doctor to graduate from the University of Coimbra, Elisa Augusta da Conceição de Andrade, did so only two decades later, in the 1880s. See <http://www.seg-social.pt/documents/10152/18931/A+mulher+em+Portugal+volume+I.pdf>, pp. 49 and 53.
34. Girton College was established in 1869 by Barbara Bodichon and Emily Davies. See Rappaport, I, 794. The creation of the College elicited another mention in the periodical, this time as Hitchin (Francisca Wood, *P*, 92: 172).
35. The problems experienced by single women in securing honest and gainful employment are highlighted more than once in the periodical, for instance when Wood commended British printing businesses employing women (*P*, 84: 139–40).
36. The pacifist newspaper *Les Etats-Unis d'Europe* had started publication in 1868.
37. João Esteves, 'Historical Context of Feminism and Women's Rights in Nineteenth-Century Portugal', p. 105.
38. This is one of the few times that the word *socialism* appears in the periodical.
39. Since some of the information overlaps with an article published in *Le Droit des femmes* a fortnight earlier, on 4 December 1869, there is a fair chance that the French periodical would have been one of the sources of information. For a transcription of the relevant article see Alessandra Anteghini, *Parità, pace, libertà: Marie Goegg e André Léo nell'associazionismo femminile del secondo Ottocento* (Genova: Name, 1998), pp. 132–36.
40. To these, she added mention of a speech delivered two years previously by the politician Benjamin Disraeli. It is unclear what speech she may have had in mind, given that Disraeli, a Conservative, had voted against extending voting rights to women.
41. See Anteghini, pp. 137–38.
42. *The Female Suffrage*, 1 March 1870, p. 8.
43. 'Editor's Preface', *The Woman Question in Europe*, ed. by Theodore Stanton, pp. v–x (p. v).
44. This citation can be traced back to Collins's famous sensation novel, *The Woman in White*, 3 vols (London: Sampson Low Son & Co, 1860), II, 19.
45. 'Folhetim', *O Zoofilo*, 14 January 1877, p. 4.
46. For an analysis of how a range of translators of *Jane Eyre* into Portuguese at times downplayed Jane's rebellious thoughts, see Ana Teresa Marques dos Santos and Cláudia Pazos Alonso, 'A Mind of Her Own: Translating the "volcanic vehemence" of *Jane Eyre* into Portuguese' (forthcoming).
47. Charlotte Brontë, *Jane Eyre* (Oxford: Oxford University Press, 2000), p. 109.
48. *O Zoofilo*, 27 December 1877, no. 24, pp. 1–2. The typo 'racionio' has been amended to 'raciocínio'.
49. Charlotte Brontë, *Joana Eyre*, *O Zoofilo*, 14 January 1877, p. 4; and 28 September 1882, pp. 1–2.
50. M. Sage Milo, '"Intellectual Acid": Cultural Resistance, Cultural Citizenship, and Emotional (Counter) Community in the *Freewoman*', *Journal of European Periodical Studies*, 1 (2017), 39–53 (p. 51).
51. Kramarae and Rakow, eds, *The Revolution in Words*, p. 3.
52. While the emancipatory path delineated by the next generation of feminists bore some fruit with the advent of the First Republic, which translated into the introduction of some progressive

legislation, Ana Paula Ferreira argues that Osório's 'equivocal, though seductive, alliance between nationalist interests and feminist demands' led to its subsequent appropriation into the maternalist ideology of the New State from the 1930s onwards (Ferreira, 'Nationalism and Feminism at the Turn of the Century', pp. 138–39). All adult women finally secured voting rights on the same footing as their male counterparts under the 1976 Constitution.

CONCLUSION

In 1874, Lady Catherine Jackson gave an account of her travels through Portugal in *Fair Lusitania*.[1] After briefly expressing her surprise at the lack of contemporary Portuguese women novelists in comparison to England, she mentioned the name of the only writer she had come across, a name veiled by a colourful pseudonym: *Fornarina de Avelar* [The Baker-Woman of Avelar]. When four years later, in 1878, Camilo Castelo Branco published his translation of Jackson's work as *A Formosa Lusitânia*, he provided additional information in a footnote, so as to satisfy the curiosity of his readers — at least in part. He indicated that the reference concerned 'um romance desconhecido da senhora D. Amélia Dulce de Serpa Pinto, que o escreveu com o pseudónimo de *Fornarina de Avelar*' [an unknown novel by D. Amélia Dulce de Serpa Pinto, who wrote it under the pseudonym of *The Baker Woman of Avelar*]. For the sake of completeness, he added: 'Simultaneamente escreviam D. Maria Amália Vaz de Carvalho e D. Guiomar Torresão, das quais a escritora inglesa não levou notícia nem informação' [Writing at the same time were D. Maria Amália Vaz de Carvalho and D. Guiomar Torresão, about whom the English writer took away neither news nor information].[2] This anecdotal evidence is telling: firstly, Lady Jackson had no inkling about the existence of *Maria Severn*, as one might perhaps have expected, given that its author, Francisca Wood, was the wife of a British gentleman. Secondly, although Camilo too seemed to be unaware of Wood, he was keen to point to the existence of female authorship in Portugal. His choices are, however, surprising for their omission of Ana Plácido, his long-term companion, as well as the silencing of the popular Peregrina de Sousa, who had just published *Henriqueta* in book-form, prefaced by Castilho (1876). There was no mention of Pusich either; instead Camilo promoted the young and promising Torresão and Vaz de Carvalho. His endorsement of Torresão, who had published her first novel, *Uma Alma de mulher*, in 1869, the same year as *Maria Severn*, was of course a public display of support, especially welcome given that in 1877, only the year before Camilo's translation, Ortigão had ridiculed her *Almanaque das Senhoras*.

Camilo's footnote proves that these two emerging female writers, who remain familiar names to this day, had registered in the public consciousness. Yet as Chapter 2 has demonstrated, women writers had already been making significant inroads for several decades and their presence in the press arguably paved the way for Torresão, Vaz de Carvalho, and indeed many others. Why is there still virtually no room for them in existing accounts of the nineteenth century? This monograph has argued for the desirability of our stepping out of the stronghold of literary historiography in order to make room for a different way of envisaging nineteenth-century print culture, by broadening our conceptualization of women writers through the study of periodicals. The model of 'generations' and of 'great works' seldom favours women. Some of the most significant women of the period are arguably best seen as (public) intellectuals, rather than merely writers. Wood deserves to be recovered and hailed as their immediate and most important precursor.

Maria Amália Vaz de Carvalho and Guiomar Torresão, in particular, would themselves surely benefit from being considered within this broader category. Their increasing cultural gravitas is attested by the fact that by the 1890s they had entered traditionally male domains of authority within print culture. Carvalho produced critical reviews of the main members of the *Geração de 70*, collated in the volumes *Alguns Homens do Meu Tempo* (1889) and *Pelo Mundo Fora* (1889). Torresão, for her part, aside from numerous critical appreciations over the years, prefaced the work of a foreign feminist journalist, Tennessee Claflin. The staunch belief that women had the same critical authority as men is something that Wood had encouraged in her young cast, as we saw in Chapter 3, and Torresão, under her mentorship, rose to the occasion. In addition, Wood herself embodied not only the rise of the woman of letters as a public intellectual but also her transformation as an identifiably political entity. As such, she cleared the way for a younger generation to pursue a role with greater public visibility even if, sadly, they failed to acknowledge her as a forerunner.

The concept of the (public) intellectual, however, seems insufficiently broad to encompass confessional writing, and leaves female discursive subjectivity unaccounted for at the other end of the spectrum. As such, Chapter 2 simultaneously argued that memorialistic writing, as practised by Josephina Neuville in *Memórias da minha vida* (1864), also deserves to be recovered, not least because it might contextualize better some of the acts of ventriloquism of the likes of Camilo Castelo Branco or Eça de Queirós. The latter's portrayal of middle-class women in particular remains profoundly one-sided and disempowering for women to this day. Simultaneously, the very use of a female pseudonym by Júlio Dinis, when expressing himself through letter-writing — a medium used privately by many women throughout the centuries, and utilized in the epistolary novel to give a voice to female subjectivity — is also interesting in this respect, raising the question of modes of expression deemed 'feminine'.

Wood was aware that she was disseminating her ideas through the periodical press in an age of rapid transformation and reform. The self-confessedly anglophile Wood sought to ensure the wider circulation of the ideas and values propagated by the liberal Victorian press, in order to instigate progress in the country of her birth. This is all the more remarkable because of her marginal position as a dissident female intellectual in a staunchly Catholic country. Ahead of the famous 1871 Casino Lectures, she marked a turning-point in terms of the conceptualization of modernity. Her writings are informed by anticlerical and more egalitarian beliefs, which are themselves shaped by a forward-looking gendered perspective. The *Geração de 70* vocally lamented the fact that Portugal, a so-called semi-peripheral country, was lagging behind the modernity of northern European thinking. Yet, as

Chapter 6 reveals, Wood was in alignment with emergent transnational feminisms, and her correspondence with Marie Goegg, André Léo and Lydia Becker, openly conducted in the pages of her periodicals, was mutually reinforcing. This fact alone begs questions concerning her lack of reception in Portugal in the context of first-wave movements: why did her writings not leave lasting traces in the Portuguese cultural memory? Were they too radical? Too feminist? Or too 'foreign'?

Wood's progressive ideology, utopian at heart and loosely influenced by Comte's notion of progress, shared points of contact with the worldview of the *Geração de 70* most notably in respect of their anticlerical positions, typified early on in Antero de Quental's celebrated postface to his *Odes Modernas*:

> Reconstrução do mundo humano sobre as bases eternas da Justiça, da Razão e da Verdade, com exclusão dos Reis e dos Governos tirânicos, dos Deuses e das Religiões inúteis e ilusórias — é este o mais alto desejo, a aspiração mais santa desta sociedade tumultuosa que uma força irresistível vai arrastando, ainda contra vontade, em demanda do mistério tremendo do seu futuro.[3]

> [Reconstruction of the human world on the eternal bases of Justice, Reason and Truth, excluding Kings and tyrannical Governments, Gods and useless and illusory Religions — that is the highest desire, the most holy aspiration of this turbulent society that an irresistible force is dragging, albeit unwillingly, in search of the tremendous mystery of its future.]

The sentiment expressed here, as this monograph has shown, was very much shared by Wood. If the radical impetus of this public intellectual appeared unseemly, then, perhaps it was merely because it originated from the mouth of a woman. To put it differently, we can postulate that, if the collective hegemonic masculinity of the *Geração de 70* pointedly ignored Wood's voice, despite their shared outlook and temporal proximity, it was primarily because of her perceived threat to the existing model of gender relations. The ideas in Wood's periodicals were indeed at times considerably more radical than Queirós's articles in *As Farpas*, not least in respect of women's emancipation, but as Lopes puts it 'Os Eças e os Ramalhos do século XIX conseguiram impor uma imagem homogénea da mulher, dos seus modos de ser e de estar que ainda figuram no imaginário de muitos' [The Eças and Ramalhos of the nineteenth century successfully managed to impose a homogeneous image of woman, and her mode of being and behaving, that remains etched in the imagination of many].[4] It is of course important to remember that not all men of that generation held conservative positions; in that respect the work of the Coimbra-educated academic José Joaquim Lopes Praça, *A Mulher e a vida ou a Mulher Considerada debaixo dos seus Principais Aspectos* (1872), is a significant milestone, even if the greater female equality advocated therein was drowned out by the cumulative effect of silver-tongued *farpas*.[5] It is likely that Praça was familiar with the ideas expounded in *A Voz Feminina*, since the periodical had circulated in Coimbra, but further research would be required to corroborate this hypothesis. Certainly the appearance of his study confirms that the rights of women, a subject matter given unrivalled public visibility by Wood, was a topic actually worthy of serious consideration.

By the late 1870s and 1880s, however, the gender-conservative agenda of the dominant *intelligentsia* meant that Torresão was relentlessly caricatured by Rafael Bordalo Pinheiro in the press. One of his cartoons in *O António Maria* portrayed her alongside Angelina Vidal, 'irmanadas na parecença física' [like two peas in a pod] as França remarks (Fig. C.1).[6]

Although Torresão's transgressive behaviour was equated to that of Vidal, the two were far from interchangeable. As a matter of fact, unlike Torresão, Vidal was a life-long political activist, who lived on to see the implantation of the Republic (1910). In many respects she was the one who provided a tangible link to the next generation of feminists, alongside Alice Pestana.[7] In the meantime, *fin-de-siècle* gender anxiety also led to a telling caricature of Torresão and the Marquês de Valada, where Torresão was depicted as wearing the (masculine) trousers and Valada the (feminine) skirt (Fig. C.2).[8] Bordalo Pinheiro's sketch signalled the prevalent fear of social disorder, arising from the disruption of assigned gender roles, preemptively ridiculed by casting aspersions on 'deviant' sexual preferences, which in the case of the Marquês de Valada were by then common knowledge.

Wood's work is likely to have fallen foul of one mechanism in particular, namely the silencing of works that deal with gender inequality and feminist questions.[9] In other words, one particular strand of her radical thinking, her feminist thought, examined in Chapter 4, was too radical *per se*. Her demands for full political equality came too suddenly and too soon to generate a following; as her husband William conceded, 'the efforts of one or two individuals in advance of the rest of the communities can produce but slight results' (*P*, 80: 123). Nonetheless in her bid to change mindsets, Wood valiantly soldiered on for two whole years. Her learning and intellectual confidence led her to frame her ideas in the occasional essay-like editorial, while debating skills came into their own through the highly effective medium of open letters. Chapter 4 and 5 demonstrate that she did not shy away from *polémica* [controversy] to promote a more egalitarian view of society, appropriating combative strategies that had remained, with few exceptions, the preserve of male journalists until then. Ultimately, the fight for the vote 'was really about redefining women and men',[10] a revolutionary proposition indeed, so the maintenance of the prevailing *status quo* required Wood's relegation to the margins.

In addition, the transgressive nature of her feminist agenda was compounded by the 'foreignness' of her alternative religiosity. Crucially, Wood's daring pronouncements remain unexamined in the context of religious studies today, even though Ildefonso notes that 'em muitos momentos, o casal Wood trouxe à baila textos em que se sobressaía um posicionamento anticlerical e antijesuítico, o que desagradava à maioria católica do país luso' [the Woods frequently brought out texts noteworthy for an anticlerical and anti-Jesuitical position, which displeased the Catholic majority in Portugal]. Lopes for her part draws further attention to the Woods' heterodox thought on religion and gender.[11] Furthermore, Valada accused Wood of foreignness not only in connection with religious dissidence, but also at the linguistic level. It is true that foreign turns of phrase creep into her work, as do false friends and other contaminations of English, or more rarely French. But then again,

FIG. C.1. Cartoon in *O António Maria*, 21 February 1884,
depicting Guiomar Torresão and the Marquês de Valada

CÁ E LÁ...

Tem sido motivo de grande festa em quasi todos os jornaes regeneradores o facto de ter o partido republicano, militando nas suas fileiras, a sr.ª Angelina Vidal.

Então que querem os senhores?...

Não ha partido politico que não tenha o seu Gabriel Claudio; e ahi está, para prova, o proprio partido regenerador, que tem um Gabriel Claudio em primeira mão...

FIG. C.2. Cartoon in *O António Maria* 21 January 1885, depicting Guiomar Torresão and Angelina Vidal

Camilo and Eça also had to contend with accusations of permeability to French, the former occasionally and the latter with greater frequency.

Wood's radical sympathies stemmed from her extensive first-hand exposure to British culture, which left its mark on her writings culturally, religiously and linguistically; conversely, however, today the diversity of her background as an *estrangeirada* might be viewed as an asset rather than a shortcoming. In the context of the history of ideas in Portugal, although shocking to more conservative sectors, her views certainly align her with pro-republican ideals ahead of the official launch of the Republican Party in 1876. Her likely allegiance to Freemasonary caused further disquiet, a disquiet tellingly articulated by the Marquês de Valada: 'será verdade que na redação desta folha ocupam um lugar importante algumas das *obreiras* da loja maçónica feminina, recentemente estabelecida em Lisboa?' [could it be true that some of the *workers* of the female Freemason lodge recently established in Lisbon have an important function in the editorial team of this paper?].[12] The links between Freemasonry, republicanism and feminism in the years leading up to 1910 are well documented, but the possibility of tracing them back to the 1860s remains hampered by the paucity of available sources. Cultural memory loss is, however, being slowly redressed, most recently by Costa's 2016 *As mulheres na maçonaria: Portugal, 1864–1950*, whose subtitle helpfully gives long overdue visibility to the involvement of women in Freemasonry in the 1860s. Although Wood's sympathies remain a matter of speculation, the present monograph has uncovered conclusive evidence of at least one Freemason in Wood's immediate family: Clarimundo Martins, the nephew to whom she dedicated her novel *Maria Severn*.

One practical impediment in terms of the survival of Wood's intervention in cultural memory was that the press was by definition ephemeral and she did not follow up with the publication of her articles in book-form. Curiously, William Wood did collate some of his own articles, but when he did so he mostly reprinted less inflammatory material, for instance articles on the history of music.[13] Arguably, the couple may have realized that without a responsive public opinion behind them, they were wasting their time. Today, however, in order to re-assess her contribution there is an urgent need for the republication of primary sources. Both Torresão and Vaz de Carvalho, by contrast, were careful curators of their public image, collating some of their stories and press contributions in book-form as they went along. In fact, the better-regarded Vaz de Carvalho, despite (or because of) her self-limiting sense of an appropriately feminine propriety, was consecrated as an honorary man by Ramalho Ortigão in his preface to her 1890 *Crónicas de Valentina* — 'V. é verdadeiramente nas letras, de todos nós o melhor' [You are truly, in our letters, the best man among us all] — a backhanded compliment if there ever was one, given that the praise bestowed followed on from the enumeration of her womanly virtues.[14]

Francisca's intellectual legacy as a feminist forerunner to the Republican generation of Castro Osório and Cabete seems to have been erased from public memory by the turn of the century, precisely when the feminist ideas and debates spreading across Europe could no longer be ignored in Portugal. Thus, when in

1902 the German-born scholar Carolina Michaëlis de Vasconcelos (similarly to Wood a transnational woman) published in *O Comércio do Porto* her overview essay about 'O movimento feminista em Portugal' [The Feminist Movement in Portugal], originally commissioned for an edited collection in Germany, her opening paragraph stated that 'O combate das massas femininas em vista de melhores condições sociais está inteiramente por organizar no mundo peninsular. [...] Elas não pensam sequer em direitos de ordem mais elevada, como seja o do sufrágio' [The battle of the female masses in search of better social conditions has, as yet, to be organized in the Peninsular world. [...] Women do not even think about higher rights, like suffrage].[15] This sweeping generalization overlooks the pioneering intervention of Francisca Wood thirty years earlier. In point of fact, Michaëlis de Vasconcelos did know about *A Voz Feminina*, to which she later alluded in passing, but unfortunately she mistakenly attributed its leadership to Torresão, listed as 'editora do jornal *A Voz Feminina* e de um *Almanaque das Senhoras* (1871) vazado em moldes antiquados' [Editor of the journal *A Voz Feminina* and the *Almanaque das Senhoras* (1871), poured into an antiquated mould].[16] Her conflation of two different products in the same sentence, neither of which she seems to have read, even though the *Almanaque das Senhoras* was still going strong then, results in a disappointing failure to appreciate and celebrate the ground-breaking content of *A Voz Feminina*.

Michaëlis de Vasconcelos fared better in terms of acknowledging her contemporaries, and even seemed *au fait* with the existence of the periodical *Sociedade Futura*,[17] although she also wrongly ascribed its editorship, to Maria Veleda and Olga de Morais Sarmento da Silveira, when initially it was in fact Ana de Castro Osório who had teamed up with Morais Sarmento. *Sociedade Futura* was certainly interested in the recovery of female precursors, but Castro Osório claimed the late eighteenth-century Leonor da Fonseca Pimentel (1752–1799) rather than Wood as a role model: 'Pimentel's support for the Republican cause and her connections to the Freemasonry seem to have been the main reasons why Castro Osório took an interest in her activities and in her role as a leading figure of the revolution that succeeded in installing a new Republic in January 1799'.[18] Of course, Castro Osório may not have been aware of *A Voz Feminina*, but even if she was, Pimentel was more clearly immediately useful for her purposes, given the conflicting images opposing true and false feminism, the latter specifically connected with the English *miss*.[19]

By the start of the twentieth century, the radical ideas and principles espoused by Wood, especially feminism and anticlericalism, had gained increasing traction and visibility but her gradual recovery still had to wait until after the 1974 Revolution. Even today, reconstruction of the impact of Wood continues to be hindered by the paucity of readily available contemporary testimonial sources. But, with the benefit of hindsight, it would be remiss to omit Wood's name in any future survey of the history of ideas in the long nineteenth century in Portugal because her conceptualization of the nation seems so modern. Wood deserves to be written back into history, for she was certainly ahead of her time in the main causes she embraced. These even included championing animal protection prior to the launch of the Portuguese Society for the Protection of Animals, a society that her petitions in the pages of *A Voz Feminina* and *O Progresso* may well have helped to get off the ground.

In the twenty-first century, when the digital age enables us to access '[digital] archives [that] house corpora brimming with potential life, spirits clamourous to return',[20] trawling through online resources has generated more contextual information about the Woods and the transnational reception of *A Voz Feminina* — examined in Chapters 1 and 6 respectively — than could ever have been anticipated at the outset of this project. Ultimately, determination and perseverance proved to be not only amply rewarded but also deeply rewarding. As such, it is my hope that this monograph will help to inspire fresh scholarship in the context of nineteenth-century studies and prompt imaginative interdisciplinary ways of (re)-conceptualizing the past in future.

One hundred and fifty years on, it is surely right to celebrate the formidable Francisca Wood and her fearless commitment to rethinking gender roles and freedom of thought. The significance of her intervention pressing for change has yet to translate into mainstream accounts of the history of ideas, but as she cogently put it in her open letter to Emilio Castelar, discussed in Chapter 5:

> São os séculos e não o *dictum* dos homens que aquilatam a verdade. Tempo virá em que as gentes se assombrem da lide social que se está passando entre os homens e as mulheres; em que se leia como uma das muitas fábulas históricas a crónica das dificuldades escabrosas que as mulheres encontram no século XIX para se fazerem crer entes racionais, inteligentes, cogitadores e capazes de responsabilidade. (*VF*, 72: 1)

> [It is the centuries, not the *dictum* of men, which measure the truth. A time will come when people will be shocked by the social battle currently going on between men and women; when the chronicle of the terrible difficulties experienced by nineteenth-century women in trying to be accepted as rational, intelligent, thinking beings, capable of responsibility, will be read as one historical fable among many.]

Wood may not quite have been the first woman to speak up, but the extent of her engagement through the most public medium at her disposal — the periodical press — was certainly unprecedented in scope and reach. More broadly speaking, this monograph has sought to offer a 'chronicle of the terrible difficulties experienced by nineteenth-century women in trying to be accepted as rational, intelligent, thinking beings, capable of responsibility' and their multiple responses against silencing. Mindful that further snippets of information concerning Wood, Neuville, and indeed many others, may re-surface in the coming years, thereby continuing to make good some of the gaps and blanks left by cultural amnesia or unconscious bias, it seems fitting as we draw to a provisional close to invoke the words immortalized by periodical culture: *to be continued...*

Notes to the Conclusion

1. Lady Catherine Jackson, *Fair Lusitania* (London: R. Bentley and Son, 1874).
2. Lady Catherine Jackson, *A Formosa Lusitânia*, trans. by Camilo Castelo Branco (Porto: Livraria Portuense, 1877), p. 107 [footnote]. There is no entry for Amélia Dulce de Serpa Pinto in any dictionary of Lusophone women writers consulted. Her surname, however, suggests that she may have been connected with the family of the famous nineteenth-century explorer, Serpa Pinto. According to a thread on the internet, she may have been his first cousin. See 'Re: Serpa Pinto [abruma]', Geneall, 16 May 2002 <https://geneall.net/en/forum/21404/serpa-pinto/#a21432/>.
3. Antero de Quental, *Odes modernas* (Lisbon: Chardon, 1865), pp. 159–60. <https://books.google.com.br/books?id=mUMuAAAAYAAJ&printsec=, Google ebook.frontcover&hl=en#v=onepage&q&f=false>.
4. Ana Maria Costa Lopes, 'Francisca de Assis Martins Wood', in *Feminae: dicionário contemporâneo*, ed. by João Esteves and others (Lisbon: Comissão para a Cidadania e a Igualdade de Género, 2013), pp. 312–18 (p. 315). <http://cid.cig.gov.pt/Nyron/Library/Catalog/winlibimg.aspx?skey=0BC86F59EEEF4B5DA62821F712ACB60E&doc=95065&img=139416>.
5. José Joaquim Lopes Praça, *A Mulher e a vida ou a Mulher Considerada debaixo dos seus Principais Aspectos* [1872], 2nd edn (Lisbon: Edições Colibri, 2005).
6. França, *Rafael Bordalo Pinheiro*, p. 112. See 'Cá e lá...', *O António Maria*, 21 January 1885, p. 21.
7. Vidal's own brand of militancy started with the periodical *A Emancipação* (1880). It provided a springboard for class-based activism that chimed with Republican demands for equality. See Mário Vidal, *Angelina Vidal*.
8. 'Carnaval Permanente', *O António Maria*, 21 February 1884, p. 64.
9. See Edfeldt, *Uma História na história*, especially the case study of the *Novas Cartas Portuguesas* in Chapter 7. Her analysis of negligent treatment is equally applicable to earlier collective enterprises such as the one undertaken by *A Voz Feminina*.
10. Kramarae and Rakow, *The Revolution in Words*, p. 3.
11. Ildefonso, 'As Mulheres na imprensa periódica do séc. XIX', pp. 25–26; and Lopes, 'Religião e género como formas de discriminação'.
12. 'A Voz Feminina e o adultério: I', *Bem Público*, 24 April 1868, pp. 331–33 (p. 333), italics in the original.
13. See William Thorold Wood, *Colecção de artigos por W. T. Wood publicados nos jornais A Voz Feminina e O Progresso de 23 de Fevereiro de 1868 a 26 de Janeiro de 1869*, 2nd edn (Lisbon: Tipografia Luso-Britânica, 1877). This anthology was first published in 1875.
14. Ramalho Ortigão, 'Prólogo', in Maria Amália Vaz de Carvalho, *Crónicas de Valentina* (Lisbon: Tavares Cardoso, 1890), pp. v–xviii, p. xvii <http://dbooks.bodleian.ox.ac.uk/books/PDFs/N11276110.pdf>.
15. Carolina Michaëlis de Vasconcelos, *O movimento feminista em Portugal*, ed. by Luís Carlos Patraquim (Paio Pires: Fradique, 2002), p. 21.
16. Vasconcelos, pp. 59–60.
17. Vasconcelos, p. 61.
18. Bezari, 'Transnational Perspectives in Early Twentieth-Century Portugal', pp. 42–43.
19. See Abranches, 'Homens, mulheres e mestras inglesas' and Tavares da Silva, *Feminismo em Portugal*.
20. A. Easley, A. King, and J. Morton, *Researching the Nineteenth-Century Periodical Press*, p. 10.

BIBLIOGRAPHY

ABRANCHES, GRAÇA, 'Homens, mulheres e mestras inglesas', in *Entre ser e estar: raízes, percursos e discursos da identidade*, ed. by Maria Irene Ramalho and António Sousa Ribeiro (Porto: Afrontamento, 2002), pp. 255–305

ADÃO, DEOLINDA, 'Ecos na escuridão: escritoras portuguesas, vozes controladas, silenciadas, ou de outra forma ignoradas', in *Judith Teixeira: ensaios críticos*, ed. by Fábio Mário da Silva and others ([n.p.]: Edições esgotadas, 2017), pp. 169–82

[ADVERTISEMENTS & NOTICES], *Daily News*, 17 June 1850

AFONSO, JOSÉ ANTÓNIO MARTIN MORENO *Protestantismo e educação: história de um projecto pedagógico alternativo em Portugal na transição do séc. XIX* (Braga: Instituto de Educação e Psicologia da Universidade do Minho, 2009)

ALORNA, MARQUESA DE, *Obras Poéticas: antologia*, ed. by Vanda Anastácio (Lisbon: Imprensa Nacional–Casa da Moeda, 2015)

'Ana Cristina Comandulli da Cunha' <https://www.escavador.com/sobre/6101641/ana-cristina-comandulli-da-cunha> [accessed 5 November 2018] (Projectos de pesquisa: para. 1)

ANASTÁCIO, VANDA, *Uma Antologia improvável: a escrita das mulheres (sécs. XVI a XVIII)* (Lisbon: Relógio d'Água, 2013)

—— 'Pensar para além das etiquetas', *Veredas: revista da Associação Internacional de Lusitanistas*, 10 (2008), 287–94 <https://digitalis-dsp.uc.pt/jspui/bitstream/10316.2/34484/1/Veredas10_artigo16.pdf> [accessed 20 November 2018]

ANDRADE, ADRIANO DA GUERRA, *Dicionário de pseudónimos e iniciais de escritores portugueses* (Lisbon: Biblioteca Nacional, 1999)

ANDRADE, MARIANA ANGÉLICA, *Murmúrios do Sado* (Setúbal: Tipografia José Augusto Rocha, 1870)

—— *Revérberos do Poente* (Porto: Joaquim Antunes Leitão, 1883)

—— *A Voz Feminina*, [8], 'A Criança adormecida', 8 March 1868, p. 4

—— [11], 'Molière', 29 March 1868, p. 3

—— [11], 'Liberdade', 29 March 1868, p. 4

—— [16], ['O assunto de que hoje vou tratar...'], 3 May 1868, p. 1

—— [23], ['Lendo o Diário de Notícias...'], 21 June 1868, p. 1

—— [24], 'O Vestuário das senhoras', 28 June 1868, pp. 2–3

—— [25], 'O Vestuário das senhoras', 5 July 1868, p. 3

—— [26], 'O Vestuário das senhoras', 12 July 1868, p. 2

—— [27], 'Portuguesas distintas', 19 July 1868, p. 2

—— [28], 'Portuguesas distintas', 26 July 1868, pp. 1–2

—— [29], 'Portuguesas distintas', 2 August 1868, pp. 2–3

—— [30], ['No escrito que aqui se tem publicado...'], 9 August 1868, pp. 1–2

—— [37], 'Pintoras notáveis', 27 September 1868, p. 3

—— [41], ['Publicou-se há pouco no Diário de Notícias...'], 25 October 1868, pp. 1–2

—— [43], 'A União ibérica', 8 November 1868, pp. 2–3

—— [46], 'João Milton', 29 November 1868, pp. 3–4

—— [52], 'Lord Byron', 10 January 1869, p. 2

—— [53], 'Lord Byron', 17 January 1869, p. 4

—— [54], ['Vou hoje tratar de um assunto de...'], 23 January 1869, pp. 1–2

—— [57], 'Um Brado a favor dos animais', 14 February 1869, pp. 1–2

—— [60], ['Agora que estamos na quaresma...'], 7 March 1869, pp. 1–2

—— [66], 'Lamartine', 18 April 1869, p. 2

—— [74], 'Saudades da infância', 13 June 1869, p. 4

—— [74], 'A Uns olhos azuis (sem serem os meus)', 13 June 1869, p. 4

'Anne-Marie Caron', in *Dicionário no Feminino (séculos XIX–XX)*, ed. by Zília Osório de Castro & João Esteves (Lisbon: Horizonte, 2005), p. 124

ANTEGHINI, ALESSANDRA, *Parità, pace, libertà: Marie Goegg e André Léo nell'associazionismo femminile del secondo Ottocento* (Genova: Name, 1998)

ARAÚJO, JOÃO DE SOUSA, *O Progresso*, [96], 'A Mulher e os seus direitos', 14 November 1869, p. 188

—— [98], 'A Emancipação da mulher', 28 November 1869, pp. 195–96

ARAÚJO, MARIA DA CONCEIÇÃO PINHEIRO, 'Tramas femininas na imprensa do século XIX: tessituras de Ignez Sabino e Délia' (unpublished doctoral thesis, Pontifícia Universidade Católica, 2008) <http://tede2.pucrs.br/tede2/handle/tede/1894> [accessed 28 November 2018]

ARDONDE, ANGELO GABRIEL UEHARA, ISADORA CARDOSO and GIOVANNI RODRIGUES BRNICCHI, eds, *Alberto Pimentel (1849–1925): tal é, em resumo, a história do rei e do seu reinado* (Campinas: Instituto de Estudos da Linguagem, 2005), Joomag ebook <https://view.joomag.com/alberto-pimentel-dossiê-com-pesquisa-historiográfica-sobre-o-autor-13-de-novembro-de-2015/0150062001445947694> [accessed 23 November 2018]

AREIAS, LAURA, and OTHERS, eds, *As Mulheres e a imprensa periódica*, 2 vols (Lisbon: CLEPUL, 2014), II (2014), ed. by Isabel Lousada and Vânia Pinheiro Chaves

ARKINSTALL, CHRISTINE, 'A Feminist Press Gains Ground in Spain, 1822–1866' in *A New History of Iberian Feminisms*, ed. by Silvia Bermúdez and Roberta Johnson (Toronto: University of Toronto Press, 2018), pp. 111–25

—— *Spanish Female Writers and the Freethinking Press* (Toronto: University of Toronto Press, 2014)

ARMADA, FINA DE, *As Mulheres na implantação da República* (Lisbon: ésquilo, 2010)

ASHTON, ROSEMARY, 'Schmitz, Leonhard (1807–1890)', in *Oxford Dictionary of National Biography* <http://www.oxforddnb.com/> [accessed 26 February 2016]

ASSIS, JOAQUIM MARIA MACHADO DE, 'Crônica', *O Futuro*, 15 March 1863, pp. 434–36

ATAÍDE, MAIA, and ANTÓNIO MANUEL GONÇALVES, eds, *Monumentos e edifícios notáveis do distrito de Lisboa*, 5 vols (Lisbon: Junta Distrital, 1962–2007), III (1963)

BARRETO, J. A. DA GRAÇA, ['... sr. e amigo...'], *O Bem Público*, 9 May 1868, pp. 348–49

BARROS, TERESA LEITÃO DE, *Escritoras de Portugal*, 2 vols (Lisbon: Tipografia Artur, 1924)

BEARD, MARY, *Women & Power: A Manifesto* (London: Profile Books, 2017)

BEBBINGTON, D. W., 'Miall, Edward (1809–1881)', in *Oxford Dictionary of National Biography* <http://www.oxforddnb.com/> [accessed 26 February 2016]

BECKER, LYDIA, *The Female Suffrage*, 1 March 1870

BEZARI, CHRISTINA, 'Transnational Perspectives in Early Twentieth-Century Portugal: The Emergence of the Periodical *Sociedade Futura* (Lisbon, 1902–04)', *Portuguese Studies*, 35.1 (2019), 39–54

BIEDER, MARYELLEN, 'Women Authors in the Romantic Tradition (1841–1884) and Early Feminist Thought (1861–1893)', in *A New History of Iberian Feminisms*, ed. by Silvia Bermúdez and Roberta Johnson (Toronto: University of Toronto Press, 2018), pp. 127–46

BIGUELINI, ELEN, 'As memórias de Josefina de Neuville (1826–após 1864): lembranças de uma transgressora', Academia.edu <http://www.academia.edu/35738040/as_memórias_de_

josefina_de_neuville_1826-após_1864_lembranças_de_uma_transgressora> [accessed 10 December 2018]

——'Tenho escrevinhado muito: mulheres que escreveram em Portugal (1800–1850)' (unpublished doctoral thesis, Universidade de Coimbra, 2017) <https://estudogeral. sib.uc.pt/bitstream/10316/79402/1/Tenho%20escrevinhado%20muito.pdf> [accessed 3 November 2018]

BIRKHEAD, T. R., and R. MONTGOMERIE, 'A Vile Passion for Altering Names: The Contributions of Charles Thorold Wood Jun. and Neville Wood to Ornithology in the 1830s', *Archives of Natural History*, 2 (2016), 221–36

'Births, Marriages & Deaths', *The Morning Post*, 28 April 1888, p. 1

BISHOP-SANCHEZ, KATHRYN, 'Mulheres invisíveis: a escrita no silêncio', *Portuguese Literary & Cultural Studies*, 12 (2007), 169–82

——'Why "The Other Nineteenth Century"?', *Portuguese Literary & Cultural Studies*, 12 (2007), pp. xiii–xxv <http://www.portstudies.umassd.edu/plcs/docs/plcs12/plcs12_introduction.pdf> [accessed 24 April 2017]

BLANCO, MARIA JOSÉ, and CLAIRE WILLIAMS, eds, *Feminine Singular: Women Growing up through Life-Writing in the Luso-Hispanic world* (Oxford: Peter Lang, 2017)

BOCK, GISELA, and ANNE COVA, eds, *Writing Women's History in Southern Europe, 19th–20th Centuries* (Oeiras: Celta Editora, 2003)

BOLLAERT, WILLIAM, *The Wars of Succession of Portugal and Spain from 1826 to 1840: With Résumé of the Political History of Portugal and Spain to the Present Time* (London: E. Stanford, 1870)

BRANCO, CAMILO CASTELO, *Obras completas*, ed. by Justino Mendes de Almeida, 18 vols (Porto: Lello & Irmão, 1982–2002)

BRITO, MANUELA ARAÚJO, FERNANDA ROBALO and CARLOTA GUIMARÃES, 'Um Jornal feminista no Portugal de 1868', *História*, 92 (1986), 48–59

BRONTË, CHARLOTTE, *Jane Eyre* (Oxford: Oxford University Press, 2000)

——*Joana Eyre*, O Zoofilo, 27 December, 1877, pp. 1–2

——*Joana Eyre*, O Zoofilo, 28 September 1882, pp. 1–2

BUCKLAND, A. R., 'Thorold, Anthony Wilson (1825–1895)', in *Oxford Dictionary of National Biography* <http://www.oxforddnb.com/> [accessed 24 April 2017]

BUESCU, HELENA CARVALHÃO, ed., *Dicionário do romantismo literário português* (Lisbon: Caminho, 1997)

BURNAY, J., 'A Família Burnay e Cabo Verde', *Geneall*, 20 February 2008 (#185499) <http://geneall.net/pt/forum/148786/a-familia-burnay-e-cabo-verde/> [accessed 26 February 2016]

BURTON, IVOR F., and DOUGLAS WOODRUFF, 'Pius IX: Pope', *Encyclopædia Britannica*, ed. by Adam Augustyn and others <https://www.britannica.com/biography/Pius-IX> [access 27 February 2018]

BYATT, A. S., *Possession* (London: Vintage, 1990)

'Cá e lá...', *O António Maria*, 21 January 1885, p. 21

CABRAL, ALEXANDRE, ed., *Dicionário de Camilo Castelo Branco*, 2nd edn (Lisbon: Caminho, 2003)

CABRAL, FERNANDA DAMAS, ed., *Ana Plácido: estudo, cronologia, antologia* (Lisbon: Caminho, 1991)

CALDAS, DELFINA VIEIRA, *A Voz Feminina*, [24], ['Ex.ma Sr.ª...'], [Correspondências], 28 June 1868, pp. 3–4

——[27], 'Luis XVI e Maria Antoinette', trans. by Delfina Vieira Caldas, 19 July 1868, p. 3

——[50], 'A Amizade', 27 December 1868, p. 3

—— O Progresso, [92], 'A Amizade', 17 October 1869, p. 174

CAMPOS, CLÁUDIA DE, *Mulheres: ensaios de psicologia feminina* (Lisbon: M. Gomes Editor, 1895)

CAMPOS, MARIA AMÉLIA, *Ana, a lúcida: biografia de Ana Plácido, a mulher fatal de Camilo* (Lisbon: Parceria A. M. Pereira, 2008)

CARDOSO, NUNO CATARINO, *Poetisas portuguesas: antologia contendo dados bibliográficos e biográficos acerca de cento e seis poetisas* (Lisbon: N. C. Cardoso, 1917) <https://archive.org/details/poetisasportugue00carduoft/page/n3> [accessed 19 December 2018]

'Carnaval Permanente', *O António Maria*, 21 February 1884, p. 64.

CARNEIRO, ANA, ANA SIMÕES and MARIA PAULA DIOGO, 'Enlightenment Science in Portugal: The Estrangeirados and their Communication Networks', *Social Studies of Science*, 30 (2000), 591–619

CARON, ANNE MARIE, *A Voz Feminina*, [37], 'Carta de M.lle A. M. Caron à Ex.ma Sra D. Mariana Angélica de Andrade', 27 September 1868, pp. 3–4

—— [57], 'Vitor Hugo e os inocentes', 14 February 1869, p. 3

—— [63], 'Mina Auck', 28 March 1869, p. 2

—— [66], ['Querida redatora...'], 18 April 1869, p. 4

—— *O Progresso*, [91], 'Ao meu discípulo', 10 October 1869, p. 169

CARVALHO, ANTÓNIO JOSÉ DE, *A Voz Feminina*, [38], 'A Victor Hugo', 4 October 1868, p. 4

—— [39], 'Um Brado patriótico: a Portugal', 11 October 1868, p. 4

—— [77], 'O Progresso', 4 July 1869, p. 112

CASTELAR, EMILIO, 'Discurso sobre la libertad religiosa y la separación entre la Iglesia y el Estado: (12-IV-69)', Biblioteca Virtual Miguel de Cervantes <http://www.cervantesvirtual.com/obra-visor/discurso-sobre-la-libertad-religiosa--0/html/feedc9c0–82b1–11df-acc7–002185ce6064_1.html#I_1_> [accessed 3 December 2018]

CASTILHO, ANTÓNIO FELICIANO DE, 'D. Maria Peregrina de Sousa', *Revista Contemporânea de Portugal e Brazil*, 6 (1861), 272–312 <http://hemerotecadigital.cm-lisboa.pt/Periodicos/RevistaContemporanea/VolIII_1861/N06/N06_master/RevistaContemporaneadePortugaleBrasil_VolIII_1861_N06.pdf> [accessed 24 April 2017]

—— *Felicidade pela agricultura* (Ponta Delgada: Tipografia da Rua das Artes, 1849) <http://purl.pt/106/4> [accessed 8 May 2017]

CAVACO, TIMÓTEO, 'Ellen Roughton (1802–1883): mãe, educadora, anunciadora do Evangelho', *Refrigério: mulheres na seara*, 161 (2016), 11–21 <https://refrigerio.ciip.pt/2016/04/refrigerio-n-0-161-abr-jun-2016/> [accessed 1 December 2018]

CHARLTON, L. E. O., ed., *The Recollections of a Northumbrian Lady, 1815–1866: Being the Memoirs of Barbara Charlton (Née Tasburgh)* (London: J. Cape, 1949)

CHAUVAUD, FRÉDÉRIC, and OTHERS, eds, *Les Vies d'André Léo: romancière, féministe et communarde* (Rennes: Presses universitaires de Rennes, 2015)

CHOULIARAKI, LILIE, 'Re-Mediation, Inter-Mediation, Trans-Mediation: The Cosmopolitan Trajectories of Convergent Journalism', *Journalism Studies*, 2 (2013), 267–83 <https://doi.org/10.1080/1461670X.2012.718559> [accessed 5 November 2018]

CLAEYS, GREGORY, 'Owen, Robert (1771–1858)', in *Oxford Dictionary of National Biography* <http://www.oxforddnb.com/> [accessed 5 November 2016]

COELHO, J. C. TEIXEIRA, *O Progresso*, [95], 'Mais um brado: às senhoras portuguesas', 7 November 1869, pp. 183–84

COELHO, MARIA DE FÁTIMA, 'O Instituto vincular, sua decadência e morte: questões várias', *Análise Social*, 61–62 (1980), 111–31 <https://www.fd.unl.pt/Anexos/Investigacao/7696.pdf> [accessed 3 November 2018]

COELHO, MARIA TERESA PINTO, *Eça de Queirós and the Victorian Press* (London: Tamesis, 2014)

—— '"Pérfida Albion" and "Little Portugal": The Role of the Press in British and Portuguese National Perceptions of the 1890 Ultimatum', *Portuguese Studies*, 6 (1990), 173–90

COLLET, F. M., 'A Pinch of Curry Powder', *The Spectator*, 15 May 1925, p. 17 <http://archive.spectator.co.uk/page/16th-may-1925/17> [accessed 5 November 2016]

COLLING, ANNE MARIE, 'Precursor do voto feminino no ocidente é um brasileiro: Domingos Borges de Barros nas Cortes Gerais portuguesas em 1822', *Anais do XXVII Simpósio Nacional de História* <http://www.snh2013.anpuh.org/resources/anais/27/1370097714_ARQUIVO_textoanpuh2013.pdf> [accessed 10 November 2018]

COLLINS, WILKIE, *The Woman in White* (London: Sampson Low Son & Co., 1860)

COMANDULLI, ANA CRISTINA, 'Maria Peregrina de Sousa (1809–1894)', *Convergência Lusíada*, 32 (2014), 208–11 <http://rgplrc.libware.net/ojs/index.php/rcl/article/download/94/95> [accessed 24 April 2017]

—— 'Presença de A. F. de Castilho nas letras oitocentistas portuguesas: sociabilidades e difusão da escrita feminina' (unpublished doctoral thesis, Universidade Federal Fluminense, Niterói, 2014)

CONNELL, RAEWYN W., *Masculinities*, 2nd edn (Cambridge: Polity, 2005)

CORREIA, RITA, [Sousa Viterbo, Francisco Marques], [Ficha histórica] <http://hemerotecadigital.cm-lisboa.pt/RecursosInformativos/Biografias/Textos/SousaViterbo.pdf> [accessed 23 November 2018]

CORTEZ, MARIA TERESA, *Os Contos de Grimm em Portugal: a recepção dos Kinder- und Hausmärchen entre 1837 e 1910* (Coimbra: Minerva Coimbra, 2001), pp. 89–117

COSTA, AMÁLIA CÂNDIDA ISABEL DA, *A Voz Feminina*, [17], ['Damos a seguinte carta...'], [Correspondência], 10 May 1868, p. 4

—— [19], ['Ex.ma Sr.ª Redatora...'], 24 May 1868, p. 4

—— [19], 'Nem sempre', 24 May 1868, p. 4

—— [22], ['O muito que hoje se fala na emancipação...'], 14 June 1868, p. 1

COSTA, ANTÓNIO DA, *A Mulher em Portugal* (Lisbon: Tipografia da Companhia Nacional, 1892)

COSTA, FERNANDO MARQUES DA, *As Mulheres na maçonaria: Portugal 1864–1950* (Lisbon: Ancora Editora, 2016)

COUTO-POTACHE, DEJANIRAH, 'Les Origines du féminisme au Portugal', in *Utopie et socialisme au Portugal du 19e siècle: actes du colloque*, ed. by J. C. Seabra Pereira (Paris: Fondation Calouste Gulbenkian–Centre Culturel Portugais, 1982), pp. 449–78

'The Country', *The Spectator*, 27 February 1836, p. 9 <http://archive.spectator.co.uk/article/27th-february-1836/9/foston-hall-in-derbyshire-the-residence-of-mr-char> [accessed 16 November 2018]

COVA, ANNE, 'The National Councils of Women in France, Italy and Portugal: Comparisons and Entanglements, 1888–1939', in *Gender History in a Transnational Perspective: Networks, Biographies, Gender Orders*, ed. by Oliver Janz and Daniel Schönpflug (New York: Berghahn, 2014), pp. 46–76

CRAWFORD, ELIZABETH, *The Women's Suffrage Movement: A Reference Guide, 1866–1928* (London: Routledge, 2001)

CREESE, MARY R. S., 'Somerville, Mary (1780–1872)', in *Oxford Dictionary of National Biography* <http://www.oxforddnb.com/> [accessed 26 February 2016]

CRISTO, ANA TERESA FERNANDES PEIXINHO DE, *A Epistolaridade nos textos de imprensa de Eça de Queirós* (Lisbon: Fundação Calouste Gulbenkian, 2010)

'Critical and Miscellaneous Notices', *Westminster Review*, 108 (1851), 130–48

CRUZ, EDUARDO DA, *Maria José Canuto, 1812–1890* (Lisbon: Biblioteca Nacional de Portugal, 2018)

——'Um "brilhante congresso": escritoras portuguesas no projeto de António Feliciano de Castilho para sua versão d' *Os Fastos* ovidianos', *Soletras*, 34 (2017), 141–65

CUNHA, SOFIA NESBITT, *A Voz Feminina*, [30], ['Terremoto nas ilhas de Sandwich'], trans. by Sofia Nesbitt Cunha, 9 August 1868, pp. 3–4

——[32], 'O Espiritualismo', 23 August 1868, p. 2

CUROPOS, FERNANDO, *L'Emergence de l'homosexualité dans la littérature portugaise (1875–1915)* (Paris: L'Harmattan, 2016)

DEMERS, FRANÇOIS, 'The Editorial and Public Debate. Introduction', *Sur le journalisme*, 5.2 (2017), 84–86

DEUS, JOÃO DE, *A Voz Feminina*, [59], ['Diz-me L. a verdade...'], 28 February 1869, p. 4

——[59], ['Senhor, Senhor...'], 28 February 1869, p. 4

—— *O Progresso*, [90], ['Mal sabes o que sofro...'], 3 October 1869, p. 166

DIAS, EURICO, 'O Archivo Pittoresco (1857–1868): subsídios para sua história' <http://hemerotecadigital.cm-lisboa.pt/RecursosInformativos/ActasdeColoquiosConferencias/textos/ConfArqPit.pdf> [accessed 22 November 2018]

DIAS, MARINA TAVARES, *Lisboa desaparecida*, 9 vols (Lisbon: Quimera, 1987–2007), III (1992)

DILLANE, FIONNUALA, 'Researching a Periodical Genre: Classifications, Codes and Relational Terms', in *Researching the Nineteenth-Century Periodical Press: Case Studies*, ed. by Alexis Easley, Andrew King and John Morton (London: Routledge, 2018), pp. 74–90

DOLLFUS, ADRIEN, 'L'Aquarium du Havre', *Histoire Naturelle* <http://informations-documents.com/environnement/histoire-naturelle/23–111%20l%20aquarium%20du%20Havre.htm> [accessed 1 December 2018]

DUARTE, INOCÊNCIO DE SOUSA, *A Mulher na sociedade civil: compendio dos seus direitos, obrigações e privilegios segundo as leis em Portugal* (Lisbon: Imprensa Nacional, 1870)

DUARTE, MARIA DE DEUS, 'Pink sunsets: configurações e (des)figurações em Mary Severn', *Revista de Estudos Anglo-Portugueses*, 14 (2005), 257–82 <https://run.unl.pt/bitstream/10362/4384/1/Revista%20de%20Estudos%20Anglo-Portugueses%20-%20Numero%2014%20-%202005.pdf> [accessed 28 April 2017]

DUBY, GEORGES, and MICHELLE PERROT, eds, *Histoire des femmes en occident*, 5 vols (Paris: Plon, 1991), vol. IV: *Le XIXe Siècle*, ed. by Geneviève Fraisse and Michelle Perrot

EASLEY, A., KING, A. and MORTON, J., 'Introduction', in *Researching the Nineteenth-century Periodical Press: Case Studies*, ed. by Alexis Easley, Andrew King and John Morton (London: Routledge, 2018), pp. 1–13

EDFELDT, CHATARINA, *Uma História na História: representações da autoria feminina na História da Literatura Portuguesa do século XX* (Montijo: Câmara Municipal do Montijo, 2006)

ELLIOTT, EBENEZER, 'The People's Anthem', *Tait's Edinburgh Magazine*, 15 (1848), 403

—— *More Verse and Prose by The Cornlaw Rhymer*, 2 vols (London: C. Fox, 1850)

'Emília Adelaide Moniz da Maia', in *Dicionário no feminino (séculos XIX–XX)*, ed. by Zília Osório de Castro and others (Lisbon: Horizonte, 2005), pp. 303–04

'Employment of Women and Children in Agriculture', *The Englishwoman's Review of Social and Industrial Questions*, 11 (1869), pp. 155–76

ENGLISH, MARY P., 'Lankester, Edwin (1814–1874)', in *Oxford Dictionary of National Biography* <http://www.oxforddnb.com/> [accessed 2 December 2018]

—— *Victorian Values: The Life and Times of Dr. Edwin Lankester* (Bristol: Biopress, 1990)

ESTEVES, JOÃO, 'Historical Context of Feminism and Women's Rights in Nineteenth-Century Portugal', trans. by Deborah Madden, in *A New History of Iberian Feminisms*, ed. by Silvia Bermúdez and Roberta Johnson (Toronto: University of Toronto Press, 2018), pp. 101–10

EVERY-CLAYTON, JOYCE E. WINIFRED, 'The Legacy of Robert Reid Kalley', *International Bulletin of Missionary Research*, 26 (2002), 123–27

FAROL, F., *O Progresso*, [81], 'Escrito do Il.mo sr. F. Farol, dirigido à "Voz Feminina" em Agosto do ano findo', 1 August 1869, pp. 127–28

FAWCETT, MILLICENT GARRETT, 'The Women's Suffrage Movement', in *The Woman Question in Europe: A Series of Original Essays*, ed. by Theodore Stanton (New York: G. P. Putnam's Sons, 1884), pp. 1–29

FERREIRA, ANA PAULA, 'Nationalism and Feminism at the Turn of the Nineteenth Century: Constructing the "Other" (Woman) of Portugal', *Santa Barbara Portuguese Studies*, 3 (1996), 120–42

FERREIRA, LEONÍDIO PAULO, 'Quando Victor Hugo elogiou Portugal por abolir a pena de morte', *Diário de Notícias*, 1 January 2017 <https://www.dn.pt/portugal/interior/quando-victor-hugo-elogiou-portugal-por-abolir-a-pena-de-morte-5580047.html> [accessed 3 November 2018]

FINCH, ALISON, *Women's Writing in 19th-century France* (Cambridge: Cambridge University Press, 2000)

'Fines Arts — Music', *The Analyst: A Quarterly Journal of Science, Literature, Natural History and the Fine Arts*, ed. by William Holl, Neville Wood and Edward Mammatt, 10 vols (London: Simpkin & Marshall, 1834–40), V (1836), 343–44

FINLAYSON, LORNA, *An Introduction to Feminism* (Cambridge: Cambridge University Press, 2016)

'Folhetim', *O Zoofilo*, 14 January 1877, p. 4

The fortieth annual report of the British Protestant School in connexion [sic] with St. George's Chapel Lisbon (Lisbon: Anglo-Portuguese Printing Office, 1877)

FOSTER, JOSEPH, ed., *Alumni Oxonienses: The Members of the University of Oxford, 1715–1886: Their Parentage, Birthplace and Year of Birth, With a Record of Their Degrees: Being the Matriculation Register of the University*, 4 vols (Oxford: Parker and Co, 1887–88), IV (1888)

—— *Register of Admissions to Gray's Inn, 1521–1889: Together With the Register of Marriages in Gray's Inn Chapel, 1695–1754* ([n.p.]: Hansard Publishing Union, 1889)

FOUCAULT, MICHEL, *The History of Sexuality: An Introduction*, trans. by Robert Hurley, 3 vols (New York: Pantheon Books, 1978–86), I (1978)

FRANÇA, JOSÉ-AUGUSTO, *Rafael Bordalo Pinheiro: o português tal e qual*, 3rd edn (Lisbon: Livros Horizonte, 2007)

FRIER, DAVID GIBSON, 'The Transition from Romanticism to Realism: Alexandre Herculano, Camilo Castelo Branco and Júlio Dinis', in *A Companion to Portuguese Literature*, ed. by Stephen Parkinson, Cláudia Pazos Alonso and T. F. Earle (London: Boydell & Brewer, 2009), pp. 120–30

G., LEONOR, A., P., [PSEUD.], *A Voz Feminina*, [5], 'Um Monumento de civilização no século 19.°, para juntar ao feixinho de curiosidades', 8 February 1868, p. 4

GARCÍA, ROSA MARÍA BALLESTEROS, 'El despertar de un movimiento social: el feminismo en Portugal', in *Discursos, realidades, utopías: la construcción del sujeto femenino en los siglos XIX–XX*, ed. by Maria Dolores Ramos Palomo and María Teresa Vera Balanza (Barcelona: Anthropos Editorial, 2002), pp. 165–212

GARRET, MARTIN, 'Mitford, Mary Russell (1787–1855)', in *Oxford Dictionary of National Biography* <http://www.oxforddnb.com/> [accessed 3 November 2018]

GASKILL, HOWARD, ed., *The Reception of Ossian in Europe* (London and New York: Thoemmes Continuum, 2004)

GOEGG, MARIE, *A Voz Feminina*, [55], ['Genebra, 19 de janeiro de 1869...'], 31 January 1869, pp. 2–3

——*O Progresso*, [97], 'Discurso da madame Goegg, presidenta [sic] da associação internacional das mulheres, pronunciado por ela mesma no terceiro congresso da liga da paz e da liberdade, reunido em Lausana', 21 November 1869, pp. 191–92

—— 'Woman's Rights in Europe', *The Revolution* [New York], 15 April 1869, pp. 228–29

—— ['Lista dos subscritores até esta data...'], *O Zoofilo*, 10 May 1877, p. 4

—— 'Literature review of John Stuart Mill, The Subjection of Women', *The Athenaeum*, 19 June 1869, pp. 819–20

GONZAGA, TOMÁS ANTÔNIO, *Marília de Dirceu* (Rio de Janeiro: Garnier, 1992)

—— *O Progresso*, [82], 'Marilia de Dirceu: Lira XVII', 8 August 1869, p. 134

GOODOLFIM, JOSÉ CIPRIANO DA COSTA, *O Celibato clerical* (Lisbon: Tipografia Universal, 1872)

—— *A Religião dos padres: a propósito do sermão anti-evangélico do Padre Serrano* ([n.p.], [n.pub.], 1870)

—— *A Voz Feminina*, [59], 'Deus e o homem', 28 February 1869, pp. 2–3

[69], 'Deus e o homem', 9 May 1869, p. 3

[70], 'Deus e o homem', 16 May 1869, p. 4

GRAÇA, JOSÉ JOAQUIM LOPES, *A Mulher e a vida ou a mulher considerada debaixo dos seus principais aspétos* (Coimbra: Livraria Portuguesa e Estrangeira, 1872)

GREIG, JAMES, *Sir Henry Raeburn, R.A.: His Life and Works, With a Catalogue of his Pictures* (London: The Connoisseur, 1911) <https://archive.org/stream/sirhenryraeburnroogreiuoft/ sirhenryraeburnroogreiuoft_djvu.txt> [accessed 4 November 2016]

GUEDES, FERNANDO, *O Livro e a leitura em Portugal: subsídios para a sua história, séculos XVIII e XIX* (Lisbon; São Paulo: Verbo, 1987)

'Guiomar Torresão', Escritoras: Women Writers in Portuguese before 1900 <http://www. escritoras-em-portugues.eu/1417106880-Cent-XIX/2015-0531-Guiomar-Torreso> [accessed 13 October 2016]

HAAN, F. DE, 'Fry [née Gurney], Elizabeth (1780–1845)', *Oxford Dictionary of National Biography*

HAMLET, JANICE D. 'Editorials', in Christopher H. Sterling, ed., *Encyclopedia of Journalism*, 6 vols (Los Angeles & London: Sage, 2009) V, 473–77

HARRISON, ROBERT, 'Banting, William (1796/7–1878)', in *Oxford Dictionary of National Biography* <http://www.oxforddnb.com/> [accessed 26 February 2016]

HENRIQUES, JOÃO PAULO, 'O pioneirismo protestante na génese de organizações univer-salistas em Portugal', *Revista Lusófona de Ciência das Religiões*, 7-8 (2005), 97-107 <https:// revistas.ulusofona.pt/index.php/cienciareligioes/article/view/4141>

HERCULANO, ALEXANDRE, *Poesias*, 2nd edn (Lisbon: Viúva Bertrand e Filhos, 1850) <http:// purl.pt/167/3> [accessed 25 November 2018]

—— *O Progresso*, [88], 'A Rosa', 19 September 1869, p. 158

HIPPEAU, C., *O Progresso*, [81], 'Educação das mulheres nos Estados Unidos: Colégio Vassar', 1 August 1869, pp. 129–30

HOOPER, KIRSTY, *A Stranger in My Own Land: Sofia Casanova, a Spanish Writer in the European Fin de Siecle* (Nashville, TN: Vanderbilt University Press, 2008)

HORSLEY, CHARLES EDWARD, 'Reminiscences of Mendelssohn by his English Pupil', in *Mendelssohn and his World*, ed. by R. Larry Todd (Princeton, NJ: Princeton University Press, 1991), pp. 237–51

HOWES, ROBERT, 'Concerning the Eccentricities of the Marquis of Valada: Politics, Culture and Homosexuality in Fin-de-Siècle Portugal', *Sexualities*, 1 (2002), 25–48

HUGHES, LINDA, 'Sideways!: Navigating the Material(ity) of Print Culture', *Victorian Periodicals Review*, 47 (2014), 1–30

ILDEFONSO, MARIA ISABEL MOUTINHO DUARTE, 'As Mulheres na imprensa periódica do séc. XIX' (unpublished master's thesis, Universidade Aberta, 1998)

—— 'As Mulheres na imprensa periódica do século XIX: o jornal *A Voz feminina* (1868–1869)', in *Novos olhares: passado e presente nos estudos sobre as mulheres em Portugal*, ed. by Teresa Joaquim and Anabela Galhardo (Oeiras: Celta, 2003), pp. 15–21

'Isabel Fry', *O Amigo da Infância*, n.d. (Lisbon: Tip. Luso-Britânica), pp. 12–13 & 21–23

'Item lot number: 383', Tennants Auctioneers <https://bid.tennants.co.uk/m/lot-details/index/catalog/69/lot/57176?url=%2Fm%2Fview-auctions%2Fcatalog%2Fid%2F69%3Fpage%3D8> [accessed 4 November 2016]

JACKSON, LADY CATHERINE, *Fair Lusitania* (London: R. Bentley and Son, 1874)

—— *A Formosa Lusitânia*, trans. by Camilo Castelo Branco (Porto: Livraria Portuense, 1878)

JANNY, AMÉLIA, *A Voz Feminina*, [13], ['Ex.ma Sra...'], [Correspondência], 26 April 1868, p. 3

JENKINS, ROY, 'Dilke, Sir Charles Wentworth, second baronet (1843–1911)', in *Oxford Dictionary of National Biography* <http://www.oxforddnb.com/> [accessed 26 February 2016]

KÄPPELI, ANNE-MARIE, 'Scènes Feministes', in *Histoire des femmes en occident*, ed. by Georges Duby and Michelle Perrot, 5 vols (Paris: Plon, 1991), vol. IV: *Le XIXe Siècle*, ed. by Geneviève Fraisse and Michelle Perrot, pp. 495–525

KIRKPATRICK, SUSAN, 'Women as Cultural Agents in Spanish Modernity', in *A Companion to Spanish Women's Studies*, ed. by Xon de Ros and Geraldine Hazbun (London: Boydell & Brewer, 2011), pp. 227–42

KRAMARAE, CHERIS, and LANA F. RAKOW, eds, *The Revolution in Words: Righting Women, 1868–1871* (London: Routledge, 1990)

LA PARRA, EMILIO, 'La Canción del Trágala: cultura y política popular en el inicio de la revolución liberal en España', *Les Travaux du crec en ligne*, 6 (2009), 68–86 <http://crec-paris3.fr/wp-content/uploads/2011/07/actes-03-La-Parra.pdf> [accessed 1 December 2018]

LEAL, MARIA IVONE, *Um século de periódicos femininos: arrolamento de periódicos entre 1807 e 1926* (Lisbon: Comissão para a Igualdade e para os Direitos da Mulher, 1992)

—— 'A Voz Feminina: jornal semanal scientífico, litterário e noticioso', *Comissão da Condição Feminina*, 3 (1981), 18–26 <http://cid.cig.gov.pt/Nyron/Library/Catalog/flexpaper.aspx?skey=CDB781C63EB344EAAAEA6D9208D065C7&doc=9636&img=139967&save=true> [accessed 5 November 2018]

LEAVITT, WILLIAM, 'History of the Essex Lodge of Freemasons', in *The Historical Collections of the Essex Institute*, 4 vols (Salem, MA: G. M. Whipple & A. A. Smith, 1859–62), III (1861), 253–72 <http://dbooks.bodleian.ox.ac.uk/books/PDFs/555028439.pdf> [accessed 1 November 2016]

LEITE, RITA MENDONÇA, *Representações do protestantismo na sociedade portuguesa contemporânea: da exclusão à liberdade de culto (1852–1911)* (Lisbon: Centro de Estudos de História Religiosa da Universidade Católica Portuguesa, 2009)

LEONARD, ANGELA M., 'Elliott, Ebenezer (1781–1849)', in *Oxford Dictionary of National Biography* <http://www.oxforddnb.com/> [accessed 26 February 2016]

LESTER, JOSEPH, *E. Ray Lankester and the Making of Modern British Biology* ([n.p.]: British Society for the History of Science, 1995)

LISBOA, JOÃO LUÍS, 'From Publishing to the Publisher: Portugal and Changes in the World of Print in the Nineteenth Century', in Márcia Abreu and Ana Cláudia Suriani da Silva, eds, *The Cultural Revolution of the Nineteenth Century: Theatre, the Book Trade, and Reading in the Transatlantic World.* (London: I. B. Tauris, 2016), pp. 69–86

'Literary Review of John Stuart Mill, *The Subjection of Women*', *The Athenaeum*, 19 June 1869, pp. 819–20

LOBO, FRANCISCO RODRIGUES, *O Progresso*, [92], ' O Poeta e o Tejo', 17 October 1869, p. 174

LOPES, ANA MARIA COSTA, 'Alguns aspectos da luta de Guiomar Torrezão pela igualdade', *Povos e Culturas*, 9 (2004), 455–70 <http://icm.fch.lisboa.ucp.pt/resources/Documentos/CEPCEP/POVOS%20E%20CULTURAS_9.pdf> [accessed 14 December 2018]

—— 'Atitude e documento invulgar: a intervenção de uma prestigiada oitocentista, Antónia Pusich, na Câmara dos Deputados', *Povos e Culturas*, 8 (2003), 207–28 <http://icm.fch. lisboa.ucp.pt/resources/Documentos/CEPCEP/POVOS%20E%20CULTURAS_8.pdf> [accessed 5 December 2018]

—— 'Francisca de Assis Martins Wood', in *Feminae: dicionário contemporâneo*, ed. by João Esteves and others (Lisbon: Comissão para a Cidadania e a Igualdade de Género, 2013), pp. 312–18 <http://cid.cig.gov.pt/Nyron/Library/Catalog/winlibimg.aspx?skey=0BC86 F59EEEF4B5DA62821F712ACB60E&doc=95065&img=139416> [accessed 28 April 2017]

—— *Imagens da mulher na imprensa feminina de oitocentos: percursos de modernidade* (Lisbon: Quimera, 2005)

—— 'Religião e género como formas de discriminação no século XIX: o casal Wood, um study case', *Gaudium Sciendi*, 2 (2012), 51–65 <http://www2.ucp.pt/resources/ Documentos/SCUCP/GaudiumSciendi/GaudiumSciendi_N2_emendas/3.Ana%20 Costa%20Lopes_copia.pdf> [accessed 26 February 2016]

LOURENÇO, ANTÓNIO APOLINÁRIO, MARIA HELENA SANTANA and MARIA JOÃO SIMÕES, eds, *O Século do romance: realismo e naturalismo na ficção oitocentista* (Coimbra: Centro de Literatura Portuguesa, 2013)

LOUSADA, ISABEL, 'Para o estabelecimento de uma bibliografia britânica em português, 1554–1900' (unpublished doctoral thesis, Universidade Nova, Lisboa, 1998)

LOUSADA, ISABEL, VÂNIA PINHEIRO CHAVES and CARLOS ABREU, eds, *As Senhoras do almanaque: catálogo da produção de autoria feminina* (Lisbon: Biblioteca Nacional de Portugal, 2014)

LYTTON, EDWARD BULWER SIR, *The Pilgrims of the Rhine* (London: Saunders and Otley Conduit Street, 1834)

MACHADO, LUÍS DE ABREU, 'Anticlericalismo', in *Dança dos demónios: intolerância em Portugal*, ed. by António Marujo and José Eduardo Franco ([Lisbon]: Círculo de Leitores, 2009), pp. 125–202

MADDEN, DEBORAH, 'Historical Context in Portugal', in *A New History of Iberian Feminisms*, ed. by Silvia Bermúdez and Roberta Johnson (Toronto: University of Toronto Press, 2018), pp. 199–203

—— 'Feminist Thought in Portugal, 1900–1926', in *A New History of Iberian Feminisms*, ed. by Silvia Bermúdez and Roberta Johnson (Toronto: University of Toronto Press, 2018), pp. 204–12

MAIA, EMÍLIA ADELAIDE MONIZ DA, *A Voz Feminina*, [24], ['Não é só nas delicadas e mimosas colunas da Voz Feminina...'], 28 June 1868, p. 1

—— [27], ['Entre diversas opiniões que se têm desenhado...'], 19 July 1868, pp. 1–2

—— [32], 'Mais algumas portuguesas distintas', 23 August 1868, pp. 1–2

—— [32], ['Começarei hoje perguntando...'], 23 August 1868, p. 1

—— [34], 'Canção do exílio', 6 September 1868, p. 4

—— [38], ['Minha muito querida tia...'], 4 October 1868, p. 4

—— [43], 'Canto materno: à minha inocente filhinha', 8 November 1868, p. 4

—— [51], '1.º Aniversário da "Voz Feminina": introdução', 3 January 1869, pp. 1–2

—— [56], 'O Carnaval: cavaco com as leitoras da Voz Feminina', 7 February 1869, pp. 1–2

—— [57], 'M.elle de Sombreuil', 14 February 1869, pp. 3–4

—— [58], 'O Século XIX', 21 February 1869, pp. 1–2

—— [63], ['Vai ser publicado em Paris...'], 28 March 1869, p. 4

—— [64], 'Coisas sérias', 4 April 1869, pp. 1–2

—— [69], 'Leituras em família', 9 May 1869, pp. 1–2

MARIANO, JULIANA DE SOUZA, 'A Personagem feminina nos romances de Maria Peregrina de Sousa: ambiguidades e dualidades' (unpublished master's thesis, Universidade do Rio de Janeiro, 2015)

MARQUES, ANTÓNIO HENRIQUE R. DE OLIVEIRA, *Dicionário de maçonaria portuguesa*, 2 vols (Lisbon: Delta, 1986)

MARQUES, F. DE ABREU, *A Voz Feminina*, [51], '1.º Aniversário da "Voz Feminina": introdução', 3 January 1869, pp. 1–2

——[56], 'O Carnaval: cavaco com as leitoras da Voz Feminina', 7 February 1869, pp. 1–2

——[58], 'O Século XIX', 21 February 1869, pp. 1–2

——[64], 'Coisas sérias', 4 April 1869, pp. 1–2

——[69], 'Leituras em família', 9 May 1869, pp. 1–2

MARQUES, LEONARDO, *The United States and the Transatlantic Slave Trade to the Americas, 1776–1867* (New Haven, CT: Yale University Press, 2016)

MARTINS, CLARIMUNDO, *A Voz Feminina*, [38], ['Minha muito querida tia...'], 4 October 1868, p. 4

MATOS, A. CAMPOS, ed., *Dicionário de Eça de Queiroz* (Lisbon: Caminho, 1993)

MATOS, FRANCISCO A. DE, *A Voz Feminina*, [24], ['Não é só nas delicadas e mimosas colunas da Voz Feminina...'], 28 June 1868, p. 1

——[27], ['Entre diversas opiniões que se têm desenhado...'], 19 July 1868, pp. 12

——[32], ['Começarei hoje perguntando...'], 23 August 1868, p. 1

MAYEUR, FRANÇOISE, 'Les Evêques français et Victor Duruy: les cours secondaires de jeunes filles', *Revue d'histoire de l'Église de France*, 159 (1971), pp. 267–304 <http://www.persee.fr/doc/rhef_0300–9505_1971_num_57_159_1872> [accessed 2 December 2018]

MCOUAT, GORDON R., 'Species, Rules and Meaning: The Politics of Language and the Ends of Definitions in 19th Century Natural History', *Studies in History and Philosophy of Science*, 4 (1996), 473–519

'The Meeting of the Nations — A Song for the Great Exhibition of Industry in 1851 — Words by Charlotte Young, Music by Wm. Thorold Wood, 1851', *Victorian Sheet Music Covers Collection*, Box 3, Item 81, Special Collections and Archives, Oviatt Library, California State University, Northridge

[MILL, HARRIET TAYLOR], 'The Enfranchisement of Women', *Westminster Review*, 109 (1851), 289–311

MILO, M. SAGE, '"Intellectual Acid": Cultural Resistance, Cultural Citizenship, and Emotional (Counter) Community in the *Freewoman*', *Journal of European Periodical Studies*, 1 (2017), 39–53

MÓNICA, MARIA FILOMENA, ed., *Dicionário biográfico parlamentar, 1834–1910*, 3 vols (Lisbon: Assembleia da República–Imprensa de Ciências Sociais, 2004–06)

MORAIS, MARIA ANTONIETA LOPES VILÃO VAZ DE, 'Os Alfaiates e as modistas em Lisboa (1775–1850): subsídio para a história do traje e da moda', *Revista de Artes Decorativas*, 6 (2012–14), 197–222 <http://citar.artes.porto.ucp.pt/sites/default/files/files/artes/CITAR/Edicoes/RAD_06.pdf> [accessed 24 April 2017]

MOREIRA, J. M. MENDES, *Origens do episcopalismo em Portugal: o despertar da igreja lusitana (1839–1899)* (Porto: [n.pub.], 1995)

MORSE, ELIZABETH J., 'Marcet, Jane Haldimand (1769–1858)', in *Oxford Dictionary of National Biography* <http://www.oxforddnb.com/> [accessed 26 February 2016]

[MUSICAL INSTITUTE], *Jornal do Comércio*, 23 March 1861, p. 4

MUZART, ZAHIDÉ LUPINACCI, ed., *Escritoras brasileiras do século XIX: antologia* (Florianópolis: Mulheres; Santa Cruz do Sul; UNISC, 1999)

[N.A.], *A Voz Feminina*, [2], ['Agradeço e li...'], [Correspondência], 12 January 1868, p. 3

——[3], ['Sra Redatora da *Voz Feminina*...'], [Correspondência], 19 January 1868, p. 3

——[5], ['O globo donde a nossa colega...'], 8 February 1868, p. 4

——[6], ['O Sr. Sousa Teles disse...'], 23 February 1868, pp. 1–2

——[6], ['Toda a correspondência...'], [Expediente], 23 February 1868, p. 4

——[7], ['O Cristianismo...'], 1 March 1868, pp. 1–2

——[7], ['Toda a correspondência...'], [Expediente], 1 March 1868, p. 4
——[8], ['Não há ninguém nos domínios de...'], 8 March 1868, p. 1
——[9], ['Dissemos no nosso último número...'], 15 March 1868, pp. 1–2
——[11], ['Qualquer pessoa que fora de Portugal...'], 29 March 1868, pp. 1–2
——[12], ['Poderá alguém dizer-me...'], 5 April 1868, pp. 1–2
——[13], ['Recebemos há tempo...'], 12 April 1868, pp. 1–2
——[14], ['Dissemos no número antecedente...'], 19 April 1868, pp. 1–2
——[15], ['Faz dó ver como uma parte...'], 26 April 1868, pp. 1–2
——[17], ['Abrindo...'], 10 May 1868, pp. 1–2
——[17], ['Damos a seguinte carta...'], [Correspondência], 10 May 1868, p. 4
——[18], ['Se os primeiros sons emitidos...'], 17 May 1868, pp. 1–2
——[19], ['Algumas das nossas distintas colaboradoras...'], 24 May 1868, pp. 1–2
——[20], ['Diz-se que as senhoras em toda a Europa...'], 31 May 1868, pp. 1–2
——[21], ['A redatora desta folha agradece...'], 7 June 1868, pp. 1–2
——[23], ['A redação da *Voz Feminina*...'], 21 June 1868, p. 1
——[23], 'Lord Brougham', 21 June 1868, p. 2
——[25], ['Com data de 19 de maio último...], 5 July 1868, p. 4
——[26], ['Domingo último...'], 12 July 1868, p. 1
——[27], ['Com a devida vénia...'], 19 July 1868, p. 1
——[26], ['Publicamos os seguintes extratos...'], 12 July 1868, p. 4
——[29], ['Diz o Sr. F. F. no Jornal de Setúbal...'], 2 August 1868, pp. 1–2
——[33], ['Do Egitaniense transcrevemos o seguinte....'], 30 August 1868, pp. 1–2
——[34], 'Observações sobre o artigo de fundo do número 33', 6 September 1868, p. 1
——[39], ['A Redação da *Voz Feminina*...'], [Expediente], 11 October 1868, p. 1
——[41], 'Questão ibérica', 25 October 1868, p. 2
——[44], ['Pedimos vénia para transcrever na nossa folha...'], 15 November 1868, p. 1
——[63], 'Associação das Senhoras Francesas', 28 March 1869, p. 3
——[63], 'Eleições em Inglaterra', 28 March 1869, p. 4
——[73], 'Mulheres Lavradoras', 6 June 1869, pp. 3–4
——[76], 'O Sexo feminino', 27 June 1869, p. 2
——*O Progresso*, [78], ['No Diário Popular...'], 11 July 1869, pp. 115–16
——[79], ['A educação do povo é a questão palpitante do dia...'], 18 July 1869, pp. 119–20
——[80], ['Com uma só exceção...'], 25 July 1869, pp. 123–24
——[82], ['O concílio ecuménico é o grande enigma'], 8 August 1869, pp. 131–32
——[82], 'Uma Senhora portuguesa médico', 8 August 1869, p. 134
——[83], ['Há um defeito inerente na natureza de todas...'], 15 August 1869, pp. 135–36
——[85], ['Depois da mudança ministerial...'], 29 August 1869, pp. 143–44
——[86], ['A questão da emancipação da mulher...'], 5 September 1869, pp. 147–48
——[87], ['Os meios por que se regulam as acções do homem...'], 12 September 1869, pp. 151–52
——[91], ['Quando temos protestado com toda a força...'], 10 October 1869, pp. 167–68
——[95], 'A Redatora deste jornal...', 7 November 1869, p. 184
——[96], ['No artigo de fundo do n.º 87 dissemos o seguinte...'], 14 November 1869, pp. 187–88
——[98], ['Recebeu-se ultimamente nesta redacção...'], 28 November 1869, pp. 195–96
——[100], ['No dia 1 de Dezembro distribuiu-se gratuitamente...'], 12 December 1869, pp. 203–04
——[101], ['Publica-se em Barcelona um jornal inteiramente devotado...'], 19 December 1869, pp. 207–08
——[102], ['Recebemos, há pouco, uma carta...'], 26 December 1869, pp. 211–12

'National Reform Conference', *The Morning Advertiser*, 24 April 1850, p. 3

NAVARRO, ANA RITA SOVERAL PADEIRA, 'Da personagem romanesca à personagem fílmica: *As Pupilas do Senhor Reitor*' (unpublished doctoral thesis, Universida Aberta, 1999)

NEUVILLE, JOSEPHINA, *Memórias da minha vida: recordações das minhas viagens*, 2 vols (Lisbon: Tipografia do panorama, 1864) <http://dbooks.bodleian.ox.ac.uk/books/PDFs/590716508.pdf>; <http://dbooks.bodleian.ox.ac.uk/books/PDFs/555057227.pdf> [accessed 28 April 2017]

—— 'Explicação sobre umas memórias', *A Revolução de Setembro*, 21 January 1859, pp. 1–2 <http://purl.pt/14345/1/j-4157-g_1859-01-21/j-4157-g_1859-01-21_item2/j-4157-g_1859-01-21_PDF/j-4157-g_1859-01-21_PDF_24-C-R0150/j-4157-g_1859-01-21_0000_1-4_t24-C-R0150.pdf> [accessed 24 November 2018]

NEWMAN, FRANCIS, *A Lecture on Women's Suffrage: delivered in Bristol Athenaeum, February 24th, 1869* (London: London Society for Women's Suffrage, 1869; repr. [n.a.]: The Francis William Newman Society, 2009) <http://www.fwnewman.org/Library/Works/SPE/LWS_2–24–69.pdf> [accessed 2 December 2018]

'New Music by William Thorold Wood', *The Spectator*, 6 May 1837, p. 22 <http://archive.spectator.co.uk/page/6th-may-1837/22> [accessed 5 November 2016]

Novo guia do viajante em Lisboa e seus arredores, Cintra, Collares, e Mafra: ornado com algumas vistas dos principaes monumentos de Lisboa (Lisbon: J. J. Bordalo, 1853)

NOYES, HENRY EDWARD, *Church Reform in Spain and Portugal: A Short History of the Reformed Episcopal Churches of Spain and Portugal* (London: Cassell, 1897)

'Obituary of Mrs Jane Wood', *Monthly Homeopathic Review*, 5 (1865), 192

ORTIGÃO, RAMALHO, *As Farpas*, 15 vols (Lisbon: Livraria Clássica Editora, 1943–46)

—— 'Prólogo', in Maria Amália Vaz de Carvalho, *Crónicas de Valentina* (Lisbon: Tavares Cardoso, 1890), <http://dbooks.bodleian.ox.ac.uk/books/PDFs/N11276110.pdf>

OSÓRIO, ANA DE CASTRO, *Às Mulheres Portuguesas*, ed. by Andreia Neves and Filipa Catarino (Lisbon: Bibliotrónica Portuguesa, 2015) <https://bibliotronicaportuguesa.pt/wp-content/uploads/2015/03/ana_de_castro_osorio_as_mulheres_portuguesas_3.pdf> [accessed 1 November 2018]

'Our Weekly Gossip', *The Athenaeum*, 6 June 1868, p. 799

OUTEIRINHO, MARIA DE FÁTIMA, 'O Folhetim em Portugal no século XIX: uma nova janela no mundo das letras' (unpublished doctoral thesis, Universidade do Porto, 2003)

—— 'Guiomar Torrezão ou memória de uma mulher de letras oitocentista', *Intercâmbio: r, 9 (1998), 163–76* <http://ler.letras.up.pt/uploads/ficheiros/5922.pdf> [accessed 24 April 2017]

OWEN, HILARY, and CLÁUDIA PAZOS ALONSO, *Antigone's Daughters? Gender, Genealogy, and the Politics of Authorship in Twentieth-Century Portuguese Women's Writing* (Lewisburg, PA: Bucknell University Press, 2011)

P., CARLOTA A., *A Voz Feminina*, [2], ['Hasteamos um pendão glorioso...'], 12 January 1868, p. 1

—— [3], ['A ilustração máxima de todos os sexos e classes...'], 19 January 1868, p. 1

—— [4], ['Temos pugnado...'], 26 January 1868, p. 1

—— [5], ['Estabelecer os princípios da mais perfeita igualdade...'], 8 February 1868, pp. 1–2

PALETSCHEK, SYLVIA, and BIANKA PIETROW-ENNKER, 'Women's Emancipation Movements in the Long Nineteenth Century: Conclusions', in *Women's Emancipation Movements in the Nineteenth Century: A European Perspective* (Stanford, CA: Stanford University Press, 2004), pp. 301–33

PALMELA, JOSÉ, *A Aristocracia do génio e da beleza feminil na antiguidade* (Coimbra: Imprensa da Universidade, 1871)

—— *A Aristocracia do génio e da beleza feminil na antiguidade*, 4th edn (Coimbra: Imprensa da Universidade, 1872)

—— *A Aristocracia do génio e da beleza feminil na antiguidade*, 5th edn (Coimbra: Imprensa da Universidade, 1876)

PARKINSON, STEPHEN, CLÁUDIA PAZOS ALONSO and T. F. EARLE, eds, *A Companion to Portuguese Literature* (Woodbridge: Tamesis, 2009)

PARTZCH, HENRIETTE, 'Danger, You Are Entering the Garbage Vortex! Salvaging the History of Women's Participation in European Literary Culture', *Nora: Nordic Journal of Feminist and Gender Research*, 4 (2017), 334–39

PATO, RAIMUNDO ANTÓNIO BULHÃO, *Memórias*, 3 vols (Lisbon: Tipografia da Academia Real das Ciências, 1894–1907), II (1894) <http://purl.pt/248/4/> [accessed 24 November 2018]

PAZOS-ALONSO, CLÁUDIA, 'Assimetrias de Género: a trajetória de Ana Plácido e o papel de Camilo', in *Representações do feminino em Camilo Castelo Branco*, ed. by Sérgio Guimarães de Sousa (Braga: Centro de Estudos Camilianos, 2014), pp. 39–63

—— 'Judith Teixeira: um caso modernista insólito', in *Obras de Judith Teixeira: poesia e prosa*, ed. by Cláudia Pazos Alonso and Fábio Mário da Silva (Lisbon: Dom Quixote, 2015), pp. 21–38

—— 'Modernity in the Making: The Women at the Heart of *A Voz Feminina* and *O Progresso*', in *As Mulheres e o moderno*, ed. by Ana Luísa Vilela, Fábio Mário da Silva and Maria Lúcia Dal Farra (Lisbon: CEPUL, 2017), pp. 37–57 <http://en.calameo.com/read/0018279775d87a8e210c2> [accessed 22 May 2017]

—— 'A Newly Discovered Novel and its Transnational Author: *Maria Severn* by Francisca Wood', *Portuguese Studies*, 32 (2016), 48–61

—— 'A Public Intellectual in Nineteenth-Century Portugal: Francisca Wood's Editorials', *Journal of Romance Studies*, 19.3 (2019), 343–68

—— 'Publish and be Damned: *Memórias da Minha Vida* and the Politics of Exclusion in Nineteenth-Century Portugal,' in *Transnational Portuguese Studies*, ed. by Hilary Owen and Claire Williams (Liverpool: University of Liverpool Press, forthcoming 2020)

—— 'Spreading the Word: The "Woman Question" in the Periodicals *A Voz Feminina* and *O Progresso* (1868–9)', *Angelaki: Journal of the Theoretical Humanities*, 1 (2017), 61–75, reprinted in *Women Writing across Cultures: Past, Present and Future*, ed. by Pelagia Goulimari (New York: Routledge, 2018)

PEREIRA, AUGUSTO XAVIER DA SILVA, *O Jornalismo português* (Lisbon: Tipografia Soares, 1896)

PEREIRA, MARIA DA CONCEIÇÃO MEIRELES, 'A Questão ibérica: imprensa e opinião, 1850–1870' (unpublished doctoral thesis, Universidade do Porto, 1995) <https://repositorio-aberto.up.pt/handle/10216/55312?locale=pt> [accessed 24 November 2018]

PIMENTEL, IRENE FLUNSER, and HELENA PEREIRA DE MELO, *Mulheres Portuguesas* (Lisbon: Clube do autor, 2015)

'Pimlico: Conservation Area — General Information Leaflet', City of Westminster, May 2004 <http://www3.westminster.gov.uk/docstores/publications_store/27%20Pimlico.pdf> [accessed 4 November 2016]

PLÁCIDO, ANA, ['Folha avulsa para recolha de assinaturas de Esperança'], Archive of Alexandre Cabral, Casa de Camilo Castelo Branco, Folder XXVIII, 94

—— *Herança de Lágrimas* (Lisbon: Sibila, 2019 [1871])

—— *Herança de lágrimas: romance original* (Guimarães: Vimaranense Editora, 1871; repr. V. N. de Famalicão: Lello & Irmão; C. M. V. N. de Famalicão, 1995)

—— 'Horas de luz nas trevas dum cárcere', *Revista Contemporânea de Portugal e Brasil*, 9 (1860), 422–24

—— *Luz coada por ferros* (V. N. de Famalicão: Lello & Irmão; C. M. V. N. de Famalicão, 1995), vol. I

—— 'Meditação', *Revista Contemporânea de Portugal e Brasil*, 2 (1862–63), 65–69

—— 'Meditação', *Revista Contemporânea de Portugal e Brasil*, 4 (1862–63), 197–200

——'*Herança de Lágrimas* (Lisbon: Sibila, 2019)

POPE, T. GODFREY P., and others, *A Communication from the Lusitanian Church* (Lisbon: [n.pub.], 1880) <http://dbooks.bodleian.ox.ac.uk/books/PDFs/590801757.pdf> [accessed 6 November 2016]

'Portugal Reached', *The Revolution* [New York], 9 July 1868, p. 11

PÓVOAS, MAURO NICOLA, 'Fontes primárias e redescobertas: o caso de Emília da Maia', in *Língua portuguesa: ultrapassar fronteiras, juntar culturas*, ed. by Maria João Marçalo and others (Évora: Universidade de Évora, 2010), pp. 1–21 <http://www.simelp2009.uevora.pt/pdf/slt56/04.pdf> [accessed 13 October 2016]

PÓVOAS, MAURO NICOLA, and LOUISE FARIAS DA SILVEIRA, 'Guiomar Torresão e as "Cartas Póstumas" do Periódico Feminino *O Mundo Elegante* (1887)', *Navegações*, 5 (2012), 101–05

PRAÇA, JOSÉ JOAQUIM LOPES *A Mulher e a vida ou a Mulher Considerada debaixo dos seus Principais Aspectos*, 2nd edn (Lisbon: Edições Colibri, 2005 [1872])

'Probate Calendars of England & Wales, 1858–1959', *Find my past* <https://search.findmypast.co.uk/search-world-Records/probate-calendars-of-england-and-wales-1858-1959> [accessed 2 December 2018]

'Proceedings of Societies', in *The Analyst: A Quarterly Journal of Science, Literature, Natural History and the Fine Arts*, ed. by William Holl, Neville Wood and Edward Mammatt, 10 vols (London: Simpkin & Marshall, 1834–1840), VII (1837), 91–102 <http://dbooks.bodleian.ox.ac.uk/books/PDFs/555020721.pdf> [accessed 5 November 2016]

PUGH, MARTIN, *The March of the Women: A Revisionist Analysis of the Campaign for Women's Suffrage, 1866–1914* (Oxford: Oxford University Press, 2000)

PURCELL, MARK, 'Thorold, Sir John, ninth baronet (1734–1815)', in *Oxford Dictionary of National Biography* <http://www.oxforddnb.com/> [accessed 26 February 2016]

PUSICH, ANTÓNIA GERTRUDES, *Galeria das senhoras na câmara dos senhores deputados ou as minhas observações* (Lisbon: Tipografia de Borges, 1848)

QUEIRÓS, JOSÉ MARIA EÇA DE, *O Crime do Padre Amaro, 2ª e 3ª versões*, ed. by Maria do Rosário de Cunha and Carlos Reis (Lisbon: Imprensa Nacional–Casa da Moeda, 2000)

—— 'Um Génio que era um Santo', in *Almanaques e outros dispersos*, ed. by Irene Fialho (Lisbon: Imprensa Nacional–Casa da Moeda, 2009)

—— *Os Maias* (Lisbon: Livros do Brasil, 1969)

—— *The Maias*, trans. by Margaret Jull Costa (Sawtry: Dedalus, 2016)

—— *O Primo Basílio* (Lisbon: Livros do Brasil, 1960)

'Quem somos', Sociedade Protectora dos Animais <https://spanimais.wixsite.com/spa-lisboa/quem-somos> [accessed 2 December 2018]

QUENTAL, ANTERO DE, *Odes modernas* (Lisbon: Chardon, 1865) <https://books.google.com.br/books?id=mUMuAAAAYAAJ&printsec=, Google ebook.frontcover&hl=en#v=onepage&q&f=false> [accessed 5 December 2018]

RAFAEL, GINA GUEDES, and MANUELA SANTOS, eds, *Jornais e revistas portugueses do século XIX*, 2 vols (Lisbon: Biblioteca Nacional, 1998–2002)

RAMOS, RUI, 'Culturas de alfabetização e culturas de analfabetismo em Portugal: uma introdução à História da Alfabetização em Portugal', *Análise Social*, 24 (1988), 1067–1145

RAPPAPORT, HELEN, ed., *Encyclopedia of Women Social Reformers*, 2 vols (Santa Barbara, CA, and Oxford: ABC-CLIO, 2001)

'Re: Serpa Pinto [abruma]', *Geneall*, 16 May 2002 <https://geneall.net/en/forum/21404/serpa-pinto/#a21432/> [accessed 5 December 2018]

[REVIEW], in *The Musical World, a Weekly Record of Musical Science, Literature, and Intelligence*, VI (1837), 108–09

REY, R. D. CÉSAR, and A. PEREIRA DA SILVA, eds, *A Esperança: semanário de recreio literário dedicado às damas*, 2 vols (Porto: Tipografia de Rodrigo José d'Oliveira Guimarães, 1865–66)

RIBEIRO, ANTÓNIO MANUEL, *O Museu de imagens na imprensa do romantismo: património arquitectónico e artístico nas ilustrações e textos do Archivo Pittoresco (1857–1868)* (Coimbra: Imprensa da Universidade de Coimbra, 2014)

RIBEIRO, MARIA MANUELA TAVARES, 'The Press: A Political Gospel', *Portuguese Literary & Cultural Studies*, 12 (2007), 265–73

—— 'A Regeneração e o seu significado', in *História de Portugal*, ed. by José Mattoso, 8 vols (Lisbon: Estampa, 1993–1994), v: *O Liberalismo*, ed. by Luís Reis Torgal and João Lourenço Roque (1993), pp. 121–29

RODRIGUES, ERNESTO, *Cultura literária oitocentista* (Porto: Lello, 1999)

—— *Mágico folhetim: literatura e jornalismo em Portugal* (Lisbon: Notícias, 1998)

ROECKELL, L., 'Bollaert, William (1807–1876)', in *Oxford Dictionary of National Biography* <http://www.oxforddnb.com/> [accessed 26 February 2016]

ROLDÃO, HELENA, [*A Esperança*: semanário de recreio literário dedicado às damas], [Ficha histórica], p. 1 <http://hemerotecadigital.cm-lisboa.pt/FichasHistoricas/AEsperanca. pdf> [accessed 6 December 2018]

ROMARIZ, ANDREA GERMANO DE OLIVEIRA, 'O Almanaque de Lembranças Luso-Brasileiro: um ensaio para um projecto maior?' (unpublished master's thesis, Universidade de Lisboa — Faculdade de Letras, 2011) <http://repositorio.ul.pt/bitstream/10451/5145/6/ ulfl106395_tm.pdf> [accessed 13 October 2016]

ROMEIRAS, FRANCISCO MALTA, 'Jesuit Historiography in Modern Portugal', *Jesuit Historiography Online* <http://dx.doi.org/10.1163/2468–7723_jho_COM_192570> [accessed 14 March 2018]

RUSS, JOANNA, *How to Suppress Women's Writing* (London: The Women's Press, 1984)

RUSSELL, WILLIAM HOWARD, *The Prince of Wales' Tour: A Diary in India; With Some Account of the Visits of His Royal Highness to the Courts of Greece, Egypt, Spain, and Portugal*, 2nd edn (London: Sampson Low; Marston; Searle and Rivington, 1877) <https://archive.org/ details/princeofwalestou00russuoft> [accessed 8 November 2016]

SALVADOR, TERESA, 'Em torno dos periódicos femininos', *Cultura: revista de história e teoria das ideias*, 26 (2009), 95–117 <http://cultura.revues.org/425> [accessed 13 October 2016]

SANTOS, ANA TERESA MARQUES DOS, and CLÁUDIA PAZOS ALONSO, 'A Mind of Her Own: Translating the "volcanic vehemence" of *Jane Eyre* into Portuguese' (forthcoming)

SANTOS, LUÍS AGUIAR, 'A Primeira geração da Igreja Lusitana Católica Apostólica Evangélica (1876–1902)', *Lusitana Sacra*, 8/9 (1996–1997), 299–360

SANTOS, MARIA EDUARDA BORGES DOS, 'Da Identidade Feminina na ficção portuguesa de oitocentos: voz(es) de mulher, perspectiva(s) de autor' (unpublished doctoral thesis, Universidad de Salamanca, 2011)

SANTOS, MARIA DE LOURDES LIMA DOS, *Intelectuais portugueses na primeira metade de oitocentos* (Lisbon: Editorial Presença, 1988)

SANTOS, MARIA HELENA C. DOS, 'Imprensa periódica clandestina no século XIX: "O Portuguez" e a Constituição', *Análise Social*, 61–62 (1980), 429–45

SAUNDERS, ROBERT, *Democracy and the Vote in British Politics, 1848–1867: The Making of the Second Reform Act* (Farnham: Ashgate, 2011)

SERRA, FERNANDO, 'Sobre as Memórias de uma Senhora', *A Revolução de Setembro*, 31 March 1858, p. 1 <http://purl.pt/14345/1/j-4157-g_1858–03–31/j-4157-g_1858–03–31_ item2/j-4157-g_1858–03–31_PDF/j-4157-g_1858–03–31_PDF_24-C-R0150/j-4157-g_1858–03–31_0000_1–4_t24-C-R0150.pdf > [accessed 24 November 2018]

SILVA, FÁBIO MÁRIO DA, *A Autoria feminina na Literatura Portuguesa: reflexões sobre as teorias do cânone* (Lisbon: Edições Colibri, 2014)

SILVA, INOCÊNCIO FRANCISCO DA, *Dicionário bibliográfico português: estudos aplicáveis a Portugal e ao Brasil*, 24 vols (Lisbon: Imprensa Nacional, 1858–1923)

SILVA, MARIA REGINA TAVARES DA, *Feminismo em Portugal na voz de mulheres escritoras do início do século XX* (Lisbon: Comissão da Condição Feminina, 1982)

'Sir Henry Raeburn (British, 1756–1823)', *Artnet* <http://www.artnet.com/artists/sir-henry-raeburn/> [accessed 19 December 2018]

SMITH, HAROLD L., *The British Women's Suffrage Campaign, 1866–1928* (2nd revd edn) (Harlow: Longman, 2010)

SOUSA, JORGE PEDRO, ELSA SIMÕES LUCAS FREITAS and SANDRA GONÇALVES TUNA, 'Diffusing Political Knowledge in Illustrated Magazines: A Comparison between the Portuguese *O Panorama* and the British *The Penny Magazine* in 1837–1844', in *Diachronic Developments in English News Discourse*, ed. by Minna Palander-Collin, Maura Ratia and Irma Taavitsainen (Amsterdam; Philadelphia, 2017), pp. 157–73

—— 'The Portuguese Press During the Monarchy: From its Origins to 1910', in *A History of the Press in the Portuguese-speaking Countries*, ed. by Jorge Pedro Sousa and others (Porto: Media XXI, 2014), pp. 11–178

SOUSA, JOSÉ B., *Almeida Garrett (1799–1854), Founder of Portuguese Romanticism: A Study in Anglo-Portuguese Cultural Interaction* (Lewiston, NY: Edwin Mellen Press, 2011)

SOUSA, MARIA PEREGRINA DE, *Retalho do Mundo* (Porto: E. P. Barbosa, 1859)

—— *Rhadamanto ou a mana do conde* (Lisbon: Tipografia Castro Irmão, 1863)

—— *Maria Isabel* (Porto: J. P. da Silva, 1866)

—— *Henriqueta: romance original precedido de biografia da autora pelo Visconde de Castilho* (Porto: António Leite Cardoso Pereira de Mello, 1876)

STANTON, THEODORE, 'Editor's Preface', in *The Woman Question in Europe: A Series of Original Essays*, ed. by Theodore Stanton (New York: G. P. Putnam's Sons, 1884), pp. v–x

STUNT, TIMOTHY C. F., 'Newman, Francis William', in *Oxford Dictionary of National Biography* <http://www.oxforddnb.com/> [accessed 2 December 2018]

TALAN, NIKICA, *Antónia Pusich: vida e obra* (Zagreb & Dubrovnik: Hrvatska Akademija znanosti i umjetnosti; Zavod za povijesne znanosti u Dubrovniku, 2006)

—— '*In memoriam* à esquecida Antónia Gertrudes Pusich', *Studia Romanica et Anglica Zagrabiensia*, 50 (2005), 145–92

TENGARRINHA, JOSÉ, *História da imprensa periódica portuguesa*, 2nd edn (Lisbon: Caminho, 1989)

—— *Nova história da imprensa portuguesa: das origens a 1865* (Lisbon: Temas e Debates, 2013)

TERENAS, GABRIELA GÂNDARA, 'Diagnoses especulares: imagens da Grã-Bretanha na imprensa periódica portuguesa (1865–1890)', 3 vols (unpublished doctoral thesis, Universidade Nova de Lisboa, 2004)

THOMSON, P., 'Kemble, John Philip (1757–1823)', in *Oxford Dictionary of National Biography* <http://www.oxforddnb.com/> [accessed 26 February 2016]

TORRESÃO, FELISMINA, ed., *Trechos literários de Alexandre Herculano e cartas do mesmo e de outros escritores ilustres a Guiomar Torresão* (Lisbon: [n.pub.], 1910)

TORRESÃO, GUIOMAR, *Uma Alma de mulher: romance original* (Lisbon: Tipografia J. G. de Sousa Neves, 1869)

—— *No Teatro e na Sala* (Lisbon: David Corazzi, 1881)

—— *Almanaque das senhoras para 1884* (Lisbon: Sousa & Filho, 1883)

—— *Almanaque das senhoras para 1896* (Lisbon: Sousa & Filho, 1895)

—— 'Biografia da Autora', in Viscondessa de Monserrate, *Estudos* (Lisbon: Tipografia do Comércio de Portugal, 1896), pp. v–xix

—— *Meteóros* (Lisbon: Tipografia Christovão A. Rodrigues, 1875) <http://purl.ox.ac.uk/uuid/907521b054ab41fab49113a69d4f5c7d> [accessed 28 November 2018]

—— *Rosas pálidas: narrativas originais* (Lisbon: Roland & Semiond, 1873)

—— *A Voz Feminina*, [4], 'Saudação', 26 January 1868, p. 1

—— [5], 'Alma de mulher', 8 February 1868, p. 1

—— [6], 'A Doida de Montmayour: drama em cinco actos, representado no teatro de D. Maria II', 15 February 1868, pp. 1–2

—— [16], 'As Pupilas do Sr. Reitor', 3 May 1868, p. 3

—— [34], 'Contos morais', 6 September 1868, pp. 2–3

—— [38], 'Setúbal na atualidade', 4 October 1868, pp. 1–2

—— [42], 'À Minha amiga e colega a Ex.ma Sr.a D. Mariana A. de Andrade', 1 November 1868, pp. 1–2

—— [46], 'Breves considerações', 29 November 1868, pp. 1–2

—— [49], 'As Senhoras inglesas', 20 December 1868, p. 1

—— [55], 'A Imprensa', 31 January 1869, p. 1

—— [73], 'A Arte dramática', 6 June 1869, pp. 1–2

—— O Progresso, [79], 'D. Gertrudes Gomes de Avelaneda (esboço biográfico)', 19 July 1869, pp. 119–21

—— [82], [Mme Brés], trans. by. Guiomar Torresão, 8 August 1869, p. 134

TRINDADE, LUÍS, Catálogo da livraria do falecido distinto bibliógrafo e bibliófilo José Maria Nepomuceno (Lisbon: Empresa Editora de Francisco Artur da Silva, 1897)

TURNER, MICHAEL J., 'Thompson, Thomas Perronet (1783–1869)', in Oxford Dictionary of National Biography <http://www.oxforddnb.com/> [accessed 26 February 2016]

UGLOW, JENNIFER, George Eliot (London: Virago, 1987)

[VALADA, MARQUÊS DE], Bem Público, 'Quem vem lá?', 7 March 1868, pp. 275–77

—— 'Quem vem lá?', 28 March 1868, pp. 300–01

—— 'Quem vem lá?', 4 April 1868, pp. 307–09

—— n.t. 18 April 1868, p. 325

—— 'A Voz Feminina e o adultério: I', 25 April 1868, pp. 331–33

—— 'A Voz Feminina e o adultério: II', 2 May 1868, pp. 339–40

—— 'A Voz Feminina', 6 June 1868, pp. 378–79

—— n.t., 30 January 1869, pp. 236–37

—— 'Os compadres calumniadores', O Bem Público, 20 February 1869, p. 259

—— ['Lemos as despedidas da Voz Feminina...'], 24 July 1869, pp. 19–20

—— 'A Livre pensadora', 22 May 1869, pp. 362–64

—— 'Veritas Odium Parit', O Bem Público, 10 June 1869, p. 399

—— ['Perguntam-nos algumas pessoas...'], 22 January 1870, p. 230

VAQUINHAS, IRENE MARIA, 'A Família', essa "pátria em miniatura"', in História da vida privada em Portugal, ed. by José Mattoso, 4 vols (Lisbon: Temas e Debates, 2010–11), III: A Época contemporânea, ed. by Irene Maria Vaquinhas (2011), pp. 118–51

—— 'Senhoras e mulheres' na sociedade portuguesa do século XIX (Lisbon: Colibri, 1999)

VAQUINHAS, IRENE MARIA, and RUI CASCÃO, 'Evolução da sociedade em Portugal: a lenta e complexa afirmação de uma civilização burguesa', in História de Portugal, ed. by José Mattoso, 8 vols (Lisbon: Estampa, 1993–94), V: O Liberalismo, ed. by Luís Reis Torgal and João Lourenço Roque (1993)

VARGUES, ISABEL NOBRE Y RIBEIRO, and MARIA MANUELA TAVARES, 'Estruturas políticas, parlamentos, eleições, partidos políticos e maçonarias', in História de Portugal, ed. by José Mattoso, 8 vols (Lisbon: Estampa, 1993–94), V: O Liberalismo, ed. by Luís Reis Torgal and João Lourenço Roque (1993)

VASCONCELOS, ARTUR TEIXEIRA DE, 'Memórias da Minha Vida', Gazeta de Portugal, 17 August 1864, n.p.

VASCONCELOS, CAROLINA MICHAËLIS DE, O movimento feminista em Portugal, ed. by Luís Carlos Patraquim (Paio Pires: Fradique, 2002)

VAZ, MARIA MÁXIMA, A Voz da Liberdade (Lisbon: Chiado, 2018)

VENTURA, ANTÓNIO, *Uma História da maçonaria em Portugal, 1727–1986* (Lisbon: Círculo de Leitores, 2013)

VIANA, JOÃO LUÍS DA SILVA, *A Voz Feminina*, [60] trans, 'Toussaint L'Ouverture', 7 March 1869, 60, pp. 3–4

—— [65], 'À Ex.ma redatora da Voz Feminina', 11 April 1869, pp. 1–2

VICENTE, ANA, *As Mulheres portuguesas vistas por viajantes estrangeiros: séculos XVIII, XIX, XX* (Lisbon: Gótica, 2001)

VICENTE, FILIPA LOWNDES, *A Arte sem história: mulheres e cultura artística (séculos XVI–XX)* (Lisbon: Athena, 2012)

VIDAL, MÁRIO DE CAMPOS, *Angelina Vidal: escritora, jornalista, republicana, revolucionária e socialista* (Lisbon: Tribuna da História, 2010)

VILAR, ANITA, ed., *Mariana Angélica de Andrade: a poetisa do Sado* (Setúbal: Centro de Estudos Bocageanos, 2009)

'Votes for Women: The 1866 Suffrage Petition', Commons Select Committee, Parliament, 31 May 2016 <https://www.parliament.uk/business/committees/committees-a-z/commons-select/petitions-committee/petition-of-the-month/votes-for-women-the-1866-suffrage-petition/> [accessed 4 December 2018]

WALKER, LINDA, 'Becker, Lydia Ernestine (1827–1890)', in *Oxford Dictionary of National Biography* <http://www.oxforddnb.com/> [accessed 26 February 2016]

WALTHAM, CHRIS, 'David Knowles' Diary 1837–1839', *Chris Waltham's Family History* <http://chris-waltham-family-history.blogspot.co.uk/2016/05/david-knowles-diary-1837–1839.html> [accessed 5 November 2016]

WEBB, R. K., 'Martineau, Harriet (1802–1876)', in *Oxford Dictionary of National Biography* <http://www.oxforddnb.com/> [accessed 26 February 2016]

'What women are doing and have done', *The Revolution* [New York], 25 June 1868, pp. 395–96

'Wood, Francisca', in *Dicionário mundial de mulheres notáveis*, ed. by Lopes de Oliveira and Gonçalves Viana (Porto: Lello & Irmão, 1967), p. 1378

WOOD, FRANCISCA DE ASSIS MARTINS, *Maria Severn*, 2 vols (Lisbon: Tipografia da Voz Feminina, 1869)

—— *A Voz Feminina*, [1], ['Bem-vindo sejas ano novo de 1868...'], 5 January 1868, pp. 1–2

—— [11], 'Educação física e moral', 29 March 1868, p. 2

—— [26], 'Os Ciúmes da minha gata preta', 12 July 1868, p. 3

—— [31], ['Diz o Sr. F. F....'], 16 August 1868, pp. 1–2

—— [35], 'Declaração', 13 September 1868, pp. 1–2

—— [35], 'Carta a Luísa', 13 September 1868, p. 2

—— [36], ['Não perdoam facilmente, diz o nosso elegante escritor...'], 20 September 1868, pp. 1–2

—— [37], 'Os Satélites', 27 September 1868, pp. 1–2

—— [38], ['Num excelente jornal de Funchal...'], 4 October 1868, p. 1

—— [39], 'Delírio-rábido-político', 11 OCtober 1868, pp. 1–2

—— [40], 'Algumas palavras dedicadas às fidalgas benevolentes actualmente em Cascais', 18 October 1868, p. 1

—— [40], 'À Ex.ma Sr.ª D. Maria N. B. Rossa', 18 October 1868, p. 4

—— [43], 'Escrito dedicado ao Il.mo Sr. J. T. Cardona, distinto folhetista da Gazeta da Beira', 8 November 1868, pp. 1–2

—— [43], 'Nova medida', 8 November 1868, p. 2

—— [45], 'As Damas em Londres', 22 November 1868, p. 1

—— [47], 'Ao Ill.mo Sr. J. T. Cardona', 6 December 1868, pp. 1–2

—— [50], 'Despedida', 27 December 1868, p. 1

—— [52], 'À Folha (jornal de Coimbra)', 10 January 1869, pp. 1–2

—— [53], 'A Uma assinante da Voz Feminina', 17 January 1869, pp. 1–2

—— [55], 'La Guêpe', 31 January 1869, p. 5

—— [56], 'The Printer's Register', 7 February 1869, p. 5

—— [57], ['Não quero disputar ao distintíssimo...'], 14 February 1869, p. 3

—— [58], 'As Senhoras inglesas e o direito eleitoral', 21 February 1869, p. 3

—— [59], 'As Senhoras inglesas e o direito eleitoral', 28 February 1869, p. 2

—— [60], 'As Senhoras inglesas e o direito eleitoral', 7 March 1869, p. 3

—— [61], 'A Religião', 14 March 1869, pp. 1–2

—— [62], 'A Religião', 21 March 1869, pp. 1–2

—— [63], 'A Religião', 28 March 1869, pp. 1–2

—— [64], 'Dai a Deus o que é de Deus e a César o que é de César', 4 April 1869, p. 3

—— [65], 'Carta a Luísa', 11 April 1869, pp. 2–3

—— [66], 'Apelo: à Ex.ma Câmara Municipal de Lisboa', 18 April 1869, pp. 1–2

—— [67], 'Apelo: aos chefes de família', 25 April 1869, pp. 1–2

—— [68], ['O Bispo de Montpellier recebeu...'], 2 May 1869, pp. 1–2

—— [68], 'O Teatro D. Maria II', 2 May 1869, p. 3

—— [72], 'Carta ao digno deputado a cortes o Il.mo Sr. D. Emílio Castelar', 30 May 1869, pp. 1–2

—— [74], ['Dear Madame Goegg...'], 13 June 1869, p. 4

—— [74], 'Aos Il.mos e às Ex.mas assinantes da Voz Feminina', 13 June 1869, pp. 1–2

—— [75], 'A Cadeira de Mendelssohn', 20 June 1869, pp. 1–2

—— [76], ['Lembro-me de ter ouvido em Londres...'], 27 June 1869, pp. 1–2

—— O Progresso, [78], 'Ao Ill.mo Sr. João A. Elliott', 11 July 1869, p. 117

—— [81], 'A Madame André Léo', 1 August 1869, p. 128

—— [84], ['Desde que o direito da mulher a regalias...'], 22 August 1869, pp. 139–40

—— [87], 'O Que se faz lá fora', 12 September 1869, p. 153

—— [88], 'À Ex.ma Câmara Municipal de Lisboa', 19 September 1869, pp. 155–56

—— [88], 'O Que se faz lá fora', 19 September 1869, p. 156

—— [89], 'As Toiradas', 26 September 1869, pp. 159–60

—— [89], 'O Que se faz lá fora', 26 September 1869, p. 160

—— [90], 'As Toiradas', 3 October 1869, pp. 163–64

—— [92], ['Publica-se há seis anos em Paris um jornal...'], 17 October 1869, pp. 171–72

—— [93], ['Vou entrar hoje num campo virgem...'], 24 October 1869, pp. 175–76

—— [94], ['Ex.mas Sras e Srs. assinantes...'], 31 October 1869, p. 179

—— [94], 'O Que se faz lá fora', 31 October 1869, p. 180

—— [95], 'To the editor of the Printers' Register', 7 November 1869, p. 184

—— [96], 'O Que se faz lá fora', 14 November 1869, p. 189

—— [97], 'A Madame André Léo', 21 November 1869, p. 192

—— [99], 'O Celibato', 5 December 1869, pp. 199–200

—— [101], 'O Que se faz lá fora', 19 December 1869, pp. 208–09

—— [102], 'O Que se faz lá fora', 26 December 1869, pp. 212–13

WOOD, WILLIAM THOROLD, Catalogue of the Musical Compositions (Lisbon: Anglo-Portuguese Printing Office, 1872)

—— Colecção de artigos por W. T. Wood publicados nos jornais A Voz Feminina e O Progresso de 23 de Fevereiro de 1868 a 26 de Janeiro de 1869, 2nd edn (Lisbon: Tipografia Luso-Britânica, 1877 [1875])

—— As Farpas e John Bull ([n.a.]: Tipografia Luso-Britânica, 1877)

—— A Voz Feminina, [25], 'Artigo dedicado às Ex.mas Sras D. M. A. de Andrade e D. A. I. da Costa, por um zeloso advogado da causa do sexo feminino', 5 July 1868, pp. 1–2

—— [26], 'Lira portuguesa', 12 July 1868, pp. 1–2

—— [28], 'A Imagem de Deus', 26 July 1868, p. 1

—— [42], 'A Independência nacional e a Ibéria', 1 November 1868, pp. 3–4

—— [48], ['Há duas maneiras de ler...'], 13 December 1868, pp. 1–2

—— [59], 'Estatística', 28 February 1869, pp. 1–2

—— [70], 'Offenbach', 16 May 1869, pp. 1–2

—— [71], 'O Leão no Jardim da Estrela', 23 May 1869, pp. 1–2

—— [73], ['To Theodore Stanton, of the *Revolution* New York...'], 6 June 1869, p. 4

—— *O Progresso*, [77], ['Já se explicou aos nossos leitores e leitoras...'], 4 July 1869, pp. 111–12

—— [80], 'To the Editor of the Printers' Register', 25 July 1869, p. 123

Websites

<https://prismaticjaneeyre.org>

<https://toponimialisboa.wordpress.com>

<http://www.seg-social.pt/documents/10152/18931/A+mulher+em+Portugal+volume+I.pdf>

APPENDIX 1

Tipografia Luso-Britânica

In order to ensure the timely publication of the weekly *A Voz Feminina*, the Woods created their own press. This appendix, listing over ninety books, pamphlets and periodicals that were published by Tipografia Luso-Britânica, is by no means exhaustive. It is merely a preliminary attempt to record materials identified in the course of the research for this book, in the hope that the information may be of interest to history of the book scholars, as well those working within translation studies or with a focus on the history of ideas.

The press was originally called Tipografia da Voz Feminina but was renamed Tipografia Luso-Britânica after the first few months. Other name variants used are Tipografia Luso-Britânica de W. T. Wood, Anglo-Portuguese Printing Office, W. T. Wood's Printing-Office. A place of publication is sometimes given: in the vast majority of cases, it is 29 Rua de São Domingos and/or 31 Rua de São Domingos. But in a few instances it appears as 28 Rua direita das Janelas Verdes.[1] It is conceivable that Tipografia Luso-Britânica might simply have moved to 28 Rua das Janelas Verdes, and the fact that at least one 1877 work had the indication 'Tip. Luso-Britânica, 28 Rua direita das Janelas Verdes' supports this hypothesis.[2] More unexpectedly, there are three instances (all from 1873) where the place of publication is recorded as Porto. Until further research is undertaken, it is difficult to establish whether a different, more short-lived, Tipografia Luso-Britânica may have existed in Porto.

The table below was compiled on the basis of searches of the online catalogues of four main libraries in Portugal: the Biblioteca Nacional de Portugal, the Calouste Gulbenkian Foundation Library, Biblioteca Municipal do Porto, and Biblioteca Geral de Coimbra (the latter under the section *miscelâneas*). Two works provided additional information, José António Afonso's *Protestantismo e educação: história de um projecto pedagógico alternativo em Portugal na transição do séc. XIX* and Isabel Lousada's *Para o estabelecimento de uma bibliografia britânica em português, 1554–1900*. The titles gleaned from these two sources are listed here, even when they do not feature in the online catalogue of any of the above libraries.

---

1. This was the official name of Rua das Janelas Verdes until 1881. See <https://toponimialisboa. wordpress.com/2016/09/28/as-ruas-direitas/>.

2. J. M. Mendes Moreira, in *Origens do episcopalismo em Portugal: o despertar da igreja lusitana (1839–1899)* (Porto: [n.pub.], 1995) makes the surprising claim that the Tipografia Luso-Britânica was 'instalada nas dependências do Convento dos Marianos, às Janelas Verdes' (p. 72). The Convento dos Marianos, acquired in 1872 by the Presbyterian Church, was located at number 2, Rua das Janelas Verdes. By then the Tipografia Luso-Britânica had been operating from Rua de São Domingos for over three years and mostly continued to give this location in subsequent years.

The list is presented by date of publication;
within each year, it follows an alphabetical order.

Date of Publication	Author and Title	Additional information
1868–69	*A Voz Feminina*, 15 November 1868 (no. 44) to 29 June 1869 (no. 76) Editor: Francisca de Assis Martins Wood	Tipografia da Voz Feminina, from no. 44 (15 November 1868 onwards) Tipografia Luso-Britânica from no. 64 (4 April 1869 onwards) Microfilm in BNP
1869	*O Progresso*, 4 July 1969 (no. 77) to 26 December 1969 (no. 102) Editors: Guilherme T. Wood and Francisca Wood	Tipografia Luso-Britânica Microfilm in BNP
1868–69	[n.a.], *O Anunciador do Povo* [1868]–1869	periodical owned by Jorge Martins Source: BNP
1869	[n.a.], *As Delícias da vida: folha mensal, científica, artística, moral e recreativa*	Source: BNP
1869	[n.a.], *O Golfo da Ambacia*, trans. by L. T. de Freitas e Costa	Lord Byron, 'Stanzas written in passing the Ambracian Gulf' Source: Isabel Lousada
1869	[n.a.], *Jornal Comercial*	Source: BNP
1869	*Almanach dos Piteireiros para... : contendo o Catecismo da Doutrina do Piteireiro / composto pelo Rei dos Piteireiros*	[source: Biblioteca Municipal do Porto]
1869	Buffon, Comte de, and others, *História natural ou descrição de todas as classes de animais*, trans. by Maria Isabel Fernandes	Publisher: Tipografia da Voz Feminina [Translated from works by Buffon, Cuvier, and the best French naturalists] Source: BNP
1869	Fernandes, Domingos Manuel, *Biografia político-literária do Visconde de Almeida Garrett*	date of publication is wrongly given as 1863 in the BNP catalogue
1869	Busch, Carlos, *As Cartas de amor*, trans. by Guiomar D. N. Torresão	Source: BNP
1869	Goodolfim, Costa, *Lendas árabes: Zahra, imitação em prosa; as duas sultanas, imitação em verso*	Source: BNP
1869	Goodolfim, Costa, *Passado e presente: poesia cómica*	Source: BNP
1869	Loureiro, Augusto, *À Beira-mar: contos, fantasias e digressões*	Source: BNP

1869	Wood, Francisca de Assis Martins, *Maria Severn*, 2 vols	Publisher: Tipografia da Voz Feminina Copies are held in Biblioteca Municipal do Porto, British Library, Fundação Gulbenkian Library (vol. II only), and Real Gabinete de Leitura, Rio de Janeiro
1870	[n.a.], *Breve devocionário para todos os dias da semana*	(29 pp.) [source: Catálogo da coleção de miscelâneas, tomo 7 (vols. Dcxcvi a Dcclxxv), by Universidade de Coimbra, Biblioteca Geral]
1870	[n.a.], *O Cozinheiro dos cozinheiros*	Contributions by Bulhão Pato, António José de Sousa Almada, Ramalho Ortigão, António Augusto Teixeira de Vasconcelos, Luciano Cordeiro and Júlio César Machado among others. Source: BNP
1870	[n.a.], *A Jovem aldeana: narração verdadeira*	5th edn Source: BNP
1870	[n.a.], *O Novo Testamento de Jesus Cristo*	[Revised and reformed edition according to the original in Greek] Source: BNP
1870	[n.a.], *Saldanha e Loulé jogando à cartas: passatempo político em prosa e verso, ornado de músicas populares; por um D. Espetador de Noronha, cavaleiro da Ordem do Chinelo*	Source: BNP
1870	[n.a.], *Vida de Napoleão III: compreendendo um resumo dos seus principais atos políticos*	Source: BNP
1870	Busch, Carlos, *Da crítica teatral em Portugal*	(44 pp.) Source: BNP
1870	Busch, Carlos, *O Espartilho da senhora: comédia em 1 ato*	Source: BNP
1870	Coelho, Francisco Adolfo, *Algumas observações acerca do Dicionário Bibliográfico Português e seu autor*	Source: British Library
1870	Coelho, Francisco Adolfo, *A Ciência alemã e a ignorância portuguesa: Hübner versus Levy,*	Source: BNP
1870	Proença, José de Azambuja, *Os Escândalos da Imprensa Nacional: carta dirigida a sua Excelência o Senhor Ministro do Reino*	(7 pp.) Source: BNP
1870	Roussel, Napoléon, *Não se deve mudar de religião mas conservar a religião de seus pais e a resposta de Jesus Cristo*	(15 pp.) [source Catálogo da coleção de miscelâneas, tomo 7.o (vols. Dcxcvi a Dcclxxv), by Universidade de Coimbra, Biblioteca Geral]

1870	Roussel, Napoléon, *Resposta de Jesus Cristo*	[source: Misc. 752, N° 12730 Coimbra]
1871	[n.a.], *Uma Antigualha e o bem que ela fez*	(16 pp.) [source Catálogo da coleção de miscelâneas]
1871	[n.a.], *As Fortificações de Paris: duas palavras sobre a guerra franco-prussiana*	Source: BNP
1871	[n.a.], *Um Homem que matava os seus vizinhos*	(23 pp.) Translated from English [source Catálogo da coleção de miscelâneas]
1871	[n.a.], *Projeto para o estabelecimento de uma escola modelo*	Microfilm in BNP
1871	[n.a.], *Vinde a Jesus*	(64 pp.) [Last page shows a hymn by M. G. L. A.; source Catálogo da coleção de miscelâneas]
1871	Busch, Carlos, *As Obras póstumas do Capitão Wolfram: comédia em 1 ato extraído de uma novela de Adrien Robert*	Source: BNP
1871	Fernandes, Domingos Manuel, *O Prémio da virtude: romance original*	Source: BNP
1871	Fernandes, Domingos Manuel, *Salve!.. Bocage: precedida de um esboço crítico*	Source: BNP
1871	Karr, Afonso, *O Monge de Kremsmunster*, trans. by Luís António Gonçalves de Freitas, 1871	(31 pp.) Source: Calouste Gulbenkian Foundation
1871	Lemon, Harry, *Espere a resposta: comédia em um ato*	[Free translation from English] Source: BNP
1871	Midosi, Paulo, *Teatro: a arte e o coração; o Sr. Procópio Baeta; a grande Duquesa de Gerolstein no penúltimo andar*	Source: BNP
1871	*A resposta branda quebra a ira / Provérbios 15. 1*	Translated from English [source Misc. 752, N° 12735, Coimbra]
1871	Robert, Adrien, trans. by Carlos Busch, *As obras póstumas do Capitão Wolfram: comédia em 1 acto*	Source: BNP
1871	Tehemje, the Egyptian wanderer, *From London to Nogueira*	Publisher: Anglo-Portuguese Printing Office Source: BNP
1871	Torre, Juan de la, *Libreria española de Juan de la Torre: catalogo general*	(20 pp.) Source: BNP
1872	Terrail, Ponson du, *A Fada de Anteil*, trans. by Pinheiro Chagas	Source: BNP

1872	[n.a.], *Esboços biográficos —* D. Thomaz Zumalacarregui	(74 pp.) Source: BNP
1872	[n.a.], *O Que é um sacramento*	(44 pp.) Transcription from the fortnightly magazine Imprensa Evangélica, Rio de Janeiro; [source Catálogo da coleção de miscelâneas]
1872	[n.a.], *Reflexões sobre a Virgem Maria*	(30 pp.) [source Catálogo da coleção de miscelâneas]
1872	[n.a.], *Sou Cristão? E como posso saber?*	(93 pp.) Translated from English [source Catálogo da coleção de miscelâneas]
1872	Boos, Martin, *A Vida*	(188 pp.) [source Catálogo da coleção de miscelâneas]
1872	Roussel, Napoléon, *O Livro dos livros*	(56 pp.) Source: BNP
1872	Wood, William Thorold, *Catalogue of the Musical Compositions of William Thorold Wood: All in Manuscript Between the Years 1835 and 1872*	Publisher: Anglo-Portuguese Printing Office Source: BNP
1873	*Psalmos e Hinos*	Quarta Edição aumentada e revista Source: José António Afonso, Protestantismo e educação: história de um projecto pedagógico alternativo em Portugal na transição do séc. XIX
1873	[n.a.], *O Amigo da casa*	(46 pp.) Translated from English [source Catálogo da coleção de miscelâneas]
1873	[n.a.], *O Amigo da infância: ilustração evangélica, dedicada às crianças*	Source: BNP
1873	[n.a.], *Cantigas a atirar: fadinhos para quem for pimpão, por um fadista de pé leve*	(4 pp.) Source: BNP
1873	[n.a.], *O Culto doméstico: andar em verdade*	(48 pp.) [source Catálogo da coleção de miscelâneas]
1873	[n.a.], *Erric, o criado russo e os duzentos lobos ou exemplo da mais nobre coragem e da mais perfeita amizade*	(16 pp.) [Transcription from the Correio Mercantil, Rio de Janeiro]; [source Catálogo da coleção de miscelâneas]
1873	[n.a.], *Isabel Fry*	Source Isabel Lousada <https://run.unl.pt/bitstream/10362/3253/4/Lousada_tese.pdf>. O Amigo de Infância includes an article with this title
1873	[n.a.], *João Bunyan*	Source Isabel Lousada
1873	[n.a.], *O Rendeiro de Craigsfoot*	Source Isabel Lousada
1873	Barroso, F. M. P., ed, *A Justiça*	Periodical Source: BNP NB According to catalogue, Porto, Tip. Luso-Britânica.
1873	*Bye-Laws of The Hope of Portugal Lodge No 1 I.O.G.T.*	Publisher: Wood's Anglo-Portuguese I.O.G.T. stands for Independent Order of Good Templars

1873	Chateaubriand, Auguste François René, *Atala*, trans. by Guilherme Braga	(82 pp.) [30 original lithographs by Gustave Doré] Source: BNP NB According to catalogue, Porto, Tip. Luso-Britânica.
1873	Collins, Wilkie, *Armadeile*	Source: BNP
1873	*Estatutos / da Sociedade Cooperativa de Consumo Dezanove de Dezembro de Responsabilidade Ilimitadada Vila de Oeiras*	[source: Biblioteca Municipal do Porto]
1873	Dickens, Charles, *Cânticos de Natal*, trans. by Eugénio Castilho	Source: BNP
1873	Figueiredo, António Pereira de, trans. *O Novo Testamento de Jesus Cristo*	Source: BNP
1873	Reis, A. Bathalha, and Oliveira Júnior, *O Campo e o jardim*	(140 pp.) Source: BNP NB According to catalogue, Porto, Tip. Luso-Britânica.
1873	Roeder, A. H., *Exercícios portugueses para leitura e análise, e para versão em línguas estrangeiras*	5th edn Source: BNP
1874	*Exposição feita perante os membros da Commissão Nacional Portuguesa do Congresso Internacional dos Orientalistas*	Source: BNP
1874	[n.a.], *Quarenta e dois artigos da igreja de Roma refutados pela escritura sagrada*	(82 pp.) Source: BNP
1874	Ferreira, J. M., *Poesia dedicada ao eterno descanso da sempre chorada filha do Sr. Bernardo Daupias*	Source: BNP
1875	[n.a.], *Almanaque da Senhora Angot para o ano de 1876*	Source: BNP
1875	[n.a.], *Caridade fraternal em auxílio dos pobres, da Igreja Evangélica Portuguesa em Lisboa*	Source: BNP
1875	[n.a.], *Salvação de graça*	[periodical from Recife, Brazil; 3 issues published: October, November and December 1875] Source: BNP
1875	[n.a.], *Vinde a Jesus*	
1875	Kalley, R. R., *Exposição de factos: relativos à agressão contra os protestantes na Ilha da Madeira*	Translation of Robert Reid Kalley, *An Account of the Recent Persecutions in Madeira*, (London, 1844) Source: BNP

1875	Monod, Adolphe, *Lucília ou a leitura da Bíblia (de inspiração protestante)*	Source Isabel Lousada
1875	Seromênho, Diogo José, *Cenas do Brasil: drama em três atos*	(28 pp.) Source: BNP
1875	Pintor Pindelo and Ferral Mining Company: report presented to the general meeting held 18th August	Publisher: W. T. Wood's Printing-Office, 1875 Available at http://purl.pt/30024
1875	Wood, William Thorold, *Coleção de artigos por W. T. Wood publicados nos jornais A Voz Feminina e O Progresso de 23 de fevereiro de 1868 a 26 de janeiro de 1869*	Source: BNP manual catalogue
1876	[n.a.], *Almanaque da Senhora Angot para o ano de 1877*	Source: BNP
1876	[n.a.], *Estatutos da Companhia de Cultura e Comércio do ópio em Moçambique: Sociedade Anónima de responsabilidade limitada*	Source: BNP
1876	F., António A. da S., *Lição a casados: comédia em 1 ato, imitação*	Source: BNP
1876	Seromênho, Diogo José, *Soma e segue*	(24 pp.) Source: BNP
1876	*Textos Bíblicos Arranjados de Maneira que Possam Facilitar o Processo de Examinar as Escrituras Sagradas e Achar de Pronto Qualquer Texto*	Source: José António Afonso, Protestantismo e educação: história de um projecto pedagógico alternativo em Portugal na transição do séc. XIX
1877	[n.a.], 'Será por ventura dificultoso a Deus consolar-te?': Job, XV.11; Consolações de Deus	(4 pp.) [source Catálogo da coleção de miscelâneas]
1877	[n.a.], *Almanaque da Senhora Angot para o ano de 1878*	Source: BNP
1877	[n.a.], *As Farpas e John Bull*	The text is in English despite Portuguese title Source: BNP
1877	[n.a.], *Está resolvida a Questão?*	(4 pp.) [source Catálogo da coleção de miscelâneas] Publisher: Tip. Luso-Britânica, 28 Rua direita das Janelas Verdes
1877	*The fortieth annual report of the British Protestant School in connexion with St. George's Chapel Lisbon… with a list of subscribers and accounts of receipts and expenditure*	Publisher: Anglo-Portuguese Printing Office, 28 Rua direita das Janelas Verdes Available at http://purl.pt/30848

1877	[n.a.], *Gazeta das Salas*	[periodical directed by Luís de Mascarenhas; 9 issues published from July to November 1877] BNP
1877	[n.a.], *Narração coreográfica da vida de nosso senhor Jesus Cristo*, trans. by J. A. S. C.	Source: BNP
1877	[n.a.], *O Zoofilo*	[Fortnightly periodical of Sociedade Protetora dos Animais. Tip. Luso-Britânica printed the 1877 issues] Source: BNP
1877	Wood, William Thorold, *Coleção de artigos por W. T. Wood publicados nos jornais A Voz Feminina e O Progresso de 23 de fevereiro de 1868 a 26 de janeiro de 1869*	Second edition of 1875 text Source: BNP
[n.d.]	[n.a.], *Como devemos entender a Bíblia sagrada?*	(15 pp.) [source Catálogo da coleção de miscelâneas]
[n.d.]	[n.a.], *A Doutrina da Igreja de Roma e a doutrina da Bíblia*	(120 pp.) [source Catálogo da coleção de miscelâneas]
[n.d.]	[n.a.], *Jéssica*	translation of Hesba Stretton's popular *Jessica's First Prayer* Source: BNP
[n.d.]	[n.a.], *O Menino da mata e o seu cão Piloto*	(32 pp.) [source Catálogo da coleção de miscelâneas]
[n.d.]	[n.a.], *O Padre Jacinto*	(16 pp.) [source Catálogo da coleção de miscelâneas]

APPENDIX 2

List of Editorials by Francisca Wood

The first number on the left indicates the issue. Where editorials have no title, the opening words are given in square brackets for ease of reference. Up until no. 35, there are only two editorials which bear Francisca Wood's signature (no.1 and no 26). But as Wood declared in no. 35 that *all* articles published anonymously up to then were in fact authored by her, earlier unsigned editorials have been incorporated into the list.

A Voz Feminina

[1], ['Bem-vindo sejas ano novo de 1868...'], 5 January 1868, pp. 1–2
[6], ['O Sr. Sousa Teles disse...'], 23 February 1868, pp. 1–2
[7], ['O Cristianismo...'], 1 March 1868, pp. 1–2
[8], ['Não há ninguém nos domínios de...'], 8 March 1868, p. 1
[9], ['Dissemos no nosso último número...'], 15 March 1868, pp. 1–2
[10] *issue missing from BNP run*
[11], ['Qualquer pessoa que fora de Portugal...'], 29 March 1868, pp. 1–2
[12], ['Poderá alguém dizer-me...'], 5 April 1868, pp. 1–2
[13], ['Recebemos há tempo...'], 12 April 1868, pp. 1–2
[14], ['Dissemos no número antecedente...'], 19 April 1868, pp. 1–2
[15], ['Faz dó ver como uma parte...'], 26 April 1868, pp. 1–2
[17], ['Abrindo...'], 10 May 1868, pp. 1–2
[18], ['Se os primeiros sons emitidos...'], 17 May 1868, pp. 1–2
[19], ['Algumas das nossas distintas colaboradoras...'], 24 May 1868, pp. 1–2
[20], ['Diz-se que as senhoras em toda a Europa...'], 31 May 1868, pp. 1–2
[21], ['A redatora desta folha agradece...'], 7 June 1868, pp. 1–2
[26], ['Domingo último...'], 12 July 1868, p. 1
[29], ['Diz o Sr. F. F. no Jornal de Setúbal...'], 2 August 1868, pp. 1–2
[31], ['Diz o Sr. F. F....'], 16 August 1868, pp. 1–2
[33], ['Do Egitaniense transcrevemos o seguinte....'], 30 August 1868, pp. 1–2
[34], 'Observações sobre o artigo de fundo do número 33', 6 September 1868, p. 1
[35], 'Declaração', 13 September 1868, pp. 1–2
[36], ['Não perdoam facilmente, diz o nosso elegante escritor...'], 20 September 1868, pp. 1–2
[37], 'Os Satélites', 27 September 1868, pp. 1–2
[38], ['Num excelente jornal de Funchal...'], 4 October 1868, p. 1
[39], 'Delírio-rábido-político', 11 OCtober 1868, pp. 1–2

[40], 'Algumas palavras dedicadas às fidalgas benevolentes actualmente em Cascais', 18 October 1868, p. 1

[43], 'Escrito dedicado ao Il.mo Sr. J. T. Cardona, distinto folhetista da Gazeta da Beira', November 1868, pp. 1–2

[45], 'As Damas em Londres', 22 November 1868, p. 1 — Gulbenkian

[47], 'Ao Ill.mo Sr. J. T. Cardona', 6 December 1868, pp. 1–2

[50], 'Despedida', 27 December 1868, p. 1

[52], 'À Folha (jornal de Coimbra)', 10 January 1869, pp. 1–2

[53], 'A Uma assinante da Voz Feminina', 17 January1869, pp. 1–2

[61], 'A Religião', 14 March 1869, pp. 1–2

[62], 'A Religião', 21 March 1869, pp. 1–2

[63], 'A Religião', 28 March 1869, pp. 1–2

[66], 'Apelo: à Ex.ma Câmara Municipal de Lisboa', 18 April 1869, pp. 1–2

[67], 'Apelo: aos chefes de família', 25 April 1869, pp. 1–2

[68], ['O Bispo de Montpellier recebeu...'], 2 May 1869, pp. 1–2

[72], 'Carta ao digno deputado a cortes o Il.mo Sr. D. Emílio Castelar', 30 May 1869, pp. 1–2

[74], 'Aos Il.mos e às Ex.mas assinantes da Voz Feminina', 13 June 1869, pp. 1–2

[75], 'A Cadeira de Mendelssohn', 20 June 1869, pp. 1–2

[76], ['Lembro-me de ter ouvido em Londres...'], 27 June 1869, pp. 1–2

O Progresso

[84], ['Desde que o direito da mulher a regalias...'], 22 August 1869, pp. 139–40

[88], 'À Ex.ma Câmara Municipal de Lisboa', 19 September 1869, pp. 155–56

[89], 'As Toiradas', 26 September 1869, pp. 159–60

[90], 'As Toiradas', 3 October 1869, pp. 163–64

[92], ['Publica-se há seis anos em Paris um jornal...'], 17 October 1869, pp. 171–72

[93], ['Vou entrar hoje num campo virgem...'], 24 October 1869, pp. 175–76

[94], ['Ex.mas Sras e Srs. assinantes...'], 31 October 1869, p. 179

[99], 'O Celibato', 5 December 1869, pp. 199–200

APPENDIX 3

List of Editorials (Alphabetically by Author)

The first number on the left indicates the issue. Where editorials have no title, the opening words are given in square brackets for ease of reference.

ANDRADE, MARIANA ANGÉLICA, *A Voz Feminina*,
  [16], ['O assunto de que hoje vou tratar...'], 3 May 1868, p. 1
  [23], ['Lendo o Diário de Notícias...'], 21 June 1868, p. 1
  [30], ['No escrito que aqui se tem publicado...'], 9 August 1868, pp. 1–2
  [41], ['Publicou-se há pouco no Diário de Notícias...'], 25 October 1868, pp. 1–2
  [54], ['Vou hoje tratar de um assunto de...'], 23 January 1869, pp. 1–2
  [57], 'Um Brado a favor dos animais', 14 February 1869, pp. 1–2
  [60], ['Agora que estamos na quaresma...'], 7 March 1869, pp. 1–2
ARAÚJO, JOÃO DE SOUSA, *O Progresso*,
  [98], 'A Emancipação da mulher', 28 November 1869, pp. 195–96
COELHO, J. C. TEIXEIRA, *O Progresso*,
  [95], 'Mais um brado: às senhoras portuguesas', 7 November 1869, pp. 183–84
COSTA, AMÁLIA CÂNDIDA ISABEL DA, *A Voz Feminina*,
  [22], ['O muito que hoje se fala na emancipação...'], 14 June 1868, p. 1
FAROL, F, *O Progresso*
  [81], 'Escrito do Il.mo sr. F. Farol, dirigido à "Voz Feminina" em Agosto do ano findo', 1 August 1869, pp. 127–28
GOEGG, MARIE, *A Voz Feminina*,
  [97], 'Discurso da madame Goegg, presidenta (sic) da associação internacional das mulheres, pronunciado por ela mesma no terceiro congresso da liga da paz e da liberdade, reunido em Lausana', 21 November 1869, pp. 191–92
MARQUES, F. DE ABREU, *A Voz Feminina*,
  [51], '1.º Aniversário da "Voz Feminina": introdução', 3 January 1869, pp. 1–2
  [56], 'O Carnaval: cavaco com as leitoras da Voz Feminina', 7 February 1869, pp. 1–2
  [58], 'O Século XIX', 21 February 1869, pp. 1–2
  [64], 'Coisas sérias', 4 April 1869, pp. 1–2
  [69], 'Leituras em família', 9 May 1869, pp. 1–2
MATOS, FRANCISCO A. DE, *A Voz Feminina*,
  [24], ['Não é só nas delicadas e mimosas colunas da Voz Feminina...'], 28 June 1868, p. 1
  [27], ['Entre diversas opiniões que se têm desenhado...'], 19 July 1868, pp. 1–2

[32], ['Começarei hoje perguntando...'], 23 August 1868, p. 1

[n.a.], *A Voz Feminina*,

    [44], ['Pedimos vénia para transcrever na nossa folha...'], 15 November 1868, p. 1

—— *O Progresso*,

    [78], ['No Diário Popular...'], 11 July 1869, pp. 115–16

    [79], ['A educação do povo é a questão palpitante do dia...'], 18 July 1869, pp. 119–20

    [80], ['Com uma só exceção...'], 25 July 1869, pp. 123–24

    [82], ['O concílio ecuménico é o grande enigma'], 8 August 1869, pp. 131–32

    [83], ['Há um defeito inerente na natureza de todas...'], 15 August 1869, pp. 135–36

    [85], ['Depois da mudança ministerial...'], 29 August 1869, pp. 143–44

    [86], ['A questão da emancipação da mulher...'], 5 September 1869, pp. 147–48

    [87], ['Os meios por que se regulam as acções do homem...'], 12 September 1869, pp. 151–52

    [91], ['Quando temos protestado com toda a força...'], 10 October 1869, pp. 167–68

    [96], ['No artigo de fundo do n.º 87 dissemos o seguinte...'], 14 November 1869, pp. 187–88

    [100], ['No dia 1 de Dezembro distribuiu-se gratuitamente...'], 12 December 1869, pp. 203–04

    [101], ['Publica-se em Barcelona um jornal inteiramente devotado...'], 19 December 1869, pp. 207–08

    [102], ['Recebemos, há pouco, uma carta...'], 26 December 1869, pp. 211–12

P., CARLOTA A., *A Voz Feminina*,

    [2], ['Hasteamos um pendão glorioso...'], 12 January 1868, p. 1

    [3], ['A ilustração máxima de todos os sexos e classes...'], 19 January 1868, p. 1

    [4], ['Temos pugnado...'], 26 January 1868, p. 1

    [5], ['Estabelecer os princípios da mais perfeita igualdade...'], 8 February 1868, pp. 1–2

TORRESÃO, GUIOMAR, *A Voz Feminina*,

    [42], 'À Minha amiga e colega a Ex.ma Sr.a D. Mariana A. de Andrade', 1 November 1868, pp. 1–2

    [46], 'Breves considerações', 29 November 1868, pp. 1–2

    [49], 'As Senhoras inglesas', 20 December 1868, p. 1

    [55], 'A Imprensa', 31 January 1869, p. 1

    [73], 'A Arte dramática', 6 June 1869, pp. 1–2

VIANA, JOÃO LUÍS DA SILVA, *A Voz Feminina*,

    [65], 'À Ex.ma redatora da Voz Feminina', 11 April 1869, pp. 1–2

WOOD, WILLIAM THOROLD, *A Voz Feminina*,

    [25], 'Artigo dedicado às Ex.mas Sras D. M. A. de Andrade e D. A. I. da Costa, por um zeloso advogado da causa do sexo feminino', 5 July 1868, pp. 1–2

    [28], 'A Imagem de Deus', 26 July 1868, p. 1

    [48], ['Há duas maneiras de ler...'], 13 December 1868, pp. 1–2

[59], 'Estatística', 28 February 1869, pp. 1–2
[70], 'Offenbach', 16 May 1869, pp. 1–2
[71], 'O Leão no Jardim da Estrela', 23 May 1869, pp. 1–2
[77], ['Já se explicou aos nossos leitores e leitoras...'], 4 July 1869, pp. 111–12

INDEX

Abranches, António Joaquim da Silva 95
Almanaque das Lembranças 13–14, 108 n. 36
Almanaque das Senhoras 91, 97–99, 139, 185, 192
Almeida, Pinto 106 n. 4
Alorna, Marquesa de 4, 5, 68, 80 n. 54, 92, 104
O Amigo da Infância (religious magazine) 16, 33–34,
    157 n. 13
The Analyst (British arts and science quarterly) 42–43,
    44
Andrade, Gomes Freire de 27, 30
Andrade, Mariana Angélica de 90, 100, 101, 104
    contributions to *VF* 91–94
    editorials in *VF* 86, 102, 162–63, 165, 227
Ângelo, Carolina Beatriz 152, 155
animal imagery 123, 125
animal welfare 16, 48, 92, 101, 140, 141–44, 156,
    192–93
Anthony, Susan 161
anticlericalism 87–89, 104, 114–17, 133–35, 188
Antoinette, Mary, Queen of France 146–47
Araújo, João de Sousa 86, 104, 227
Arnoso, Count of 48
art, F. Wood's interest in 32
Assembleia Literária (periodical) 59, 77
Assis, Joaquim Maria Machado de 4
Association of Portuguese Journalists and Writers 11,
    99
Ataíde, Margarida de (pseudonym) 79 n. 51
    see also Chagas, Manuel Pinheiro
The Athenaeum (British periodical) 160–61, 171, 172–
    73, 174, 176
attacks on female writers 58–59, 70, 75, 88, 98–99
    see also Bem Público, hostility to *VF* from
Avelada, Diana de (pseudonym) 55
    see also Dinis, Júlio
Avellaneda, Gertrudis Gómez de 96

Balsemão, Catarina 68, 92
Banting, William 32
Barreto, J. A. da Graça 157 n. 23
Barros, Domingos Borges de 29
Barros, Teresa Leitão de 63, 76
Beard, Mary 65
Becker, Lydia 160, 167, 168, 177
Bem Público, hostility to *VF* from 1, 88–90, 115–16,
    125, 140, 151–53, 155, 177, 181, 188, 191
    see also Valada, Marquês de

Beneficência (periodical) 59
Bible, feminist readings of 114–16
Bodichon, Barbara Leigh Smith 147, 160, 182 n. 23,
    183 n. 34
Bollaert, William 26
Branco, Camilo Castelo 9, 15, 55, 61–63, 64, 66, 99,
    185
    and Plácido 2–4, 67, 68, 185
    statue of 2, *3*, 4
Brazil 23 n. 66, 63–64, 68, 71, 74–75, 90–91, 93,
    131–33
    press links with 16, 87
Britain:
    Campsall Hall, South Yorkshire 41–43
    English attitudes in Portugal 171
    F. Wood's time in 25, 26, 29–33, 159–60, 167, 191
    governesses from 154–55
    sugar boycott 33, 142–43
    women's progress in 84, 125, 147, 162, 167, 176
British Ultimatum, 1890 49, 155
Brontë, Charlotte, *Jane Eyre* 16–17, 47–48, 178–80
Brougham, Lord Henry 34–35, 43
Browne, Maria 4, 68
bullfighting 143, 157 n. 13
Byatt, A. S. 19

Cabete, Adelaide 152, 155, 191
Caldas, Delfina Vieira 97, 102
Camões, Luís Vaz de 94
Campos, Cláudia de 72, 81 n. 79
Campos, Narcisa Amália de Oliveira 107 n. 30
Campsall Hall, South Yorkshire, UK 41–43
The Campsall Society for the Acquisition of
        Knowledge 42–43, 44
Canuto, Maria José da Silva 13–14, 109 n. 62
Cape Verde 29, 59, 87, 95
Cardoso, Nuno Catarino 106 n. 10, 107 n. 23
Caron, Anne Marie 90–91, 96, 100–01, 105
cartoons *189*, *190*
Carvalho, António José de 104
Carvalho, Maria Amália Vaz de 4, 11, 89–90, 97,
        107 n. 30, 113, 177, 185–86, 191
Casino Lectures, 1871 47, 156 n. 2, 177, 186
Castelar, Emilio 18, 93–94, 141, 148–51, 152, 193
Castilho, António Feliciano de 58, 60, 63, 76, 78 n. 34,
        91, 98
Castro, Luís de Almeida de Melo e 106 n. 12

Catholic Church:
  disestablishment campaigns 35, 134–35, 150, 172
  male hegemony in 114–17, 133–35, 145–48
  see also anticlericalism
celibacy vows criticised 133–34
Chagas, Manuel Pinheiro 79 n. 51, 96, 220
Charlton, Lady Barbara Tasburgh 41
Chinese foot-binding 146
Chiosso, James 43
Christianity, see Catholic Church; religion
Civil Code (Portugal), 1867 6–7, 118
Claflin, Tennessee 99–100, 186
Coelho, Francisco Adolfo 47
Coelho, J. C. Teixeira 86, 104, 175, 227
Coelho, Joaquim Guilherme Gomes 55
  see also Dinis, Júlio
Coimbra, Portugal 6, 87, 88, 119, 187
Collins, Wilkie 16, 178
colonialism, Portuguese 74
  see also slavery
Comissão para a Cidadania e a Igualdade de Género
  21 n. 39
commercial journalism, rise of 9, 139
Comte, Auguste 89, 187
Connell, Raewyn W. 111
  see also hegemonic masculinity
context and women writers 56, 58, 135
Corn Laws, UK 35, 44, 46
Coronado, Carolina 94
Costa, Amália Cândida Isabel da 86, 162–63, 227
Costa, António da, A Mulher em Portugal 76, 98
Costa, Ermelinda Pereira da (pseudonym), see Branco,
  Camilo Castelo
Cristo, Monte, see Fonseca, Manuel Pinto da
A Cruzada (periodical) 12, 59, 173
'Cruzada das Mulheres Portuguesas' 173
Cunha, Sofia Nesbitt 39, 90, 100, 101
curry powder for the hungry 36

Davies, Emily 174, 183 n. 34
'Declaração' (VF editorial) 25, 84, 86, 90–91, 100, 101,
  105, 163
Deffand, Marie de Vichy-Chamrond, marquise du 151,
  152
Deus, João de 79 n. 51, 96, 97, 105
Diário de Notícias (newspaper) 8–9, 15, 139
Dias, Gonçalves 91
Dickens, Charles 16, 31
Dilke, Sir Charles Wentworth 171
Dinis, Júlio 55, 66–67, 96, 97, 186
discrimination against women in Portugal 117–34
Disraeli, Benjamin 183 n. 40
dolls 71, 112
  see also playthings, women treated as
Doncaster Lyceum, UK 42
La Donna (Italian periodical) 159, 176

Le Droit des femmes (French periodical) 96, 159, 169,
  176, 177, 183 n. 39
Du Châtelet, Émilie 151, 152

Eça de Queirós, José Maria, see Queirós, José Maria
  Eça de
editorials, impact of in nineteenth century 111, 139–40
editorials in VF and O Progresso 86, 89, 225–29
  by Andrade:
    'Um Brado a favor dos animais' 92
  by male contributors 104
  by Torresão:
    'A Imprensa' 166
  by F. Wood:
    ['Aos Il.mos e às Ex.mas assinantes da Voz
      Feminina...'] 88
    'Apelo: à Ex.ma Câmara Municipal de Lisboa'
      141–42, 143
    'Apelo: aos chefes de família' 142
    ['Bem-vindo sejas ano novo de 1868...'] 112
    ['O Bispo de Montpellier recebeu...'] 145–48
    'A Cadeira de Mendelssohn' 31
    'Carta ao digno deputado a Cortes o Il.mo Sr. D.
      Emílio Castelar' 148–51
    'O Celibato' 133
    ['O Cristianismo...'] 87, 114–15, 225
    'As Damas em Londres' 125, 136 n. 7
    'Declaração' 25, 84, 86, 90–91, 100, 101, 105, 163
    'Delírio Rábido-Político' 163–65
    ['Desde que o direito da mulher a regalias...']
      125–29
    ['Domingo último...'] 87
    ['Ex.mas Sras e Srs. assinantes...'] 152, 175
    ['Não perdoam facilmente, diz o nosso elegante
      escritor...'] 103
    ['A redatora desta folha agradece...'] 102
    'Os Satélites' 121–22
    'A uma assinante da Voz Feminina' 116, 117, 140
  by William Wood:
    'Artigo dedicado às Ex.mas Sras D. M. A. de
      Andrade...' 162–63
education, W. Wood's 41–43
education, women's:
  in Britain 173–74, 176
  contrasted with men's 118–22, 130, 145–48, 172
  literacy levels in Portugal 6–7
  and motherhood 67, 113–14, 149–50
  Woods' private school 38–39, 96
Eliot, George 26, 37, 45
Elisa, Henriqueta, see Sousa, Henriqueta Elisa Pereira
  de
Elliott, Ebenezer 44–45
Elliott, Eliza 101–02, 183 n. 29
Elliott, João A. 101–02, 171–72
England, see Britain
The Englishwoman's Review (British periodical) 87, 170

Epinay, Louise, marquise d' 151, 152
A Esperança (literary magazine) 64–66, 68–69, 77, 83
evangelical publications 16, 47

Farol, António Fernandes de Figueiredo Ferrer 86, 104, 136 n. 7, 227
As Farpas (periodical) 47, 98, 139, 155, 187
fashion 85, 92, 101, 112, 121, 160
Faucit, Helena 30
Fawcett, Millicent Garrett 168–69
Feio, Maria 106 n. 10
Felix, Rachel 30
femininity, perceptions of 9–10, 59, 63, 113–14, 115–16, 122–25, 149–50, 172
feminism:
    first-wave 1, 13, 14, 18, 105, 106, 106 n. 10, 113, 156, 173, 187
    'true' and 'false' 155, 165, 192
Fénelon, François 101
Fernandes, Maria Isabel 16
Ferreira, Gertrude Duarte 53 n. 80
Figueiredo, António Cândido de 91, 93, 104
folhetins [serials or commentary columns] 11, 14–15, 23 n. 61
    on Neuville's memoirs 70
    by Peregrina de Sousa 60, 61, 63
    by Torresão 95, 96
    in *VF* 56, 85, 99
Fonseca, Manuel Pinto da 72, 73
'foreignness' of Wood's ideas 57, 115, 120–22, 143, 151, 155, 170, 187, 188–89, 191
    see also transnationalism
Fornarina de Avelar (pseudonym) 185
Foucault, Michel 134
France, women's progress in 80 n. 54, 91, 100–01, 116, 145, 146–47, 151–52, 159, 169, 175–76
    Le Droit des femmes (French periodical) 96, 159, 169, 176, 177, 183 n. 39
Freemasonry 27, 29, 60, 151, 152–53, 191, 192
Freewoman (British periodical) 180–81
Freitas, Rodrigues de 177
French Revolution, 1848 29, 35, 44, 77 n. 12, 146–47, 150, 152
Fry, Elizabeth 33–34, 55
O Futuro (Brazilian periodical) 68

G., Leonor A. P. (male pseudonym) 89, 106 n. 14
Garrett, Almeida 1, 27, 29, 96
Gazeta de Portugal 69
Gazeta literária do Porto 9
gender, *see* intellect and gender; hegemonic masculinity; femininity, perceptions of
    and double standards 83, 118, 119
Geração de 70 47, 56–57, 58, 98–99, 111, 177, 180, 186–87
    see also Ortigão, Ramalho; Queirós, José Maria Eça de

Germany 128, 176
Girton College, Cambridge 174
Goegg, Marie 86, 159, 166–67, 169, 170, 175, 177, 227
Gonzaga, Tomás Antônio 105, 131–33
Goodolfim, José Cipriano da Costa 104
governesses, English 70, 154–55
Grimm's tales, Wood's rewriting of 51 n. 30, 87

Haiti 169
Hardy, Thomas 36
hegemonic masculinity 18, 59, 63, 111–12, 129–34, 140, 187
    in the Church 114–17, 133–35, 144–48
Herculano, Alexandre 63, 70, 92, 105
heroism 131–33
Hippeau, Célestin 173–74
horses, mistreatment of 143
Horsley, Charles Edward 31–32
Howitt, Mary 46
Hugo, Victor 20 n. 22, 93–94, 175
Hurston, Zora Neale 4

intellect and gender:
    'feminine roles' 9–11, 59, 63, 112–16, 122–25, 149–50, 172
    'literata' (lettered woman) 9, 10, 62, 99
    'literato' (man of letters) 9, 98, 153–54
    men championing women 29, 98, 102–05, 117, 147, 162
    'mulher de letras' (woman of letters) 9, 11, 186
    recovering female writers 92, 98, 185–86, 192
International Association of Women 166
Italy 159, 176

Jackson, Lady Catherine 185
Jacome, J. C. de Freitas 102
Janny, Amélia 89
Jesuitism 116–17, 188
job-titles femininized 125–27
Jornal das Senhoras 85
Jornal do Comércio 8–9, 15, 37–38

Kalley, Robert Reid 16
Kemble, John 30
Knowles, David 43–44
Kyllmann, Philippine 168

Ladies' Gallery, Portuguese Parliament 58–59
Lamballe, Princess 146, 151
Lankester, Edwin 41–43
laws, England:
    Matrimonial Causes Act, 1857 36, 159, 167
    Reform Bill, 1832 25, 32–33, 42
    Reform Bill, 1867 147, 160
laws, Portugal 5–6
    Civil Code, 1867 6–7, 118

Penal Code, 1852 115
press laws liberalised 9
League for Peace and Freedom 166, 174–75
Leavitt, William 29, 152
Léo, Mrs André 169, 175
Levaillant, Clementina 71, 73
Lewes, George 26
'liberty, fraternity and equality' 150
libraries:
    accessing women's works in 15, 57–58, 60,
        107 n. 23, 171, 217
    Portuguese women's access to 119–21
Liga Portuguesa da Paz 156, 175
Lisbon:
    'a city so little likely to be stirred by sentiment' 160,
        177, 180
    impact of railways on 6
    press links with 7–8, 76, 87
literacy in Portugal 6
'literata' (lettered woman) 9, 10, 62, 99
'literato' (man of letters) 9, 98, 153–54
Lopes, António José Fernandes 70
Lopes, Teixeira 3
L'Ouverture, Toussaint 169
Lusitanian Church 47
Lytton, Edward Bulwer 95

Machado, Júlio César 67, 71, 83, 93, 97, 102–03, 117
Madrepora Society 63–64
Maia, Emília Adelaide Moniz da 90–91
male dominance, see hegemonic masculinity
male privilege 117–22
Malibran de Bériot, Madame 44
Manchester Suffrage Committee 160, 163, 167, 168
Marcet, Jane 167
Maria Severn (F. Wood)
    autobiographical details in 17, 29, 31, 32, 152, 171,
        191
    politics in 6, 32–33, 35–36
    pronunciation notes 34
    reception 15, 93, 185
    serialisation of 14–15, 16, 56, 85, 87, 176
    wife-selling in 36
Marques, F. de Abreu 86, 104, 227
Martineau, Harriet 37, 167, 168, 169
Martins, Clarimundo 29, 49, 152
Martins, D. António Alves (Bishop of Viseu) 129
Martins, Narciso 29
Martins, Joaquim Pedro de Oliveira 99
Matos, Francisco A. de 86, 104, 136 n. 7, 162, 163,
    227–28
Matrimonial Causes Act (England), 1857 36, 159, 167
memoirs:
    Neuville 57, 69–77, 186
    Roland 152

memory loss, cultural 27, 60, 69, 72, 100, 135, 155,
    187, 191
    see also silencing of female writers; recovery of
        female writers
men championing female intellectuals 29, 98, 102–05,
    117, 147, 162
Mendelssohn, Felix 31–32
mentoring 100–02
Meredith, Louisa Anne 46
Miall, Edward 35, 172
Mill, Harriet Taylor 37, 159
Mill, John Stuart 147, 160, 162, 163, 172–73
    The Subjection of Women 162, 173, 176, 179
Mitford, Mary Russell 44, 46
Moderno, Alice 22 n. 58, 156 n. 11
Molière 91–92, 148
Monteiro, Sttau 27
Morning Advertiser (English newspaper) 46
The Morning Post (English newspaper) 48–49
motherhood and intellect 59, 63, 67, 113–14, 122–25,
    149–50, 172
Mozzoni, Anna Maria 159
'a mulher livre ao lado do homem livre' 11, 17, 113–14,
    125–34, 136 n. 7, 161, 166–67, 181
music 26, 31–32, 37, 38, 39, 43–46, 191
The Musical World (weekly magazine) 44

A Nação (newspaper) 139
The National Reform Organisation 46
networking, women using periodicals for 76–77, 87,
    96, 100
Neuville, Josephina 56, 57, 69–75, 76, 186
Neves, J. G. de Sousa 97
Newgate Prison, England 34
Newman, Francis 130–31, 172, 176
Ninon de Lenclos, Anne 151, 152

open letters 47, 65, 101, 104, 117, 169, 140–56, 170–73,
    175, 177, 193
Ortigão, Ramalho:
    on Carvalho 177, 191
    'Coisas Inocentes' 66–67
    As Farpas 47, 98, 139, 155, 187
    John Bull 48
    O Mistério da Estrada de Sintra 15
Osório, Ana de Castro 106, 135
    Às Mulheres Portuguesas 1, 113, 114, 118
    A Semeadora 105, 176
    Sociedade Futura 13, 192
Owen, Robert 42, 43, 55
Oxford University 174

P., Carlota A. (male pseudonym) 86, 87, 89, 228
pacifism 174–75
Palmela, José 93

O Panorama (periodical) 70, 87
Parati, second Count of 152
Pato, Raimundo António Bulhão 69
Pelletan, Eugène 147, 151
Penal Code, 1852 (Portugal) 115
Penny Magazine (British periodical) 34–35, 43
Peregrina de Sousa, Maria, *see* Sousa, Maria Peregrina de
Pereira, Augusto Xavier da Silva 7
periodical press, impact of 7–9, 32, 35, 76–77, 111, 139–40
periodicals and magazines:
  Almanaque das Senhoras 91, 97–99, 139, 185, 192
  O Amigo da Infância (religious magazine) 16, 33–34, 157 n. 13
  The Analyst (British arts and science quarterly) 42–43, 44
  A Esperança (literary magazine) 64–66, 68–69, 77, 83
  Assembleia Literária (periodical) 59, 77
  The Athenaeum (British periodical) 160–61, 171, 172–73, 174, 176
  Bem Público (periodical) 1, 88–90, 115–16, 125, 140, 151–53, 155, 177, 181, 188, 191
  Beneficência (periodical) 59
  A Cruzada (periodical) 12, 59, 173
  Diário de Notícias (newspaper) 8–9, 15, 139
  La Donna (Italian periodical) 159, 176
  Le Droit des femmes (French periodical) 96, 159, 169, 176, 177, 183 n. 39
  The Englishwoman's Review (British periodical) 87, 170
  As Farpas (periodical) 47, 98, 139, 155, 187
  Freewoman (British periodical) 180–81
  O Futuro (Brazilian periodical) 68
  Morning Advertiser (English newspaper) 46
  The Morning Post (English newspaper) 48–49
  The Musical World (weekly magazine) 44
  A Nação (newspaper) 139
  O Panorama (periodical) 70, 87
  Penny Magazine (British periodical) 34–35, 43
  O Português (periodical) 29
  Punch (weekly magazine) 36, 160
  The Spectator (British magazine) 41, 50 n. 22
  The Quarterly Review (British periodical) 174
  Revista Contemporânea de Portugal e Brasil (periodical) 63, 68, 78 n. 33, 80 n. 57
  A Revolução de Setembro (newspaper) 70, 80 n. 54, 88, 102
  The Revolution (American periodical) 88, 159, 161, 170, 181
  A Semeadora (periodical) 105, 176
  Sociedade Futura (periodical) 192
  Westminster Review (English periodical) 37, 45–46
  O Zoofilo (periodical) 16–17, 47, 48, 143–44, 157 n. 16, 178–80, 224
  see also A Voz Feminina; *O Progresso*

Pestana, Alice 2, 156, 175
petition for female suffrage, UK 18, 147, 160, 162, 167, 168, 171
Pimentel, Alberto 65
Pimentel, Leonor da Fonseca 192
Pinheiro, Rafael Bordalo 99, 188
Pinto, Amélia Dulce de Serpa 185
Pires, Henrique 71–72
Plácido, Ana Augusta 2–4, *3*, 56, 57, 67–69, 70, 76, 102–03, 185
playthings, women treated as 127, 128–29
poetry 85, 90–94, 95, 104–05, 131–33, 162
'political woman' 92, 125–29, 163–64
Pope Pius IX 145–48
portrait of W. Wood 39, *40*, 41
O Português (periodical) 29
Portuguese Revolution, 1974 11
poultry, mistreatment of 142–43, 144
Praça, José Joaquim Lopes 187
Prata, Maria Adelaide Fernandes 64, 65–66, 89
prisons, women's 34
O Progresso:
  closure of 134, 151, 153–55, 175–77
  editorials in 86, 104, 125–29, 133, 143, 152, 175, 226
  'O que se faz lá fora' rubric 87, 161, 173–76, 214
  VF changes to 83, 84, 85, 88–89, 92
pronunciation notes 34
prostitution 127
Protestant Christianity, women's roles in 114–15
pseudonyms 62, 86, 104, 178, 185, 186
  use of female by men 55, 66–67, 89, 186
public opinion as man-made 117–18
Punch (weekly magazine) 36, 160
Pusich, Antónia Gertrudes 2, 12–13, 56, 58–60, 66, 68, 152
  periodicals of 57, 77, 86, 173

The Quarterly Review (British periodical) 174
Queirós, José Maria Eça de 1, 6, 7, 39, 48, 112, 186
  As Farpas 187
  O Crime do Padre Amaro 135, 178
  O Mistério da Estrada de Sintra 15
  O Primo Basílio 139, 178
  Os Maias 38, 73–75, 144
  statue of 2, *3*
Quental, Antero de 187

Radcliffe, Ann 46
Raeburn, Sir Henry 39–41
railways, impact of 6, 87
Rarey, John Solomon 32
recovery of female writers 14, 75, 92, 98, 185–86, 192
Reform Bill (England), 1832 25, 32–33, 42
Reform Bill (England), 1867 147, 160
refugees, political 29

Regeneração [Regeneration] period 1, 5–11
regional papers:
    Portugal 7, 88
    Britain 160–61
religion:
    evangelical publications 16, 47
    women's roles in Protestantism 114–15
    see also Catholic Church
're-mediation' 12
restrictions on Portuguese women 118–22, 144
retweeting, early equivalent of 160–61
Revista Contemporânea de Portugal e Brasil (periodical)
    63, 68, 78 n. 33, 80 n. 57
A Revolução de Setembro (newspaper) 70, 80 n. 54, 88,
    102
The Revolution (American periodical) 88, 159, 161, 170,
    181
revolutionary songs 123–24
revolutions:
    French Revolution, 1848 29, 35, 44, 77 n. 12,
        146–47, 150, 152
    Portuguese Revolution, 1974 11
    Spanish Revolution, 1868 148–49
Ristori, Adelaide 30
rodapé 22 n. 61, 85
Roland, Madame 151, 152
Roughton, Ellen/Helena 114
Russ, Joanna 4
Russia 176

'sabichona' (know-it-all) 9–10
Sand, George 67–68, 92
Santana e Vasconcelos, Jacinto Augusto, see Vasconcelos,
    Jacinto Augusto Santana e
Sarmento, Olga Morais 13, 192
Schmitz, Leonhard 42
A Semeadora (periodical) 105, 176
sexual scandals:
    Neuville 69–73, 76
    Plácido and Camilo 67
    Valada 155, 188
Sibila imprint 57
silencing of female writers 76, 100, 135, 155, 185–86,
    188
    see also memory loss, cultural
Silva, Inocêncio Francisco da 69
Silveira, Maria Olga Morais Sarmento da, see Sarmento,
    Olga Morais
Simões, Francisco 3
Sinfrónio sketch (VF) 129
slavery:
    abolition in Britain 32–33, 142–43
    abolition in Haiti 169
    abolition in Portugal 6
    slave imagery 102, 126, 150, 172
    slave-trading 73–74

Smith, Frederica 114
'socialism', in O Progresso 175
Sociedade Futura (periodical) 192
Society for the Diffusion of Useful Knowledge 34
Society for the Protection of Animals (Sociedade
    Protectora dos Animais) 16, 48, 143–44, 156, 180,
    192–93
Society of Jesus 116
Somerville, Mary 37, 167
Sousa, Henriqueta Elisa Pereira de 64, 65, 66
Sousa, Maria Peregrina de 56, 57, 60–64, 68, 69, 76,
    185
    contributions to A Esperança 65, 66, 69
Spain 94, 123–24, 125
Spanish Revolution, 1868 148–49
The Spectator (British magazine) 41, 50 n. 22
spiritism/spiritualism 101
Staël, Germaine de 67–68
Stanton, Elizabeth Caddy 161, 170
Stanton, Henry 170
Stanton, Theodore 15, 88–89, 170–71, 177
statues:
    Branco and Plácido 2, 3, 4
    Eça de Queirós 2, 3
Stowe, Harriet Beecher 80 n. 54, 170
suffrage campaigns, see women's suffrage campaigns
sugar boycott, England 33, 142–43
Switzerland 159, 176

Tait's Edinburgh Magazine 45
Teixeira, Judith 27, 76
telegraph, impact of the 6
Tennyson, Alfred, Baron 174
theatre 30
Thompson, Thomas Perronet 35–36, 44, 46, 55
Thorold, Anthony Wilson 48–49
Thorold, Jane, see Wood, Jane Thorold
Thorold, Sir John 39
Tipografia da Voz Feminina 15–16, 157 n. 13, 217, 218,
    219
Tipografia de J. G. de Sousa Neves 97
Tipografia Luso-Británica 15–16, 34, 47, 48, 157 n. 13,
    178, 217–24
'to say something is to do something' 14, 135
Torres, Lília 90
Torresão, Guiomar 2, 4, 11, 93, 95–100, 105, 107 n. 28,
    157 n. 22, 185–86, 191
    Uma Alma de Mulher 56, 83, 95, 96, 97, 135
    Almanaque das Senhoras 91, 97–99, 139, 185, 192
    caricatures of 188, 189, 190
    editorials in VF 86, 90, 165–66, 228
translations:
    by C. T. Wood (Jr) 43
    Jane Eyre 47, 178–80
    at Tipografia Luso-Británica 16–17
    in VF 87, 95, 101, 101–02, 104, 166, 169, 170, 175

transnationalism 13–14
    of feminism 159–81, 186–87, 189, 192
    and Freemasonry 152–53
    Neuville's memoirs 70–71, 72, 73–74
    in open letters 84, 141, 145–51, 153–56
    of Peregrina de Sousa 63–64, 76
    of Torresão 99
    see also 'foreignness' of Wood's ideas
Twamley, Louisa Anne 46

UK, see Britain
United States 99–100, 159, 161, 163, 170, 172–74

Valada, Marquês de 115, 124, 155, 188, 190
    see also Bem Público, hostility to VF from
Vasconcelos, Artur Teixeira de 69–70
    use of female pseudonyms 79 n. 51
Vasconcelos, Carolina Michaëlis de 192
Vasconcelos, Jacinto Augusto Santana e 69, 72
Vassar College, US 173–74
Viana, João Luís da Silva 86, 104, 169, 228
Vidal, Angelina 2, 12–13, 117, 188, 189
Vilar de Allen, Viscount of 64
Viterbo, Francisco Marques de Sousa 65
votes for women, see women's suffrage campaigns
A Voz da Liberdade (Madeira paper) 7
A Voz Feminina (VF)
    change of title 83, 84, 85, 88–89, 92
    editorial vision 83, 84–89, 135–36, 140
    female contributors to 89–102, 226–28
    in feminism debate 159–81
    hostility from Bem Público 1, 88–90, 115–16, 125,
        140, 151–53, 155, 177, 181, 188, 191
    male contributors to 102–05, 170, 226–28
    reviews of 87–88
    see also editorials in VF and O Progresso

Waltham, Chris 43
Westminster Review (English periodical) 37, 45–46
wife-selling 36, 159, 167
Wilberforce, William 33
Wollstonecraft, Mary 102
The Woman Question 159–81
women against emancipation 124–25

women's suffrage campaigns:
    Portugal 29, 58, 93, 96
    transnational debate on 99–100, 147–51, 160–81
    UK 18, 37, 147, 160, 162, 163, 167, 168, 171
Wood, Arthur Thorold 39, 41, 43, 49, 51 n. 36
Wood, Camilla 41
Wood, Caroline 41
Wood, Charles Thorold (Jr) 39, 40, 41, 43
Wood, Charles Thorold (Sr) 39, 41–42, 43
Wood, Emily 41, 43, 51 n. 36
Wood, Francisca de Assis Martins:
    birth and death 27, 28, 49
    family background 29
    and first-wave feminism 1, 13, 14, 106, 156, 173
    later years 47–48, 177–80
    male supporters 102–05
    marriage 26–27
    mentoring of younger female writers 96, 100–02,
        186
    relocation to Portugal 37–39
    resignation as editor 88
    time in England 26–27, 29–33, 159–60, 167, 191
    see also A Voz Feminina (VF); editorials in VF and O
        Progresso; Maria Severn (F. Wood)
Wood, Jane Thorold 39, 41–42
Wood, Neville 39, 41
Wood, William Thorold 40
    editorials by 86, 162–63, 228–29
    family background 25–27, 39–43
    later years 47–48
    marriage 26–27
    and music 26, 31–32, 37, 39, 43–46, 191
    open letter to Stanton 15, 88–89, 170–71
    relocation to Portugal 37–39
    support for female intellectuals 83, 88, 188
    tombstone 27, 28, 48
Wood, Willoughby 39, 41, 43

Young, Charlotte 46

O Zoofilo (periodical) 16–17, 47, 48, 143–44, 157 n. 16,
        178–80, 224
    translation of Jane Eyre 47, 178–80

9 781781 887998